FAITH AND KNOWLEDGE

FAITH AND KNOWLEDGE

Mainline Protestantism and American Higher Education

DOUGLAS SLOAN

Westminster John Knox Press
Louisville, Kentucky

Book design by Drew Stevens
Cover design by Kevin Darst, KDEE Design Inc.

First edition

Published by Westminster John Knox Press
Louisville, Kentucky

This book is printed on acid-free paper that meets the American National Standards Institute Z39.48 standard. ♾

PRINTED IN THE UNITED STATES OF AMERICA

94 95 96 97 98 99 00 01 02 03—10 9 8 7 6 5 4 3 2 1

Library of Congress Cataloging-in-Publication Data

Sloan, Douglas, date.
     Faith and knowledge : mainline Protestantism and
American higher education / Douglas Sloan. — 1st ed.
          p.   cm.
     Includes bibliographical references.
     ISBN 0-664-22035-5 (alk. paper)
     1. Church and college—United States—History—20th century.
2. Liberalism (Religion)—Protestant churches—History—20th
century.   3. Liberalism (Religion)—United States—History—20th
century.   4. Knowledge, Theory of (Religion)—History of
doctrines—20th century.   5. Education, Higher—United States—
History—20th century.   6. Education (Christian theology)—History
of doctrines—20th century.   I. Title.
LC383.S56   1994
377'.1'0973—dc20   94-8682

In memory of my brother
Phillip Leland Sloan

Contents

Preface

In March 1953, the first issue of *The Christian Scholar* was published by the newly established Commission on Higher Education of the National Council of the Churches of Christ in the U.S.A. In his lead editorial, J. Edward Dirks wrote, "Signs are accumulating . . . that a great theological boom is now upon us. Already it may confidently be claimed that the twentieth century is the greatest age of theology since the thirteenth." Out of this twentieth-century "theological renaissance," as Dirks and others were to call the theological boom, *The Christian Scholar* proposed to undertake a twofold task: to explore the meaning of the Christian faith in its implications for contemporary American higher education and, from the engagement that was to ensue, "to seek new and deeper meanings in the Gospel itself."[1]

Nearly fifteen years later, like the theological renaissance for which it labored, *The Christian Scholar* would come abruptly to an end. During these years, however, it was one of many expressions of the last, major concerted attempt by mainline Protestant churches to engage twentieth-century American higher education at its center and on a broad front.

When J. Edward Dirks launched *The Christian Scholar,* the church's new involvement with American higher education was already well under way. It had begun in the 1930s in connection with the growing "theological boom" of which Dirks wrote, and it continued to build. By the 1950s the Protestant churches were beginning to carry out an enthusiastic and many-sided engagement with American higher education in a variety of ways and on a scale of which many persons, both in the churches and outside, have not always been aware. Theologians, college and university faculty and administrators, church leaders, denominational and ecumenical religious groups, political action movements, campus ministers, and laypersons in many fields were all involved. In the political and cultural turmoil on the nation's campuses during the 1960s the church's higher education activities flared in intensity, even seeming for a moment to gain new energies, and then they suddenly began to disintegrate. By 1969 the church's large-scale engagement with American higher education was all but finished.

This book tells the story of this last, major attempt by mainline Protestantism to have a significant influence on American higher education. The primary focus throughout is on the relationship between faith and knowledge—on the ways in which the mainline Protestant churches did, and did not, deal with the faith-knowledge relationship. It was the faith-knowledge relationship that lay at the heart of the church's endeavors in higher education. The church's claim to have a legitimate voice in higher education depended on its ability to demonstrate an essential connection between faith and knowledge. More important, the faith-knowledge relationship, as it came to expression in modern higher education, also ultimately would determine the place of religion in modern culture generally.

The conception of knowing and of knowable reality that has come during the past centuries to dominate modern culture and education has left little place for the concerns and affirmations of religion. The dominant conception of knowing that has shaped modern consciousness and culture, while quite powerful, has been extremely narrow. In the prevailing modern view of how and what we can know, the quantitative, the mechanical, and the instrumental are accorded full standing. All those things, however, that involve—as Huston Smith has put it—values, meaning, purpose, and qualities are regarded as essentially having little to do with knowledge, except as they can be reduced to more basic and more real material and mechanistic entities.[2]

Above all, a purely quantitative, mechanistic, and instrumental way of knowing, by definition, cannot deal with the qualities of experience, including not only the familiar qualities of nature, such as color and sound, but also the larger constellations of qualities we class under the headings of meaning, value, life, consciousness, self, and spirit. The qualities of experience are usually consigned to the unknowable, and often they are regarded even as sources of illusion and irrationality. The dominant conception of how and what we can know has thus given rise to views of reality that have little room for all that makes human experience peculiarly human. The affirmations of religious faith have been called into question and thrown on the defensive by the dominant modern conception of knowing; so too have ethics, the arts, literature, and personal-communal meaning and values—all the realms of experience involving the qualitative.

In the nineteenth and twentieth centuries there have been various responses to the growing dominance of this narrow modern conception of knowing and the materialistic, mechanistic worldview with which it has been associated. One type of response has been that of various forms of antimodernism—the rejection of the modern world and the attempt either to resist it actively or to opt out of it. Within Protestantism a major type of this kind of response has been religious fundamentalism, essentially an effort to counter the mechanical worldview with an alternative worldview drawn from a literalistic reading of the Bible and earlier modern conceptions of natural theology.

A second major response has been simply to embrace some form of scientific naturalism. Some naturalists have always been thoroughgoing proponents of a radical mechanical philosophy and a positivistic, scientistic approach to the whole of reality. Others, including some Protestant theologians, embraced naturalism and a scientific epistemology while maintaining that it is possible to speak meaningfully (and scientifically) about values, purpose, and even the Divine. Since some of these value-committed naturalists, though not all, had to smuggle in their own values from covert, often unacknowledged, nonscientific sources, they were actually a variation on the third major response to the modern mind-set.

The third response, probably the most common one, certainly for mainline Protestantism and for many others as well, has been to adopt some version of what can be called a two-realm theory of truth. This is the view that on the one side there are the truths of knowledge as these are given predominantly by science and discursive, empirical reason. On the other side are the truths of faith, religious experience, morality, meaning, and value. The latter are seen as grounded not in knowledge but variously in feeling, ethical action, communal convention, folk tradition, or unfathomable mystical experience.

The strength of the two-realm approach is that it has helped to keep alive whole dimensions of human experience and meaning that the dominant view of knowable reality cannot encompass. The twofold theory of truth, however, has always had an abiding twofold weakness. While it represents resistance against the modern mind-set, it justifies and perpetuates the basic dualism that is a chief hallmark of the modern world: the split between subject and object, fact and value, theory and practice, self and other, science and the humanities, and so on, including, of course, the deep abyss between faith and knowledge.

More important still, the balance between the two realms of truth is unequal. The realm of faith, meaning, and values is constantly put on the defensive and undercut by the incursions of a narrow, positivistic knowledge and its accompanying materialistic worldview. Without a grounding in accepted, potentially knowable reality, the objects of faith, ethics, and art are always verging toward the epiphenomenal and the unreal. In this has been the central crisis of faith in the modern world.

There has been a possible fourth response to the modern mind-set. This would be the development of qualitative ways of knowing that are every bit as rigorous and compelling as the quantitative. Well-developed qualitative ways of knowing could in principle include the quantitative, providing meaning and direction for it, since quantities are, after all, only a particular subset of the qualitative. And this response could open up the possibility, otherwise closed to the modern mind, of reaching beyond the senses to real knowledge of the non-sensory and supersensible realities that constitute both the beauty and life in nature as well as the marrow of all religion, ethics, art, and meaning. Apart, however, from a few faltering and inchoate gestures in this direction (some of them actually in the nineteenth century), this possibility of developing new, deeper, and more capacious ways of knowing has seldom been taken up and pursued.

At the end of World War I, the split between modern knowledge and faith was clearly evident to many folk, and the threat to faith that this posed was being widely felt. It was during the years immediately following the war, however, that the Protestant theological renaissance began. By the mid-1930s it was in full momentum.

The new theologians were convinced that they could combine modern science and scholarship with the fundamental affirmations of the Christian faith. They set themselves the task of showing that the Christian faith is relevant to modern understanding because it provides the best account available of the human condition. On the one side, they rejected fundamentalism as antimodern. On the other side, and at the same time, they rigorously criticized the modernist pretensions of human reason, whether these took the form of a mechanistic and deterministic naturalism or an idealism that unquestioningly identified the achievements and values of modern culture with the Divine. Coming to grips with modern knowledge and its implications for faith was, therefore, the theologians' most important challenge. It was a challenge they felt equal to.

It was a challenge also that would catapult the new theologians and those influenced by them directly into an encounter with modern higher education. By the time the theological renaissance was beginning to flower, American higher education had become firmly established as the primary institutional center for developing the knowledge on which a modern scientific-technological society depends. Consequently, the university was also becoming the main channel of opportunity and access to that knowledge and the prime custodian and controller of it. A theological movement that seriously challenged the basic assumptions of modern culture would be drawn willy-nilly into a full-scale engagement with modern higher education. And this is, of course, what happened. The purpose of this study is to tell the story of that engagement and, in so doing, to explore some of the fundamental issues of faith and knowledge in modern culture.

Two expressions that I use in this study—"the theological renaissance" and "mainline Protestantism"—are not without problems, and a few words about them may be necessary. The Protestant "theological renaissance" of roughly the second quarter of the twentieth century was closely associated with the theological movement known as neo-orthodoxy. The movement, however, was broader than the term neo-orthodoxy suggests, and few even of the major theologians involved were entirely comfortable with that label. As Langdon Gilkey has observed, "the literature of neoorthodoxy composed most of the leading Protestant theological productions (except in Chicago) in Europe, England, and America, from 1918 (in Europe) and 1935 (in America) until roughly 1960."[3] Included were theologians and religious thinkers as diverse as the Europeans Karl Barth, Emil Brunner, Rudolf Bultmann, Nicolai Berdyaev, Gustav Aulén, Anders Nygren, Donald and John Baillie, and C. H. Dodd, and the Americans Reinhold and H. Richard Niebuhr, Paul

Tillich (European-American), John Bennett, Douglas Horton, Robert Calhoun, and many others.

Perhaps the theological renaissance can be most accurately described as having had important origins in the rise of European neo-orthodoxy, but it soon came to include many persons to whom the name neo-orthodox cannot be applied, and many persons who actually opposed neo-orthodoxy. I shall use the term "theological renaissance" to describe the whole period we are looking at, and I will attempt to employ the term "neo-orthodoxy" only when neo-orthodox themes in the strict sense are clearly evident.

Although we are focusing on Protestantism, the theological renaissance, in actuality, was part of a much larger Judeo-Christian theological renewal. Such Jewish thinkers as Martin Buber, Abraham Heschel, and Will Herberg should also be included on the list, not only for their work as Jewish theologians but also for their direct influence on the American Protestants. Similar considerations apply to the work of leading Roman Catholic thinkers such as the theologians and philosophers Jacques Maritain, Etienne Gilson, and Gabriel Marcel, to say nothing of the novelists Graham Greene and François Mauriac. Although the theologians caught up in the theological renaissance by no means agreed fully, they all shared the conviction that the Christian tradition could speak with power to the modern human being.

While the influence of the European theologians was initially important for the American movement, and continued to be, the American theological renaissance came to have its own distinctiveness. It is the American expression of the theological renewal, particularly as exemplified in the work of its three major representatives, H. Richard Niebuhr, Reinhold Niebuhr, and Paul Tillich, that is most important for this study. Of course, in concentrating upon those within Protestantism who were influenced, directly or indirectly, by the theological renaissance, I am actually dealing with a limited segment of mainline Protestantism itself. As a consequence, I do not explore the full range of the attitudes toward higher education of those many mainline Protestants, church leaders and laity, who were not caught up fully in the theological renaissance, but whose support was essential to all the church's endeavors in higher education. The engagement with higher education arising out of the Protestant theological renaissance, however, dealt with issues of faith in the modern world to which every religious group, sooner or later, for better or worse, would have to respond.

The expression "mainline Protestantism" is a somewhat vague term, and as William R. Hutchison has observed, it sometimes carries connotations that are normative as well as descriptive. Nevertheless, it is an unavoidable and useful term, and I employ it entirely in the sense of the purely descriptive definition formulated by Hutchison as including "the group of churches and network of leaders that appear, prima facie, to have dominated American Protestantism in the early twentieth century, and to have enjoyed considerable religious and cultural authority in the environing society."[4] The definition makes no normative claims but does enable the term to serve the purposes of historical identification.

The mainline Protestant experience has implications for others who, had time and energy permitted, could well have been included in this story. The long and distinctive African-American Protestant tradition in higher education is, for example, not dealt with in this study. Although African-American Protestants have had their own often unique achievements and problems in higher education, the mainline experience looked at here reveals many crucial issues in the split between modern conceptions of knowledge and concerns for human meaning, ethics, and justice that are not irrelevant to the African-American experience in modern society and higher education. A complete study would also have included much more than I do on the fundamentalist and evangelical experience in higher education, especially in light of the growth of evangelicalism and its expanding activity in higher education after the 1960s. However, I do touch on the evangelical experience in the concluding chapter, exploring there why evangelicals today cannot expect to escape the faith-knowledge issues that confronted mainline Protestants in mid-century.

Finally, the full story would include the involvement of Roman Catholic and Jewish groups in twentieth-century higher education. Both the theological renaissance and mid-twentieth-century efforts at educational reform included Roman Catholics and Jews, as well as Protestants, often with all three working cooperatively and mutually influencing one another. This is why it would be a mistake to interpret the mainline Protestant engagement with higher education merely as an attempt to recoup a bygone Protestant cultural hegemony (though to be sure such motives were present). Clearly what was at stake concerned others besides Protestants, although they were the main players in the engagement. The fundamental issue had to do with the place of religion itself within modern culture and higher education.

The mainline Protestant engagement with higher education provides a sustained and multifaceted case study of the many dimensions of the relationship between faith and knowledge. Besides being a good story in its own right, the Protestant engagement with American higher education that drew its primary inspiration and outlook from the theological renaissance touched the deepest issues of the faith-knowledge relationship, and in a way that has implications of importance far transcending mainline Protestantism itself. That the Protestants in the end failed in this effort in no way diminishes—perhaps it even heightens—what may be learned from their experience.

Other perspectives than the one I have chosen on the relationship between the churches and twentieth-century American higher education are, of course, possible. The different stories that could be told from these varying perspectives would each have its own value. I do not think, however, that all perspectives are of equal significance or that it is a matter of indifference from which perspective one chooses to view and relate ideas and events. The perspective I have chosen for this study, I am convinced, is of central significance to an adequate understanding of religion and modern culture, and certainly of the American Protestant churches and twentieth-century higher education. Other important stories about the churches and American higher education certainly can and will be told. Nevertheless, if these other possible stories are to grasp the central issues in the relation between the church and modern higher education, and between religion and modern culture more generally, they will ultimately have to deal in some way with the story of the churches' handling of the relationship between faith and knowledge.

A final introductory comment may be in order. The study throughout examines the problems posed to faith by the dominant modern conceptions of knowing and knowledge. We now live in a time in which the word from many quarters is that the modern mind-set has been overcome and that we are entering a radically new time and culture that can only be described as postmodern.

This may be the case. The question, however, is whether and in what ways this widely heralded postmodernism is truly postmodern (that is, truly postpositivist, postreductionist, and postrelativist). To what extent is it primarily certain aspects of modernism drawn out to their logical conclusions? Do postmodern ways of knowing and assumptions about reality truly transcend modern assumptions, or is what passes for postmodernism more accurately described as a compounding in the utmost extreme of the modern mind-set and its predicaments? What are the implications for faith? Can we distinguish between a spurious postmodernism and a genuinely new and life-giving postmodernism? These are all extremely large questions in themselves. Nevertheless, the experience of the mainline Protestant churches in their mid-twentieth-century engagement with American higher education can shed some light on such questions. For this reason, in the concluding chapter, I have ventured to hazard a few reflections on Protestantism and its postmodern prospects, and on what a truly positive (not positivistic) postmodern approach to the faith-knowledge issue would require.

The story begins well before this century and, as we have just noted, points into the future. Chapter 1 therefore, provides some essential nineteenth-century background on religion, higher education, and the development of the theological renaissance. Chapter 2 looks at the beginning efforts to bring the theological renaissance to bear on developing a thoroughgoing but constructive intellectual critique of modern higher education. Chapter 3, then, examines the unfolding of the actual campaign carried out by the churches on many fronts within the university. The pivotal chapter 4 critically explores the main theological approaches at the time to the faith-knowledge issue. The primary subjects of this chapter are the major American leaders of the theological renaissance, Reinhold Niebuhr, his brother H. Richard

Niebuhr, and Paul Tillich, as well as their successors, the self-named secular and death-of-God theologians, and a small but important marginal group, the radical empiricists. Chapters 5 and 6, focusing respectively on the religious student and faculty endeavors, describe the collapse of the Protestant theological-educational reform efforts. The concluding chapter reflects on the present and the future, looking especially at the faith-knowledge issues in the light of the current claims that we are now entering a postmodern era in which a whole new approach to knowing and reality is in the making.

NOTES

1. *Christian Scholar* 36, no. 1 (March 1953) : 4–5. Strictly speaking, as the volume number indicates, *The Christian Scholar* was not an entirely new creation but was the continuation in new format of the journal, *Christian Education*, published since 1917. Not only in format but in content and purpose as well, it was essentially an altogether new journal.

2. Huston Smith, "Excluded Knowledge: A Critique of the Modern Western Mind-Set," *Teachers College Record* 80 (February 1979). Reprinted in Huston Smith, *Beyond the Post-Modern Mind* (New York: Crossroad, 1982), 62–91.

3. Langdon Gilkey, *Naming the Whirlwind: The Renewal of God Language* (Indianapolis and New York: Bobbs-Merrill Co., 1969), 89, n. 9. Leonard Sweet describes neo-orthodoxy as "highly diverse and difficult to put into a single framework." Leonard I. Sweet, "The Modernization of Protestant Religion in America," in *Altered Landscapes: Christianity in America, 1935–1985*, ed. David W. Lotz, et al. (Grand Rapids: Wm. B. Eerdmans Publishing Co., 1989), 23

4. William R. Hutchison, ed., *Between the Times: The Travail of the Protestant Establishment in America, 1900–1960* (Cambridge: Cambridge University Press, 1989), x.

Acknowledgments

I want to express my gratitude to the Lilly Endowment, Inc., for the generous support that made the research and writing of this study possible. My deep gratitude goes especially to Robert Wood Lynn, who, as Senior Vice President of the Lilly Endowment, first suggested that I consider exploring the involvement of the Protestant churches in twentieth-century American higher education. Even after his retirement from the Lilly Endowment, Robert Lynn continued to lend encouragement and critical insight to my work as it progressed. I also want to express my special gratitude to Craig Dykstra, who succeeded Robert Lynn at the Lilly Endowment, and to Jeanne Knoerle, Program Director at Lilly, for their continuing encouragement and support of the project.

A number of persons contributed in essential ways to the writing of the book. I am indebted to the work of Arthur Zajonc, Robert Zuber, Winton Solberg, Wesley Hotchkiss, and Frank Dent, who did specific case studies for my research bearing on various particular aspects of the churches' relationships to American higher education, to which I refer in the book.

Verlyn Barker, William Bean Kennedy, Robert Wood Lynn, James Burtchaell, Jeanne Knoerle, Robert Zuber, Wesley Hotchkiss, George Marsden, Fred Paddock, and John Cobb read various versions of the manuscript as it took form, and I have profited much from their criticisms and suggestions. Verlyn Barker has throughout provided much-appreciated encouragement and intellectual and moral support.

Lastly, I also want to mention in gratitude a number of persons with whom I had opportunities at various times to converse or correspond, and from whom I received insight, criticism, and often crucial information and, in a couple of instances, helpful memories. These persons include: Merrimon Cuninggim, Dorothy Bass, Jackson Carroll, Charles Courtney, the late Barbara Hargrove, Jack Harrison, Joseph Hough, Jack Lewis, William N. Lovell, Hugh Noble, Parker Palmer, Robert Rue Parsonage, Robert Rankin, Mark R. Schwehn, Robert Seaver, Harry Smith, Huston Smith, Wilfred Cantwell Smith, Hal Viehman, and the late Amos Wilder.

None of the persons named in these acknowledgments are in any way responsible for shortcomings in the book, and none of them necessarily agree with my telling of the story or with my interpretation of it.

CHAPTER 1

The Church, the University, and the Faith-Knowledge Issue: The Background

The history of American higher education, until well after the middle of the nineteenth century, can scarcely be understood apart from the history of American Protestantism. Besides the family, the church, state, and college were often viewed as the main institutional pillars of early colonial America, with the college serving to prepare trained leaders for the other two. By the early nineteenth century the connection between higher education and the institutions of church and state had become less direct. Nevertheless, colleges, which were by that time being founded by the scores in the expanding new nation, were looked to for the preparatory professional training, as well as for the moral formation and cultural learning deemed vital to a healthy and advancing society.[1]

The various Protestant denominations, often competitive, yet, at the same time, divergent expressions of more commonly shared pan-Protestant cultural assumptions and ideals, played a central role in the founding, administering, and teaching tasks of antebellum American higher education. Churches cooperated with local communities in the establishment of colleges, raised funds for their continuing support, and provided much of the college faculty and almost all the college presidents. Until after the Civil War the major concerns of the churches were usually also represented in the central intellectual work of higher education—in the teaching of divinity, moral philosophy, political economy, the classical languages, and usually even in the teaching of science. College teachers and leaders often took as much responsibility as did ministers and seminary professors for addressing issues of faith and knowledge, for discussing the moral uses of knowledge, and for reconciling supposed conflicts between science and religion.

By World War I, in little more than fifty years, this had ceased to be the case. The faith-knowledge issue was still for the church a matter of crucial importance; for American higher education it was no longer. What had once been the mutually shared concern and responsibility for achieving a proper relationship between faith and knowledge, a balance also once thought necessary for a meaningful and vital culture, had split apart. The church was now the sole guardian of faith; the college and university the prime champions of knowledge. As a consequence, the church found itself in the twentieth century on the periphery of American higher education, to be sure, welcomed, or at least tolerated for its adjunct services in the moral and social care of students, but excluded almost entirely from the central intellectual tasks that had come to define the essence of the modern university.

Beginning in the 1930s, however, and gaining momentum throughout the next three decades, the neo-orthodox theological renaissance held forth the promise that the Christian faith could be presented in an intellectually rigorous and respectable way, and that the Protestant church, therefore, in renewed and vital engagement with the university, could reclaim a major role in giving shape and meaning to modern culture. The nature, course, and consequences of this, the last serious, self-directed involvement of the churches with American higher education, is the subject of this book. In this chapter we will look at the nineteenth- and early twentieth-century background of that engagement. We will focus, first, on the antecedents and development of the neo-orthodox theological movement itself and on the ensuing theological renaissance in American Protestantism, and, second, on the nineteenth- and early twentieth-century transformation of American higher education, exploring throughout the importance of the relationship between faith and knowledge.

THE BEGINNINGS OF
THE THEOLOGICAL RENAISSANCE

The Victorian Faith Synthesis

By the end of the nineteenth century, it seemed to many liberal and forward-looking people that whatever strains and tensions might once have existed, even if only recently, between the knowledge provided by modern science and the ideals and norms upheld by the traditions of the churches, had at last been put to rest. For large numbers of people a belief in the beneficent power of science seemed to go together with a whole array of hopes for the advance of society. This confidence in the future, often designated and described as the Victorian faith in progress, was actually a synthesis of scientific knowledge, religious idealism, and social reform concerns that had come to provide for many Europeans and Americans their basic outlook on the world.[2]

One of the clearest and most succinct expressions of the new faith synthesis was provided as early as 1877 by Charles William Eliot, the young president of Harvard University. That year Eliot gave the keynote address at the ceremonies marking the opening of the new wing of the American Museum of Natural History on the still sparsely settled, upper west side of Manhattan.[3] The occasion elicited from Eliot an almost archetypal expression of the nineteenth-century faith synthesis. In a talk of only a few minutes, Eliot set forth the central tenets of the new faith.

First, science was recognized and proclaimed as the dominant mode of knowing in the modern world. "In every field of study," said Eliot, "in history, philology, philosophy, and theology, as well as in natural history and physics, it is now the scientific spirit, the scientific method, which prevails." Second, the new science was to be applied to the solution of humanity's most pressing social problems. It was to be a wedding of social reform with the new capacities promised by science for the management, control, and organization of the future. At the time, Eliot located this promise primarily in the Darwinian emphasis on heredity and its possibilities for an applied eugenics that would

> throw additional safeguards around the domestic relations; embrace the natural interest in vigorous family stocks; guide wisely the charitable action of the community; give a rational basis for penal legislation; and promote the occasional production of illustrious men and the gradual improvement of the masses of mankind.[4]

While the faith in scientifically guided social progress would come to embrace more than Eliot's emphasis on Darwinian evolution and heredity, the evolutionary emphasis would remain strong. And Eliot's particular invoking of it brought out clearly the preeminently managerial character of the new faith in social progress through the application of scientific knowledge.

The last point in Eliot's talk underscored the third basic characteristic of the new faith: it was a synthesis of faith in science, in progressive human ideals and cultural values, and in God—and each was thought to lead to and require the others. Modern science, Eliot said,

> has proved that the development of the universe has been a progress from good to better, a progress not without reactions and catastrophes, but still a benign advance toward ever higher forms of life with ever greater capacities for ever finer enjoyments. It has laid a firm foundation for man's instinctive faith in his own future. . . . It has thus exalted the idea of God—the greatest service which can be rendered to humanity.[5]

The new faith was a blend extracted from many different sources. In describing the distinctive outlook of American life from 1898 to 1918, John Higham has written that it was an "amalgamation of idealism and technique," a mixing of a faith in human religious, moral, and social ideals with a faith in technical efficiency, scientific expertise, and bureaucratic organization.[6] The sources of the new faith-blend were many: an Enlightenment faith in human reason and dignity; older religious visions, especially Protestant postmillennial expectations of the coming kingdom of God on earth, to be heralded, as Jonathan Edwards himself once put it, in the progress of learning, virtue, and civic harmony; perhaps a peculiar American penchant, at least according to foreign visitors, for the empirical, the practical, and the technical; civil religious faiths and hopes nourished and confirmed by the triumphs of the American Revolution and more recently of the Civil War; varieties of nineteenth-century philosophical and popular idealism; the energies and expectations released by rapid industrial, geographic, and demographic expansion; and, above all, the palpable and impressive achievements of science and technology themselves.

What Eliot's statement made clear was the easy movement among all these many components of the new synthesis. Faith in God transferred easily, with all of its religious and numinous energies intact, to faith in science. And the advances in science and technology in turn confirmed the highest of human religious and ethical ideals.

What Laurence Veysey has described as "the emergence of the American university," of which Eliot himself was a major figure, was still in its early stages at the time of Eliot's Museum address.[7] By the end of the century, however, the new university would become the most influential force in American higher education and, in that capacity, would also assume a leading role in the propagation of the new faith.

The university would become the center of scientific discovery and thus the wellspring of the scientific knowledge thought so necessary to social reform and progress.[8] The university would become the training center for the scientific experts who would produce the new knowledge and who would have to take the lead in applying it skillfully to the solution of society's most critical problems.[9] And, finally, the university would itself stand as the temple, the emblematic expression for the American people of the modern joining of piety and learning, faith and knowledge, idealism and technique. As William Rainey Harper, president of the new University of Chicago, put it at the turn of the century: "The university is the prophet of this democracy, and as well, its priest and its philosopher . . . in other words, the university is the Messiah of the democracy, its to-be-expected deliverer."[10] A little less revivalistically, yet reflecting much the same spirit, Nicholas Murray Butler remarked in 1904 that "the university has succeeded to the place once held by the cathedral as the best embodiment of the uplifting forces of the modern time."[11] Most significant is that Butler was by then simply employing what already had become a common figure of speech in university rhetoric.

There was an anomaly in all this. The blend of scientific knowledge and idealism comprised many really conflicting elements, the contradictions of which were not resolved but merely covered by the general faith in progress. More serious was the plain, though largely overlooked, fact that nineteenth-century science, when viewed within its prevailing interpretive framework, was fundamentally at odds with religious and ethical ideals of any kind. This was clear to all who had eyes to see and who were able to look without flinching.

The Mechanical Philosophy

From its origins, modern science had been exclusively quantitative. In fact, modern science had its beginnings precisely in the distinctions between primary qualities (mass, weight, extension, number, and so on) and secondary qualities (color, sound, form, meaning, and everything else not amenable to being counted, measured, and weighed). The latter, the secondary qualities, were thought to exist mainly in the human mind and, hence, to be too tinged with subjectivity ever to be known with any certainty. Secondary qualities, consequently, were to be rigorously excluded from the purview of the scientific method. Only the primary qualities—in short, quantities—were regarded as inhering in objective reality; therefore, they alone were considered capable of being scientifically known. Furthermore, within this method all observations of the world were to be interpreted exclusively in terms of mechanical cause and effect, physical causality being the only kind that lent itself to quantitative objectification.

Although Immanuel Kant in the late eighteenth century established the activity of the subjective mind in the process of knowing, he did so by nailing all knowledge ever more decisively to the framework of finitude, to sense experience and abstractions from sense experience. After Kant, the quantitative, mechanical view of nature as essentially a law-bound system of matter in motion remained intact, and this view continued to extend its sway as the scientific view of reality. The Darwinian theory of evolution, in many ways the culmination of nineteenth-century science, in effect represented the extension of the mechanical, materialistic philosophy to everything—to life, to consciousness, and to human ideals and values.[12]

As long as science could be viewed as merely one way, albeit a very powerful way, of coming to know a certain, limited domain of reality, namely, the quantitative and the mechanical, its challenge to other ways of knowing and experiencing the world would have been limited. However, the Enlightenment's exaltation of a narrow conception of reason, identified increasingly with scientific reason, helped pave the way for the nineteenth-century positivist demand that all experience without remainder be tested, as Auguste Comte, the father of positivism, put it, by "the positive data of science."[13]

The central claim of all varieties of positivism since has been that science is not merely one way of knowing a certain limited dimension of the world, a useful abstraction for limited purposes, but the sole reliable method for knowing anything at all. And hand-in-hand with this has usually gone a kind of corollary claim that, as the sole source of all that counts as knowledge, science alone can provide a valid, all-encompassing view of reality, the so-called scientific worldview.

By its nature, however, a purely empirical, quantitative, and mechanistic way of knowing cannot deal with the essence of religion or of most philosophy. By definition, a purely quantitative science cannot in itself deal with the qualitative, with, for instance, the qualities of nature, red, blue, sound, and so forth, or with the qualities of life, with truth, beauty, goodness, with the intrinsically meaningful, with purpose, with value. At the most quantitative science can only interpret these qualities instrumentally or as mere surface signs of an underlying quantitative reality.[14] As Alfred North Whitehead later described the scientific worldview that was becoming increasingly widespread in the nineteenth century, its picture of the universe was that of nature as "a dull affair, soundless, scentless, colourless; merely the hurrying of material, endlessly, meaninglessly."[15] This scientific worldview clearly challenged any religion and philosophy that sought a deeper reality of quality and meaning within or behind the material appearances.[16]

The wonders of scientific advance and its technological achievements hid from most people the underlying conflict of science with religious affirmations and sensibilities. The majority of people most likely did not concern themselves with such matters, or at most gave them only a passing thought. The religiously inclined, whether a liberal idealist or a Bible-reading churchgoer, could view the scientific, industrial, and technological progress of the times as part of the working out of the divine plan, the one seeing it as the evolutionary progress of the highest human and divine ideals, the other as the manifestation of divine purpose and the coming of God's kingdom on earth.

Nevertheless, some did see and draw the implications from the challenge inherent in the scientific, mechanical worldview. In fact, one way of understanding the many idealist philosophies of the nineteenth and early twentieth centuries is to see them precisely as attempts to maintain the reality of a world in which meaning could still be found and secured beyond or within the desolate universe described by science. For example, William James's religious-ethical pragmatism, otherwise so different from the idealist philosophies, as well as his lifelong involvement with parapsychology, was an attempt to find realms of meaning invulnerable to the inroads of the mechanical philosophy.[17] Among those who also saw clearly the implications of the mechanical philosophy were a few thoroughgoing scientific naturalists at one end of the spectrum and at the other a few theological conservatives. In ironic juxtaposition to one another, both grasped, as most liberals did not, what the scientific worldview actually meant for human meaning and purpose. The consistent naturalists accepted the futile inevitability of a mechanistic and meaningless universe running down according to the Second Law of Thermodynamics; the religious conservatives rejected it in favor of a counter worldview drawn from their understanding of scripture. There were, of course, also a few dour and prescient souls like Henry Adams, who suspected that not only in the mechanical worldview, but, more importantly, in the scientific method itself, the human being had gotten its hands on something it would not be able to control.[18]

Such thoughts did not shake the optimism and expectations of most people. Nevertheless, for a few people, these thoughts raised difficulties and undeniable nagging questions. For those religious believers who accepted the methods and promises of science, it was especially important to be able to show that science, religion, and human ideals and hopes not only could be reconciled but also were basically mutually supportive.

Evolutionary Theological Reconstruction

A battery of Protestant theologians and popular religious writers began to take up the challenge of showing that science and religion went together. The task was made simpler because most scientists in this country were themselves religious people who saw no inherent conflict between science and religion.[19] Soon many theologians and religious thinkers began to see in the theory of evolution itself the key to reconciling science and religion. The initial waves of shock and religious reaction against Darwinism that erupted during the first decades after the publication of the *Origin of Species* began to subside as the work of reconciliation proceeded.[20]

Liberal clergymen and scientific popularizers, such as Henry Ward Beecher, George A. Gordon, Lyman Abbott, and John Fiske, began to apply evolutionary science to the whole of traditional theology. At the same time several important theological chairs in American seminaries were filled by persons dedicated to reconciling traditional theology with evolutionary science and with the new application of scientific history to the study of the Bible: persons such as Henry Churchill King at Oberlin, William Adams Brown at Union Seminary in New York, and William Newton Clarke at Colgate.[21]

The theological reconstruction that was carried out by these persons was thoroughgoing. Traditional views, such as the authority of the scriptures and the doctrines of creation, sin, and salvation, were all overhauled in the light of the evolutionary vision. The central concept in the evolutionary reconstruction of theology was that of the immanence of the Divine in the whole process of cosmic and social evolution. All of creation was seen to be gradually but ineluctably advancing, under the guidance of the divine presence in the human being and in nature, toward an ever-increasing realization of human ethical and religious ideals and social harmony. The evolutionary concept applied in the scientific study of scripture yielded the idea of a progressive revelation of the divine purposes.

The optimistic faith in human action and the emphasis on an ethicized religion tied in directly with other nineteenth-century movements for social and institutional reform. So successful were the theological reconstructionists, for example, that the major social gospel writers and progressive reformers of the early twentieth century could largely assume that the conflict between science and religion had been overcome. Instead of the science-faith issue, these writers could now focus mainly on the burning social and ethical issues of the times.[22] Some, like Walter Rauschenbusch, who emphasized the modern relevance of such traditional Christian doctrines as sin and redemption, were able to do so because they could assume that the problem of reconciling Christian faith with science had been resolved.[23] All shared the optimism and progressive idealism of the evolutionary theological outlook.

The Social Gospel, undergirded by the new theological reconstruction of science and religion, helped stoke the larger social reform movements of the early twentieth century with religious energy. And the underlying work of theological reconstruction helped make possible an easy move back and forth between religious and more secular-oriented reform activities and concerns, including, especially, education.

In this regard the liberal theologians rendered a crucial service in smoothing the way for an ever-wider acceptance of the university as the major producer and popularizer of the knowledge so necessary for the building of an industrial democracy. There were those who suspected that the university's aversion to denominational ties bespoke a deeper rejection of religion as such; persons, who, for example, decried "the godless state university" and who viewed the university's exaltation of science over scripture and doctrine as outright unbelief.[24]

The evolutionary reconstructionists' reconciliation of faith and science, and their championing of a nonsectarian, cultural religion helped to deflect and mitigate such attacks, and to enable those so inclined to see the university as a chief bulwark of the faith-knowledge synthesis. In his 1900 inaugural address as chancellor of the State University of Nebraska, Baptist theologian and former president of Brown University, Elisha Andrews, gave clear testimony to what he regarded as the success of the reconcilers' work: " . . . owing to a happy change in the spirit of science and in the spirit of religion, the schism between these two vital interests at universities as in the general world of thought is less and less angry as the years pass, science growing devout and religions comprehensive and sweet."[25]

The theological reconstructionists were able to describe science and technological advance as supportive of religion and ethics through their taking up an evolutionary view of the divine presence at work in nature, history, and intellectual development. By adopting an evolutionary view, they were, most importantly, also able to claim that they had harmonized religion with Darwinism. Theirs was indeed a theory of evolution, but it was *not* a Darwinian theory of evolution.

The theologians' version contained values, ideals, and metaphysical assumptions that really had no ground in a purely quantitative, mechanistic science and its Darwinian evolutionary offspring. These large ideals the theologians imported into the scientific worldview from sources outside it.[26] By speaking the language of evolution and evolutionary theory, however, they could appear to be building real bridges between Darwinism and scientific knowledge, on the one side, and faith and ethics, on the other. As long as they could point to what seemed to be patent evidence of evolutionary social and moral progress, their well-intentioned sleight of hand would remain largely undetected.

The Breakup of the Evolutionary Synthesis

After World War I the grand nineteenth-century synthesis of scientific knowledge, religious and philosophical idealism, and progressive, social-reform optimism began to unravel; but it did not come apart all at once. Although the story of the dissolution of the Victorian faith-knowledge synthesis has been often told, several aspects of this story warrant underscoring for the light they shed on the development of neo-orthodoxy and its attempt to engage the faith-knowledge problem anew.

The catastrophes of the war itself, and on top of them the social and psychic dislocations that followed, the depression, and eventually the rise of Hitler and the clouds of further war, drastically undermined the pretensions of any easy faith in progress. All these made it ever more difficult to maintain a belief in an immanent good working itself out in the evolutionary perfection of nature and human history. The early epithet, "crisis theology," which was frequently used to describe the stirrings of what would become neo-orthodoxy, reflected the movement's origins in a growing, widespread sense after World War I that the modern world was in deep trouble.

For some time after the war, however, the influence of the evolutionary reconstructionists and related theological liberals remained strong, and, indeed, throughout the first quarter of the new century, dominated much of mainline Protestant theological education—especially in the Methodist, Congregational, and Baptist churches.[27] William Adams Brown, for example, continued to publish well into the 1930s. Other liberal theologians and popular preachers, such as Albert C. Knudson, Harris Franklin Rall, and especially Henry Emerson Fosdick of the Riverside Church in New York, also enjoyed wide following and influence.

These, and those who took their bearings from them, have often been described as "evangelical liberals" because of their determination to preserve the claims of traditional Christian doctrines, even as they restated them in light of their embrace of the ideals and achievements of modern science and culture.[28] They saw themselves, for instance, as staunchly Christocentric in their constant emphasis on Jesus as the highest expression of the nature and will of God and of the human potential for kinship with God. And while they revised the traditional doctrine of sin to square it with their optimistic assessment of the advances of modern civilization and the future evolutionary potential of human religious-ethical development, they nevertheless insisted that the human being requires redemption and needs divine inspiration to attain its highest potential. In other words, they were by no means out-and-out scientific humanists.

As the earlier liberal optimism and confidence began to fade for many people after the war, however, the liberal theologians themselves were forced increasingly to be more rigorous in what they chose to find acceptable in modern culture. Moreover, it was no longer so easy to assume that religious faith and ethical values, on the one hand, and scientific knowledge, on the other, were mutually supportive. The hard edge of the scientific method and scientific worldview was becoming increasingly difficult to overlook.

The purely quantitative and mechanistic assumptions of science began to come increasingly to the fore, shorn now of their idealistic trappings. And this nonidealistic view of science was being embraced by more and more persons as desirable. Increasingly after World War I, the optimistic, evolutionary ethical view of science began to give way to the insistence that science is value-free, objective, and wholly empirical.[29] The behavioral position in psychology, for instance, powerfully articulated by John Watson during the war years, did away with all non-empirical notions of self, ideals, and purpose.[30] Likewise, an older view of sociology as a kind of scientific moral philosophy yielded to the view of a social science modeled entirely on the physical sciences as objective, empirical, and ethically neutral.[31] In his presidential address to the American Sociological Society in 1929, for example, William Ogburn said, "Sociology as a science is not interested in making the world a better place in which to live. . . . Science is interested directly in one thing only, to wit, discovering new knowledge."[32] In anthropology, sociology, and psychology, all taking their lead from the physical sciences, the emphasis was increasingly toward reducing all beliefs, religions, and value commitments to what were regarded as more empirical and real physical, biological, and economic needs and realities. The conflict between science as the only way of knowing reality, on the one side, and, on the other side, human values, meaning, and the qualitative had become pronounced.

The rise and spread in the 1920s and 1930s of various forms of philosophical and theological naturalism reflected the growing dominance of scientific assumptions about the world and the possibilities of human knowledge. The central tenets of the naturalists, as their name indicates, were that "nature is all there is," and that science is the only bona fide source of knowledge of any kind. For the naturalists, therefore, the only knowledge persons can have of the world at any given time is what science tells them. In the thought of John Dewey, F.J.E. Woodbridge, Morris R. Cohen, and others, the naturalist position began to be fully articulated.

Many liberal theologians responded to the scientific and naturalist challenge by trying to show that religious affirmations, like those of science, also are based solidly on empirical data. The data were those said to be afforded by religious experience and by the evidences of personal moral transformation and ethical action in the world.[33] On this basis several theologians attempted to develop their own theological naturalism.

This new theological naturalism was represented especially in the work of Yale's D. C. Macintosh, and Chicago's Shailer Mathews and Henry Nelson Wieman.[34] Macintosh wanted to develop theology as itself an experimental and empirical science that could satisfy the epistemological norms of natural science. Mathews, likewise, embraced what he called "modernism" in theology as "the use of the methods of science to find, state and use the permanent and central values of inherited orthodoxy in meeting the needs of the modern world."[35] Wieman, drawing on the process theology of Alfred North Whitehead, attempted to establish that proper theological statements were themselves scientific, that is, empirical, objective, and verifiable. These theological naturalists were struggling to recognize the claims of natural science as definitive for all knowledge, and still to find a place, within the conditions set by science, for traditional, even evangelical, religion. As such, and by definition, it was a tension-filled undertaking.

By the mid-1930s, then, the liberal spectrum ran all the way from popular idealism and evangelical liberalism at one end to a more rigorous and carefully wrought theological neonaturalism at the other. But this latter end of the spectrum also ran out, in the work of people like Edward Scribner Ames, Eustace Haydon, George Burnam Foster, and, perhaps, at times, even Shailer Mathews, into unabashed nontheistic, scientific naturalism and humanism.[36] The line between the religious naturalists and the secular, and at times even antireligious, naturalists was becoming difficult to draw. Increasingly, nonreligious, scientific naturalists charged religious liberals with being inconsistent in their affirmations of science by failing to jettison completely the baggage of their evangelical religious heritage.

In the 1920s another challenge arose from the opposite direction. This challenge came from Protestant conservatives, self-named as "fundamentalists," who charged that in their wholehearted embrace of human reason, civilization, and science—especially historical science as applied to the study of scripture—the liberals had actually abandoned historic Christianity itself. That the liberal spectrum could seem to shade off unbrokenly into outright scientific naturalism added force to the fundamentalists' accusations.

However, the fundamentalists' adherence to a pre-Darwinian conception of science, their dogmatic reassertion of certain Christian doctrines ("the fundamentals"—often congealed seventeenth-century versions of these doctrines), and their insistence on the inerrancy of the Bible in its literalistic reading—all these factors made it easier for the liberals to depict the fundamentalists' attacks as basically unlearned and ignorant and not a serious intellectual challenge. That most Protestant churchgoers were more conservative than liberal, if they were theologically minded at all, did seem to make fundamentalism for a time a serious power threat to control of the churches. Still, it was a threat the liberals were able to deal with.[37]

By this time, however, liberalism was coming under fire from yet another direction—from Protestant theologians who were claiming to be both modern and at the same time firmly rooted in the traditional biblical and doctrinal sources of the historic Christian tradition. These latest critics could not easily be dismissed as fundamentalists, though some attempted to do so.[38] Neither, however, could they be welcomed by the liberals as simply another needed corrective of the liberal position; their criticisms of the liberals' cultural

Christianity were too severe for that. The neo-orthodox theological revival was gathering momentum.

The Theological Renaissance

Writing from the vantage of the 1970s, Sydney Ahlstrom once identified 1934 as the *annus mirabilis* of neo-orthodoxy. Shortly thereafter, however, and using the same expression, William J. Wolf declared 1936 to be the annus mirabilis.[39] A good case could be made for either, since by the mid-1930s the neo-orthodox theological renaissance in America was well under way. The year 1936 saw the publication in English translations of Karl Barth's *Credo* and the first volume of his *Church Dogmatics*, Emil Brunner's *The Divine Imperative*, Nicolai Berdyaev's *The Meaning of History*, and Søren Kierkegaard's *Philosophical Fragments;* the following year would bring the English translation of Martin Buber's *I and Thou*. In these were represented some of the most important European sources of the theological revival, although English translations and studies of the work of Barth, Kierkegaard, and others, such as that of Albert Schweitzer, all inimical to liberalism, had already been made available by American theologians.[40]

Just as important, young American theologians themselves, even in the 1920s, were starting to develop their own criticisms of liberal theology. Thus, they had begun to place their unique American stamp on the budding theological renaissance. Already the brothers Reinhold Niebuhr and H. Richard Niebuhr were emerging as among the most important of the new theologians. Especially influential in these early years were Reinhold Niebuhr's *Moral Man and Immoral Society* (1932)—later characterized by Sydney Ahlstrom as "probably the most disruptive religio-ethical bombshell of domestic contribution to be dropped during the entire interwar period"— and H. Richard Niebuhr's *The Kingdom of God in America* (1937).[41] In these works the Niebuhrs eloquently indicted what they regarded as the spiritual emptiness and shallow moralism of liberal-progressive religion and the "cultural Christianity" that they saw it fostering. They were soon to be joined by Paul Tillich, whose influential book *The Religious Situation* H. Richard Niebuhr had translated into English in 1932. Two years later Tillich fled Hitler's Germany to come to Union Theological Seminary in New York City. There, and later at Harvard and the University of Chicago, he would become a renowned American-German theologian. Other young American theologians also were rallying to the banner of theological renewal.

Besides their experience of cultural and social crises, the new theologians shared several theological emphases that set them apart from earlier Protestant liberalism. They all shared a rediscovery of a deep meaning in the images and stories of the biblical narratives and in the classic doctrines of the Christian tradition, a meaning that they were convinced the liberals had either forsaken, or had squandered by watering it down beyond recognition.

Over against the liberal emphasis on an immanent divinity working through nature and human history, the neo-orthodox stressed the divine otherness and transcendence. Over against the liberals' optimistic appraisal of human reason and goodness, the neo-orthodox brought a vivid sense of the human capacity for evil, especially as it found group expression in institutional power and social structures. Over against the liberals' faith in an ongoing evolutionary advance, the neo-orthodox stressed discontinuity, crisis, the inbreaking of transcendent divine judgment. They positively affirmed and wanted to safeguard human freedom and responsibility. Above all, they affirmed the reality of transcendent being and love as providing the only ultimate meaning and coherence to human existence.

Of great importance for these neo-orthodox beginnings of the American theological renaissance were Karl Barth's early emphasis on God as the "wholly other," and Kierkegaard's rejection of every form of culture Christianity and his demand for authentic human decision and existence against all objectifying, depersonalizing rationalistic systems. These were set within a larger context of a renewed appreciation and reappropriation of certain classic theological texts, especially those of Augustine and of the Protestant Reformation. Just as important as these European influences for the Americans, however, were their own traditions as Americans, and their own experience and appraisal of their mid-twentieth-century historical situation.

Even in their appropriation of European neo-orthodox thinking the Americans tended to select those positions and views most congenial to their own traditions and experience. Most leading American theologians, for example, seemed receptive to Emil Brunner's view, as against that of Karl Barth, that a healthy respect for God's transcendence is compatible with an emphasis on the divine presence and the possibility of a natural theology. Reinhold Niebuhr in his monumental Gifford lectures, *The Nature and Destiny of Man*, delivered early in the 1940s, drew extensively on such emphases from Emil Brunner.[42] This is not to say that there was not sharp argument among the new American theologians about such issues. Nevertheless, there existed from the beginning within the American theological renaissance an opening for those who, while dissatisfied with much of the earlier liberalism, did not wish to repudiate all liberal concerns with society and nature and who did not welcome the label neo-orthodox.

Moreover, all the new theologians, whatever the shades of differences among them, considered themselves moderns who wanted to affirm human reason, modern science, and modern scholarship, even when these were applied to thinking about religion. This stood them squarely in an unbroken, though reconstructed, continuity with central emphases of the American liberal tradition. It also distinguished them from fundamentalists and other antimodernists.[43]

Especially important in the American theological renaissance, including most of its strictly neo-orthodox forms, was an abiding concern for social action and social justice. Reinhold Niebuhr had established this as a fundamental emphasis from the beginning.[44] Here can be discerned, for instance, an important connection of American neo-orthodoxy itself with the traditional practical and pragmatic streams in American life (including political and philosophical pragmatism). It is here also, perhaps even more importantly, that most American neo-orthodoxy can be seen standing in a revised, but unbroken continuity with the earlier Social Gospel. Although tempered and checked by Reinhold Niebuhr's cautions against the pride that infects the best of intentions, and by his devastating diagnoses of the recalcitrance of institutional and structural injustice—even when cast in the context of what Donald Meyer later described as the neo-orthodox "search for political realism"—the connection of the American theological renaissance with the earlier Social Gospel and its hope and optimism about the possibilities of historical improvement, however carefully these now had to be envisaged, remained in place.[45]

Finally, a broad but central emphasis running throughout the theological renaissance was a high estimation of the crucial importance of personal existence and of personal-communal relationship and responsibility. The great truths of the scriptures, of the biblical images and stories, and of the Christian tradition were to be grasped, not in literal, propositional statements, but in personal decision and response. Religious truths, images, and doctrines were, as Reinhold Niebuhr said, to be taken "seriously but not literally." They were to be interpreted existentially and symbolically, in such a way that their meaning for human existence would be revealed, and the possibility of authentic personal response would be evoked. The Kierkegaardian, existentialist background was an essential foundation of the initial neo-orthodox undertaking. In this connection Martin Buber's treatment of the religious dimension in terms of an I-Thou encounter also became a major component of the new American theological armory. These existentialist emphases, symbolically rendered and understood were central to neo-orthodoxy itself. They also provided important potential points of contact within the theological renaissance for a broad spectrum of other theological positions.

As Reinhold Niebuhr formulated the new theologians' critical enterprise: An idealism (philosophical or popular) that identified the human being and the achievements of human culture with the Divine, and a naturalism that denied human freedom, responsibility, and the possibility of transcendence—both alike were to be rejected. The theologians set themselves the task, and were convinced of its possibility and necessity, of showing that the Christian faith is relevant to the modern world as the best account available of the human condition.

The experiences of the Great War and of a worldwide economic depression had rendered the affirmations of idealism increasingly vulnerable to criticism. Not so easy, however, was the criticism of naturalism because of its association with the methods and results of science that the theologians wanted to affirm.

Harder still was the positive task of making the Christian faith, as conveyed by scripture and tradition, compelling to the modern mind. In all of this the theologians had to come to grips with the faith-knowledge relationship. The challenge that faced them was whether they could bring the two together in a truly integral union, or would succeed only in fashioning yet another, and, perhaps, this time the last version of the grand nineteenth-century amalgamation of faith and knowledge, destined in its turn to unravel and fall apart.

The dominance of science in the culture still posed the knowledge-faith problem in its sharpest form. Whatever else was to be said about them, this the liberal theologians of the late nineteenth and twentieth centuries, who had attempted to join idealism and naturalism, had clearly grasped. In their 1937 festschrift for the naturalist theologian, D. C. Macintosh, the editors, two of them, H. Richard Niebuhr and Robert L. Calhoun, themselves to be leading figures in the theological renaissance, wrote that the importance of Macintosh's work was that he had been able "to align the problem of religious knowledge with science." "The scientific method," they wrote, "is now acknowledged to be the method by which knowledge must come."[46] The issue was clear. If science is the chief form of knowledge for the modern mind, what do religious faith and ethics have to do with knowledge, and in what way?

Interestingly, it was the arch-naturalist John Dewey, soon to become the *bête noire* of many neo-orthodox theologians, who put the issue as clearly as anyone: "Certainly," he wrote, "one of the most genuine problems of modern life is the reconciliation of the scientific view of the universe with the claims of the moral life."[47] Elsewhere Dewey wrote, "If the physical terms by which modern science deals with the world are supposed to constitute that world, it follows as a matter of course that qualities we experience and which are the distinctive things in human life, fall outside of nature." The result, he pointed out, is to deny to our view of nature just "the traits that give life purpose and value." In their place arises "the belief that nature is an indifferent, dead mechanism."[48] Dewey saw the problem, and he spent his life trying to find a solution. How successful he was is another story.

Whether the new theologians, however, would see the knowledge problem as clearly as either their predecessors, such as Macintosh, or their adversaries, such as Dewey, would prove to be crucial, especially in their involvement with higher education. And higher education would be the central arena within which the faith-knowledge issues would have to be engaged.

THE TRANSFORMATION OF
AMERICAN HIGHER EDUCATION

The Emergence of the University

By the 1930s American higher education had undergone a fundamental transformation. The new research university had become firmly established as the cognitive center of a culture shaped increasingly by science and technology. It also had become more and more the social-professional-opportunity center of that culture. The further development of older academic disciplines, the proliferation of new ones, especially in the sciences and social sciences, and the creation of new professional and vocational schools within the universities and without—all had transformed both the curricular and the institutional landscapes of higher education.[49]

In the nineteenth century the land grant colleges and state universities had pioneered in bringing a diversity of new practical and occupationally oriented subjects directly into the curriculum—engineering, home economics, agriculture, commerce. Other institutions quickly followed the universities' example.[50] The spread of the elective system and the development of the departmental system fostered further specialization and proliferation of new subject areas.[51] Among the many new types of institutions founded alongside the traditional college and the new research university were normal schools and teachers' colleges, nursing schools, business and technical schools, and junior colleges, almost all of these with a technical and practical emphasis.[52] Even though many small colleges maintained that they were centers of the traditional liberal arts, their actual course offerings, which included more and more vocational and prevocational courses, revealed that they too could not resist the new educational currents.[53]

The "service" ideal of the progressives and Social Gospel reformers had been eagerly taken up by higher education. The university now not only claimed to be the source of the new scientific knowledge needed for the guidance of modern society and for the solution of its most pressing problems but also led the way in developing new institutions—university extension service, experiment stations, home demonstration and agricultural county agents—to bring the new knowledge to the wider public. The development of new occupations in American society, all of them pressing to be recognized on an equal footing and with the same privileges of the older professions, further enhanced the place of higher education in American culture. The university, organizing itself professionally by academic disciplines, was increasingly called on, and was more than ready, to assume the role of training, standardizing, and providing the credentials for all professions, academic and others. By the 1930s American higher education was being looked to by the American people as one of the chief portals to social status, professional standing, and occupational opportunity.[54]

The prestige of the new university had been firmly established, and throughout the first decades of the twentieth century all the institutions of American higher education enjoyed an ever-growing esteem in the eyes of the American public, especially of the middle and upper middle class public.[55] After the war, and into the 1920s and 1930s, the depression notwithstanding, enrollments in American higher education swelled. From about 597,800 students in 1919–1920, enrollment in American higher education nearly tripled to 1,500,000 in 1939–1940.[56] As Lawrence Cremin points out, most of the new students were in technical, vocational, and professional fields, especially engineering, education, commerce, and business.[57]

Although the majority of American students were enrolled in the more numerous colleges, the research university was already setting the standards, the ethos, and the reward system for the rest of American higher education. The prestige and growing influence of the university were firmly anchored in its commitment to science as the primary source and model for all its endeavors, including the university conception of research and social service—service to the nation, to industry, to the professions, and to the public. "What propelled the university movement," Edward Shils has written, "was a drift of opinion toward the appreciation of knowledge, particularly knowledge of a scientific character."[58]

By the 1930s, moreover, there had emerged in American culture what Roger Geiger has called the "privately funded research system," an interlocking network of universities, foundations, and industry.[59] Committed to introducing scientific efficiency and rational standardization into the organization and management of American public, industrial, and educational life, a number of powerful philanthropic foundations—especially the Carnegie Foundation for the Advancement of Teaching and the Rockefeller General Education Board—began to support a select number of universities they deemed best equipped to carry out the research efforts required for the attainment of their goals.[60]

Geiger shows that by 1930 fewer than twenty American universities were receiving the lion's share of research funding from the foundations and industry. It was basically these same select universities that would continue throughout the rest of the century to be recipients of most research funding— including, increasingly after World War II, funds from the federal government.[61] Above all, this relatively small number of research universities would be the flagships and standard-bearers for what counted as most important in the whole of American higher education. That the story of the rise to leadership of these research universities can be told almost entirely, as Geiger does, in terms of scientific and technological research, with scarcely a passing mention of the humanities, is as revealing as anything of the dominance of scientific methods of inquiry in setting the norms for what counted as research and knowledge within American higher education.

It was also within the universities that the new social and behavioral sciences of psychology, sociology, anthropology, political science, and economics began to develop and to find a place for themselves.[62] In their origins these subjects had been treated as topics within the old required moral philosophy course taught in the eighteenth- and nineteenth-century college to the senior class by the college president. With the expansion of the universities in the 1870s and 1880s, however, these subjects soon emerged in their own right; and after World War I they took their place within the university as separate academic disciplines with claims to their own domains and methodological identities. The formation of the Social Science Research Council in 1923 marked the coming of age of the social science disciplines within the university and the increasing ability of psychologists, political scientists, and sociologists to further secure their positions within academia with increased foundation funding for research.[63] Essential to the new social sciences was the view that the methods of natural science provide the only reliable means for the serious study of human beings and human society.

Like so much in the universities at the turn of the century, the fledgling social sciences were at first imbued with the strong social reform concerns of the Social Gospel and progressive reform movements. A number of the new, young academic social scientists carried with them the missionary reform idealism of the liberal Protestantism in which they had grown up. Many were influenced, through their study in German universities, by German historical and developmental concepts, which often seemed to undergird an evolutionary reform optimism. And a few of them were committed to more radical, left-leaning political activism. All of this melded for a time to put the new social sciences solidly within the nineteenth-century synthesis of faith in scientific progress, idealism, and social reform.[64]

Even in the 1890s, however, many young academics had begun to dissociate themselves from Social Gospel reform causes and to turn toward a more rigorous emphasis on scientific research and on developing their professional ties. One reason for the pulling back of many young academics from social reform was their vulnerability to the pressures of more conservative university administrators and trustees. Another was the need they felt to concentrate more of their energies on establishing their own firm professional identity and standing within the university. The progressive conception of the university as the producer of expert scientific knowledge for social use further provided a rationale for these young social scientists to begin to conceive of themselves as doing more good by withdrawing from overt social reform and concentrating instead on the production of useful knowledge through scientific research.[65] Most important in turning the social scientists toward a strictly academic and disciplinary orientation, however, was the conception of science itself as objective, empirical, and value free.

By the 1920s this empiricist, objectivist, and ethically neutral conception of science had come to dominate and to give shape to the social sciences. The increasingly pronounced emphasis within the social sciences in the 1920s of behavioralist and quantitative conceptions of scientific method further strengthened this orientation.[66] Applied social science itself was being conceived mainly as the more efficient scientific manipulation and management of human society in the interests of goals and purposes supplied by sources other than the social sciences themselves. Increasingly, as we have seen, many social scientists began to deny any responsibility for raising questions of meaning, ethics, and social purpose because such issues were thought to lie beyond the domains of the social science disciplines. Taking the physical sciences as his model, for example, the social scientist George A. Lundberg said in 1929:

> It is not the business of a chemist who invents a high explosive to be influenced in his task by considerations as to whether his product will be used to blow up cathedrals or to build tunnels through the mountains. Nor is it the business of the social scientist in arriving at laws of group behavior to permit himself to be influenced by considerations of how his conclusions will coincide with existing notions, or what the effect of his findings on the social order will be.[67]

To be sure, most natural and social scientists probably regarded science, as they had from the beginning, with the faith that by its nature science was inherently progressive. But, at the same time, the notion of the sciences, including the social sciences, as ethically neutral also relieved the scientists themselves from having to justify this faith—which, by the canons of a purely quantitative science, they would have been hard put to do—just as it absolved them from raising questions of purpose and value altogether.

The sway of the scientific method within the university also made itself felt in the humanities. Interestingly, the conception of the scientific study of history, religion, and literature received its first major introduction into nineteenth-century American higher education by young American theologians fresh from study tours in German universities, where the new scientific methods were first being developed, primarily in biblical and literary criticism.[68] Further attempts to place history, and eventually other humanistic subjects, on a scientific basis continued. To the extent that they were not amenable to being made scientific, the humanities—literature, art, philosophy, religion—were not forced out of the university, but they were put constantly on the defensive and were repeatedly challenged to demonstrate that they deserved as solid and respectable a place in the curriculum as the sciences. Years later the historian Laurence Veysey would describe the continuing plight and fragmentation of the humanities in modern higher education. "Those who reject the dominant scientific conception of knowledge," Veysey would write, "can only wander off in a score of mutually unrelated directions."[69] Most religious, mystical, symbolical, and artistic modes of thought and knowing found little place at all within the university, except as objects of observation and analysis.[70]

Religion and the University

From a number of perspectives it would be accurate to speak of the growing secularization of American higher education by the 1920s. Many of the century-long accoutrements of the traditionally close relationship between the churches and the colleges were dissolving or rapidly being cast away—compulsory chapel, the hiring of clergymen as college and university presidents, the required teaching of divinity and of moral philosophy.[71] The Carnegie Foundation retirement plan put forward in 1906 was intended to standardize American higher education by encouraging those colleges that might become, as Ellen Lagemann has described it, " 'true universities' in which science might flourish."[72] A major stipulation of the plan was that participating institutions had to be free of all denominational control. A number of colleges, such as Brown, Centre, Coe, Drake, Rochester, Rutgers, Wesleyan, and others severed their denominational ties and became eligible to receive the proffered retirement funds.[73]

Furthermore, the traditional religious, curricular goals of many colleges began to disappear in the face of students' growing interest in practical and technical courses, and in the opportunities for social advancement and assimilation that going to college offered.[74] One survey of college catalogues indicated that between 1910 and 1920 there was a more than 50 percent decline in the number of colleges affirming that higher education included religious aims.[75] Moreover, many faculty members were showing increasing indifference and hostility, not only to institutional religion, but to religious questions and issues themselves. An oft-quoted study concluded that by 1916 nearly 90 percent of sociologists, biologists, and psychologists doubted the existence of God.[76] By the 1930s students interested in religious questions would find little encouragement either from most of their professors or from the course offerings available in the college catalog.[77]

Whether the students themselves during these years maintained a vital interest in religious issues, despite widespread faculty attitudes and their own vocational concerns, is a more difficult question. In the early part of the century many college-sponsored, or college-encouraged, religious activities remained available for most students, not only at church-related colleges, but also at many state institutions. Many local churches welcomed students to services, and even held special classes for the students. Before World War I, large numbers of faculty at many colleges and universities also were active in these local churches and frequently taught Sunday schools, but evidence suggests that after the war this tended to become less and less the case.[78]

Well into the first quarter of the twentieth century, the main source of direct religious influence on the campus was the interdenominational student Christian association. The first Young Men's and Women's Christian Associations in this country were founded in the larger American cities during the 1850s, where they offered to young people in the urban centers a variety of opportunities for worship, study, recreation, and education.[79] Beginning at the state universities of Virginia and Michigan in the late 1850s the student Christian associations also spread to the nation's colleges and universities. By 1900 some 1,300 association chapters had been founded on college and university campuses with over 100,000 members, almost half the number of students in all of American higher education. By World War I such chapters existed on most campuses, usually with full-time secretaries organizing many-sided religious, and, increasingly, student welfare and social programs.[80] Also present on many campuses was the Student Volunteer Movement, founded in 1889 to enlist students in the burgeoning worldwide missionary outreach of the Protestant churches. And, during the first decade of the century, the various individual denominations and religious groups, at first Protestant, then Catholic and Jewish groups, began to organize their own campus programs to reach students.

For the years after World War I, however, students' actual religious views and commitments are difficult to ascertain. In a review of a number of articles and studies dealing with student attitudes, John Evans concluded that throughout the entire period between the wars "students remained basically interested in and loyal to religious commitments despite the secularistic philosophy the professoriate imposed on them."[81] However, Paula Fass, in her study of youth of the 1920s, while noting that many college students of the time were regular or semiregular churchgoers, nevertheless, describes the steady erosion of student religious interests and enthusiasms by the pressure of fraternity and sorority life, sports, parties, and other extracurricular and social activities.[82] "The typical college undergraduate," wrote the editor of the student newspaper at Methodist Duke University in 1928, "has too much to do, both of work and amusement, to consider religion other than something 'that isn't done' in college."[83] Yet Fass also observes that "political radicalism was very often a Christian phenomenon, and the most sustained impulses toward internationalism and national reform were connected with denominational or inter-denominational conferences. . . ."[84] In 1936 a study showed that over 85 percent of the students in American higher education identified themselves by their religious preferences.[85] It would seem that despite many competing interests and wide faculty indifference, students maintained a steady interest in religion, which on occasion could be mobilized in striking fashion, but which for the most part manifested in conventional ways, and was, like so many of the students' other interests and concerns, essentially a foreign presence within the university.

While it makes sense in many respects to speak of the growing secularization of higher education, from another perspective this can be very misleading. In important ways the university itself became a major religious phenomenon of American culture. David Levine, in his study of the American college during the first part of the century, has written that as an avenue for social and occupational status (read salvation?), "education became the secular religion of twentieth-century American society."[86] Tied in with this looking to higher education for social and material opportunity were other, deeper sentiments. However much the older idealism, traditional religion, and conventional morality may have been called into question by the war and its aftermath, the university still carried the nineteenth-century faith in education and science as intrinsically good and the bulwarks of democracy and cultural advance. This enabled most people simply to continue to ignore the hard edge of science that was now actually showing itself. Levine quotes Roscoe Pound the legal educator as observing in 1936 that "in its hold upon popular faith and popular imagination, organized higher learning has the place in American society of today which organized religion had in the society of the middle ages."[87]

Still more serious as a genuine religious phenomenon was the role of the university as the temple of knowledge. The university scientist increasingly came to play the part of the seeker, the initiate, and the seer. In the first years of the university, the research ideal itself was regarded and extolled by its votaries as a path of initiation, which it was: a discipline requiring a quasi-religious devotion of the first order. G. Stanley Hall of Clark University wrote that research was "the very highest vocation of man."[88] In a similar vein, Albion Small, of the University of Chicago and founder there of America's first university department of sociology, urged, "Remember the research ideal, to keep it holy!"[89] While most scientists would probably have been more modest than their colleague, Columbia University zoologist Henry Fairfield Osborn, who in 1913 nominated the modern natural scientist for "the new order of sainthood," they were probably as certain as Osborn that they were, indeed, the rightful guardians of the one true path to knowledge.[90] It is true that this older, nineteenth-century, idealistic rhetoric faded (though it never disappeared entirely), but the substance remained. The investment of the university with religious function and office was not temporary. As custodians of the dominant scientific way of knowing, and constituting the modern tribunal for determining the definition of all true and acceptable knowledge, the universities had become, in Edward Shil's words, "the heirs of the churches."[91] American higher education would perforce, therefore, be the unavoidable and prime testing ground for the new theology.

The Churches and Modern Higher Education

The loss by the Protestant churches of the prominent position they had long enjoyed in American higher education was also part of a larger process of displacement of the churches from their earlier position of influence and control within American culture generally.[92] It is important to note, however, that, within American higher education at any rate, the churches had not always resisted this process of displacement. In important ways, both liberal and conservative churches had gone along with, even cooperated actively in, their own removal from the center of things.

Liberal Protestants, for instance, could and usually did view the establishment of the new university—nondenominational, devoted to scientific research, and exerting its influence at many points in modern industrial society—as evidence of the progress of civilization and the coming of the kingdom of God on earth. Many of the early state university presidents and higher education reformers, for example, were persons of religious faith who saw no contradiction between the university and, as President James B. Angell of the University of Michigan put it, "the work of promoting our Christian civilization." President Cyrus Northrop of the University of Minnesota (from 1882 to 1911), active congregational layman, at one time moderator of the Congregational National Council, felt that the university should not be sectarian, but that it should be a center of Christian culture. And, a final example, Henry Churchill King, whom we have already noted as a major theological voice in the liberal effort to reconcile religion and science, was also president of Oberlin College, an influential Congregationalist, an adviser to the Carnegie Foundation, and a proponent of its rationalizing and standardizing policies in higher education, which he regarded as part of the ethical ideal of progress and truth.[93]

But more conservative Protestants seem also to have made their willing contribution to the displacement of the churches from the center of American higher education. Nineteenth-century Protestant revivalism, with its split between a narrow, technical utilitarian reason for dealing with this world and an emotional conversion experience as the heart of religion, made it possible to accept, even to favor, the promotion of an exclusively technological and utilitarian reason as long as provision was made elsewhere by the churches for nurturance of the soul. These Protestants might even tend to favor the new utilitarian emphases of the state universities over the older liberal arts colleges, if humanistic traditions in liberal education were also seen—and there were strong, long-standing Protestant traditions for thus seeing them— as suspiciously pagan and as threats to robust piety. "Ironically," Franklin Littell has argued,

> it was the misguided piety of revivalist Protestantism which . . . gave the first great impetus to the state colleges and universities. The pious were determined that their sons and daughters would receive the technical training they needed in order to make their way in the world and equally determined that they should not be exposed to the hazards of classical and liberal learning. So the state colleges were voted massive subventions by the Federal Congress and state legislatures controlled by Methodists and Baptists and Disciples and others who wanted their children to have training in agricultural science, mechanical engineering and other "useful" skills without the danger of exposure to Greek philosophy, Latin letters, Roman jurisprudence, and other classical pursuits.[94]

Even if Littell may be somewhat overstating the case, it is clear that, whatever misgivings some may have had, Protestants of almost all persuasions very early flocked to the new state universities.[95] The student body of the University of Illinois in the late nineteenth century, for example, was made up predominantly of Protestants—Methodists, Baptists, Presbyterians, Congregationalists, and Disciples.[96] In 1900 the new chancellor of the University of Nebraska remarked, "To read the religious statistics of the university for last year you would think we were the collegium de propaganda fide for the entire western hemisphere."[97] What he was primarily pointing to was the number and diversity of Protestant students on campus. Church-related colleges continued steadily to lose students to public institutions throughout the twentieth century. In 1900, 80 percent of American undergraduates were in church-related colleges; within about forty years, 60 percent were in other private and state universities.[98]

During the early years of the century both liberal and many conservative Protestants could, therefore, view the growing dominance of the new scientific, technological, utilitarian trends in American higher education with some equanimity, even with satisfaction, as compatible with their own religious and social views—and in the process not worry themselves too much about any loss of an integrating humane education experience. By the 1930s the churches' relationship to the university was in many ways severely circumscribed, by now partly out of necessity, but all along partly by the churches' own earlier, ready accommodation to the situation.

Nevertheless, the church continued to invest considerable attention and energy in those areas where it did remain active in higher education. The church's main strategies in higher education were now three. The first was primarily pastoral, to provide "a home away from home," concentrating on the students' religious and moral lives as essentially distinct from their intellectual and curricular pursuits. Early in the century, the church began, in Clarence Shedd's expression, "to follow its students" with campus ministers, campus churches, and various forms of campus centers.[99] In 1905 the Presbyterians appointed a university pastor at the University of Michigan, and other mainline Protestant denominations soon began to do likewise. Most denominations also began to organize denominational centers, often called "foundations," for their campus ministers and students.[100] Further-more, in the 1920s most Protestant denominations began to form intercolle-giate movements, such as the Lutheran Student Movement (1922) and the Methodist Student Movement (1927), joining the work of their different campus ministers and foundations.

The emphasis in most of this work was mainly on Bible study, worship, personal counseling, and providing social opportunities. There was little during these early years of a concerted or determined effort to engage the intellectual life. There was, however, growing concern among many campus ministers and students about the lack of denominational cooperation, which seemed to them an expression of sectarianism inappropriate in a university setting. A few early attempts began to be made in the direction of greater ecumenical efforts.[101] A basis was beginning to be laid for later interdenomi-national endeavors of wider scope, which would eventually culminate in a national student Christian federation. This, however, would have to wait, for ecumenical progress during the 1930s was halting.

The founding of the University Christian Mission in 1938 was a major interdenominational step, one which also inadvertently revealed the basically outsider position from which the church was working in American higher education. Formed by the Federal Council of Churches, the University Christian Mission sent visiting interdenominational teams to hold a "religious emphasis week" once a year at different college and university campuses. "Religious emphasis week" was by that time an ironically apt expression of the Protestant church's conception of its task within the university and of the position it actually held there.

If the first main strategy of the church in higher education was basically pastoral, the second did have an intellectual focus. This was the attempt to provide opportunities for the teaching and study of religion within the college and university curriculum. In this area the displacement of the church in American higher education had been especially striking. The prominent place of religion in American higher education from the beginning, including in many state universities as late as the 1870s, had, by the 1890s, almost within one generation, substantially altered. The change, of course, was not so dramatic in church-related colleges, which continued to offer various courses in religion. Even in these institutions, however, new vocational and technical curricular emphases had begun to undermine the importance of the teaching of religion. In other private colleges and state universities, the teaching of religion and opportunities for raising religious concerns were meager in the extreme.

Early in the century several different kinds of efforts began to be undertaken for making the teaching of religion available in non-church-related colleges and universities.[102] One approach was to arrange for students at state universities to receive credit for courses in religion given at a nearby church-related college. This arrangement had a number of problems, not the least of them being that it raised legal questions concerning the separation of church and state. Another related approach was for churches near campuses (especially churches with strong faculty-student congregations) to offer courses, which the universities would sometimes also recognize for credit. The Disciples church may have been the first to promote this approach at the end of the nineteenth century with the establishment of "Bible chairs" adjacent to many state university campuses. The University of Illinois initiated yet another approach that was followed by many universities during the 1920s and 1930s. In this plan the various denominational foundations, including the Catholic and eventually the Jewish, cooperated with the university trustees and senate to offer religious courses for credit. Yet another approach was the founding of independent interdenominational—and, increasingly, interfaith—schools of religion affiliated with state universities. The interfaith school of religion founded at the state university of Iowa in 1923 was the leading example of this type of endeavor.

A final pattern for the teaching of religion was the founding of nondenominational chairs and departments of religion within colleges and universities themselves. Although the founding of such departments began as early as the 1880s, it was only later in the twentieth century that this would become the major pattern for the teaching of religion in American higher education.

It is not clear how many students these various efforts reached, or how effective they were. A widely cited study indicated that by 1936 in only two states was no credit course work in religion available for state university students. This study concluded that, while in Catholic colleges almost all students, and in Protestant colleges one out of two students, took some courses in religion, in other private colleges and in state universities the figures were respectively one out of eight and one out of twenty students.[103] Another study of some two hundred colleges and universities showed that no more than half the students in denominational, private, and state schools combined took even one course in religion, and that in the state institutions the figure was 84 out of 1,000.[104] Despite the various efforts, the teaching of religion remained peripheral to the mainstream of American higher education.

Early in the 1920s, however, the groundwork was being laid for gaining a much firmer place for the teaching of religion in the college and university curriculum. The chief inspiration for this new impulse was the work of Charles Foster Kent, Woolsey Professor of Biblical Literature at Yale. Kent was the moving force in the founding of a National Council of Schools of Religion in 1922, which two years later became the National Council on Religion in Higher Education. Kent's major concern was that intellectually sound and rigorous instruction in religion should become an integral part of American higher education, especially within state and nondenominational institutions. His deeper concern was that such an approach to religion was essential if American higher education was to provide a genuine ethically enlightened preparation for professional life in every field.[105]

Kent's initial intention was to ensure trained teachers for independent schools of religion at state universities, such as at Iowa, Indiana, and elsewhere. However, the work of the National Council of Religion in Higher Education soon began to extend into other areas as well. Although Kent died in 1925, the council was well-established by then. The council soon began to develop a program of Kent Fellows, providing support for graduate study in religion for gifted young scholars.[106] This program would provide an essential foundation for the growth of departments of religion and religious studies after World War II. It was also during these years that the major argument was developed for the teaching of religion in American higher education as central to the humanities and, thus, indispensable to the wholeness of all higher education, including professional education.

The third main strategy of the churches in higher education was to maintain the church-related liberal arts college. The major arguments that were being made for the church-related college would remain basically unchanged throughout the following half-century. One was that the church-related college was in a better position than secular schools to promote an atmosphere of faith and morals within which the intellectual and social life of the student could be pursued. A second argument was that the church-related college could provide an integrating liberal arts education rooted in the traditions of Christian humanism and thus could offer a needed antidote to the fragmenting and secularizing influences of vocational and research specialization.

Still another argument for the church-related college was to adopt the progressive slogan of higher education in "service to the nation" and to argue that in maintaining colleges the church helped fulfill its ethical mandate to serve the larger society. The ambiguities in the concept of service did not really surface until the late 1960s, and only then after "service" had become a rallying cry of secular theology. Already, however, the marks of the church-related college were proving elusive, and the beginning of a half-century search for the definition and purpose of the church-related college was under way.

Despite the considerable attention given to them, these three areas of the church's involvement with higher education lay on the periphery of the university and its chief concerns. And this was cause of growing uneasiness among many church leaders and theologians.

As World War II came to an end, there was a strong and growing sense everywhere that higher education would be more important than ever in postwar American culture. The GI Bill was enrolling a whole new student population, and a new awareness was dawning of the social opportunities offered by higher education. The universities had proved their usefulness in the war effort and were now recipients of what promised to be ever larger infusions of money from federal and state governments. And there was a widespread sense of concern, anxiety, and enthusiasm about the role of higher education in solving pressing social and cultural problems, as reflected especially in the Harvard Report of 1945 and the President's Commission on Higher Education of 1946.[107]

It is not particularly surprising, then, that in all of this the Protestant churches began to evince a fresh sense of their responsibilities—and new possibilities—within American higher education. This sense was sharpest among those who had come under the influence of the theological renaissance, which was now in full swing.

In many respects the emphases of the theological renaissance were tailor-made for engagement with higher education. Most importantly, the theological renaissance was preeminently an intellectual movement. Its champions were erudite and scholarly, many of them deeply knowledgeable about major issues of modern thought and culture. In attempting to engage higher education they could rightly claim to be addressing and speaking to the central, not the secondary, concerns of the university. And they were capable as few before them of mobilizing an awareness of the religious origins of Western, and especially of American, higher education. Moreover, most of the leading theologians of the new movement were faculty at so-called university divinity schools—seminaries such as Union in New York, Harvard,

Yale, Chicago, Vanderbilt, Princeton—and well-situated to speak to the university, as well as to help place their own graduate students in university departments of religion and literature, which they did increasingly in the 1950s and early 1960s.[108]

The renewed opening up in the "Harvard Report," for instance, and in the discussions it generated, of the issues of general education, the relation between science and the humanities, and the ethical, even religious, dimensions of knowledge, signaled that, perhaps, the time was ripe for the American religious tradition in higher education to rediscover and reassert itself in new ways.

NOTES

1. See, for example, David Potts, " 'College Enthusiasm!' as Public Response, 1800–1860," *Harvard Educational Review* 47 (February 1977): 28–42; Douglas Sloan, "Harmony, Chaos, and Consensus: The American College Curriculum," *Teachers College Record* 73, no. 2 (December 1971): 221–51; James McLachlan, "The American College in the Nineteenth Century: Toward a Reappraisal," *Teachers College Record* 80, no. 2 (December 1978): 287–306.

2. See, for example, the articles in Daniel Walker Howe, ed., "Special Issue: Victorian Culture in America," *American Quarterly,* 27 (December 1975).

3. Charles William Eliot, "Address on the Opening of the New Building," *American Museum of Natural History 8th and 9th Annual Reports* (1878), 49–52

4. Ibid., 50–51.

5. Ibid., 52.

6. John Higham, "Hanging Together: Divergent Unities in American History," *Journal of American History* 61 (June 1974): 5–28.

7. Laurence Veysey, *The Emergence of the American University* (Chicago: University of Chicago Press, 1965).

8. Robert Church, *Education in the United States: An Interpretive History* (New York: Free Press, 1976), 227ff.

9. Ibid.; also Robert Church, "Economists as Experts: The Rise of an Academic Profession in American Economics, 1870–1917," in *The University in Society,* ed. Lawrence Stone (Princeton, N.J.: Princeton University Press, 1976), 2:571–610; and Benjamin Rader, *The Academic Mind and Reform: The Influence of Richard T. Ely in American Life* (n.p.: University of Kentucky Press, 1966).

10. James P. Wind, *The Bible and the University* (Atlanta: Scholars Press, 1987), 127.

11. Quoted in John Whitney Evans, *The Newman Movement: Roman Catholics in American Higher Education, 1883–1971* (Notre Dame, Ind.: University of Notre Dame Press, 1980), 4.

12. John Greene, *Science, Ideology, and World View* (Berkeley, Calif.: University of California Press, 1981), passim, esp. 129–57.

13. See Lesek Kolakowski, *The Alienation of Reason: A History of Positivist Thought* (Garden City, N.Y.: Doubleday & Co., 1968); Allan Bullock, "The Future of Humanistic Studies," *Teachers College Record* 82, no. 2 (winter 1980): 173–90.

14. See Huston Smith, "Excluded Knowledge: A Critique of the Modern Western

Mind Set," *Teachers College Record* 80, no. 3 (February 1979): 419–45. Also reprinted in Huston Smith, *Beyond the Post-Modern Mind* (New York: Crossroad, 1982), 62–91.

15. Alfred North Whitehead, *Science and the Modern World* (New York: Macmillan Co., 1925), 80.

16. Also see Greene, *Science, Ideology, and World View.*

17. See Robert McDermott, "Introduction," in William James, *Essays on Psychical Research* (Cambridge, Mass.: Harvard University Press, 1986), xiii–xxxvi.

18. For example, Henry Adams, *The Education of Henry Adams* (1906; Boston: Houghton Mifflin Co., 1961), 489–98.

19. Charles Rosenberg, *No Other Gods: On Science and American Social Thought* (Baltimore: Johns Hopkins University Press, 1976).

20. This is not to say that a few did not see clearly that Darwinism itself was antithetical to religion, and this recognition was not all on the side of religious conservatives. Princeton's conservative and rationalist theologian Charles Hodge pointed out bluntly and correctly that, in its own terms, "Darwinism is atheism," but Hodge was joined in this evaluation, for example, by Borden Parker Bowne, founder of personalism, a major twentieth century school of theological liberalism. Bowne described Darwinism as "Life without meaning; death without meaning, and the universe without meaning. A race tortured to no purpose, and with no hope but annihilation. The dead only blessed; the living standing like beasts at bay, and shrieking half in defiance and half in fright." Quoted in Paul Boller, *American Thought in Transition: The Impact of Evolutionary Naturalism, 1865–1900* (Chicago: Rand McNally & Co., 1989), 23.

21. Walter Marshall Horton, "Science and Theology," in Samuel McCrea Cavert and Henry Pitney Van Dusen, eds., *The Church through Half a Century: Essays in Honor of William Adams Brown* (New York: Charles Scribner's Sons, 1936), 93–109; Henry Churchill King, *Reconstruction in Theology* (New York: Macmillan Co., 1901); William Adams Brown, *Christian Theology in Outline* (New York: Charles Scribner's Sons, 1906).

22. For example, Henry Churchill King, *Theology and the Social Consciousness* (New York: Macmillan Co., 1902); Gerald Birney Smith, *Social Idealism and Changing Theology* (New York: Macmillan Co., 1913); Walter Rauschenbusch, *Theology for the Social Gospel* (New York: Macmillan Co., 1917).

23. Horton, "Science and Theology," 100–101.

24. The place of religion in the state universities is exceedingly complex. For outstanding treatments of the issues, see Winton U. Solberg, *The University of Illinois, 1867–1894: An Intellectual and Cultural History* (Urbana, Ill.: University of Illinois Press, 1968), and idem, "The Conflict between Religion and Secularism at the University of Illinois, 1867–1894," *American Quarterly* 18 (Summer 1966): 183–199.

25. Elisha Benjamin Andrews, "Inaugural Address," The University of Nebraska, in *Builders of American Universities*, vol. 2: *Inaugural Addresses, State Universities*, ed. David Andrew Weaver (Alton, Ill.: Shurtleff College Press, 1952), 305.

26. This has been a common practice ever since. See Greene, *Science, Ideology, and World View*, esp. 158–93.

27. Winthrop Hudson, *Religion in America* (New York: Charles Scribner's Sons, 1981), 271–79.

28. Hudson, *Religion in America*, 271–76; Claude Welch, "Theology," in *Religion*, ed. Paul Ramsey (Englewood Cliffs, N.J.: Prentice-Hall, 1965), 227ff.; Kenneth Cauthen, *The Impact of American Religious Liberalism* (New York: Harper & Row, 1962), 27–28. Also see Lloyd J. Averill, *American Theology in the Liberal Tradition* (Philadelphia: Westminster Press, 1967), 126–31.

29. See Edward A. Purcell, Jr., *The Crisis of Democratic Theory, Scientific Naturalism and the Problem of Value* (Lexington, Ky.: University of Kentucky Press, 1973), 15ff.

30. See the interesting discussion ibid., 34–38.

31. See Douglas Sloan, "The Teaching of Ethics in the American Undergraduate Curriculum, 1876–1976," in *Ethics Teaching in Higher Education*, ed. Daniel Callahan and Sissela Bok (New York and London: Plenum Press, 1980), especially the section on "Ethics and Social Sciences in the New University," 15ff.

32. Quoted in Ernest Becker, *The Lost Science of Man* (New York: George Braziller, 1971), 28.

33. Welch, "Theology," 228–29. One can see in this a continued development of the two main Protestant options after Kant for establishing the reality of religious affirmations: If, according to Kant, the truths of knowledge are restricted to the sense world, the truths of religion must be sought either in religious experience, à la Schleiermacher, or in ethical action, à la Ritschl.

34. See Cauthen, *The Impact of American Religious Liberalism*, 147ff.

35. Ibid., 152.

36. See Welch, "Theology," 234–35; Hudson, *Religion in America*, 276–79.

37. See Hudson, *Religion in America*, 372.

38. See, for example, Averill, *American Theology*, 19.

39. Sydney Ahlstrom, *A Religious History of the American People*, vol. 2 (Garden City, N.Y.: Doubleday & Co., Image Books, 1975), 437ff.; William J. Wolf, "The Theological Landscape 1936–1974: An Address," in *Theology and Culture: Essays in Honor of Albert T. Mollegen and Clifford L. Stanley*, ed. W. Taylor Stevenson *Anglican Theological Review*, Supplementary Series, 7, November 1976: 32.

40. For examples, see Karl Barth, *The Word of God and the Word of Man*, translated with an introduction by Douglas Horton (Boston, Chicago: Pilgrim Press, 1928); and Wilhelm Pauck's study of Barth, *Karl Barth, Prophet of a New Christianity* (New York and London: Harper & Brothers, 1931); also see Ahlstrom, *A Religious History*, vol. 2, 432–33.

41. Ahlstrom, *A Religious History*, vol. 2, 436; Both Niebuhrs had already begun to raise questions about liberal theology: Reinhold Niebuhr in *Leaves from the Notebook of a Tamed Cynic* (Chicago and New York: Clark & Colby, 1929) and H. Richard Niebuhr et al., in *The Church against the World* (Chicago and New York: Willett, Clark & Co., 1935).

42. See Richard Fox, *Reinhold Niebuhr: A Biography* (San Francisco: Harper & Row, 1987), 237–38.

43. On the scope of antimodernism in late nineteenth- and early twentieth-century American culture, see Jackson Lears, *No Place of Grace: Antimodernism and the Transformation of American Culture, 1880–1920* (New York: Pantheon Books, 1981).

44. This emphasis appeared not only in *Moral Man and Immoral Society* (New York: Charles Scribner's Sons, 1932), but also in his earlier *Leaves from the Notebook of a Tamed Cynic* (1929). Niebuhr maintained it continually thereafter, beginning with *An Interpretation of Christian Ethics* (New York and London: Harper & Brothers, 1935).

45. Donald B. Meyer, *The Protestant Search for Political Realism, 1919–1941* (Middletown, Conn.: Wesleyan University Press, 1988 [1960]).

46. Julius S. Bixler, Robert L. Calhoun, and H. Richard Niebuhr, eds., *The Nature of Religious Experience* (New York: Harper & Brothers, 1937), xi–xii.

47. John Dewey, *Philosophy and Civilization* (New York: Capricorn Books, 1963; originally published 1931), 43.

48. John Dewey, *Quest for Certainty; A Study of the Relation of Knowledge and Action* (New York: Capricorn Books Edition, 1960; originally published 1929), 255–56, passim.

49. See Laurence Veysey, *The Emergence of the American University* (Chicago: University of Chicago Press, 1965); Roger L. Geiger, *To Advance Knowledge: The Growth of American Research Universities, 1900–1940* (New York and Oxford: Oxford University Press, 1986); Konrad H. Jarausch, ed., *The Transformation of Higher Learning, 1860–1930* (Chicago: University of Chicago Press, 1983); Ellen Condliffe Lagemann, *Private Power for the Public Good: A History of the Carnegie Foundation for the Advancement of Teaching* (Middletown, Conn.: Wesleyan University Press, 1983).

50. Lawrence A. Cremin, *American Education: The Metropolitan Experience, 1876–1980* (New York: Harper & Row, 1988), 555ff.; Merle Curti and Vernon Carstensen, *The University of Wisconsin: A History, 1848–1929,* 2 vols. (Madison, Wis.: University of Wisconsin Press, 1949).

51. For a good account of the origins, purposes, and consequences of the elective system, see Hugh Hawkins, *Between Harvard and America: The Educational Leadership of Charles William Eliot* (New York: Oxford University Press, 1972).

52. See Cremin, *American Education,* 562–64; David O. Levine, *The American College and the Culture of Aspiration, 1915–1940* (Ithaca, N.Y.: Cornell University Press, 1986), 162ff.

53. Levine, *The American College,* 60–62; Willis Rudy, *The Evolving Liberal Arts Curriculum: A Historical Review of Basic Themes* (New York: Teachers College, Columbia University, 1960); George E. Peterson, *The New England College in the Age of the University* (Amherst, Mass.: Amherst College Press, 1964).

54. Burton Bledstein, *The Culture of Professionalism: The Middle Class and the Development of Higher Education in America* (New York: W. W. Norton & Co., 1976).

55. See Levine, *The American College,* 130–32.

56. Cremin, *American Education,* 248; Levine, *The American College,* 39.

57. Cremin, *American Education,* 248; Levine, *The American College,* 41. "Between 1918 and 1925, new collegiate departments of commerce were opened. . . . Enrollment in engineering climbed from 29,784 to 49,139 between 1918 and 1920, an increase of 65%," reports Levine.

58. Edward Shils, "The Order of Learning in the United States: The Ascendency of the University," in Alexandra Oleson and John Voss, *The Organization of Knowledge in Modern America, 1860–1920* (Baltimore and London: Johns Hopkins University Press, 1979), 46, also see 32; also see Jarausch, *The Transformation of the Higher Learning,* 202.

59. Roger L. Geiger, *To Advance Knowledge* (New York: Oxford University Press, 1986).

60. Ernest Victor Hollis, *Philanthropic Foundations and Higher Education* (New York: Columbia University Press, 1938); also see Clyde W. Barrow, *Universities and the Capitalist State: Corporate Liberalism and the Reconstruction of American Higher Education, 1894–1928* (Madison, Wis.: University of Wisconsin Press, 1990), esp. 60ff.

61. Harold Orlans, *The Effects of Federal Programs on Higher Education: A Study of Thirty-six Universities and Colleges* (Washington, D.C.: Brookings Institution, 1962); also see idem, *Science Policy and the University* (Washington, D.C.: Brookings Institution, 1968).

62. See Dorothy Ross, "The Development of the Social Sciences," in Oleson and Voss, *The Organization of Knowledge,* 107–38; Jurgen Herbst, *The German Historical*

School in American Scholarship: A Study in the Transfer of Culture (Ithaca, N.Y.: Cornell University Press, 1965); Paul Buck, *Social Sciences at Harvard, 1800–1920*, (Cambridge, Mass.: Harvard University Press, 1965); Sloan, "The Teaching of Ethics."

63. Ross, "The Development of the Social Sciences," 125.

64. Herbst, *The German Historical School;* Mary O. Furner, *Advocacy and Objectivity: A Crisis in the Professionalization of American Social Science, 1865–1905* (Lexington, Ky.: University of Kentucky Press, 1975), chap. 2; Benjamin Rader, *The Academic Mind and Reform: The Influence of Richard T. Ely in American Life* (Lexington, Ky.: University of Kentucky Press, 1966).

65. See Robert L. Church, "Economists as Experts: The Rise of an Academic Profession in America, 1870–1917," in *The University in Society,* ed. Lawrence Stone (Princeton, N.J.: Princeton University Press, 1974), vol. 2, esp. 573, 596; Furner, *Advocacy and Objectivity,* 290–92; Rader, *The Academic Mind and Reform,* 130–58.

66. Ross, "The Development of the Social Sciences."

67. G. A. Lundberg, R. Bain, and S. Anderson, eds., *Trends in American Sociology* (1929), quoted in Robert K. Merton, *Social Theory and Social Structure* (Chicago: Free Press of Glencoe, 1963), 543.

68. See Natalie Ann Naylor, "Raising a Learned Ministry: The American Education Society, 1815–1860" (Ed.D. diss., Teachers College, Columbia University, 1971); Herbst, *The German Historical School.*

69. Veysey, a positivist, sees no other possibility. See Laurence Veysey, "The Plural Organized Worlds of the Humanities," in Oleson and Voss, *The Organization of Knowledge,* 57.

70. See Shils, "The Order of Learning," 44–45.

71. Dorothy Bass, "Teaching with Authority? The Changing Place of Mainstream Protestantism in American Culture," *Religious Education* (summer 1990); Hugh Hawkins, "Charles W. Eliot, University Reform, and Religious Faith in America, 1869–1909," *The Journal of American History* 51, no. 2 (September 1964): 191–213; John Whitney Evans, *The Newman Movement: Roman Catholics in American Higher Education, 1883–1971* (Notre Dame, Ind.: University of Notre Dame Press, 1980), 9.

72. Lagemann, *Private Power for the Public Good,* 40.

73. Hollis, *Philanthropic Foundations and Higher Education,* 38, 54.

74. See Rudy, *The Evolving Liberal Arts Curriculum.*

75. Evans, *The Newman Movement,* 4.

76. James H. Leuba, *The Belief in God and Immortality* (Boston: Sherman, French & Co., 1916), 221–81; Levine, *The American College,* 76; William Houston, *The Church at the University* (Columbus, Ohio: Westminster Foundation of Ohio, 1926), 14.

77. See Evans, *The Newman Movement,* 68.

78. Ibid.; Houston, *The Church at the University,* 14.

79. See Cremin, *American Education,* 96–98.

80. See Seymour A. Smith, *Religious Cooperation in State Universities: An Historical Sketch* (n.p.: University of Michigan, 1957), 4.

81. Evans, *The Newman Movement,* 65.

82. Paula Fass, *The Damned and the Beautiful: American Youth in the 1920s* (New York: Oxford University Press, 1977), 42–46, 136–39.

83. Ibid., 138.

84. Ibid., 334–35.

85. Gould Wickey, "A National Survey of the Religious Preferences of Students in American Colleges and Universities, 1936–37," *Christian Education* (October 1937). A survey in 1939 of students at eighteen different institutions (four state universities and

the rest denominational colleges), concluded that these students "seem to be strongly favorable toward the church," and "they believe in the reality of God," though students at southern and denominational colleges were more religious than those at state universities and northern colleges. Erland Nelson, "Student Attitudes toward Religion," *Genetic Psychology Monograph* 22 (1940): 323–423.

86. Levine, *The American College*, 87.

87. Ibid.

88. Quoted in Richard Storr, *Harper's University: The Beginnings; A History of the University of Chicago* (Chicago: University of Chicago Press, 1966), 159; also see Hugh Hawkins, "University Identity: The Teaching and Research Functions" in Oleson and Voss, *The Organization of Knowledge*, 297.

89. Quoted in Hawkins, "University Identity," 289.

90. Henry Fairfield Osborn, *The New Order of Sainthood* (New York: n.p., 1913).

91. Shils, "The Order of Learning," 31.

92. See Dorothy Bass, "Teaching with Authority?"; also idem, "Ministry on the Margin: Protestants and Education," in William R. Hutchison, *Between the Times: The Travail of the Protestant Establishment, 1900–1960* (Cambridge: Cambridge University Press, 1989), 48–71.

93. See Harris Kaasa, et al., "Humanism: A Christian Perspective," U.S. Department of Education, Office of Educational Research and Improvement, Washington, D.C. (1981), 50–51; Bass, "Ministry on the Margin"; Henry Churchill King, *Reconstruction in Theology* (London: Macmillan & Co., 1901).

94. Franklin Littell, *From State Church to Pluralism* (New York: Doubleday & Co., 1971), 126–27.

95. And they came largely to seek technical, vocational, and professional education. See, for example, the observation of Houston, *The Church at the University*, 26–27.

96. Winton U. Solberg, "The Conflict Between Religion and Secularism at the University of Illinois, 1867–1894," *American Quarterly* 18 (Summer 1966): 188. Solberg comments: "The atmosphere was not congenial to Catholics, Jews, and agnostics." A survey of Ohio State University as late as 1926 produced a similar picture of the student body's religious composition, although by then the number of Jewish and Catholic students had also increased substantially. Houston, *The Church at the University*, 18.

97. Weaver, *Builders of American Universities* 2:305.

98. Clarence P. Shedd, *Religion in the State University* (New Haven, Conn.: Hazen Foundation, 1947), 5.

99. Clarence P. Shedd, *The Church Follows Its Students* (New Haven, Conn.: Yale University Press, 1938); also Smith, *Religious Cooperation in State Universities;* Shedd, *Religion in the State University;* Milton C. Towner, ed., *Religion in Higher Education* (Chicago: University of Chicago Press, 1931).

100. Wesley Foundation (Methodist); Westminster Foundation (Presbyterian); Roger Williams Foundation (Baptist); Pilgrim Foundation (Congregational); Newman Clubs (Catholic—1905); Hillel Foundation (Jewish—1923, University of Illinois).

101. The founding of the United Religious Work at Cornell University in 1919, for example, brought together staff representing the Catholic and Jewish groups, the YMCA and YWCA, and most mainline Protestant groups. The founding in 1920 of the united "Student Christian Movement in New England," made up of the YMCA and YWCA, and four denominations, was followed by similar organizations in the Middle Atlantic States and New York State. Various other types of interreligious councils began to appear during the 1920s at other campuses. During the 1930s the National

Conference of Christians and Jews also began work on many campuses for developing deeper mutual understanding of these groups. Another development during the 1930s was for college and university administrators themselves, in both independent and many state institutions, to take on the responsibility of appointing administrative officers—directors of religious activities, university chaplains, and counselors—to direct and coordinate religious work. See Smith, *Religious Cooperation in State Universities*, 27–34; 37–39; 56.

102. At Iowa each religious group, Catholic, Protestant, and Jewish, supported teachers of religion, selected by the religious communions, but appointed by the university according to its professorial criteria. In addition a director was appointed and paid for by the university. For descriptions of the various approaches, see Clarence P. Shedd, *Proposals for Religion in Postwar Higher Education*. Hazen Pamphlet no. 11 (New Haven, Conn.: Edward W. Hazen Foundation, 1945); idem, *Religion in the State University;* Edward W. Blakeman, "Religious Education in Tax-Supported Colleges and Universities," in *Orientation in Religious Education,* ed. Philip Henry Lotz, (New York: Abingdon-Cokesbury, 1950); Thornton W. Merriam, "Religion in Higher Education Through the Past Twenty-five Years," in *Liberal Learning and Religion,* ed. Amos N. Wilder (New York: Harper & Brothers, 1951), 3–26.

103. Gould Wickey and Ruth A. Eckhart, *A National Survey of Courses in Bible and Religion in American Colleges and Universities* (Printed for the Indiana Council on Religion in Higher Education, 1936).

104. Blakeman, "Religious Education," 370.

105. On Kent's work and that of the National Council on Religion in Higher Education, see Merriam, "Religion in Higher Education"; Martha H. Biehle, "Fifty Years: 1923–1973; A Brief History of the National Council on Religion in Higher Education and the Society for Religion in Higher Education," mimeographed manuscript, Society for Values in Higher Education, Georgetown University, Washington, D.C.

106. As part of this program the council also provided regular series of conferences, consultations, and placement activities for teachers of religion, and the beginnings of a research and publication program. See Biehle, "Fifty Years."

107. *General Education in a Free Society: Report of the Harvard Committee* (Cambridge, Mass.: Harvard University Press, 1945); President's Commission on Higher Education, *Higher Education for American Democracy,* 6 vols. (Washington, D.C., 1947); Also see Levine, *The American College,* 210–20.

108. George Lindbeck, *University Divinity Schools: A Report on Ecclesiastically Independent Theological Education* (n.p.: Rockefeller Foundation, 1976), 25–26, 28.

CHAPTER 2

The Church and the Crisis in the University

ASSESSING THE SITUATION: OPTIMISTS AND PESSIMISTS

A major assessment of the churches' new, postwar possibilities and prospects within American higher education appeared in 1947 with the publication of *The College Seeks Religion,* by Merrimon Cuninggim.[1] At the time, Cuninggim was professor of religion at Pomona College, and he was soon to become dean of Perkins School of Theology at Southern Methodist University in Dallas. Fifteen years later he became director of the Danforth Foundation. In these positions Cuninggim would be an important figure in the new theological-educational enterprises of the 1950s and 1960s.

In his book Cuninggim analyzed what he discerned as a widespread, serious reevaluation of American higher education provoked by the war, a reevaluation coming from many quarters, both from within the church and from within the institutions of higher education themselves. It was his judgment that because of this reevaluation, religion had come to occupy "a larger place in the college's thinking and practice than at any time in the twentieth century." He felt, therefore, that the outlook for the future of religion within American higher education was exceedingly promising.[2] This was the optimistic note on which the study opened and closed. Although his work, then and since, has been criticized for this optimistic appraisal of the situation, Cuninggim provided some weighty documentation for his judgment.

For one thing, Cuninggim could point to the growing evidence of the recent development of an ecumenical, international student Christian movement. The old Student Volunteer Movement from the nineteenth century continued as a major link between American and international students. But in addition, from the 1920s on, the World Student Christian Federation (WSCF) had become increasingly influential among Christian student groups in Europe. And, as we shall see, the ecumenical interests and the continental connections of the theological renaissance in America would help ensure that the WSCF would have an important influence on American student Christian movements as well.

Cuninggim could also point to increasing ecumenical work by the churches within American higher education itself during the 1930s and 1940s. The founding of the University Christian Mission (UCM) in 1930 we have noted. In 1935 a voluntary, interdenominational organization of campus ministers, the Church Society for College Work, was established. In 1944 the National Intercollegiate Christian Council of the YMCAs and YWCAs, working with other church boards and with the WSCF, formed a national Faculty Committee on Religion in Higher Education. This committee immediately became active in organizing faculty-student study groups on campuses around the country. The same year the 1942 War Emergency Council for Student Christian Work was reorganized and expanded into a new United Student Christian Council (USCC), the largest cooperative undertaking by the American churches to that time.[3]

Another extremely important source of the churches' cooperative work in higher education was the Edward W. Hazen Foundation with its offices in New Haven and its close connections with Yale Divinity School. The Hazen Foundation often worked with the American Council on Education and the National Council of Religion in Higher Education. The latter, we have seen, was the main group at the time promoting the regular teaching of religion in the college and university. Between 1945 and 1949, these three groups jointly sponsored a series of more than fifty "Faculty Consultations on Religion in Higher Education" on campuses around the country.[4] In the late 1930s and 1940s the Hazen Foundation also had developed a series of widely circulated, and often cited, pamphlets, written by leading national scholars, dealing with various aspects of the place of religion in higher education.[5] Another project of the Hazen Foundation and the American Council on Religion was the preparation of a study by well-known scholars, based on the main reading materials used in college courses, of the place of religion in various, specific academic disciplines.[6]

Important as Cuninggim found the churches' widening activities, he was especially encouraged by the growing interest in religion that he detected among the faculties and administrators of American higher education itself. He was able to discuss in detail significant religious programs at ten major American universities, including Yale, Princeton, Syracuse, Duke, Northwestern, and Chicago.[7] He also was heartened by the extent to which important colleges, such as Harvard in its Report on *General Education* and Amherst College in a similar study of the curriculum, were beginning again to raise the underlying questions of the philosophy of education.[8] In Cuninggim's view, the widespread "spirit of secularism," which he felt had been characteristic of the college earlier in the century, was on the wane.[9] Although he did permit himself a few second thoughts about the decline of secularism in higher education, Cuninggim was overwhelmingly convinced that "the time of profound interest in religion has arrived," and that "prospects for the achievement of a vitally religious atmosphere in higher education were never brighter."[10]

The efforts of the Protestant churches to have a new impact on American

higher education were, indeed, beginning in earnest. Cuninggim had perceived this, and his book documented the extent to which it was occurring. In
this he was on solid ground. What was not so certain was that the American
colleges and universities themselves would be as welcoming of the new
overtures from religion as he wanted to think.

There were others who certainly disagreed. Writing a couple of years after
Cuninggim, Bernard Iddings Bell commented, "The American university
does not in reality care a button about religion. . . . It looks on religion as one
of the minor amusements, like china painting or playing the flute, pleasant for
those who enjoy that sort of thing, but not an intellectual or a practical
necessity."[11] Even more serious, many of the churches' forays into higher
education, which Cuninggim had cited as corroboration for his optimism,
were themselves turning up evidence about higher education much more
supportive of Bell's than of Cuninggim's assessment.

The Hazen study of the reading materials used in college courses reported
a state of almost unrelieved religious naïveté and illiteracy in every academic
discipline.[12] Robert L. Calhoun of Yale, analyzing the most widely used
books in the history of philosophy, described the majority of them as openly
hostile toward religion, when they were not hopelessly sentimental or
ignorant about it.[13] Henry Margenau of Yale, reviewing the most-used
readings in the physical sciences, confessed that, while he had not anticipated
much in the way of religious references, "the clear abstinence from utterances
of metaphysical import on the part of writers in the field . . . has been a mild
surprise."[14] In history and literature, the authors reported that religion simply
received "the silent treatment," and in the various social sciences a similar
picture emerged. "The typical 'social scientist,'" William A. Horton, an
economist, observed, "not merely has never studied but is not even aware of
the great tradition of religious thought." He concluded that in the domain of
religion "the mental age of the American college student is probably around
ten, and that of his instructors not much more."[15]

Goodwin Watson wrote of the field of psychiatry that "The avoidance of
religion in contexts where it would normally be discussed shows an almost
pathological sensitivity."[16] And of their discipline of anthropology, Margaret
Mead and Jean Rhys noted that, while anthropologists continued their
traditional interest in describing religious phenomena, they did so with
concepts that were thoroughly outmoded. "No new theoretical interest in
religion," they wrote, "has developed to replace the nineteenth-century
problems." And, they concluded, "This is very likely to result in an
alienation of the students' interest in religion as a subject for study, an
alienation which is of course intensified by the secularization of psychology
and sociology."[17]

In his introduction to *College Reading and Religion*, Donald Cottrell, dean of
the College of Education at Ohio State University, summarized the results of
the disciplinary surveys.

It is evident that religion is a neglected field of reading and study on the part of college students. The lightness of touch and even ignorance with which intellectual issues having a religious bearing or import are dealt with would seem little less than astonishing when the expansion of scholarship in general is taken into account.[18]

That the surveys in every case had been conducted, not by theologians or church leaders, but by outstanding figures in the various academic disciplines themselves, lent an indisputable authority to the Hazen volume.

Another independent study of the religious beliefs and practices of faculty members, not in state and secular institutions this time, but in church-related colleges themselves, presented similarly discouraging findings. Even, perhaps especially, in these colleges, concluded the director of the study, Edwin Espy, "There is little evidence of a profound intellectual wrestling with the problems of relationship between faith and fact, 'revealed' truth and 'scientific' truth, religious method and educational method, religion and an integrated curriculum."[19] Not even the colleges closest to the church could offer alternatives to what appeared to be the mainstream tendencies of the day.

Even more disturbing, if anything, were the results of the three-year consultation program on religion in higher education, which included campuses of almost every type and in every region of the country. In their discussions with faculty groups and individuals, the consultants found little interest in or understanding of religion in any depth. At the first national conference of college chaplains held at Yale Divinity School in 1948, the theologian Albert C. Outler summarized the reports of the fifty-two consultations. In them, he said,

Education is revealed as being largely secularist, positivist, and incompatible with an adequate world view. The curriculum is dangerously departmentalized. The administration is polite but indifferent. . . . As for the faculty, they are indifferent or hostile—more regularly the former. . . . The most regular complaint is the intellectual insularity of the faculty; they are too easily complacent about their ignorance and irresponsibility regarding other subjects.

Outler saw in this situation "a strategic opportunity and an awful responsibility" for the college and university chaplain.[20]

Merrimon Cuninggim also reported at this chaplains' conference. He spoke in much the same vein as Outler, that "the temper of today's college is predominantly secular." Cuninggim again, however, emphasized his hope that it was becoming an "uneasy secularism." "Our students," he said, "are more reluctant than before to adopt paganism; our colleges are more uneasy than formerly in the secular state."[21] In the remarks of both Cuninggim and Outler can be sensed a growing and aggressive confidence that the need was great and the time was ripe for renewed efforts on the part of the churches to engage American higher education.

The degree of receptiveness by higher education to religion was the main issue of difference between Cuninggim and others. But both seemed to be agreed, and it was this that Cuninggim's reiterated hopefulness stressed, that real openings now existed as never before for new ventures into higher education by the churches. And an emerging and ever stronger theme of these discussions—one that had been secondary, when not absent, in most churches' earlier endeavors in higher education—was that the new efforts on behalf of religion would have to make the intellectual domain a central concern. As Outler put it: "Who can forcefully assert that no real education can dispense with religion and no real religion can be ignorant of the concerns of the intellect?"[22]

Out of this conference, as a yet further step in the marshalling of religious forces for the coming engagement, came a new organization: the National Association of College and University Chaplains and Directors of Religious Life, open to campus religious workers in the United States and Canada. It is important to note that it was the intellectual emphases of the new theology that were struck at this conference of campus workers. A rethinking of the nature of the churches' place and responsibilities within higher education was beginning to broaden. The Americans were, therefore, well-primed for the catalytic boost their concern with higher education was about to receive from Christian faculty and student leaders in Europe.

THE CRISIS IN THE UNIVERSITY:
"HELPING THE UNIVERSITY TO BE THE UNIVERSITY"

The new theological outlook had been connected with a direct concern for higher education very early. In fact, the outlines of what were to be the main emphases of the churches' new endeavors in higher education were already being adumbrated well before World War II. As early as 1929, Willem Visser 't Hooft, crisis theologian and later General Secretary of the World Council of Churches, had called for Christians to reclaim the "intellectual life" as "just as urgent as the . . . calling to carry Christianity into social and international relationships." "There is," he wrote, "just as much need of an 'intellectual gospel' as there is for a 'social gospel.'" He called both for a student movement that would "make study a main part of its programme," and for the organization of fellowships of Christian professionals, and especially for "a Christian Professors Movement."[23]

Similar concerns spread among leaders of the British and American student Christian movements, and the concerns began to bear some fruit even during the war years. The leaders of the British SCMs were especially active in addressing what they called "the university question." Many of their concerns found expression in a 1943 book by Arnold Nash, chaplain to the SCM and lecturer in economics at the University of Toronto, *The University and the Modern World,* a provocative, social-theological analysis of the university and its problems.[24] Three years later John Coleman, formerly a university professor of mathematics and at the time Secretary of the World Student Christian Federation, published a widely used and cited study guide based largely on Nash, *The Task of the Christian in the University.*[25]

In England a group of prominent university professors formed the Christian Frontier Council, sometimes dubbed "the Dons' Group." Outstanding members of the Dons' Group—John Baillie, H. A. Hodges, Dorothy Emmett, A. D. Vidler, Daniel Jenkins, and others—authored a series of "University Pamphlets," dealing with central issues of the university and its curriculum from the perspective of the Christian faith.[26] The joint work of the English SCMs and the Dons' Group culminated in the 1949 publication of *The Crisis in the University* by Sir Walter Moberly, an Oxford philosopher and chair of the prestigious national University Grants Committee.

Moberly's book was a learned and penetrating analysis of the crisis in the modern university as symptomatic of a larger crisis in modern Western culture itself—of which the war was the most vivid recent reminder. In this sense Moberly's book represented a major Christian entry into a larger critical discussion of Western culture and the modern university that had been under way among leading Western cultural critics for some time—and Moberly himself placed his work in this wider context.[27]

This crisis in the university, as Moberly—and the other SCM writers—saw it, lay primarily in the dominance within the university and modern culture of science as a worldview that could not deal with questions of human meaning and value, but that at the same time had become the source of the notion that a spurious scientific objectivity and value-neutrality should govern the pursuit of all knowledge. This value-neutral stance, said the critics, created a vacuum that is soon filled either by nihilism or by unexamined assumptions drawn unconsciously from somewhere—if not surreptitiously or unknowingly from the liberal Western traditions, then ultimately from some other less benign, frequently much more absolutistic source. The lack of a unifying, integrating principle in the modern university, and the increasing fragmentation of its curriculum and research undertakings, were in this light especially ominous symptoms of just such a vacuum waiting to be filled. The critics pointed to the capitulation of the German and eastern European universities to totalitarian and nationalistic ideologies and governments as compelling recent evidence that the vacuum need not, and most likely would not, be filled indefinitely by an unconscious faith in liberal, progressive democracy.

Several basic themes developed by Moberly—and often stated earlier by Visser 't Hooft, Nash, Coleman, and members of the "Dons' Group"— became fundamental in shaping American Protestant leaders' conception of the church's task in higher education.

First was the emphasis enunciated by Visser 't Hooft, who had said that the churches' proper relationship and mission to higher education must be above all in the intellectual realm. As Nash put it, the primary question for the church was now, "How can the Church help students find their Christian vocation as students in the sphere of 'secular' scholarship itself?"[28] And Moberly underscored and expanded this not only by including faculty and professional laity as well but also by stressing the centrality of the intellectual task for faith itself.[29] "All Christians in universities," he wrote, "should be, or at least should set themselves to become lay theologians."[30]

Behind the intellectual emphasis was a twofold conviction that, on the one hand, the university was the most powerful institution in modern culture precisely because it was the cognitive center of modern culture; and that, on the other hand, the university was evading its responsibilities to raise and explore "the basic questions of human existence" and of cultural purpose. The deepest needs of modern society for ethical insight and meaning were not being addressed by the cultural institution best equipped and most responsible for doing so. Hence, the major responsibility of Christians in the university was not to convert but, as exemplary scholars and students, to call the university to its true vocation as seeker of truth in every domain of life. In Moberly's phrase, which would quickly become a mainstay in the SCM vocabulary, the first task of the Christian scholar and student was to work "to enable the university to be the university."[31]

This meant, among other things, joining with others in addressing what for many critics had become the major problem of the modern university, the lack of an integrating principle to give the university educational coherence and larger purpose. Dominated more and more by technical, utilitarian interests, and in thrall to the doctrine of value-free inquiry, the university, in Moberly's perspective, mirrored within itself the drift and fragmentation of the larger modern world. Many of the problems of the university, which critics had pointed to since early in the century—a fragmented curriculum, overspecialization, excessive technicism and vocationalism, a depreciation of teaching, and so forth—were, in this view, functions of the lack of an inner integrating educational principle. The entire general education movement of twentieth-century American higher education can be understood, in fact, as in large part an attempt to find just such an integrating educational principle.[32]

The Christian critics affirmed this larger search for a new source of unity and hoped to join in. Some spoke of the need for an "integral university" as opposed to the rudderless "multiversity"; some of the need for "a coherent philosophy of life"; others of the need for "a new world view."[33] Instead of the integral university, Moberly said, "What we have, in fact, today is the chaotic university." He added: the universities "can give no light or guidance to a directionless world, so long as they are themselves directionless and are content to remain so."[34] All agreed that a deeper, clearer, integral self-understanding of the nature of the intellectual task itself was necessary if "the university was to be the university."

A primary way Christians could contribute to this deeper understanding was to bring to light and examine the basic presuppositions that underlie and are present in all intellectual endeavor.[35] Here was an early attempt to call into question what Ernst Lehrs has called the modern "onlooker consciousness" and its claims to a totally objective and value-free knowledge.[36] All knowing, the argument ran, rests ultimately on certain basic presuppositions about reality. These presuppositions are most likely to be latent and largely unconscious, the taken-for-granted assumptions of our ordinary, everyday common sense—of the kind described by T. E. Hulme, "[We] do not see them but other things through them"; what William James called "the premises which are never mentioned"; Barfield's "collective habits" of the modern mind—all the more powerful for their being unconscious.[37] They determine our interpretation of the world, even our selection and shaping of what we see in the world.

Exposing the underlying presuppositions actually at work in all the different scholarly disciplines would then make possible a rigorous and open dialogue between naturalistic, idealistic, technological, nihilistic, personalistic, biblical, and other assumptions. Their adequacy as sources of illumination and understanding could then be explored. The aim now was not so much to establish the dominance of one view over others as to ensure a fair encounter and open dialogue among all. The result, however, would not be the vacuous neutrality fostered by a misconceived objectivism, because it was assumed that a genuine commitment to seek truth also would be at work. But this also threw back on the Christian in the university the responsibility of being first and foremost a good student and scholar.[38]

As Moberly and the other SCM writers conceived the intellectual task of the Christian in the university, they included within it the importance of social awareness and social action. For the intellectual emphasis to become effective, it could not remain merely in the realm of lofty, but disembodied ideals. It would have to engage and transform both the concrete structures and practices of the institutions of higher education themselves, as well as the institutional connections between higher education and the wider society.

So the theme of social awareness and action was present from the beginning in the university concerns of the WSCF and other SCM writers. Coleman, for instance, had defined the integral university as one committed to "fundamental research" as a counter to the utilitarian, government, and industrial research predominant in the modern university. In so doing he had further urged that courses be made "relevant" (twenty years later a key word of the American student movement) to the real needs of society and the actual problems of students.[39] Nash, introducing a theme that also would become ever stronger among American activists, had stressed in 1943 the importance of the sociology of knowledge in uncovering the social origins and interests at work in supposedly value-neutral ideas.[40] The task of bringing to light the hidden presuppositions of thought had included from the beginning, therefore, a keen sense of the connections between ideas and power, ideas and interests.

But Moberly himself was always insistent that the social emphasis had to be understood in relation to the central and defining intellectual purpose of the university. "Certainly," Moberly had written, "*Theoria* is not superior to *Praxis* . . . ; but it does not follow that it is subordinate." And he had written further, "The university has indeed a social responsibility, but . . . this is first and foremost a responsibility for focussing the community's intellectual conscience." Granted, the university does many other things for the community, but Moberly maintained, nevertheless, "The university will betray the community, as well as lose its own soul, if it allows itself to be so anxious and troubled about many things as to miss the one thing needful." The distinctive responsibility of the university, he unwaveringly held, "is to be the university." By that he meant the preeminent place in society where the criticism and evaluation of ideas, and the intellectual virtues rooted in the search for truth, are nurtured and passed on. Social concern and action had their rightful place within the university but always in intimate connection with the university's primary responsibility for the intellectual life.[41]

Immediately on its appearance, Moberly's book began to receive attention in both England and America.[42] Moberly certainly did not initiate the American churches' new involvement with higher education. On the American scene, his book fell into an excited discussion, which was already well under way, of most of the main issues and questions he dealt with. Nevertheless, his articulation of the issues, bringing together, in considerable detail, the historical, theological, and educational considerations, was a fundamental influence in shaping the Americans' subsequent understanding of the university question.

Moberly's work served mainly as a catalyst for the Americans, focusing and galvanizing their thinking, and, above all, demonstrating decisively for them that the theological renaissance of the mid-twentieth century could have direct and far-reaching implications for the whole of modern higher education. Like almost all European influences before it, both in American higher education and in theology, the Moberly analysis was taken up and quickly absorbed into the larger American scene, often being transformed, even disappearing as such in the process. Still, the publication of *The Crisis in the University* can be seen as a kind of benchmark of the beginning in earnest of mainline American Protestantism's concerted postwar efforts to engage American higher education anew.

By the mid-1950s a solid institutional base, with a number of supporting pillars, was in place, from which the American churches could carry out and direct this engagement. Probably most important was the long-standing presence on almost all the nation's college and university campuses of the various denominational and interdenominational student movements, campus ministries, social and service agencies, and related activities and organizations. These were all beginning to show stirrings of new energies and ideas prompted by the theological renewal. A second pillar of support was the influence of the now well-established work of the Hazen Foundation, the Danforth Foundation, and the National Council of Religion in Higher Education. All three, through their various programs of student support, scholarly research, conferences and publications, were making increasing financial, institutional, and personnel resources available for the effort, as Edward W. Hazen had once put it, "to aid the cause of religion in higher education."[43]

A third pillar in this structure of institutional supports—in the eyes of many, one of the most promising—was the growing work of the Commission on Higher Education of the National Council of Churches and the creation, in connection with the Commission, of the Faculty Christian Fellowship (FCF). In the fall of 1951 the United Student Christian Council called on the various denominational higher education agencies and boards to organize some kind of association of faculty men and women throughout the country, whose work would be "oriented upon the basis of genuinely Christian and ecumenical perspectives" and which would "find its primary rooting in the Protestant Churches."[44]

In response, the Faculty Christian Fellowship was organized at Berea College in Kentucky in October 1952 as an autonomous (not denomination-ally based) organization of college and university faculty to study the Christian faith in the modern university and especially in relation to the various academic disciplines.[45] The following June the Faculty Christian Fellowship held its first conference. The same year, under the direction of Hubert C. Noble, the newly formed Department of Campus Life of the Commission on Higher Education of the National Council of Churches made the Faculty Christian Fellowship one of its chief responsibilities. The new journal of the Department of Campus Life, *The Christian Scholar*, became the FCF's unofficial organ, supplemented by a regular newsletter, the *Faculty Forum*, which was circulated to campuses and faculty members throughout the country.[46]

The organizers of the new Faculty Christian Fellowship movement explicitly attributed the inspiration for it to the earlier call by Visser 't Hooft for such an organization, to the model of the Dons' Group in England, and to the ecumenical experience of the USCC.[47] If any group was to carry out the work of what many from Moberly on were to see as the major task of the Christian in the university—to uncover and examine the basic presupposi-tions of the modern mind and to relate the Christian faith to the specific academic disciplines—it would be the Faculty Christian Fellowship. The organization was begun with much enthusiasm, and for the first ten years there seemed to be indications that the hopes for it were well-founded.

Participants in the new efforts to relate religion to higher education were very much aware at the time of the importance of these institutional supports to their work. The author of an important study of the Christian teacher in higher education, for example, dedicated his book to: "The Danforth Foundation, The Faculty Christian Fellowship, The Hazen Foundation, The National Council on Religion in Higher Education; Pioneers in the renaissance of religion in American higher education."[48] Other authors also pointed to this same configuration of institutions as prime evidence of new impulses moving in the churches' involvement with higher education.[49]

THE BEGINNING INTELLECTUAL ENGAGEMENT WITH THE UNIVERSITY

The early 1950s also saw the beginning of a growing body of literature on religion and education written by Christian college and university faculty and some administrators. This literature promised a new departure from much of what had appeared before in that it attempted, in the manner of Moberly, to move to the offensive. These new writers were now attempting to go beyond a mere analysis of the existing place of religion within higher education to a more comprehensive and fundamental critique of the university. They also were beginning a positive exploration of what was required if a truly fruitful engagement by the churches with higher education was to take place—in scholarship, in the specific disciplines, in the responsibilities of teaching, in student-faculty relationships, in administration, and so on. The new theological imperative—for college and university faculty and administrators themselves to take up as central to their concerns the intellectual task of being a Christian in the university—appeared to have fallen on fertile soil.[50]

There were opportunities for mixed motives in all this. The desire to engage the university anew on its own terms could mingle quite easily with the longing to be taken back into the fold, to recoup the lost status once enjoyed by the church in higher education. The danger was always present that the necessary desire to demonstrate outstanding scholarship on the university's terms would in the end take the edge off any really radical questioning of the dominant university intellectual canons, modes of knowing, and academic reward systems. That one would willy-nilly reap the rewards by being a good scholar, and thus be tempted to settle for that, was the modern university version of an old religious dilemma made famous by John Wesley, Pennsylvania Quakers, and Max Weber. These were temptations and problems that eventually would have to be considered.

In this new outpouring of works on the place of the Christian in higher education, important attempts were begun by faculty, for example, to explore the implications of their religious faith for the content and method of their own academic disciplines. Some were collections of essays, such as that edited by Hoxie N. Fairchild under the auspices of the Hazen Foundation, *Religious Perspectives in College Teaching*, with contributions by such outstanding and well-known scholars as Talcott Parsons of Harvard, Kenneth Boulding of Michigan, George F. Thomas of Princeton, Robert Ulich of Harvard, E. Harris Harbison of Princeton, Theodore Green of Yale, John Hallowell of Duke, and others. Perhaps even more important was the appearance, particularly in the humanities, of substantial monographs exploring in detail the implications of religious perspectives for specific disciplines and subject areas by such scholars as Stanley R. Hopper, Nathan Scott, Amos Wilder, J.V.L. Casserley, John A. Hutchinson, Albert C. Outler, and others.[51] In addition there were books, again mainly by college and university faculty, and some by seminary professors, dealing with other important, but more general issues in the relation between religion and higher education—issues such as the responsibilities of the Christian teacher, theological perspectives on the university and campus life, the intellectual tasks of the Christian teacher and student, the relation between faith and knowledge, and the social responsibility of the Christian intellectual and lay theologian.[52]

Although there was considerable diversity among them, all these authors were deeply influenced by the theological renaissance. The three most important twentieth-century American theologians—the brothers Reinhold and H. Richard Niebuhr and Paul Tillich—exerted an especially strong influence in the writing of most American academics who concerned themselves with the Christian faith and higher education. The neo-orthodox project of reclaiming the traditional, especially the biblical, sources of faith in a way suitable to modern life and consciousness streamed throughout this burgeoning new literature on religion and higher education.

Almost all the authors involved were bound together by their common conviction that any significant new approach by the church to higher education would have to be one that made the intellectual task primary. Nearly all would have agreed with Perry D. LeFevre in saying, "Every Christian intellectual . . . has an obligation to bring the life of his mind into an active and positive relationship to his ultimate concern, his basic trust, his commitment to what nourishes, sustains, and creates the ground of his life," in short, to his deepest religious faith.[53]

All were united also in the conviction that an unusual and opportunity-laden moment was at hand for the churches to reassert themselves in the college and university. As Kenneth Irving Brown put it, "The time is ripe in American education for a reorganization of our program that shall take larger concern for values, purposes, and ideals, and an even larger concern for the presentation of a world view which shall include a recognition of God and His expectation of man."[54] In the conception made compelling to many of these authors by Paul Tillich, theirs seemed to them to be, indeed, a moment of *kairos*—the auspicious time, the potentially revelatory moment.

Three dominant concerns ran through this literature: (1) the further development of the analysis and critique of modern higher education, largely along the lines laid down by Moberly; (2) the epistemological-theological problems of the relationship between faith and knowledge; and (3) the place of religion and theology, both as separate subjects and within the other academic disciplines.

The American Critique of the University

Actually the Americans followed Moberly's critique fairly closely, elaborating and adjusting it when necessary to fit the special circumstances of their situation. The two major emphases in their criticisms were again the call to examine the fundamental presuppositions of knowledge and the need to find an integrating principle to help stem the intellectual and administrative fragmentation of the university and its wider, culturally disintegrating effects. What was originally the Student Christian Movement challenge, articulated definitively by Moberly, to bring to light the unexamined presuppositions at work in the modern mind, and in higher education particularly, became a regular refrain of the American critics during the 1950s. In this the Americans added little to the substance of the Moberly-type analysis, but they did pursue its implications in several directions.

The call to seek out the dominant, hidden assumptions of modern knowledge and research served a number of purposes. For one, it enabled the critics to point out the spurious nature of what they called "the cult of objectivity" that held sway throughout the teaching and research ethos of the university.[55] The refusal to deal with the most basic questions of meaning and ethical purpose for fear that it would violate the scholar's vaunted objectivity meant, the critics argued, that the university simply abdicated its responsibility for the social and ethical uses to which its knowledge was put. It meant also that the university could neither help students ask nor help them answer the most basic questions, such as What knowledge is of most worth? or Why study anything at all that does not have immediate utilitarian payoff? This silence on the most basic questions of purpose could only exacerbate the trend toward cultural drift and fragmentation.

The dominant conception of objectivity, the critics maintained, was spurious on more than one count. It meant, for example, that the real metaphysical and religious depths of all the disciplines never were plumbed, on the mistaken notion that to do so required noncognitive commitments that violated rational objectivity. Hence the most interesting and important dimensions of the disciplines were never developed. There are, the critics said, "latent or implied theological issues in every one of the disciplines," and it is essential that these "be dealt with in every division, department, and course where they arise naturally."[56]

Furthermore, under cover of the reigning notion of objectivity all kinds of hidden assumptions and commitments were in actuality often smuggled in, albeit unknowingly, by the supposedly detached, objective teacher and researcher. As George Thomas, professor of religion at Princeton, put it, "The idea of teaching without presuppositions is an illusion. If a professor does not base his interpretation of his field upon presuppositions derived from Christian theism, he will base it upon presuppositions derived from some other perspective."[57] In other words, "the cult of objectivity" really was a cloak for the introduction into the classroom of "concealed religions"— naturalism, scientism, positivism, rationalism, humanism, and so forth.[58] Even the silence itself of the university—of its teachers and curriculum—was not value neutral, but was in fact a commitment to the view that religion is unimportant. "The student," wrote Thomas, "who is not shaken by open attacks upon religion may be affected deeply by the complete silence about religion he meets everywhere."[59]

This attack on the "cult of objectivity" also permitted the critics to make the case that the Christian scholar's own religious commitment was not a violation of objectivity rightly conceived. On the contrary, they maintained, the only kind of objectivity worthy of the name requires becoming conscious of one's own deepest presuppositions about reality and laying them out for all to see and test. Rather than precluding, in the name of a factitious value-neutrality, any concern about the uses to which knowledge is put, a genuine objectivity must include a concern for the full ethical and value implications of the research involved. The attempt to show that the Christian scholar can—indeed, must—be at once committed *and* objective in the fullest sense of both terms was almost an obsession among the Christian critics of the university during these years.[60]

The demand to examine the presuppositions at work in modern education was also part and parcel of the search for an integrating vision for the university. Building again on Moberly and the other SCM writers, the American religious critics could maintain that they were not alone in seeing a fragmenting specialization and absence of unifying purpose as one of the most serious problems facing modern education and society. Moreover, it was not, should anyone be inclined to see it as such, a problem apparent and of interest only to the religiously concerned.

Here the Christian critics joined forces with many other, often secular, critics of the university. The Harvard Report had been a prime witness to the seriousness with which many nonreligious educational leaders viewed the intellectual and curricular drift within modern higher education. The Christian reformers could quote outstanding social commentators such as Walter Lippmann, for example, that because in American higher education, "There is no common faith, no common body of knowledge, no common moral and intellectual discipline," there is in the wider society an enormous and growing "cultural vacuum."[61] Becoming conscious of the underlying presuppositions of thought was seen as essential to the possibility of discovering the unifying conceptions and integrating principles worthy of filling that expanding vacuum.

The emphasis on probing the underlying presuppositions of all thought also enabled the Christian critics to bring their own presuppositions, their reappropriation of the Christian tradition, directly to bear on the issues of modern higher education. It was here that their theological debt to the neo-orthodox attempt to reclaim the central doctrines of the Christian tradition, but in terms intelligible to the modern mind, was perhaps most apparent.

Against the lack of meaning and the nihilism they saw in the naturalistic and positivistic assumptions dominant in the university, they could juxtapose the affirmation of ultimate meaning and purpose contained in the Christian doctrines of creation and redemption, which they saw revealed decisively in the biblical accounts of the creation and of the life, death, and resurrection of the Christ Jesus. Against a reductionistic scientism, which viewed the human being as merely a function of other more basic mechanical, biological, or economic forces, they could juxtapose the vision of the human being as created in the image of God and, thus, uniquely capable of meaningful, moral, and spiritual striving. Against an overweening modernist faith in the capacities of human goodness and human reason, against what one author called "the secularist's freewheeling optimism about the nature of man,"[62] they could juxtapose the view of the human being as sinner, always overreaching and inevitably corrupting his own highest capacities and social relationships. Against the human propensity to seek power and place and to pursue utopian and totalitarian social schemes, they could juxtapose the doctrine of the sovereignty of God and its rejection of the manifold forms of human idolatry.

A realistic accounting of the narrow and self-serving interests at work in the best of intentions and in the highest of ideals was essential to the neo-orthodox attempt to affirm the sovereignty of God and to show the empirical manifestations of the doctrine of original sin. The "grandeur and misery of man," the title of a popular book on the relationship between the Christian faith and psychotherapy, was thus a fundamental theme of the critics—the grandeur elucidated often as the human capacity for personal decision and authentic I-Thou relationships, the misery as the human being's inevitable tendency to abuse and manipulate these relationships.[63]

All of this had implications for a Christian critique of the university, for it could be spelled out in a diversity of attempts to put in their proper place the claims of what one early, fairly widely read, and thoroughly neo-orthodox book for students called "the gods of the campus."[64] At the same time the other side of this theological criticism of the university was that it demanded a corresponding criticism of any anti-intellectual tendencies within the church itself.

A strong desire existed among the theological reformers of every stripe, and all the more so among the university reformers, to combat what they perceived as a widespread anti-intellectualism within the church and among students. They were determined to oppose any attitude that viewed the intellectual life as harmful, or even secondary, to the religious life (and for many students inimical as well to the social contacts often regarded on campus as necessary to worldly success). The reformers were determined that they not be taken for religious sentimentalists. They, therefore, felt themselves compelled to be hard on any tendencies coming from churchly sources that "would put the intellectual at the bottom of the list," below such otherwise admirable concerns as character development, "working with people," and social and community service.[65] Especially galling to them were church colleges that betrayed "a lack of interest in hard intellectual struggle," and that justified their own second-rate academic performance in the name of a nonintellectual stress on religion and morality. As theologian Joseph Haroutunian of McCormick Seminary argued, appealing to Jonathan Edwards's conception of the human being as "God's intelligent creature": "Education that does not issue in intelligence is a farce and a folly."[66]

The American critics took seriously the earlier SCM writers' call for "lay theologians"—Christian faculty members, students, and people in all the professions interested in and knowledgeable about theological issues and their wider intellectual and cultural ramifications. One upshot of the emphasis on countering anti-intellectualism in the churches and theological illiteracy among lay faculty and students was the addition of yet another genre to the growing body of literature we have been considering; namely, the publication of theological books expressly for lay people.[67]

Despite their criticism of American higher education, the theological-educational reformers evinced an unmistakable optimism about the possibilities of transforming and energizing the university. The entire tenor of their criticisms, and the clear expectation that they would be heard and taken seriously, revealed a confidence that the university, for all its problems and shortcomings, would yet be a major center for cultural renewal, and that the rejuvenated Christian faith of the theological renaissance would find a place within the university. Howard Lowry had been one of the first to give expression to the confidence that impelled the reformers. He wrote,

> If education seriously seeks for meaning and significance, if it pretends to regard the whole of human life, if it wants to be universal enough to do the work of a "university," how can it avoid paying attention to the Hebrew and Christian traditions and to the present working of religion in men's lives? These are the thoughts that give hope to Christians as they see how things are running in higher learning just now.[68]

Faith and Reason

Some of the new theological reformers increasingly realized that the success of their entire enterprise hinged on how effectively they could come to grips with the knowledge-faith relationship. The modes of knowing and the conceptions of knowledge dominant in the university disciplines, and in the worldviews that they also represented and contributed to, left little place for the affirmations of faith and ethics. The pervasiveness in modern culture and education of naturalistic assumptions about the nature of the human being, positivistic-scientistic assumptions about knowing, and popular, utilitarian, and materialistic assumptions about the purposes of learning—all of which the religious reformers tended to lump together under the shorthand term, secularism—had long forced religious concerns and affirmations to the periphery of higher education.

The challenge posed by the philosophical school of logical positivism during the 1930s, 1940s, and 1950s in many ways sharpened the issue. With their aggressive assertion that all non-empirical, nonverifiable language is nonsense, the logical positivists simply ruled out of the court of intelligible discourse, not only religion but also all metaphysical, ethical, and poetical statements. These were regarded either as meaningless or as mere "emotivism"—the expressions of arbitrary, subjective feelings.[69] Although the vogue of the earlier logical positivism soon gave way to the more careful, refined, and critical outlook of linguistic analysis, the challenge to the meaningfulness of all religious and metaphysical language remained as strong as ever. Even if in the university the actual numbers of informed devotees of logical positivism and linguistic analysis remained relatively few, there were many indeed whose disciplines and own outlooks were rooted in the assumptions of a more general, largely unconscious, positivism and materialistic reductionism. The conceptions of reason and of knowing dominant in the university left little room and grounding for the traditional affirmations of faith or conceptions of ethics. Unless the affirmations of faith could be shown to have connection and standing in what was conceived as knowable reality, they would gravitate ever more to the realms of the purely emotivist, the nonessential, and the unreal.

With the drastic modern restriction of reason and knowing exclusively to sense experience and abstractions from sense experience, the ancient question, always a difficult one, of the relationship between faith and knowledge, took a decisive new turn. Several theologians responded to the challenge to address the faith-knowledge issue anew.[70] How the major American theologians, Paul Tillich and the Niebuhrs, dealt with the problem we must eventually ask. At this point, however, it is possible to get a glimpse of how many of the active church leaders, college and university faculty, and others involved directly in the theological-educational reform of higher education were dealing with the question, and how, among some of them, the work of the leading theologians was being appropriated and finding expression.

By the mid-1950s more and more of the theological reformers were actually trying their hands at grappling with the problem. LeFevre, writing in 1958 on the faith and responsibilities of "the Christian teacher" in higher education, concluded that the most important issue of all "has to do with the relation of the knowledge or truth disclosed in and through the so-called secular disciplines and religious knowledge or truth." "How," he asked, "is

the knowledge or truth with which the secular disciplines deal to be related to
the knowledge or truth with which theology deals?"[71]

The same year a collection of lectures given a couple of years previously at
a conference of some three hundred Protestant scholars from nearly sixty
different campuses was published under the title *Toward a Christian Philosophy of Higher Education*.[72] The foreword of the book began with no less than
the claim that "Christianity has *a science of knowledge* relevant to the present
and valid for the seeker of truth today."[73] This promised far more than any of
the book's contributors delivered, though all of them seemed convinced that
the development of a "Christian science of knowing" was the order of the
day.

Nevertheless, the book marked a genuine move among some to come to
grips with the knowledge as well as the faith side of the relationship.
Reflecting the shared conviction of all the contributors, one wrote, "We
cannot have a sound world view unless we construct an epistemology."[74] But
it was J. Edward Dirks, editor of *The Christian Scholar* and also director of the
program in religion and higher education at Yale Divinity School, whose
chapter presented one of the clearest statements at the time of why the issue
was of overriding importance for the reform of higher education.

The task of developing a theological grounding, Dirks wrote, "that can
support the meaning and task of education in our time demands that we give
our attention to the difficult problem posed by the relation of faith and
reason." The split between faith and reason, he added, underscoring why the
issue could not be avoided by anyone seriously concerned about the place of
religion in higher education, has meant that "the field has been left open to
scientific naturalism and humanistic rationalism to develop an epistemology
which excludes the concerns of faith from the realms of rational inquiry."
And, he said, since institutions of higher education can serve the wider
culture only in their own distinctive way, that is, through the conceptions of
knowledge that dominate the academic disciplines, we find at the cultural
level "that nearly the whole of man's energies are being used, in the name of
reason, for 'the practice of the *absence* of God,' as someone has defined
secularism. An appeal to reason is demanded if we would articulate the
meaning and the implications of Christian faith in our time."[75]

How reason would be dealt with in the knowledge-faith relationship was
the main question. By this time several approaches to it had developed
among the theological-educational reformers.

Of these, one of the earliest (it had its main roots in the nineteenth
century), and in many ways most persistent (it continually makes its reappear-
ance in the present), may be described as the "facts-value approach." This
position held that knowledge (usually as defined by scientific methods)
provides the facts about the world, while faith and religion (along with
philosophy and poetry) supply the values that gave the facts whatever
meaning and significance they might have. This approach did not seek to

overcome the split between faith and knowledge so much as to assign to each side its own particular functions and then to argue that the faith-value side was just as important as the knowledge side.

It was an approach that assumed an epistemology of naive realism in which the facts—the objects—as given in perception and the notion of values were taken as essentially unproblematic. It sidestepped any deeper critical examination of the conceptions of empirical observation and reason themselves, and of the simple, independent facts and objects these were supposed to provide. Nor did this position address the difficulty that in this simple view of empirical reason and observation the whole realm of values remained amorphous and vague and, almost by definition, purely subjective and arbitrary. It was a naive approach, and it left the gap between knowledge and faith as wide as ever, while begging most of the important questions that would have to be answered in attempting to bridge the gap.

A simple fact-value distinction seems to have been especially appealing to many scientists writing during the late 1940s and early 1950s on the conflict between empirical science and religious faith.[76] It was a position that tended to crop up again and again in various forms even among thinkers who were otherwise usually more probing in their handling of the epistemological questions.[77] One early attempt to tighten up the "fact-value approach" was to hold that the non-empirical side of the relationship is also factual, that is, as one writer put it, "Values, goals, purposes, intentions, the self, are facts."[78] Without a more rigorous demonstration, however, of how this might be the case, this tactic seemed to involve more word play than substance.

Another more complex version of the facts-value approach was one that held that while the facts and objects of the world may be given directly and simply by empirical reason and observation, they do not mean anything until they are interpreted. According to this view, interpretation is necessary at every level, and as we eventually move to consider the ultimate significance of the facts, then we have perforce to rely on integrating, high-level assumptions about the ultimate nature of reality drawn from the realms of metaphysics and religion. The hope from this point of view was that the "Christian worldview" would prove more adequate than others as a source of such interpretation.[79]

This last position was essentially a restatement of the call to bring to light the hidden presuppositions of thought. It did serve to show the presence of all kinds of worldviews and metaphysical assumptions at work where it was often asserted by "the cult of objectivity" that there were none. But this position was frequently framed in such a way that knowledge of the facts and interpretation of the facts still remained essentially separate. As George F. Thomas, professor of religion at Princeton and an exponent of this position, argued, for example, religion does not add new facts in any subject. Instead, he said, religion "provides an interpretation to *all* the facts of the subject by indicating their relation to God as the ultimate Being upon whom they depend."[80] But this substitution of "facts-meaning" for "facts-value" left the old Cartesian abyss as wide as ever. And it did little to put to rest the suggestion of something arbitrary, even ideological and irrational, at the level of all worldviews and overarching belief systems to which appeal was made to provide ultimate meaning. This suggestion of arbitrariness was not lessened by the tendency of some to employ the Moberly-SCM insistence that "everyone has presuppositions" as little more than a slogan to establish the inescapability of faith, without taking the next step to ask, "On what grounds are we to select among our presuppositions and worldviews?"[81]

The better theologians did attempt these next steps, but others were not so rigorous. A quality of arbitrariness and emotivism clung to much of the talk about faith and ultimate presuppositions, which were said to interpret the meaning of the world, but which had little or nothing to do with knowledge about the world. A sense of this arbitrariness in talk about worldviews would soon figure importantly in the later secular theologians' repudiation of all ultimate meanings as ideological and unproductive, as something to be jettisoned entirely and to be replaced by instrumental meanings and the day-to-day problem-solving involved, as they supposed, in living in the secular world.

Even in the early years of the 1950s a number of reformers did begin to develop much more penetrating conceptions of the faith-knowledge relationship than those offered by a simple fact-value, fact-meaning approach. Some saw, for example, that the role played by understanding in knowing involved a good deal more than merely clothing supposedly neutral facts with the meaning and values supplied by a particular, externally applied worldview. It was seen by some that there is no such thing as a value-free disciplinary method, since even—or especially—at the methodological level are to be found all kinds of hidden, normative (and not merely descriptive) assumptions about the nature of truth.[82] Moreover, this meant not only that facts and values are mutually interpenetrating at every step of inquiry but, even more important, that the methodological assumptions of the disciplines help determine at the outset the nature of the facts themselves. In other words, in a phrase of the psychologist Gardner Murphy, quoted by LeFevre, "the data are a function of the method used."[83]

While most reformers focused their methodological criticisms on those disciplines dealing primarily with the human world of personality and culture, a few did begin to glimpse that a similar probe of basic assumptions also might apply to the natural sciences.[84] As one writer framed it, the radical question they began to raise was "What is the relation of scientific conceptualization to reality itself?"[85] The posing of this kind of question offered the possibility of a fundamental reexamination of the academic disciplines all along the line. But it was only a beginning awareness of what was needed and possible. The further development of this awareness also would depend on the way major theologians of the movement dealt with the relationship between theology and the natural sciences.

At the end of the 1950s it was still not clear whether enough concerned Christian faculty would be interested in and capable of doing the hard work of raising really radical questions about their disciplines. The task may have been a larger one than most realized at the time, and many obstacles stood in their way. One of the weightiest of these obstacles they supplied themselves.

Associated with the fact-value approach was a form of expression that was exceedingly popular among the reformers, but that in the end had extremely unfortunate consequences for their cause—though they seemed never to have noticed. This was the oft-repeated declaration that while there are Christian interpretations of the results of the different university disciplines, there are no specifically Christian methods of inquiry as such. It was a conviction and a manner of speaking that recurred repeatedly in one form or another. "In terms of the investigation carried on, the methods used," wrote Lowry for example, "there is, of course, no such thing as 'Christian chemistry' or 'Christian biology.' "[86] Similarly, another writer said, "There is no such thing as 'Christian physics, economics, politics or logic; there is only physics, economics, politics, or logic.' For the technical work of a scholar in any field is the same whether he is a Christian or not."[87] The same way of talking recurred over the decade in the pages of *The Christian Scholar:* In 1954— "There is no 'Christian physics' or 'Christian Psychology' "; in 1963— "There is no Christian stone-masonry any more than there is a Christian physics or a Christian sociology. It is even an open question whether there is such a thing as Christian art. . . ."[88] This was a form of thought and expression that continues to be a favorite among Protestant theologians down to the present.[89] It is a view that on the face of it seems so unexceptionable, indeed, appears so highly laudable and compelling, that the serious problems it poses to resolving the faith-knowledge issue remain extremely difficult to discern and disclose. It may, therefore, be worth a slight digression to look more closely at what it entailed.

The motives behind this way of talking were several and all commendable. One was the strong desire by the reformers not to be seen as in any way promoting religious indoctrination. They wanted to make absolutely clear that the claims on the scholar, and especially on the Christian scholar, were first and foremost those of truth, and that the claims of truth are not to be predetermined by any dogmatic formula or framework to which the results of research must be made to conform. To underscore the theological grounding for this anti-indoctrination conviction, they were fond of another expression, "All truth, wherever it is found, is God's truth," another worthy saying, which, as we shall see shortly, also had its problems.[90]

Another motive in the disclaimer that the Christian scholar has no specifically Christian method was to affirm without reservation the importance of scholarly and technical competence and to permit no possibility of excusing technical shoddiness and poor scholarship in the name of a misconceived piety or morality. As always, the reformers wanted to go on record as affirming wholeheartedly the impressive achievements of human reason and the accomplishments of modern science and scholarship. The theological imperative for this they saw in the doctrine of divine creation and the essential goodness of the created world. By the same token they also wanted to affirm their solidarity in the brokenness and limitations, not only of creaturehood itself but of sinful human creatures having to cope with the down-to-earth problems of finite existence. Thus, a guest editor of *The Christian Scholar* wrote that Christian scholars, and especially Christian colleges, "need to embrace once more the earthiness of their vessel, i.e., their essential identification of subject matter, methods, and ends with the pagans in the world of learning."[91] Finally, it was only by disavowing any suggestions of a sectarian conception of learning that they could hope to be accepted and influential in the mainstream of modern higher education—a motive certainly subject to abuse, but in itself worthy enough. So what then was the problem?

The problem was that this way of speaking tended to be accompanied by a hidden, unexamined assumption of its own. This was the assumption of a fact-value, fact-meaning dichotomy in which it was taken for granted that the modes of knowing and conceptions of knowledge dominant in the modern academic disciplines are essentially adequate and relatively unproblematic sources for all knowledge about the world. The more this way of speaking took on, as it increasingly did, a formula- or slogan-like quality, uttered without careful thought, the more it reinforced this assumption.

As a consequence, the repetition of this formula tended to undercut, and made it difficult to carry out in any really radical way, one of the major admonitions of the reformers themselves; namely, that a deep and critical examination of the fundamental presuppositions and methods of the academic disciplines, including those of science, be vigorously pursued. It encouraged in effect a "hands-off policy" with respect to the disciplines, a blunting and foreclosure at the outset of any radical questioning of them. The possibility that there are other ways of knowing and other conceptions of what can be known than are allowed as valid by the instrumentalist, positivist, and empiricist epistemologies dominant in the university disciplines became ever more difficult to entertain. Because of the repeated use of this formula new capacities of imagination, insight, and perception other than those already sanctioned by the established methodological traditions of the disciplines were almost never explored.

Similar considerations also apply to the oft-repeated statement that "All truth is God's truth." This was intended as a salutary reminder that Christians do not possess the entire truth, and that Christians must welcome the illumination that often comes from the non-Christian. Moberly had stressed this. As the heathen peoples might be the instruments of God's judgments on Israel, "so," he said, "Marx or Nietzsche or Freud may have a word for our generation, to refuse to hear which would be to be deaf to the voice of God."[92] Yet such a statement that all truth is God's truth required for its usefulness a searching, critical examination of various claims to truth and of their underlying conceptions of true knowledge. This Moberly himself had been quite clear about.

Without such an accompanying critical awareness, the sloganlike use of the statement, which increasingly became the usual one, resulted simply in an uncritical and unconscious baptism, as God's truth, of whatever conceptions of truth and claims to truth happened to hold sway in the university and culture at any particular time. When this happened, then the call for a critical examination of the assumptions of modern scholarship degenerated into a mere promotion of all scholarship as, in the words of one, less than critical, theological enthusiast, "the veritable work of God."[93]

All of this does not mean that the critical examination of the university disciplines was totally ignored; it is to say that this work lumbered under some heavy burdens, often imposed by the best of intentions.

Despite shortcomings and unfinished business, however, important beginnings were made to undertake an ongoing analysis of the academic disciplines from the vantage of the Christian faith. Not surprisingly, it was *The Christian Scholar* under the editorship of J. Edward Dirks that provided a main forum for the development of this analysis and critique.[94]

Toward the end of the decade, Dirks himself, in fact, presented his own carefully thought-out approach to the faith-knowledge issue, which he cast in terms of the relationship between faith and reason.[95] Dirks's statement exemplified the best thinking of Christian faculty reformers at the time on the issue. We introduced this section with Dirks's clear grasp of the central importance of the issue for the churches' engagement with higher education. Surveying the history of major approaches to the problem, Dirks went on to reject categorically all attempts to find a solution by separating faith and reason. Making such a separation, he said, creates "a tragic dualism both for the modes of human knowledge and for man himself," because it creates a split between the cognitive on the one side and the emotional and volitional on the other, all of which are involved together in the quest for knowledge.

Against a narrow conception of an abstract intellectuality, Dirks was arguing for the view that knowing involves the participation of the whole human being. By the same token, he held that faith, defined essentially as trust, which all persons possess in one form and degree or another, is, therefore, also involved in the work of cognition and knowing, and at many different levels. At the most basic level, faith as trust is indispensable for even the first steps in the work of knowing; and, at the ultimate level, faith provides "a world view," "an inclusive orientation to life," by which life is shaped and understood. At this point he repeated a by-now standard affirmation of neo-orthodoxy that the real conflict is not between faith and nonfaith but between opposing faiths. For knowing to occur, however, faith must be accompanied by reason, which, working with the "materials supplied by faith," serves as our sole means of criticism, analysis, organization, and understanding. Dirks called his "the dialectical approach" to the relationship between faith and reason, one in which the two are linked together in mutual support, each essential to the other.

Dirks's was a helpful and summary presentation of many crucial questions. And, if only because it sought an integral joining of faith and reason, his "dialectical approach" was an advance on some other attempts to deal with the issue. Nevertheless, there were problems in his treatment. For one thing, although Dirks declared that faith "supplies the materials" with which reason must work, he never indicated concretely what the nature of this noetic content of faith might be. The hints he gave were decidedly ambiguous. Faith as trust would seem to be quite different from the materials which it is supposed to supply to reason. In suggesting at points some inclusive, meaning-giving worldview, as one type of material supplied by faith to reason, he did little more than others to dispel the sense of arbitrariness in the decisions faith makes among competing worldviews.

Perhaps the most important unresolved problem was Dirks's ambiguous handling of the concept of reason itself. He was painfully aware of the destructive consequences for faith when reason is defined so narrowly and in such a constricted way that it has no place for the things of which faith speaks. He also recognized that it is precisely such a narrow conception of reason that dominates modern higher education and culture.

> When the history of modern thought is finally written in the future, it will undoubtedly be obvious that modern epistemology, in all areas of knowledge, is a story of the triumph of naturalism. . . . The whole of reality will be seen as having been viewed within a context of spatiotemporal events, subject to measurement and analysis by scientific means, and their relations governed by laws that, if they can be known at all, are elaborated in mechanistic and mathematical terms.

His appraisal of the culturally and religiously devastating consequences of this is worth quoting at length because it again pinpoints vividly the central problem.

> The end result will be apparent: a form of reductionism of all reality to the single plane of nature, the knowledge of which is limited to the positive sciences. For such a world view—the total elaboration of all the implications of a universe from which God himself has been banished and whose throne is taken by man himself—the role of faith is without meaning.[96]

However, despite this clear recognition of the problem, Dirks speaks throughout of the necessity for a mutual, dialectical partnership of faith and reason without once asking how the dominant, modern conception of reason is to be transformed, or whether it can be transformed, in such a way as to encompass and support as knowable reality the dimensions of experience with which faith as trust seeks to be involved.

Yet, on Dirks's analysis it is clear that, unless this transformation can take

place, faith cannot enter into partnership with reason without being undermined and destroyed in the process. As the 1950s came to a close, the
question of the possibility of the transformation of the dominant modern ways
of knowing remained the central issue still facing the church in the modern
world.

The Case for Theology in the University

The third main concern behind the intellectual emphasis was to show that
the theological enterprise itself was not only intellectually respectable, but
also indispensable to the complete university. Again, of course, there was
plenty of room for mixed motives: a genuine conviction that theology had
something of crucial importance to contribute to the university and to modern
culture, mingled with anxiety, resentment, jealousy, and a sense of inferiority
in not being taken seriously.

Some critical and sticky problems of definition were involved in making
the argument for theology in the college and university. After all, the last
thing the new theologians and reform faculty wanted was to be accused of
sectarian or denominational parochialism, much less of denominational
aggrandizement. Consequently, theology was sometimes defined as almost
synonymous with a philosophy that took into account basic religious realities.
The classic statement of this position had been the 1938 work of the liberal
Union Seminary theologian, William Adams Brown, *The Case for Theology in the
University*.[97] Even Robert Hutchins, in his preface to Brown's book, after
having rejected the notion of theology in the university two years earlier,
implied that he found Brown's conception acceptably latitudinarian and close
to what he himself meant by metaphysics.[98] Since Brown wrote his book
partly as an explicit response to Hutchins, this was no small concession on the
latter's part.

Sometimes, in the hands of the more biblically based neo-orthodox,
theology was defined more strictly as the Western Judeo-Christian tradition,
but even here these theologians usually insisted on saying that by theology
they meant Protestant, Catholic, and Jewish religious perspectives.[99] Moreover, the close affinity the neo-orthodox had with the whole modern
existentialist movement also enabled them to include within the compass of
theology those philosophies in which basic questions of human meaning and
commitment were raised and explored. H. Richard Niebuhr defined the role
of theology in the university as that of servant, not to rule or to dictate, but to
raise the questions of meaning and purpose needed for the university to fulfill
its proper tasks.[100]

One important outcome of all this was that the definition of theology
remained sufficiently broad that the arguments for it applied with equal,
perhaps even more force, to the case for the teaching of religion generally in
the university. The spokesmen for theology in the university were them-

selves, in fact, often the most active in working for the establishment of departments of religion and religious studies. The creation of new departments of religion during the 1950s and 1960s throughout the institutions of American higher education owed much to their efforts.[101]

The basic argument for theology in the university was that theology has important things to say, not only in its own right but with vital implications for understanding the world, and that it ought to be allowed to say them.[102] In other words, theology dealt with the "basic questions" of human existence that concerned the innermost responsibility of the university, and it could do so in an intellectually rigorous way; therefore, not to permit these questions to be raised was intellectually inexcusable. "Can colleges and universities," asked Howard Lowry in this vein, "be open-minded enough to open their minds to the deepest questions raised by men and to thorough consideration of the classic answers given to these questions over the years?"[103] If so, then they were duty-bound to welcome theology to full standing in the curriculum. "If," argued George Buttrick, preacher to Harvard University, "utilitarian and hedonistic ethics are taught, to say nothing of the nobler ethic of John Dewey and Ralph Barton Perry, why not New Testament ethic? It would pass muster!"[104]

A related version of this argument for the educational necessity of theology in the curriculum was simply the broad one that theology historically constituted a significant member of the humanities, which, if omitted, left a gap that was educationally inexcusable.[105] This was a venerable argument in the theology-religion arsenal.[106] The subjects of the modern college and university curriculum, Lowry said, summarizing his statement of this argument, "are so thoroughly shot through with religious allusions and concepts that they cannot be understood by religious illiterates."[107] It was an argument, therefore, that demanded not only special departments of religion, but also that religious perspectives had their rightful and necessary place in individual courses and subjects.[108]

The argument held further that in the American cultural experience, no less than in the European, theology had from the beginning been a major formative force. Without a knowledge of theology, therefore, one simply lost a major source of understanding of both the larger history of American culture, and especially the history of American higher education itself. Consequently, the theological renaissance sparked a renewed call during the 1950s to give special attention to the theological roots of American higher education.[109] It is important to note that neither the concern nor the arguments for the place of theology in the university were new with the theological reformers. Their main contribution was not so much new arguments as new energies to advance the older ones.

Above all, it was hoped that theology might provide, if not the integrating principle for a coherent curriculum, a base around which such integration might be nurtured and developed. As we have seen, the loss of integration and intellectual-cultural cohesion in modern higher education had for some time been of deep concern to a variety of people, religious and secular alike. However, it will also be recalled, that the most influential and recent secular statement of the need for a recovery of an integrating principle in the university, the Harvard Report on General Education, explicitly rejected the idea that in the modern world religion could provide the "unifying purpose and idea" of higher education. "Whatever one's views," said the Harvard Report, "religion is not now for most colleges a practicable source of intellectual unity."[110] It was necessary, therefore, to show that, while the Harvard Report was correct about the need for intellectual integration in the university, it was mistaken in its low estimate of religion as an important potential source of that integration.

Sir Walter Moberly had laid out the lines for an answer to the Harvard Report, and most American reformers were in accord with his view of how theology might serve as the unifying center for the university. Moberly had emphatically rejected the idea of trying to impose Christian doctrine as the core of the university's life and curriculum. Such a so-called Christian university would in any case, he felt, be impossible in the modern situation; worse, however, it would be highly undesirable. "Domination by theologians," Moberly wrote, "is no less objectionable than domination by any other group. Any implied claim to infallibility is unchristian, since it clashes with Christian insight into human creatureliness and human corruption. . . ."[111] What was possible and needed, Moberly argued, was for the university to become truly liberal and interested in the basic questions of life. A genuine interest in the ultimate issues, and in their wider cultural implications, would become the source of a growing sense of ordered priorities for the life and tasks of the university.

In this setting, communities of Christian scholars and students within the university, equally devoted as Christians and as scholars, would make their contribution, which Moberly was convinced, would be essential to the university's search for human meaning and goodness. For Moberly, religion and Christian theology in the university would serve not as a way to capture the university for Christian purposes in any religiously coercive sense, but rather, again, "to help the university to be the university." Running throughout Moberly's analysis was a hankering after an older humanistic university ideal, but, as he saw it, the Christian's task in the university was to work to reclaim that ideal in a way suitable to modern conditions and needs.

Most American reformers followed Moberly in this interpretation of the integrating role of theology in the university.[112] A few, however, were more optimistic—or more imperial, as the case may be—about the possibilities of a direct Christian influence within American higher education. For them the American scene offered unique advantages denied the Europeans. For Kenneth Brown of the Danforth Foundation, one of these advantages was that Europeans tended to regard creedal statements and doctrine as the core of the Christian life, whereas Americans were much more practical and pragmatic, and thus stressed religious experience, action, and the spirit of Christianity as of the essence. Brown agreed with Moberly that education should not put doctrine at the core of education for this would, indeed, mean the dogmatic imposition on others of one's beliefs. But, he felt, American Christians, unlike the Europeans, could envisage having a direct and wide-spread influence in the university through their life and example, their active pursuit of the Christian principles of justice and love, and, as Brown put it, their commitment to "the contagious personality of Jesus Christ as the vision of greatness."[113] They had only to begin building their communities of commitment.

Brown was joined in the mid-1950s by many others who saw unique advantages, also unavailable to the Europeans, in the presence in American higher education of hundreds of church and independent colleges.[114] In these they saw the possibility that a deliberate commitment to a Christian outlook and spirit could be made the controlling purpose of an institution of higher education without the sacrifice of educational openness and freedom. While these smaller, independent, and committed institutions could not be emulated directly by the large universities, they would serve as examples of how Christian commitment could undergird scholarship and community. What this actually meant, and how it was to be done, was vague, but an optimistic hope in its achievement remained strong among many reformers throughout the fifties.

Many of the more crusty, American neo-orthodox may have bristled at the evidence of an unreconstructed theological liberalism in Brown's apparently casual attitude toward doctrine. But, in actual fact, most of them, as much as Brown, also valued highly the possibilities of Christian social action and community building within higher education. Later on many of the leading new "secular theologians" would take up their own version of "the conta-gious personality of Jesus Christ." Furthermore, almost all those writing on higher education during these years, however hard their criticisms of the university, evinced an optimism about the possibilities of education and of the religious spirit that was typically, if not uniquely, American.

During these years the Americans certainly remained enthusiastic about the possibilities and prospects of the theological renaissance itself. While the new theological movement was largely confined to academics, little doubt seemed to exist among its adherents that intelligent people throughout the church would welcome the chance now being made available to them to become "lay theologians." We have noted the early panegyrics of *The Christian Scholar* pronouncing this the greatest theological century of all time. As late as 1960, Professor Alexander Miller of Stanford University, and a major voice at the time among the theological university reformers, was expressing similar views. Miller was commissioned in 1957 by the USCC to write a study book for their 1960–61 study theme, "The Church's Mission in the Colleges and Universities," with the hope that it might be an "American Moberly."[115] In his book, *Faith and Learning*, Miller was so sanguine about the strength of the theological renaissance as to predict that, "The danger to the Christian enterprise in the university over the next immediate period will come not so much from its intellectual enemies, as from the fact that it may have things too easily its own way." He lamented that there were not more militant secularists around to keep the church on its toes.[116] His was probably the last such expression of unbridled confidence about the theological future.

CONCLUSION

If the hopes for the theological renaissance and its engagement with American higher education were to be fulfilled, three things would be necessary.

First, it would be essential that the faculty continue to grapple with the knowledge side of the faith-knowledge relationship. It was a question they had taken up, but which many of them had yet to recognize as the all-important issue that it was, and which none had yet adequately considered. As long as this issue remained unresolved, it would be difficult to establish a secure place for religion and theology in the curriculum, except, perhaps, as they were regarded as having "historical value." It would also be difficult to avoid the suggestion that the faith affirmations of the reformers were not, in spite of all disclaimers to the contrary, merely the dogmatic assertion of arbitrary and abstract belief systems. Most serious of all, without the necessary work on the knowledge issue, the things spoken of by faith would remain peripheral or even unreal in relation to the culturally acknowledged world of known and knowable experience.

Second, it would be essential that the leading American theologians themselves give major attention to the knowledge side of the faith-knowledge relationship. The entire higher education reform movement depended on the work of these theologians. Since a main emphasis of the theological-educational reform was not only to examine the presuppositions of the various academic disciplines but also to secure a firm place for theology itself within higher education, the imperative to provide a convincing theological treatment of the faith-knowledge relationship was all the more urgent.

Third, it would be important that the central epistemological and faith issues be conveyed clearly and persuasively to two important groups, and that these issues be taken up and pursued by them. It was crucial that at least some important figures in the larger educational community be drawn into the dialogue and that the reform efforts not remain simply a conversation among the like-minded. It was also essential that there be an understanding and sense of the importance of the intellectual issues, especially among the religious student movements, the campus ministries, and the wider faculty

Christian movements, where a strong emphasis on social action was beginning to make itself felt. Establishing and maintaining the unity between the intellectual and the social action emphases was of utmost importance. The intellectual required the social action emphasis for its effective institutional embodiment, while the social action emphasis separated from the intellectual would eventually find itself stranded, with no real justification for making the university its main arena of expression.

We will examine each of these in reverse order. In the next chapter we look at the social action, organizational, and communication emphases of the churches' new involvement with the university. In the following chapter we will examine in greater detail what kind of foundation was provided in the work of leading American theologians for the engagement with higher education, especially looking at how these theologians conceived of faith and its relationship to reason and knowledge. And in the succeeding chapters we shall look at and reflect on the outcome of all this.

NOTES

1. Merrimon Cuninggim, *The College Seeks Religion* (New Haven, Conn.: Yale University Press, 1947). This was the publication of a doctoral dissertation completed four years earlier at Yale University Divinity School.

2. Ibid., 30.

3. Much of this cooperative work grew out of the interdenominational War Emergency Council for Student Christian Work. As Cuninggim noted shortly after the founding of the USCC, "Nearly all student groups support or take part in the World Student Christian Federation, the World Student Service Fund, the Student Volunteer Movement, and the University Christian Mission." Cuninggim, *The College Seeks Religion*, 44–45; Also see Seymour A. Smith, *Religious Cooperation in State Universities: An Historical Sketch* (n.p.: University of Michigan, 1957), 63–72. There were other groups, such as the Church Society for College Work (founded 1935), a voluntary, interdenominational organization of campus ministers.

4. John W. Nason, "Religion in Higher Education: The Program of Faculty Consultations," *The Educational Record* 27, no. 4 (October 1946): 425.

5. The titles of the Hazen pamphlets published before 1950 included: P. J. Braisted, *Religion in Higher Education* (1942); R. L. Calhoun, *Religion in Higher Education* (1942); [Colloquium], *Conversation on Higher Education and Religion* (1942); J. S. Bixler, *The Resources of Religion and the Aims of Higher Education* (1942); P. M. Malin, *Teaching Economics with a Sense of the Infinite and the Urgent* (1947); Ordway Tead, *The Relation of Religion to Education* (1945?); G. N. Shuster, *Education and Religion* (1945); C. P. Shedd, *Proposals for Religion in Postwar Higher Education* (1945); Ordway Tead, *Spiritual Problems of the Teacher* (1945); Reinhold Niebuhr, *The Contribution of Religion to Cultural Unity* (1945); R. H. Gabriel, *Spiritual Origins of American Culture* (1948); Ordway Tead, *Toward First Principles in Higher Education* (1947?); G. K. Chalmers, *The Prerequisite of Christian Education* (1947?); Ordway Tead, *Education for Character* (1947?); Sir Richard W. Livingstone, *Some Thoughts on University Education* (1948).

6. Donald Cottrell, ed., *College Reading and Religion;* The Edward W. Hazen Foundation and the American Council on Religion (New Haven, Conn.: Yale University Press, 1948).

7. Cuninggim, *The College Seeks Religion,* 183–218.

8. Ibid., 260–61.

9. Ibid., 259–63.

10. Ibid., 95, 263.

11. Bernard Iddings Bell, *Crisis in Education* (New York: McGraw-Hill Book Co., 1949), 152–53.

12. Cottrell, *College Reading and Religion.*

13. Ibid., 17.

14. Ibid., 66.

15. Ibid., 261.

16. Ibid., 136–37.

17. Ibid., 296–97.

18. Ibid., x.

19. R. H. Edwin Espy, *The Religion of College Teachers* (New York: Association Press, 1951), 170.

20. Albert C. Outler, "The Chaplain's Ministry in Building Religious Foundations for Higher Education," in *New Directions for Religion in Higher Education: A Report of the First National Conference of College and University Chaplains and Directors of Religious Life* (New Haven, Conn.: Yale Divinity School, 1948), 20–21. Also see idem, *Colleges, Faculties, and Religion* (New Haven, Conn.: Edward W. Hazen Foundation, 1949).

21. Merrimon Cuninggim, "The Religious Climate of the Post-War College," in *New Directions for Religion in Higher Education,* 7–9.

22. Outler, "The Chaplain's Ministry," 21.

23. Willem Adolph Visser 't Hooft, *None Other Gods* (New York and London: Harper & Brothers, 1937), 137–38.

24. Arnold S. Nash, *The University and the Modern World* (New York: Macmillan Co., 1943).

25. John Coleman, *The Task of the Christian in the University* (Geneva: World Student Christian Federation, 1946).

26. See Sir Walter Moberly, *The Crisis in the University* (London: SCM Press, 1949), 8–9.

27. See, for example, Robert Maynard Hutchins, *The Higher Learning in America* (New Haven, Conn.: Yale University Press, 1938); Norman Foerster, *The Future of the Liberal College* (New York and London: D. Appleton-Century, 1938); José Ortega y Gasset, *Mission of the University* (Princeton, N.J.: Princeton University Press, 1944); Walter M. Kotschnig, ed., *The University in a Changing World* (London: Oxford University Press, 1932); [Harvard University], *General Education in a Free Society: Report of the Harvard Committee* (Cambridge, Mass.: Harvard University Press, 1945). Moberly, *The Crisis in the University,* 23, 41, passim.

28. Nash, *The University and the Modern World,* 283.

29. For example, Moberly, *The Crisis in the University,* 261–73.

30. Ibid., 71.

31. Ibid., 26, 106, 121–26, 161, passim.

32. See Douglas Sloan, "The Teaching of Ethics in the American Undergraduate Curriculum, 1876–1976," in *Ethics Teaching in Higher Education,* ed. Daniel Callahan and Sissela Bok (New York and London: Plenum Press, 1980).

33. Coleman, *The Task of the Christian in the University,* 10; Moberly, *The Crisis in the*

University, 295; [Editorial], *The Christian Scholar* 39 (March 1956): 4; Alexander Miller, *Faith and Learning* (New York: Association Press, 1960), 28–29, and chapter 4, "The Integral University." Franklin Woo observes that Coleman used the term "the multiversity" twenty years before it acquired notoriety at the hands of Clark Kerr. Franklin Woo, "From USCC to UCM: An Historical Inquiry with Emphasis on the Last Ten Years of the Student Christian Movements in the U.S.A. and Their Struggle for Self-Understanding and Growing Involvement in Social and Political Issues" (Ph.D. diss., Teachers College, Columbia University, 1971), 184.

34. Ibid., 50, 295.

35. The articulation of this task in terms of "uncovering basic presuppositions" may have first come from such SCM writers as Moberly and Nash, but it soon became a stock SCM expression. See, for example, Moberly, *The Crisis in the University,* 66–68; Nash, *The University and the Modern World,* 29–30; Coleman, *The Task of the Christian in the University,* 48ff.; *Christian Scholar* 37 (March 1954): 4; 38 (June 1955): 83; Miller, *Faith and Learning,* 48–49, 90; Hubert C. Noble, "Evangelism on the College Campus," *Theology Today* 11 (April 1954): 62–75; J. Gordon Chamberlin, *Churches and the Campus* (Philadelphia: Westminster Press, 1963), 152. A somewhat later treatment of this same conception of theology as a critique of dominant presuppositions at work in the university, but one done with great care and precision, is Charles S. McCoy, *The Meaning of Theological Reflection.* Faith-Learning Series: A Series Examining the Academic Disciplines (New York: Faculty Christian Fellowship, 1964).

36. Ernest Lehrs, *Man or Matter* (New York: Harper & Row, 1950).

37. See note 33; also Owen Barfield, *History, Guilt, and Habit* (Middletown, Conn.: Wesleyan University Press, 1979), 73.

38. The theme runs through all the literature of the time dealing with the church and the university.

39. Coleman, *The Task of the Christian in the University,* 55, 61.

40. Nash, *The University and the Modern World,* 225ff.

41. Moberly, *The Crisis in the University,* 74, 126.

42. See, for example, [National Intercollegiate Christian Council], *Synopsis and Study Outline for the Book* The Crisis in the University *by Sir Walter Moberly* (New York: National Student Council YM/YWCA, n.d. [probably 1950]). This lists committees, conferences, and study groups across the country studying the topic. Also J. Robert Nelson, ed., *The Christian Student and the University* (New York: Association Press, 1952).

43. Quoted in Kenneth Irving Brown, *Not Minds Alone: Some Frontiers of Christian Education* (New York: Harper & Brothers, 1954), 24.

44. Ibid.; *The Christian Scholar* 36, no. 1 (March 1953): 55.

45. Descriptions, activities, and hopes for the Faculty Christian Fellowship may be found in *The Christian Scholar* and the *Faculty Forum* (see note 46 below). Also see, Rene de Visme Williamson, "Christianity and Higher Education: The Faculty Christian Movement in the United States," in *Association of American Colleges Bulletin* 41, no. 1 (March 1955): 88–97.

46. The *Faculty Forum* was published by the Division of Higher Education of the Methodist Church and the Board of Christian Education of the Presbyterian Church, U.S.A., "as a contribution to the movement among college and university professors."

47. *The Christian Scholar* 36, no. 1 (1953): 155, 323.

48. Perry D. LeFevre, *The Christian Teacher: His Faith and His Responsibilities in Higher Education* (New York and Nashville: Abingdon Press, 1958).

49. See, for example, Kenneth Irving Brown, *Not Minds Alone,* 21–34.

50. An early attempt at a comprehensive treatment of the main issues confronting the churches within the university was Howard Lowry, *The Mind's Adventure: Religion and Higher Education* (Philadelphia: Westminster Press, 1952). At the time Lowry was president of Wooster College and formerly professor of English at Princeton University, and an expert on Matthew Arnold. He had been urged to write his book by E. Fay Campbell, director of the Division of Higher Education of the Board of Christian Education of the Presbyterian Church, U.S.A. For guidance in the task Lowry had put together a large advisory committee of well-known church leaders, theologians, and academics. Lowry's book was upstaged in its appearance only a few months by Moberly's *The Crisis in the University*. So it missed having the impact as a trailblazer, which it might otherwise have enjoyed. Since Moberly's was also in actuality the more comprehensive and penetrating of the two, it continued to receive most of the attention that otherwise might have gone to Lowry's book.

The publication of *The Mind's Adventure* was significant, nonetheless. Dealing with many of the same theological, educational, and organizational issues as had Moberly, and drawing on similar resources (including Nash and Coleman among others), Lowry's book represented, in both origins and content, the extent to which a consensus was beginning to emerge, joining theologically concerned faculty, administrators, and church leaders, about the major issues facing them in higher education and about ways of approaching these issues. Of similar significance in documenting this emerging consensus was the publication of the 1954 book, *Not Minds Alone: Some Frontiers of Education* by the new director of the Danforth Foundation and former president of Hiram College and Denison University, Kenneth Irving Brown. See note 43 above. At the same time other books dealing with similar topics also were appearing.

51. Hoxie N. Fairchild, ed., *Religious Perspectives in College Teaching* (New York: Ronald Press Co., 1952); also see the similar collection, Paul M. Limbert, ed., *College Teaching and Christian Values* (New York: Association Press, 1951). See, for example, Stanley R. Hopper, ed., *Spiritual Problems in Contemporary Literature* (New York: Harper & Brothers, 1952); Nathan Scott, *Modern Literature and the Religious Frontier* (New York: Harper & Brothers, 1958); Nathan Scott, ed., *Tragic Vision and the Christian Faith* (New York: Association Press, 1957); Amos Wilder, *Modern Poetry and the Christian Tradition* (New York: Charles Scribner's Sons, 1952); J.V.L. Casserley, *Morals and Man in the Social Sciences* (New York: Longmans, Green & Co., 1951); Albert C. Outler, *Psychotherapy and the Christian Message* (New York: Harper & Brothers, 1954); David E. Roberts, *Psychotherapy and a Christian View of Man* (New York: Charles Scribner's Sons, 1950).

52. LeFevre, *The Christian Teacher;* Chad Walsh, *Campus Gods on Trial* (New York: Macmillan Co., 1953); Robert Hamill, *Gods of the Campus* (New York: Abingdon-Cokesbury Press, 1949); Lowry, *The Mind's Adventure;* Kenneth Irving Brown, *Not Minds Alone.* The title of Brown's book suggests that he may have consciously seen himself providing a necessary widening to the intellectual emphasis indicated by Lowry's title.

53. LeFevre, *The Christian Teacher,* 36.

54. Kenneth Irving Brown, *Not Minds Alone,* 18.

55. See, for example, Lowry, *The Mind's Adventure,* 72.

56. Ibid., 34; Fairchild, *Religious Perspectives in College Teaching,* 13.

57. Fairchild, *Religious Perspectives in College Teaching,* 22.

58. See, for example, ibid., 21–22; Lowry, *The Mind's Adventure,* 81; Kenneth Irving Brown, *Not Minds Alone,* 107–10; LeFevre, *The Christian Teacher,* 72.

59. Fairchild, *Religious Perspectives in College Teaching*, 12.

60. Over the years *The Christian Scholar* returned repeatedly to the relationship between commitment and objectivity. See, for example, *The Christian Scholar* 37, no. 1 (March 1954): 4; 38 (March 1955): 3; 42, no. 1 (March 1959): 3, and in this same issue, Merle E. Brown, "Objectivity and Commitment," 7–15. Also see references above.

61. See Fairchild, *Religious Perspectives in College Teaching*, 4.

62. Lowry, *The Mind's Adventure*, 26.

63. David Roberts, *The Grandeur and Misery of Man* (New York: Oxford University Press, 1955).

64. Hamill, *Gods of the Campus*.

65. See, for example, Lowry, *The Mind's Adventure*, 49–51; Kenneth Irving Brown, *Not Minds Alone*, 52–53, 67ff.

66. Joseph Haroutunian, "A Protestant Theory of Education," in *Toward a Christian Philosophy of Higher Education*, ed. John Paul von Grueningen (Philadelphia: Westminster Press, 1957), 36. Haroutunian added: "In fact, I should like to insist upon this essential function of education against those pious souls who think that 'moral and religious training' is more their business than the training of the mind for integrity and creativity. . . . Creative intelligence is a glory without which the face of man is dull as a cement wall and the whole of him is a foretaste of death." This was vintage neo-orthodox rhetoric.

67. See, for example, Balmer H. Kelly, ed., *The Layman's Bible Commentary*, 25 vols. (Richmond: John Knox Press, 1959); Robert McAfee Brown, ed., *Layman's Theological Library*, 6 vols. (Philadelphia: Westminster Press, 1956–57); Reinhold Niebuhr, ed., *Christian Faith Series*, 5 vols. (Garden City, N.Y.: Doubleday & Co., 1955–1959).

68. Lowry, *The Mind's Adventure*, 51.

69. Alisdair MacIntyre has written, "Emotivism has become embodied in our culture." Alisdair MacIntyre, *After Virtue: A Study in Moral Theory* (Notre Dame, Ind.: University of Notre Dame Press, 1981), 21.

70. See, for example, Richard Kroner, *The Primacy of Faith* (New York: Macmillan Co., 1943); Nels F. S. Ferré, *Faith and Culture* (New York: Harper & Brothers, 1946); Erich Frank, *Philosophical Understanding and Religious Truth* (New York: Oxford University Press, n.d.); John Hutchison, *Faith, Reason, and Existence* (New York: Oxford University Press, 1956).

71. LeFevre, *The Christian Teacher*, 39.

72. Grueningen, ed., *Toward a Christian Philosophy of Higher Education*.

73. Ibid., 7, my italics.

74. Edwin H. Rian, "The Need: A World View," in Grueningen, ed., *Toward a Christian Philosophy of Higher Education*, 20–21.

75. J. Edward Dirks, "Faith and Reason," in Grueningen, ed., *Toward a Christian Philosophy of Higher Education*, 45–46.

76. See, for example, many of the articles by scientists in Limbert, *College Teaching and Christian Values*, and Fairchild, *Religious Perspectives in College Teaching*.

77. LeFevre, for instance, reverts at points, in what is a usually much more careful analysis, to what seems to be a simple identification of theology with values and social sciences with knowledge. LeFevre, *The Christian Teacher*, 71–72.

78. Robert B. MacLeod, "Experimental Psychology," in *Religious Perspectives in College Teaching*, ed. Hoxie N. Fairchild, 283.

79. See, for instance, *The Christian Scholar* 36, no. 2 (1953): 83.

80. George F. Thomas, "Religious Perspectives in College Teaching: Problems

and Principles," in *Religious Perspectives in College Teaching*, ed. Hoxie N. Fairchild, 14–15.

81. I remember one of my professors in sociology of religion at Yale University Divinity School in the mid-1950s exclaiming impatiently to his class one morning, "I am so tired of the SCM types always saying, 'everyone has presuppositions.' Of course they do. Then what?"

82. For example, LeFevre, *The Christian Teacher*, 38, 72ff.

83. Ibid., 73.

84. See, for example, *The Christian Scholar* 41, no. 3 (September 1958); Edwin E. Aubrey, "Scientia, Scientific Method, and Religion," in *Liberal Learning and Religion*, ed. Amos Wilder (New York: Harper & Brothers, 1951), 27–55; Charles Birch, "Creation and the Creator," *The Journal of Religion* (April 1957), 85–98; LeFevre, *The Christian Teacher*, chapter 5, "The Christian Teacher and the Natural Sciences," 76–86.

85. LeFevre, *The Christian Teacher*, 83.

86. Lowry, *The Mind's Adventure*, 104.

87. Thomas, "Religious Perspectives in College Teaching," 16.

88. *The Christian Scholar* 37, no. 1 (March 1954): 75; 46, no. 4 (winter 1963): 276.

89. Merrimon Cuninggim: "There is no such thing as 'Christian biology' or 'Christian fine arts' or even 'Christian economics,' certain frightened pseudo-Protestants to the contrary notwithstanding." *The Protestant Stake in Higher Education* (n.p.: Council of Protestant Colleges and Universities, 1961), 53. The formula gets repeated again and again. In 1988 Cornel West wrote, "There is no such thing as 'Christian' social analysis, just as there is no such thing as Christian mathematics, Christian physics, or Christian economics." Cornel West, *Prophetic Fragments* (Grand Rapids: Wm. B. Eerdmans Publishing Co., 1988), 113.

90. For example, LeFevre, *The Christian Teacher*, 32, 34; Kenneth Irving Brown, *Not Minds Alone*, 43; *The Christian Scholar* 39, no. 3 (September 1956): 167; 50, no. 4 (December 1957): 260; Cuninggim, *The Protestant Stake in Higher Education*, 52.

91. *The Christian Scholar* 41, Supplement (autumn 1958): 185–86.

92. Moberly, *The Crisis in the University*, 104–5.

93. Miller, *Faith and Learning*, 152–53.

94. Over the years special themes and even whole issues of *The Christian Scholar* were devoted to such topics as "Poetry and Modern Thought," "The Relationship of Faith, Knowledge, and Language," "The Christian in Philosophy," "Tensions and Community in Academic Life," "History, Historicism, and the Christian Perspective," "The Christian Faith and Human Law," "Christianity and The Arts," "Christian Faith and Natural Science," and others.

95. J. Edward Dirks, "Faith and Reason," in Grueningen, ed., *Toward a Christian Philosophy of Higher Education*, 45–62.

96. Ibid., 54.

97. William Adams Brown, *The Case for Theology in the University* (Chicago: University of Chicago Press, 1938).

98. Ibid., v–viii; It may be of some interest to note in passing that Hutchins seems to have maintained this positive attitude toward religion in education, at least sufficiently for defenders of religion in higher education to continue to quote him over the years. See, for example, Cuninggim, *The College Seeks Religion*, 75, 108; Lowry, *The Mind's Adventure*, 94, 96.

99. For example, see Miller, *Faith and Learning*, 136; Charles S. McCoy, *The*

Meaning of Theological Reflection, Faith-Learning Series; A Series Examining the Academic Disciplines (New York: Faculty Christian Fellowship, 1964), 21. McCoy was critical, for example, of those of his colleagues who misunderstood theology as being exclusively Christian, since this led, he felt, to "the unfortunate characterization of church and university respectively as 'community of faith' and 'community of learning' "—a separation and encapsulation of both that was directly inimical to the theological renaissance's basic understanding of the church's intellectual task in the university.

100. H. Richard Niebuhr, "Theology in the University," in idem, *Radical Monotheism and Western Culture* (New York: Harper & Row, 1970), 93–99, first published as "Theology—Not Queen but Servant," *The Journal of Religion* (December 1943). Niebuhr's definition, however, had its own problems. What did servant mean? Servants are sometimes known for their obsequiousness. If servant did not include a probing criticism of the conceptions and uses of knowledge dominant in the university, it could "serve" mainly to provide religious legitimation and sanction for what the scientists and technicists were going to do anyway—a kind of Western version of Mitsubishi Zen.

101. See, Claude Welch, *Graduate Education in Religion: A Critical Appraisal* (Missoula, Mont.: University of Montana Press, 1971), 38–39; also see Paul Ramsey and John F. Wilson, eds., *The Study of Religion in Colleges and Universities* (Princeton, N.J.: Princeton University Press, 1970), 12–14. I deal with the teaching of religion in the university in more detail in following chapters.

102. For representative statements of this view, see Moberly, *The Crisis in the University*, 263ff.; Miller, *Faith and Learning*, 104ff.; George Arthur Buttrick, *Biblical Thought and the Secular University* (Baton Rouge, La.: Louisiana State University Press, 1960), 13, 20–21, 23.

103. Lowry, *The Mind's Adventure*, 37.

104. Buttrick, *Biblical Thought and the Secular University*, 21.

105. For representatives of this type of argument, see Harold H. Ditmanson, et al., *Christian Faith and the Liberal Arts* (Minneapolis: Augsburg Publishing House, 1960); the chapters by the various authors in Christian Gauss, ed., *The Teaching of Religion in American Higher Education* (New York: Ronald Press Co., 1951); Lowry, "Liberal Education and Religion," chapter 3 in *The Mind's Adventure*; Edwin E. Aubrey, *Humanistic Teaching and the Place of Ethical and Religious Values in Higher Education* (Philadelphia: University of Pennsylvania Press, 1959); Miller, *Faith and Learning*, 144.

106. It was the one voiced, for example, by a group of faculty members at Princeton in 1935, who maintained in a special committee report on religion in the university, that their fields of philosophy, literature, art, and history could only be adequately understood in connection with the theological-religious traditions of Western culture. Their report eventuated five years later in the appointment of a professor of religious thought at Princeton University. Gauss, *The Teaching of Religion in American Higher Education*, 85; Cuninggim, *The College Seeks Religion*, 76–77.

107. Lowry, *The Mind's Adventure*, 70.

108. See especially the chapters in Limbert, *College Teaching and Christian Values* and in Fairchild, *Religious Perspectives in College Teaching*.

109. See, for example, George H. Williams, *The Theological Idea of the University* (New York: Commission on Higher Education, National Council of Churches, 1958). Also, for example, Robert McAfee Brown, "The Reformed Tradition and Higher Education," *The Christian Scholar* 41, no. 1 (March 1958): 21–40.

110. Harvard Report, *General Education in a Free Society*, 39.

111. Moberly, *The Crisis in the University*, 104–5.

112. For expressions of the importance of religion in what Coleman had called the "integral university," see Miller, *Faith and Learning*, 105; Lowry, *The Mind's Adventure*, 84–87. See Coleman, *The Task of the Christian in the University*, 33, 44–45.

113. Kenneth Irving Brown, *Not Minds Alone*, 40–41.

114. For example, see Lowry, *The Mind's Adventure*, 50–51; Kenneth Irving Brown, *Not Minds Alone*, 41; LeFevre, *The Christian Teacher*, 8; Rian, "The Need: A World View," in *The Christian Century* 37, no. 1 (March 1954): 14, passim.

115. Miller, *Faith and Learning*, xiii.

116. Ibid., 130.

CHAPTER 3

The Church Engages
Higher Education:
The Campaign Is Launched

THE BACKGROUND: THE ACADEMIC REVOLUTION

In the twenty years after World War II, two major developments in American higher education occurred. Although both had prewar origins, they grew in intensity in the postwar years and, working together, amounted almost in themselves to a transformation in higher education. The first was the nearly complete triumph of the research university in determining the primary ethos and goals of American higher education. The second was a vast expansion in numbers of students entering the nation's colleges and universities.

In 1957 David Riesman described American higher education as a snake with the leading research universities, such as his Harvard, at the head, and the other, lesser institutions following as the tail.[1] Enormous differences existed, of course, among the variety of institutions represented in this picture. Nevertheless, all took their leads from the head and tried to emulate it, each attempting to move farther and farther up the tail toward a more prestigious place near the front of the procession. Normal schools attempted to become colleges, teachers colleges to become state colleges, and state colleges to become state universities. Liberal arts colleges submitted to becoming "university colleges," feeders to the university graduate schools, and they were themselves permeated more by the research and publication reward system than by the old ideal of teaching. And the universities vied with one another to be identified as the most deserving recipients of funding from government and foundations. In 1968, Riesman, with Christopher Jencks, published *The Academic Revolution*, documenting the dominant influence on college and university campuses of members of the academic profession, and the nearly total triumph throughout the whole of modern higher education of the research university ideal and ethos.[2]

The other development was the rapid acceleration of the century-long trend from elite higher education to mass higher education. This development manifested itself both in the increasing numbers of students attending institutions of higher education as well as in the continuing introduction of all kinds of practical, vocational subjects at nearly every level of higher education. Returning veterans were followed by the grown-up baby boomers, and at the same time, the doors of higher education were being opened to entirely new types of students—older, minority, and working students.

Total enrollments in American higher education rose from 2.7 million in 1949 to 3.2 million in 1959, and to an astounding 8.1 million in 1970.[3] The community college movement grew rapidly as it promised community service courses as well as university transfer opportunities for talented individuals requiring academic remedial work. Professional and vocational courses flourished at every level. Higher education was looked to more and more to solve America's most pressing social problems. Above all, higher education was called on to provide the high-level, theoretical knowledge so necessary for the nation's scientific, technological, economic, and military strength.

All these goals were reflected in the major pieces of federal legislation enacted during this period for aid to higher education. The National Defense Education Act of 1958 was a direct response to the Soviet Union's success in launching Sputnik and brought a billion dollar federal program to the support of science, mathematics, and foreign language instruction. The Higher Education Act of 1965 not only provided direct assistance to students and institutions but also attempted to encourage colleges and universities to apply their knowledge to the alleviation of growing urban problems. Monies from private foundations for applied research in the social sciences became more and more available.[4]

Both of these developments, the dominance of the research ideal and the drive toward mass and popular higher education, were in some ways reinforcing, but in certain, important respects were also incompatible, if not outright contradictory. The one was avowedly academic, theoretical, and elite; the other was experiential-social, practical-applied, and popular-democratic. Harboring both developments and the ideals they represented in the same system of higher education was no simple matter. It meant continuing conflict and power struggles between the representatives of the two positions. And it further exacerbated the sense of a lack of unified purpose within modern higher education.

In 1963, however, Clark Kerr, chancellor of the University of California, in his book, *The Uses of the University*, suggested that this was not an unhappy, but rather an advantageous state of affairs. Earlier critics of the university had used the expression "multiversity" in a basically pejorative sense.[5] For them the term signified a higher education system that grew by accretion with no real inner principles of cohesion and with no overall sense of direction or purpose. Kerr, however, gave the term "multiversity" a new twist, attempting to make a virtue of it.

While he quipped that the parking lot was often the only thing the different divisions of the university had in common, Kerr, nevertheless, suggested that this was a strength. The pragmatic character of the university, the lack of clarity about its mission, and the ability of the myriad denizens of the university to rely on a bureaucratic ethic of live and let live without demanding ideological concord, this, he submitted, constituted the genius of the university. This enabled the members of the university to innovate and to respond to new impulses without their having to fit into some predetermined set of priorities or conceptual framework. This lack of unity enabled the university to serve a diversity of social interests, accommodating within itself many, often competing purposes and parties. Kerr's analysis would soon come under fire as an apology for the university's service primarily to industry, government bureaus, and the military. Although his assessment of the value of the multiversity was contested, his description of it as an institutional reality was not.

With the "academic revolution," however, there came a much deeper point of unity than the term multiversity suggested, whether used pejoratively or approvingly. This was that all of modern education had come to be pervaded by a single conception of knowledge. The popular way of expressing this view of knowledge was to say that "knowledge is power." Increasingly, the dominant definition of knowledge pervading all of modern education was (and remains) that "knowledge is power." Every other conception of knowledge found itself placed on the defensive, if not squeezed out of modern education entirely. Moreover, the chief purpose of higher education was now, as a widely used expression began to put it, "the production of knowledge" for the continuing control of nature and the furthering of social advance.[6]

As it developed during the late 1940s and through the 1950s, the academic revolution confirmed the emphasis of the theological renaissance on the need of the churches to develop a reinvigorated but entirely new approach and relationship to American higher education. The sheer extent and momentum of the expansion of higher education also underscored what a daunting challenge the theological reformers were taking on. Nevertheless, during the 1950s it did not appear at all to be an impossible task. A many-sided campaign by the churches began to unfold, one that involved the student Christian movements, a revitalized campus ministry, new faculty undertakings, and the churches' most direct institutional base in higher education, the church-related college.

THE STUDENT CHRISTIAN MOVEMENTS
AND THE CAMPUS MINISTRY

After the war the various denominations began to develop their campus ministries, appointing more campus workers and building new centers on campus, some of them quite elaborate and expensive, to house their activities. Much of this growth was a function of the relative affluence and expansive mood of the churches during this period. From the point of view of the denominations, their mission to the campus was still conceived largely in older notions of evangelism and of providing for students a "church home away from home."

According to Hal Viehman, for many years Presbyterian campus minister, and later a key executive of the Presbyterian Board of Higher Education, the older assumptions and patterns of thinking that characterized the different denominations were reflected very clearly during these years in their various strategies for campus ministry, and even in their architectural decisions: the Lutherans focusing much of their student work in local churches adjacent to campuses; the Methodists building large foundation centers as assembly halls and communal enclaves; the Presbyterians, always the more academic, not building so much but attempting rather to separate their campus ministries from local churches in order to work more directly with faculty and theologically interested students.[7] Whatever the persistence of older patterns, however, the new campus ministers who were being appointed by the denominations were increasingly recent seminary graduates deeply influenced by the theological renaissance. They began to carry its concerns and understandings directly into the campus work of their denominations.

From the beginning there were built-in tensions between the new campus ministry and the congregations that supported them. The "religious revival of the 1950s" was accompanied by a remarkable surge in churchgoing and membership growth among mainline Protestant denominations. This religious revival of the 1950s has often been depicted as shallow and conventional.[8] Even at the time, it provided much sport and rich grist for the critical mills of neo-orthodox theologians and savvy campus ministers eager to demonstrate to the modern student that true religious sensibilities have little to do with popular piety. Nevertheless, however superficial it may have been, the religious revival, and the increase in churchgoing it produced, was an important source of the money necessary for the churches to expand their support of theological education and the organizational outreach of the campus ministry. This situation not only was fraught with many occasions for bad faith but also would require, for the long-term effectiveness of the campus minister, that the congregations and supporting denominational agencies begin to understand and back the new approach to higher education.

One step in this direction was the attempt of theological reformers and some church leaders to redefine and recast the meaning of evangelism.[9] Until this time evangelism had been conceived and practiced by the churches largely after the manner of nineteenth-century revivalism, even though, for most mainline Protestant churches by mid-twentieth century, it was no longer proper to insist on an emotionally charged conversion experience as the necessary accompaniment of the faith decision. Nevertheless, the older pattern prevailed of regarding evangelism largely as winning individual souls to the faith, with an emphasis on "personal decision."

This older conception of evangelism was considered by the new theological-educational reformers as unfortunate on several counts. It was highly individualistic and, thereby, failed to reckon with the larger social and cultural context of the individual. It lacked both social awareness and a socially critical capacity. It usually slighted the importance of thinking, when it was not outright hostile to the intellectual life, stressing feelings and social conformity instead. It lent itself unabashedly to institutional aggrandizement, as the separate denominations competed to sign up new converts on their church rolls. All in all, in the view of the reformers, the notions of evangelism that had come overwhelmingly to characterize much church activity in the twentieth century were not suited to modern human experience, and made no sense at all in the context of modern higher education.

The reformulation of evangelism by those influenced by the theological renaissance began with the rejection of any notion of an abstract, isolated individual seen as the prime object of conversion. Instead, the new evangelism would take in the needs of the larger community and of the individual situated within the context of that community.

As a consequence, the importance of the university for the theological renaissance was once more underscored. The university was seen as "the most strategic point in our culture," as "the cognitive center of the modern world."[10] The new evangelism, therefore, would have to begin by attempting "to take the university seriously," to work "to understand the university—its nature, its purposes, its problems."[11] Furthermore, the principal work of the new evangelism would have to be carried by people within the university, not by churchly intruders from without who had no real, integral connection with the university. "Christian witness," wrote one of the new church executives of higher education, "must be made by persons who are at home in the university community and who accept its disciplines of scholarship."[12] The new evangelism would, therefore, take the intellectual tasks of both the university and the church with utmost seriousness.

This meant that the church must in a sense be instructed by the college and university about the deeper intellectual dimensions of the meaning of evangelism. The college is committed, and the church must be similarly committed, wrote theologian Julian Hartt, "to the development of the intellectual life, that is, to the deepening of understanding and the broadening of knowledge for the enrichment of existence."[13] The attempts to reformulate the meaning of evangelism also provided an opening for broadening the intellectual dimension to include not only the verbal, but all symbols of communication that speak to modern persons, especially the forms of modern art and symbolic social action.[14]

The neo-orthodox understanding of the social dimensions of sin further undergirded the attempt to redefine evangelism away from a narrow, individualistic emphasis. Some reformers drew especially on the work of the European neo-orthodox theologian, Hendrick Kraemer, who insisted that individualistic conceptions of evangelism, which stressed "personal decision," make no connection with "the new type of man" who is caught up in the complex web of modern society, and who no longer has "any stamina for personal decisions."[15] Instead, they argued, evangelism must be reconceived as "structural evangelism." Structural evangelism meant concentrating not on the conversion of the isolated individual, but rather on reforming the structures of society having to do with justice, equality, and peace.[16] In the new conception of evangelism the dual emphasis on the tasks of intellectual understanding and social awareness moved to the fore. The relation between the two, however, remained extremely vague.

The redefinition of evangelism tended also to reinforce the strong impulses that already had begun to arise among the various student movements themselves for a more ecumenical understanding and expression of the denominations' student work on campus.[17] As a consequence, the interdenominational, ecumenical organization of the national student Christian movements, which had already started before the end of the war, continued to expand.[18]

The United Student Christian Council (USCC), the interdenominational organization of American student work founded in 1946, joined in 1959 with the old Student Volunteer Movement and the Interseminary Committee of the YMCA and YWCA to form the National Student Christian Federation (NSCF).[19] The next year four denominations merged to create the United Campus Christian Fellowship (UCCF), which then represented its four members as one within the NSCF, a further expression of the strong ecumenical spirit now running through the student movements.[20] The organization of such interdenominational groupings reflected the deepening conviction among both students and campus ministers that, in the modern university situation, old denominational divisions no longer had much meaning.[21]

The NSCF was a concrete expression of these new views and commitments. The NSCF was especially important in tying the American student Christian movements more directly to the international student movement through the WSCF. Moreover, the NSCF attempted to include among its campus members faculty and students who did not belong to churches officially linked with the NSCF as an organization.[22] Most important, the new federation also gave added impetus to the two emphases of study and social concern that had marked the new theological orientation of the theological renaissance from Visser 't Hooft on.

The study and literature secretary of the old Student Volunteer Movement was now located within the NSCF. The study secretary's task included developing study books for the older USCC quadrennial conferences, which the NSCF now took on for a much broader constituency. It also entailed providing extensive, ongoing study materials for this wider membership, including a regular newsletter, *Wind and Chaff*.

The study emphasis within the NSCF, however, was itself pushed more and more toward a focus on social issues and social activism. During the early 1950s within the United Student Christian Council, the predecessor of the NSCF, this had not been so much the case; a strong concern with social issues had yet to develop. At those points within the USCC, however, where the influence of the World Student Christian Federation made itself felt, a budding social awareness, even in these early years, can be discerned.

The chair of the political commission of the WSCF was an American, William Stringfellow. A lawyer and accomplished lay theologian, Stringfellow was instrumental in introducing political-social concerns among the leadership of the American student movements. Stringfellow, however, himself very much in the neo-orthodox mold, always insisted that the political be set within a theological context.[23]

The political emphasis continued to become increasingly important. As early as 1951, one of the main study books edited by the study secretary of the USCC, J. Robert Nelson, was on the topic "The Christian Student and the World Struggle."[24] In 1955 the theme adopted for the 17th Quadrennial Conference of the USCC was "Revolution and Reconciliation." For this conference the study and literature department produced three books, the titles of which clearly reflected an increasing interest in political-social activism: *Encounter with Revolution; Revolution and Redemption*; and *Shock and Renewal*.[25] It was reported that about twenty-two thousand copies of these books were distributed to some four hundred ecumenical study groups on campuses across the country.[26]

The next quadrennial conference, held in Athens, Ohio, in 1959, and now under the auspices of the newly formed NSCF, took as its theme "The Mission of the Church in the Whole World." This conference signaled the beginning of the NSCF's full-fledged embrace of political-social activism. The main study book for the conference, *Outside the Camp*, by Charles West of Princeton University, stressed the importance of the church's "being in the world" and engaging the major concrete social-political issues that it found there.[27] At the Athens Conference nine such "priority issues" were identified and forums created for discussing them: technical upheaval; racial tension; militant non-Christian faiths; new nationalism; modern secularism; responsibility for statesmanship; universities and students; displaced, uprooted, rejected peoples; and communism.[28] Another major study book for the conference, *Evangelism and Politics* by Philippe Maury, interpreted the former largely in terms of the latter.[29]

Present at the 1959 Athens conference were Martin Luther King, Jr., James Lawson, Andrew Young, and others of the Student Christian Leadership Conference (SCLC), which one month later, in February 1960, began its series of lunch counter sit-ins in Greensboro, North Carolina. Shortly thereafter, the NSCF established a "Legal Aid and Scholarship Fund" to help students who had been arrested and expelled from their schools (an act triggered by the arrest and expulsion from Vanderbilt of SCLC leader James

Lawson, who had formerly been a missionary to India and a traveling secretary of the old Student Volunteer Movement). The NSCF staff and student officers kept in close touch with the sit-in movement, and in September voted the NSCF a "full member" of the newly founded Student Nonviolent Coordinating Committee.[30] From that point on, the NSCF would plunge ever deeper into the maelstrom of political and social unrest beginning to envelop the country. In 1966 the NSCF reorganized as the University Christian Movement (UCM) in order to encourage further the work of ecumenical cooperation and social activism on the college campus.

From the very founding of the NSCF there were ambiguities in its organization and outlook that were never resolved and that would become ever more apparent and troubling. These are worth noting because they were symptomatic of the work of the student movements and campus ministry in general. One area of ambiguity was the relationship of the NSCF to the denominational churches. A major purpose in the organization of the NSCF had been to achieve greater autonomy for student leadership of the Christian movement within higher education. At the same time, all the denominations had strong affiliation with their student movements and were the sole source of support for them. Many perceptive denominational executives in higher education attempted to provide the student movements with full resources, while at the same time pulling back to allow space for student leadership and self-determination of the movements to develop. This ill-defined space was a continuing point of tension and of potential conflict between the student movements and the supporting denominations.

Another area of ambiguity was that of the relationship of the NSCF to its nondenominational members and to the non-Christian groups and movements within the university with which it increasingly sought to work. The criteria for working with these others on common aims were never clearly formulated, indeed they were scarcely considered. This posed many problems—with whom to work and not to work, what kind of connection to establish with them, and so forth. But perhaps the most important problem would be: From whom would the NSCF take its primary directions? From its own integral identity and inner judgment of what was required, or from the perceptions and claims of others? By the mid-1960s this would become an excruciating question.

Finally the NSCF embodied an ambiguity running throughout the whole student movement. This had to do with the lack of clarity about the connection between the intellectual task of the Christian in the university and the social action emphasis of "being in the world." Moberly, it will be recalled, had been fairly precise about the relationship. The primary task of the Christian in the university, in his view, was to focus on the unique tasks, needs, and responsibilities of higher education; this would provide a touchstone for arranging the order of priorities for social action on issues concerning the university. In the American student movements, however, there was not even this clarity about the relationship between the intellectual and social tasks. A tendency, therefore, always existed for the two to fall apart and to lose their inner connection. As the social turmoil of the 1960s broke in all its fury, this would become an exceedingly critical problem.

During the 1950s and into the early 1960s, however, these ambiguities and problems had yet to become apparent. Instead, during these years the work of the campus ministries and their associated student movements gained in momentum, manifesting an enthusiasm and energy that the new theology fed and shaped. Reflecting the new ecumenism, which we have seen at work in the evolving of the NSCF, the various denominational campus ministers began to reorient their work increasingly away from preoccupation with students only of their churches and to direct their efforts more and more toward interdenominational endeavors and toward the whole academic community.

Not only did the traditional forms of campus ministry begin to take on new life, but also novel and experimental forms of campus ministry began to develop and spread. Perhaps the most dramatic of these was the intentional, or covenantal, community of students devoted to study, worship, and life together. Foremost among these was the Christian Faith and Life Community at the University of Texas in Austin.[31]

Founded by campus minister W. Jack Lewis in 1952, the College House of the Christian Faith and Life Community soon had about thirty women and forty-five men students engaged in the program every year until it ended in 1964. The purpose of the program was to develop a theologically informed and mature individual who could articulate his or her faith and bring it to bear on life, whether as a student, or later as a responsible church member, parent, and citizen. The original Moberly-SCM emphasis on being a theologically sophisticated and committed Christian within the university, which meant also being a good student and scholar, was very much at the heart of the Austin experiment.

In addition to making their regular university studies a basic priority, students in the program also followed a special course of theological studies, all set in the framework of a residence hall where together the students lived, ate, worshiped, and studied. Care was taken, however, to ensure that time spent in the College House program was limited in order to enable the students to participate fully in curricular and extracurricular affairs at the university and to avoid even the suggestion of a monastic community withdrawn from campus life. The central emphasis placed on university study was reflected in the high number of students in the program who were regularly on the dean's honor roll.[32]

In 1956 Joseph Mathews, theologian at Perkins School of Theology at Southern Methodist University in Dallas, joined Lewis to head up the program of theological studies for the Christian Faith and Life Community.[33] A rigorous course of study in theology was developed, with readings from contemporary theologians such as H. Richard Niebuhr, Reinhold Niebuhr, Paul Tillich, Rudolph Bultmann, Dietrich Bonhoeffer, and others. The theological program included lectures, essays, seminar discussions, worship, and individual counseling. Almost a dozen faculty members were added, including a few seminary interns, all of various denominations, who provided a group ministry for the students, and who followed their own program of group study as well. The Austin community also published a newsletter, *Letter to Laymen*, sent to individuals and groups of laity interested themselves in becoming lay theologians. And in 1958 a Laos House was added to the program for adult lay persons and clergy, where they too could come to be confronted by Joe Mathews' existentialist neo-orthodox theology in special forty-four hour intensive, marathon sessions.

The Austin Christian Faith and Life Community became the model for a score or more of others. Following the Austin example, similar intentional communities were established at other colleges and universities in the South, as well as, for example, at Brown, MIT, Yale, Wisconsin, and the state university of Iowa. Nonresidential, but covenantal communities, also established to share disciplines of work, worship, and study, were to be found at Emory, the University of Minnesota, the University of Wisconsin, and Temple.[34] "The Community of Lay Scholars" in North Carolina and the "Guild of Lay Theologians" at the University of Texas were among the better known examples.[35] All were attempts to bring the new theological awareness to bear on a concern for the life of the mind and for the meaning of personal-communal life as these were actually experienced by university students.

Another experiment in new approaches to the campus ministry was the development of research centers devoted to the life of the university, the life of the church, and the relationship between them. The model was the Christian Faith and Higher Education Institute founded by Jack Harrison at the Michigan State University in East Lansing.[36] Harrison first went to Michigan State University as the Presbyterian university pastor where he joined an ecumenical campus ministry group. But he soon became dissatisfied with the group, and he began to explore with a number of faculty members from various disciplines, and with Harold H. Viehman, head of the Presbyterian Department of Campus Christian Life, what new forms were required for a ministry to higher education that involved faculty as much as campus ministry. Out of these conversations, largely at Viehman's and Harrison's inspiration, came the proposal for the establishment of a number of regional study centers across the country that would pioneer a new initiative in campus ministry. In 1962 Harrison became the director of the first center, the Christian Faith and Higher Education Institute, which was located at Michigan State University in a deliberate effort on Harrison's part to have the centers situated at the heart of state-related higher education institutions.

The institute strove to create a research context in which "persons could learn to think theologically what they are doing" and from that context to produce high quality academic publications related to the tasks of the church and university in the modern world.[37] It also attempted to provide self-study resources for both academic institutions and the campus ministry. The institute was first sponsored by the United Church of Christ and the United Presbyterian Church U.S.A., and eventually came under the sponsorship of the United Ministries in Higher Education, which comprised nearly a dozen Protestant denominations working cooperatively in higher education.

With the guidance of a study and strategy committee made up of outstanding university and church leaders, the institute conducted a number of research projects, not only at East Lansing but at other colleges, universities, and theological seminaries that drew on its resources: forming small faculty committees to study the relation of the faith to the different disciplines, organizing faculty conferences, developing dialogues between Christians and non-Christians on campuses, publishing the results of such work, and lending support to the publication of related work by others. The institute as Harrison conceived it was an attempt by the church to be present in the university, and to try to serve and be served by the university, without having a grand plan that might miss the real needs of the moment. It was an attempt to take seriously the call for the church "to be in the world." The institute was in existence from 1962 to 1972.

A variety of other experimental campus ministries also existed: the voluntary association, often centered in social action; the ecumenical council on campus; the team ministry; the student church; and others.[38] One which enjoyed considerable vogue for a short time during the early 1960s, and then passed quickly from the scene, was the "coffee house ministry." From only a handful in 1963, one thousand coffee house projects sponsored by churches and student ministries on college campuses across the country were reported to exist only three years later.[39]

The coffee house ministry seems to have caught on as a tangible expression of the redefined concept of evangelism and the related theological imperative for Christians to "be in the world." It sought to offer a place where students could meet within the atmosphere of the campus rather than of the church; a place that would, it was hoped, encourage "talking about one's faith" in connection with students' real concerns and without conventional religious expectations; a place where folk singing, poetry, painting, and the dramatic arts could be presented and enjoyed as nonlecture and nonsermonic forms of communication; and a place where the concept of the theologically sophisticated laity could be practiced, since those who did the work in the coffee house programs were expected to be students and faculty, not just campus ministers.

All said, however, the coffee house ministry was something of a halfway house: not otherworldly, to be sure, but not fully in the world either. This was sensed by campus ministers who spoke of graduating from the coffee house ministry to the "bar and tavern ministry."[40] The coffee house was, to be sure, an attempt by the churches to respond to the rising demand among students for new forms of communal experience, but it was at bottom a decidedly tame response. The rapid demise of the coffee house and the inability of the churches to envisage something either more culturally radical or, better, more culturally insightful, and the growing tendency to rely instead on a fairly naive notion of political action, were all indications of how little prepared the churches were to come to grips with the deep cultural and spiritual crisis of the times.

One of the most interesting of all the initiatives of the American student movement was *motive* magazine.[41] It began in 1941 as a journal published by the Methodist church for the Methodist student movement. Under its four major editors after the war—Harold Ehrensperger, Roger Ortmayer, Jameson Jones, and B. J. Stiles—*motive* became a leading expression within the whole American Christian student movement of some of the most creative potentials of the theological renaissance.

In 1965 *motive* was the single runner-up to *Life* as the recipient of the Columbia School of Journalism's "Magazine of the Year" award; and in 1966 *Newsweek* observed that "in *motive*, a monthly journal published for college students by the church's Division of Higher Education, Methodists have developed the most creative and unfettered magazine sponsored by any denomination."[42] That same year the Methodist church made arrangements for *motive* to be the official journal for the newly formed United Christian Movement (UCM). By this time, however, *motive* had long since served unofficially as the virtual national magazine of the entire American student Christian movement. Its circulation was never large—twenty thousand at the most—but it was regarded as a pacesetter by all the mainline Protestant campus movements. It should not go unremarked: as many faculty as students seem to have read *motive*.

From the 1950s on *motive* became distinctive for its commitment to the arts—especially the visual arts—as a medium for exploring basic issues of theology, education, and personal-social meaning. Even as the magazine began in the early 1960s to become a voice for the civil-rights movement, and to venture ever further into direct concern with other immediate social issues, it did so with an undiminished artistic emphasis and panache.

motive was always controversial. Its avant-garde literary and artistic orientation as well as its earnest theological critiques of church, university, and society did not sit well with all its readers. Some students protested that the magazine was "way out," "too arty." Nor did it endear itself to all church officials who had to receive the complaints of parents and conservative lay groups, of which there were a number, that the magazine's unconventionalism undermined the faith and morals of their children.[43] As the social turmoil of the 1960s increased, B. J. Stiles, who took over as editor in 1961, furthered the tradition, with the help of his art editor, Margaret Rigg, of attempting to make the artistic excellence and orientation of *motive* a powerful form of symbolic protest against apathy and injustice.[44]

Under all four of its main editors *motive* represented one of the few places within the theological renaissance where the importance of imagination—aesthetic and moral—in our knowledge of reality received some sustained attention and exploration. At the same time, however, the prevailing notion of imagination in *motive* was expressionistic—more the imaginary than the imaginal—and, hence, in the long run may have worked against the arts as having real implications for the knowledge side of the faith-knowledge relationship.

The tasks facing the student movements and campus ministry would be immensely complicated by growing student unrest. The 1950s, in many ways deserving of their reputation as the time of panty raids and the silent generation, nevertheless, concealed more student thoughtfulness and social concern than seems to have been readily apparent.[45] The uprisings of Hungarian and Korean students, the House Un-American Activities Committee protests in San Francisco, above all the black student leadership in sit-ins and freedom rides, the appeal of the Peace Corps—all began in the 1950s and early 1960s to awaken student concerns about what they might do to improve the world.

In 1962 one student wrote, "There is a latent student activism in America. . . . Who or what force will utilize and direct this latent power?"[46] Soon the latent would manifest, and the question would demand an answer. Within a few years the continuing civil rights struggle, the heightening of the war in Vietnam, a spreading drug culture, a society-wide change in sexual mores with students taking the lead, generational conflicts, a growing disillusion with the major institutions of the society, especially including higher education, would all add fuel to student unrest.[47] The entire effort of the church then would depend largely on what its student movements and campus ministry would understand the church's primary task in the university to be in relation to these other movements and larger social events.

THE FACULTY

The Faculty Christian Fellowship

For more than a decade after its founding in 1952 the Faculty Christian Fellowship (FCF) was active and appeared to be growing. Throughout these years the FCF continued to see as its main task the Moberly-SCM mandate to uncover the basic presuppositions of the various academic disciplines and to explore the tensions existing between them and those of the Christian faith. The underlying "hypothesis," as William Kolb, sociologist at Carleton College, and one of the leaders of the Faculty Christian Fellowship, expressed it, was that "if the Judaic-Christian image of man is valid, it will order the empirical data more successfully than do the present presuppositions and assumptions of the various disciplines."[48] Thus the defining purpose of the Faculty Christian Fellowship continued to be seen as that of carrying out the central intellectual task of the church's engagement with the university. That this would require much more than the simplistic notion of applying alternative worldviews to interpreting the empirical data does not seem to have ever been clearly grasped. Still, it was a starting point and one that had the promise of an ever deeper and more radical probing of the fundamental assumptions about knowing and about knowable reality at work in modern higher education.

Many outstanding, nationally known scholars were involved in the work of the Faculty Christian Fellowship, some as regulars, others intermittently. The executive committee, for instance, included such scholars as E. Harris Harbison (Princeton), Kirtley Mather (Harvard), Nathan A. Scott (Howard and Chicago), George F. Thomas (Princeton), and Elizabeth H. Zorb (Vassar). Many other well-known scholars also were active from time to time in various specific projects.

Well into the 1960s, the Faculty Christian Fellowship seems to have been rather successful in turning out large numbers of faculty for numerous regional and national conferences on campuses across the country. The topics of these meetings covered many different aspects of religion and higher education.[49]

In 1954 the executive committee estimated that the FCF already had groups on nearly half the nation's major campuses. This was a soft estimate and no doubt revealed the enthusiasm of the executive committee; yet the movement was clearly taking hold and expanding at this early time.[50] The actual size of the movement at its largest, however, is difficult to gauge. In 1964, perhaps the FCF's peak year, *The Christian Scholar* reported a paid circulation of about four thousand and a free circulation for the *Faculty Forum* of more than thirty-seven thousand. Such figures would seem to indicate by the early 1960s a respectable and growing movement, involving a fairly large number of faculty members on many campuses across the country.[51] However, an ambiguity of commitment seems to have permeated the movement from the beginning, leading to ever greater frustration for its leaders. As early as 1961, an editorial in the *Faculty Forum* complained,

> The executive committee of the FCF is about ready to abandon the effort to develop a membership, since never at any one time have there been as many as four hundred members—this despite the fact that perhaps fourteen hundred annually participate in the various faculty conferences and hundreds more express genuine interest otherwise.[52]

Whatever the levels of administrative frustration, the Faculty Christian Fellowship seems to have been off to a good start by the early 1960s. The questions facing the FCF would be whether it could keep to its central task of a critical examination of the disciplines and their underlying assumptions about knowing and who within the FCF would be the main ones to take up and carry the burden of this work, since it was not something that could be expected of a mass membership. In this respect it will be especially important to consider in due course what kind of guidance on the relationship between faith and knowledge was being given by the major Protestant theologians, from whom the whole movement took its bearings.

The Teaching of Religion

The study and teaching of religion as a full-fledged part of the college and university curriculum—long a main goal of those touched by the theological renaissance—had begun by the 1960s to be a reality. In 1965 Robert Michaelsen, chair of the newly reorganized department of religious studies at the University of California at Santa Barbara, spoke of "a quiet revolution in American universities."[53] He was referring to the steady growth during the preceding decade in the founding of departments of religion and religious studies in American higher education, a growth that was particularly dramatic on the campuses of state universities, and one which was especially accelerating even as Michaelsen was commenting on it.

The early 1960s witnessed the consolidation of several different groups that had long been working for the study of religion in higher education. In 1963 the American Academy of Religion was formed, as a reorganization of the older National Association of Biblical Instructors, to become the major professional body of professors of religion. The previous year the Fellows of the National Council on Religion (the Kent Fellows) and the Fellows of the Danforth Foundation merged to form the Society for Religion in Higher Education. The enlarged society provided new impetus for the long-standing interests of its constituent members: the place of religion in public institutions, the establishment of religion as an indisputable member of the humanities, and the training of college teachers of religion with an emphasis on the application of university disciplines to the study of religion. In 1969 the professional organization of the teaching of religion took yet another step with the consolidation of several other societies to form the Council on the Study of Religion.[54]

By the mid-1960s nearly 90 percent of public institutions offered courses in religion and about 30 percent had departments of religion. Much of the growth, furthermore, was in the strongest and largest institutions.[55] Most significant, however, was the fact that religion had been established as an emerging subject area in its own right on a standing with other subjects in the curriculum of higher education. The older views of the study of religion as primarily evangelistic or as pastoral and professional training for religious educators had given way to the conception of religion as another scholarly, academic discipline.

There were several reasons for the success of the efforts to gain acceptance for the study of religion as a proper field of study in the liberal arts curriculum. Supreme Court decisions of the early 1960s, especially the *Schempp* case of 1963, had removed legal constraints on the teaching about religion in public institutions; thus, state university administrators were relieved of many of their anxieties about violating the constitution.[56] Probably another reason was the expansion of the social sciences during the period, coupled with a dawning awareness of the long traditions of the study of religion from the perspectives of anthropology, psychology, and sociology, and a concomitant desire to expand and apply these approaches to the study of religion even more thoroughly.[57] Although the subjects of the humanities were overshadowed during these years by the vogue of the social sciences, the humanities, of course, retained their place as proper courses in the curriculum. The argument that religion was integral to the humanities was one that the sophisticated no longer wished to challenge.

The impact of the theological renaissance on the twentieth-century growth of the study of religion in higher education ought not to be overlooked. Indeed, it may have been decisive. Many observers have commented on the influence of leading theologians, especially of Paul Tillich and of Reinhold and H. Richard Niebuhr, in demonstrating the intellectual rigor and respectability of theology and in stimulating interest in religious phenomena in almost every area of human experience.[58] The theological probings of H. Richard Niebuhr and his pathbreaking work in sociology of religion, Reinhold Niebuhr's cultural critiques and application of theological perspectives to the understanding of politics and society, and Paul Tillich's wide-ranging interests in his development of the theology of culture—all had the effect not only of revealing a new intellectual vitality in theology but also of awakening an awareness of the religious dimensions of the other subjects in the curriculum—literature, art, philosophy, history, and the social sciences themselves.

Also important was the work of the university divinity schools, where the theological renaissance had its strongholds, in the training of the majority of the first wave of teachers to staff the new university departments of religion.[59] Some of the most vital teaching of religion and of ethics in American higher education during the two decades after the war took place in the new university departments of religion staffed by young graduates imbued with the intellectual and religious excitement of the theological renaissance.[60]

Although it is difficult to pin down exactly, an important influence on the expansion of religious studies in the best universities was undoubtedly the upsurge of student interest in religion in the 1960s, the period in which religious studies were established decisively as an essentially unquestioned division of the university curriculum. This was also a period that witnessed a new phenomenon among American university students: a widespread desire for sources of religious meanings beyond the mainstream Judaic and Christian traditions. This religious enthusiasm found expression both in a search for new cultural forms and values as well as in a burgeoning interest in Eastern religious philosophies, esoteric Western traditions, and a variety of modern claims to new revelation.[61]

Few places existed in mid-twentieth-century American culture, including within the university, capable of acknowledging, much less responding to students' natural hunger for meaning and purpose, or even to their curiosity about how other peoples might make sense of their lives. The new religious studies departments, however, promised just such a response, and for a time in the cultural exuberance of the 1960s, students flocked to them. In the five years between 1964 and 1969 religious course enrollments in private, nonde-nominational colleges and universities increased by 45 percent. In public institutions, however, the increase in religious enrollments was a remarkable 150 percent.[62]

Anecdotes abound regarding student interest in religion during these years. Henry May has recently recalled Paul Tillich's triumphant reception on the Berkeley campus in the mid-1960s.[63] In 1966 one-third of the student body at the University of Rochester petitioned the university to add courses in religion.[64] At the universities of Michigan, Yale, Stanford, Hawaii, and others, students gathered to hear such religious luminaries as Hans Küng, Harvey Cox, Bishop James A. Pike and, as always, Paul Tillich.[65] Early in 1966 *Time* magazine reported, "The scholarly study of religion, shorn of both catechism and clericalism, is fast becoming a major subject in secular U.S. colleges and universities."[66] Observers then and since have described the student unrest of the times as bearing most of the earmarks of religious revival.[67]

With allowances being made for a large range of variations at individual institutions, the overall pattern in the development of religious studies exhibited three basic stages.[68] Although the scholarly study of religion—the psychology, sociology, anthropology, and history of religion—had its origins and found some expression within nineteenth-century higher education, it did not shape the predominant pattern or outlook regarding the teaching of religion on college and university campuses. Well into the twentieth century the study and teaching of religion in American higher education was regarded primarily as a means of evangelism and moral education conducted by and for the benefit of individual religious and church groups.

After World War II, a very different kind of teacher and conception of religion began to prevail. The new faculty in departments of religion in the postwar years not only were imbued with the theological excitement of their seminary studies, during what were still the golden years of the twentieth-century theological renaissance, but also carried with them the characteristic neo-orthodox understanding of the place and task of theology and religion in the university.

From this perspective, the study of religion within the university would raise the basic questions of the purpose, meaning, and value of modern education and thereby provide a center from which an integrating perspective on the tasks and responsibilities of the university might be developed. The study of religion also would provide an opportunity to uncover and explore the underlying presuppositions of the various academic disciplines. This would provide a hearing for the presuppositions of the Judeo-Christian tradition on an equal basis with other explanatory assumptions at work in the university. There was even a hope that in such a dialogical contest of presuppositions those of the Judeo-Christian tradition would emerge as providing, in a much more specific sense, the most satisfactory integrating perspective for modern higher education. Its demand for openness and for intellectual, scholarly rigor at every level moved this position well beyond the earlier evangelistic, pastoral, and professional conceptions of the study of religion in the college and university.

Reflecting this understanding, as well as the seminary training of many of the faculty, the curriculum of most religion departments during the 1950s and early 1960s concentrated on Western Christian theology and the history of Christian thought, especially the traditions associated with Augustine, Aquinas, and the major Reformation figures, biblical studies, ethics, and modern existentialism, with usually a few courses on comparative religion.[69] Efforts were made to reflect the pluralistic nature of the university by introducing more courses in Judaism and Catholicism, a broadening very much in harmony with the neo-orthodox Western-oriented ecumenism. As we also have noted, the intellectual seriousness of the theological renaissance and the religious-ethical earnestness of its emphasis on the divine-human encounter infused the religious studies departments with a vigor and excitement that were often lacking elsewhere on the campuses, not least in many philosophy departments. "Thus," wrote John Wilson, "departments of religion effectively tutored the consciences of several generations."[70]

By the mid-1960s, however, the study of religion in higher education already had entered a third stage. The course offerings began to be broadened to include much greater attention to non-Western, archaic, and esoteric Western traditions; and the other academic disciplines, especially the social sciences, moved increasingly to the fore as the primary basis for understanding religious phenomena. The study of religion was now beginning to take its place within the university as a full-fledged, professional and academic field (if not discipline) in its own right, alongside and on par with other academic fields of study.

The broadening of the curriculum, however, reflected more than the academic professionalization of religious studies. By the early 1960s there was already a growing sense among many students, as well as many faculty, that, in spite of the theological renaissance, the mainstream theological and institutional religious traditions of the West seemed increasingly out of touch

with—or in the catchword of the moment, irrelevant to—the realities of
modern life. This religious dissatisfaction was expressed in part in the sudden
rise of secular theology. It was also manifest very differently in the countercultural turn toward non-Western and archaic religious sources. Both reactions found a resonance in the new departments of religious studies. One
young teacher of religion wrote,

> For most of us the parental discipline against which we have been rebelling is
> that of theology. Given a solid grounding in biblical studies and dogmatic
> history ourselves, with only an occasional apologetic tilt at psychology and other
> religions, we have awakened from our sectarian slumbers to discover a fascinat-
> ing land of myth and folklore outside the seminary walls.[71]

Thus, at least in the early and mid-1960s, a new kind of evangelism went
hand in hand with the movement to make religious studies a bona fide
academic discipline, an evangelism of meaning. Pluralism in the guise of
academic breadth and objectivity served both interests.

Yet, if the study of religion had eliminated earlier ambiguities, it was now
shot through with others. Three are of special importance. One such area of
ambiguity had to do with the tension between the professor of religious
studies serving as a "messiah of meaning" and at the same time striving to
become a professional as defined by the dominant canons of the academic
guild.[72] Without maintaining some version of the neo-orthodox attack on the
"cult of objectivity," and this attack was becoming less and less in evidence,
the young teacher seeking to be a proper academic professional could not also
serve unambiguously as the pastor and spiritual guide many students were
looking for. The new curricular pluralism seems to have covered over the
tension between these two demands on the teachers of religious studies.
Under the umbrella of pluralism they could be purveyors of all manner of
enticing meaning, while maintaining the stance of the academic professional.
But while pluralism may have disguised and alleviated the tension, it did not
dissolve it.

A second area of ambiguity concerned the relation of religion to the rest of
the university. In the final stage of the development of religious studies the
cherished hope of the theological-educational reformers that the study of
religion would furnish the basis for a new intellectual and ethical integration
of the university was given up. The passing of this hope, which in fact had
provided much of the energy for the initial postwar expansion of religious
studies in the university, was sudden and, as far as this author can tell, largely
uncommented on. This older hope was probably filled with all kinds of
theological, perhaps even cultural and institutional, imperialistic interests,
and its abandonment, at least in the old form, was no doubt justified. Its
absence, however, with nothing to replace it, raised several questions: What
was to become of the original criticism of the drift and fragmentation of the
university? Had it simply become passé? More specifically, what was to be the

relationship of the study of religion to the other academic disciplines? Would the study of religion be mainly and essentially grist for their methodological mills? Would there be any fundamental and mutually modifying interaction between religion and the other disciplines at all? This points to the third area of ambiguity.

This third ambiguity was the most important. It had to do with the tension between the desire to grasp and elucidate the essence of the religious domain and the methods by which this was to be accomplished. The central question was whether the dominant modes of knowing and Enlightenment conceptions of reason, which were being employed in making religion an accepted university field of study, did not themselves render much of the full and most essential subject of religion inaccessible. It was not a question, however, that many were asking.

These unresolved ambiguities would become increasingly apparent.

Religion and the Arts

The theological renaissance inspired an interest in the arts among many Protestant theologians and religious leaders unlike anything seen since the transcendentalists. The neo-orthodox emphasis on the biblical stories and images as revelatory of the divine-human relationship spurred a wider interest in the religious significance of all cultural symbolism.[73] Myth, ritual, and art of every kind now became raw material for the theological search for the inner meaning of existence and the primary sources for the analysis of the metaphysical and religious assumptions of modern culture. Reinhold Niebuhr's homiletic skills in making the biblical imagery existentially compelling to his religious and secular admirers alike provided concrete evidence of the power of the symbol as bearer of meaning. Paul Tillich's interest in non-ecclesial modern art as fundamentally religious—revealing of the deepest religious sensitivities and commitments of modern culture—was probably even more important in stimulating and sustaining the new theological interest in the arts.

One of Tillich's main lessons, quickly and enthusiastically absorbed by the theological reformers, was that the religious significance of art, especially in the modern world, is independent of its subject matter. In the modern world, explicitly "religious art" was often as not a reflection of artistic and religious shallowness and impoverishment. For Tillich, the artist's style revealed the "ultimate concern," the deepest faith commitments, of the artist's time and culture. For Tillich, the theological analysis of culture consisted largely in the attempt to decipher the religious meanings of the artistic styles of particular cultural periods.[74] Tillich perhaps above all others helped instill an awareness that every person and culture, even the most materialist, live ultimately by symbols, images, myths, and rituals.[75]

The theological renaissance, therefore, had several tasks in its relation to the arts: to decipher the styles and symbols by which modern culture lives and that reveal its deepest commitments and substance; to connect with those artists in the world who through their art are plumbing, albeit often unwittingly, the religious depths of human existence; and to bring the church into an educated, critical, and vital engagement with the symbolic expressions that shape modern consciousness and culture. "It is in such manifestations at all levels," wrote Amos Wilder, "that the moral and spiritual life of the age discloses itself."[76] This required the church to give renewed attention not only to the art and artists of the times but also to its own use of symbolism in worship and ritual. Liturgy and the ecclesiastical arts were to be purged of all sentimentalism and escapism and brought into a renewed connection with the everyday world in which the twentieth-century human being lives.

For some, like Wilder, the church's new awareness of the arts, and involvement with them, posed a still more demanding task. The arts, almost as much as religion, were themselves caught in the modern dualism of objective fact and subjective meaning. For the churches to continue to regard the arts as mere embellishments, propaganda aids to evangelism, and inspirational escapism from the demands of daily life would be, as Wilder put it, to capitulate to "the banishment of the arts and worship from a materialistic world, from a rational-technological age."[77] To overcome the modern dualism, and to recover the symbolic potency of both the arts and religion, demanded the realization that the proper contrast is not between imagination and knowledge, but between a true and false imagination. And this in turn required "the re-education of the emotions," "the re-education of the imagination."[78] This would be no small task, but its recognition, even among a few, went to the heart of the matter.

With the formal constitution in 1950 of the National Council of the Churches of Christ in the United States of America (NCCCUSA), out of the old Federal Council of Churches, the new theological awareness of the significance of the arts began to find institutional expression.[79] At the beginning an executive committee of the Department on Worship and the Arts was set up within the National Council Division of Christian Life and Work, with Marvin Halverson, theologian and respected art critic, as its executive director and Paul Tillich as a vice-chairman.[80] The department was organized into six commissions devoted to architecture, art, literature, music, drama, and worship, through which Halverson was to begin a program of study and education to help bring the churches into a creative and critical relationship with the arts and with modern artists.[81] Under Halverson's leadership the new department began very quickly to develop an ambitious program in religion and the arts.

Particularly auspicious for its future were the distinguished persons of faith and aesthetic sensitivity and accomplishment Halverson was able to bring into the work of the department: artistically knowledgeable theologians and religious thinkers such as Paul Tillich of Union Seminary, Joseph Sittler of the University of Chicago, and Amos Wilder of Harvard University; theologically sophisticated literary scholars such as Nathan Scott of the University of Chicago, Stanley Romaine Hopper of Drew, and Cleanth Brooks of Yale; and leading figures from the wider world of art and culture, such as Norris Houghton, actor and founder of the pioneering off-Broadway Phoenix Theater in New York City, drama critic John Mason Brown, prize-winning writer Robert Penn Warren, Alfred H. Barr, a founder of the New York Museum of Modern Art, actors Raymond Massey and Mildred Dunnock, *Theatre Arts* editor Rosamond Gilder, and British playwright E. Martin Brown. Other persons prominent in the arts, such as Eero Saarinen in architecture, Thornton Wilder in drama, Robert Shaw in music, and W. H. Auden in literature also advised the department from time to time. It would be hard to imagine a more outstanding group of persons for such a venture in religion and the arts.

In 1955 Amos Wilder drafted a memorandum setting forth a comprehensive understanding of the task of the Department on Worship and the Arts and its importance for the life of the church in the modern world.[82] The Wilder memorandum, circulated among the department members, is a noteworthy document on several counts. It was filled throughout with the confidence that because of the theological renaissance the Protestant churches were at last in a position to engage creatively the modern world, and in this case specifically the world of the arts. It underscored the new theological awareness of the crucial importance of the symbol as the primary vehicle of meaning and value in all of society. It analyzed the particular and problematic place of the arts within modern, scientific and secular society. It stated the particular responsibilities of the church with respect to the arts, both within its own life and in the wider culture.

Wilder began his memorandum with a reminder of the religious significance of the arts: "When we say 'art,' we say 'symbol,' we say 'meaning,' we say 'communion.' The arts, old and new, good and bad, are peculiarly the carriers of meaning and value in our society as in all societies."[83] He then referred to Paul Tillich's call for the churches to forge a vanguard of persons able to interpret the religious significance of contemporary art and to enter into dialogue with "the influential movements of our time in art, literature and criticism." Such a vanguard could not be created, said Wilder, as long as the churches continued in an older professional and pragmatic attitude limited to concern with "the ecclesiastical arts" and with the rhetorical and illustrative uses of the arts. Instead, what is now required is a deep understanding of the symbolic expressions of culture in which "at all levels the moral and spiritual life of the age discloses itself." There now exist, he said, two major resources for the church in developing this understanding: the popular arts and media as mirrors of the age, and the creative work of the most responsible artists of our time who are providing an "actual assessment of the human situation." In this light, Wilder argued, the church had a fourfold task.

The first task of the church was to see in the arts "the indices and symptoms" of the deepest meaning and commitments of the culture and through the arts to learn to know and understand our time more adequately. The second task was for the Christian not only to know contemporary culture but to contribute actively to its critical assessment and the reshaping of it. Here Wilder felt the theological renaissance offered powerful new resources for such "a Christian criticism of life," but he stressed a note seldom heard as yet even within the new theology. "To bring a Christian criticism to bear," he said, "solely in terms of social and political factors is to forfeit engagement with the common life where confusions are even greater and where motivations are perhaps even more fallible." In other words, artistic insight and renewal must ground and accompany social and political action, if political action is to be truly new and enduring.

The third task of the church was to contribute directly to the health and vitality of the arts by encouraging significant artists and by raising the unfortunately low aesthetic sensibilities and creativity prevailing within the church itself. At this point Wilder dealt directly with the relation between faith and knowledge in the modern world, indicating the consequences for both religion and the arts of the modern dualism between a narrow conception of knowledge and the other domains of human experience.

If the church has not taken this third task seriously, Wilder said,

> it can only be because so frivolous a view of the arts and of the whole domain of the imagination has prevailed. The fateful cleavage between reason and emotion, sense and sensibility, the practical and the spiritual order, has consigned the arts in the minds of many to a marginal and decorative or inspirational role.

Wilder pushed his analysis of the "fateful cleavage" and its consequences further. "Once the divorce between intellect and imagination had been consecrated," he wrote,

> that part of man identified with intellect very naturally fell under the sway not only of science but of the technology that arose from science and finally of the civilization and patterns and values associated with it. A vast prestige attached itself to the conquests of science and its techniques and offered a seductive ideology or way of life. But this culture has been one which because of its very axioms ("knowledge is power"; "evidence is measurable") starved out the esthetic life which therefore had to establish a precarious or defiant life for itself in the sentiments. The arts of a rationalized society had either to take the line of a celebration of technological man—a kind of propagandistic art—or offer themselves as a private solace, or (as in the modern mass-media) as vehicles of sensationalism for anonymous multitudes seeking a vicarious substitute for genuine personal life.

The best of modern art, he noted, however, has been attempting to reclaim this lost territory, and the church must especially, therefore, "further all vital movements in the arts today and identify itself with the most significant symbolizations."

Some years later, building explicitly on Wilder's analysis, a theologian and member of the executive committee of the Department on Worship and the Arts, Joseph Sittler, would suggest that within the arts are to be discovered the possibilities of a wider and deeper way of knowing than that confined to a narrow rationalistic intellect. Love and obedience, maintained Sittler, are not mere subjective feelings and attitudes, but are potentially cognitive capacities. "The way to knowledge," he maintained, is deeply related to them.[84] Sittler seems to have been groping toward a conception of genuine qualitative knowledge, genuine knowledge of the most important realms of human experience, made possible through the development of just those capacities and feelings most present in the religious and aesthetic domains. This possibility of qualitative knowing was not a conception that found wide response among other representatives of the theological renaissance, but it may be significant that when it was nascently put forward, it was by one of those who had turned to a recovery of the meaning dimension of the arts.

Related directly to this third task, the fourth task of the church in the arts is to heal the separation that has arisen between the church and the creative artists of our society. Again Wilder voiced the confidence that the theological renaissance has brought about a new situation in which such a rapprochement had become a real possibility, for it had produced thinkers who had "both restated the faith with new power and interpreted the times so significantly that the secular world had found itself addressed."

The memorandum was slightly edited and published by the department under the title *The Church, The Arts, and Contemporary Culture*.[85] This statement represented the most careful and comprehensive thinking about the church and the arts, and it served as the standard to which appeal would repeatedly be made in the years ahead in defining, explaining, and seeking support for the work of the Department on Worship and the Arts.

From the start there were signs of some internal difficulties facing the Department on Worship and the Arts within the National Council of Churches. The concentration in early reports of the work of the department on publications, study guides, bibliographies, and conferences, and the repeated stress that these be developed in cooperation with local and regional councils of churches and denominational agencies may have reflected a real intent to bring the department's work to the local, congregational level. At the same time it may also have hinted at the budgetary constraints from the beginning on any emphasis on the arts within a bureaucratic organization traditionally oriented toward social service projects and evangelism, with very little long-standing concern or understanding for the aesthetic, the contemplative, and the intellectual.[86]

Furthermore, not all leaders of the National Council were sympathetic or comprehending of the radical nature of the church's mission in the arts as envisioned by Halverson, Tillich, Wilder, and other members of the department. When Wilder's memorandum was published, his strong urging that "the church further all vital movements in the arts today and identify itself with the most significant symbolizations" was softened to a plea for the church to be "receptive" and "sensitized" to art and symbols. There is little evidence that Roy G. Ross, General Secretary of the National Council of Churches, understood the significance of the arts as seen by the new department, and there is little evidence to suggest that other divisions of the Council felt the work of Worship and the Arts to have been of particular relevance to their concerns.[87]

There was support, however.[88] And, although Halverson, because of budget problems, had to rely on collaborative ventures with other church groups and outside agencies, the department's program began to develop. Among its early projects were cooperative undertakings that led to a series in *Life* magazine on art dealing with Christ; a series in *Architectural Forum* on theology and architecture; a commission (together with the National Methodist Student Movement) of an oratorio on the Wesleys by Union Seminary theologian Tom Driver; and the publication by Meridian Press of *Religious Drama 1*, edited by Halverson (which was followed in successive years by volumes 2 and 3). The Commission on Literature, with the support of the Danforth Foundation, sponsored a seminar in religion, drama, and literature at Drew University. And the department worked widely in consultation with a number of religious journals and with local and regional church groups in developing projects in music and drama.[89]

The interest in religion and the arts was appearing elsewhere as well. The Riverside Church in New York City began in 1955 to sponsor an annual anthology of poetry by college writers, judged by people like Marianne Moore and Mark Van Doren. Local and regional church groups, sometimes with the help of Halverson, more often without, began to organize lecture series on the arts, sponsor theater groups, and hold exhibitions of painting and sculpture. The New Hampshire Congregational-Christian Conference in association with Dartmouth College provided in 1956 a series of monthly lectures for pastors on modern literature.[90] Joseph Sittler reported a two-day meeting in Greenwich Village in 1961 between a group of theologians and the jazz musicians Jerry Mulligan, Dizzy Gillespie, Louis Armstrong, and Thelonious Monk.[91] By the early 1960s the concern for the relation between religion and the arts was finding broader expression within the organization of the church, as, for example, with the founding of Religious Communities for the Arts in the United Church of Christ.

In 1962 Marvin Halverson left his position with the National Council of Churches. Truman B. Douglass, who had been chair of Halverson's executive committee soon resigned as well. Their departure may have been motivated in part by frustration with the slow pace with which the churches were responding to the call for a new relationship to the arts. But the move did enable Halverson to seek wider, extraecclesiastical connections and support for the concern with religion and the arts by working to found the Society for the Arts, Religion and Contemporary Culture (ARC). Especially active with Halverson in founding ARC were Truman Douglass and Paul Tillich, and other theologians and artists including John Dillenberger, Robert Penn Warren, Denis de Rougement, Robert Motherwell, and others. Under their leadership, and with Alfred J. Barr of the New York Museum of Modern Art as its first president, ARC began to develop a regular program of activities devoted to the arts and the theology of culture.

At about the same time the president of the National Council of Churches, J. Irwin Miller, an industrialist with strong interests in theology and the arts, appointed a special committee on the Council's Role in the Field of Religion and the Arts.[92] The committee report, most of the substance of it based on Wilder's original memorandum, was submitted in late 1963 and called for a full Department of the Arts within the Council. Its primary focus was still to be on healing the split between the modern intellect and the realms of meaning, aesthetic awareness, and faith encompassed in the experience of the arts. By the early 1960s, then, in spite of some difficulties, the effort to bring about a new relationship between theology and art gave much evidence of beginning to take hold, both within the churches and through a growing variety of contacts with the wider artistic world itself.

The project had implications for the churches' engagement with higher education as well, since the arts had always held a secondary and shaky position among the priorities of the modern research university. The recovery, through the arts and a reinvigorated theology of culture, of an awareness of the symbol as, in Wilder's phrase, the prime "carrier of meaning and value," promised invaluable resources for the reconceptualization of the nature, sources, and uses of knowledge in modern culture and education. Fragile though it was, a real effort had been initiated to bring the theological renaissance to bear on the arts. And it had been undertaken in a way filled with potential for a fundamental overcoming of the split between faith and knowledge, with the arts in their fullness as the essential bridge between the two.

Church-Related Colleges

One fairly immediate effect of the theological renaissance was to stir new interest in the nature and purpose of the specifically church-related college and to inspire new hopes for its future. In his earlier (1947) look at religion in American higher education, Merrimon Cuninggim's usual optimistic appraisal of things faltered at the one point where he had to contemplate the church-related college. "The actual situation with respect to church-related colleges today," he wrote then, "is not a happy one."[93] And others agreed: the sense of identity, Christian or otherwise, of the church-related college was

vague and uncertain, the quality of education it offered was often undistin-
guished, and its care of students seldom better than elsewhere. Often the
claim to be a church-related college meant no more than that chapel was
available, some courses in religion were offered, and the professors were
morally respectable. Within only a few years, however, a very different sense
of the situation and its possibilities was taking hold.

Howard Lowry in his 1950 book on religion and higher education gave
expression to this new outlook by challenging the church college, above all, to
affirm its identity as a Christian college and to seek to become a model
education community exemplifying the relevance of the Christian faith for
the whole of higher education.[94] Lowry's conception of the identity of the
Christian college required some effort—the Christian college would be
centered around a group of learners, both teachers and students, "who
confess Jesus Christ as their Saviour and Lord"; it would be open to free
inquiry and abjure all manner of indoctrination; it would require for its faculty
Christians or persons sympathetic to religious inquiry; and it would have a
deep obligation to liberal learning. Although there were many fuzzy edges
here, his call for the church-related college to stand for something, and to
know what it stood for, was a clear affirmation that the church-related college
had a unique opportunity in American higher education that it ought
not—and need not—squander. His had been one of the first intimations of a
new sense emerging of the possibilities of the church-related college.

In 1954 *The Christian Scholar* published a special issue devoted to the topic
of the "Christian college." The editor of this issue wrote, "The church-
related colleges are discovering new vitality as they seek to bring the
Christian faith and understanding to bear upon their total life. . . ."[95] The
same year the First Quadrennial Convocation of Christian Colleges, the
culmination of a four year study undertaken under the auspices of the
Commission on Christian Higher Education of the National Council of
Churches, was held at Denison University with more than two-hundred
church-related colleges represented. The proceedings of this first Quadrennial also were published as a special issue of *The Christian Scholar*.[96]

In his address at the convocation on "the theological foundations of higher
education," theologian Albert Outler pointed to the impact of the theological
renaissance on the new thinking about Christian higher education. Reflecting
on the changes during the ten years since he began his original visits to
campuses in 1944, which had resulted in his extremely critical assessment of
the state of religion in most colleges and universities right after the war,
Outler now said, "My clearest impression of the decade since [1944], is the
amazing spread and intensification of concern about the Christian dimensions
of higher education. . . ." "We are participants," he added, "in a major
educational revolution—with many crucial phases of the revolution yet to
come." The most significant sign of the revolution, Outler suggested, was
that Christian educators were beginning to consider "the theological basis of

what Christian educators do."[97] Others—educators, church leaders, and theologians from this country and Europe and Asia—spoke at the convocation and in much the same vein.

In 1958 a Second Quadrennial Convocation of Christian Colleges was held at Drake University, and its proceedings too were published as a special issue of *The Christian Scholar*.[98] These three special issues of the *Scholar*, spring and autumn of 1954 and autumn of 1958, provide a rich compendium of the best thinking on the nature and task of the Christian college emanating from the theological renaissance. What is most striking about these issues of the *Scholar*, especially in comparison with later studies of church-related higher education, is the extent to which the serious intellectual tasks facing the church in higher education were taken up as being of the essence of any satisfactory conception of Christian higher education and the Christian college.

Running throughout both convocations was the sense that the Christian college had the opportunity as never before to play a uniquely creative role in American higher education, but only if it made a concerted effort, as Jerald Brauer of the University of Chicago stated it, "to understand the Christian faith in relation to the curriculum and to the totality of Christian life."[99] Attention accordingly was given at both convocations to the importance of developing within higher education a community of concern for the search for truth and for the needs of the whole person. Also affirmed as essential was the necessity of avoiding indoctrination of any kind and of making the Christian college itself a model community wherein devoted Christian scholars welcomed the presence among them of those who did not share their faith.[100] Considerable attention was given also to the responsibility of the Christian and of the Christian colleges for the uses to which knowledge was put in the life of the world at large.

At both convocations, much attention was devoted to the intellectual task that was thought to belong to the core of any conception of a Christian college. The Christian commitment in higher education, Robert Lowry Calhoun of Yale said, will mean "the effort to develop in *all* fields of instruction, recognition and concern for what we have become accustomed to speak of as Christian perspective."[101] This, he and others pointed out, would demand a critical engagement with the content and the modes of knowing of the various university disciplines. The familiar task of uncovering worldviews and hidden presuppositions was emphasized by many participants, as was the need to seek within the fragmentation of the curriculum an underlying unity of the disciplines as an expression of faith in the unity of God's truth. Another major topic of the convocations was the responsibility of the Christian college to concentrate on developing a framework for high quality instruction in the liberal arts that would raise the ultimate issues and basic questions of life that are the substance of the arts.

These emphases, as noted, made the relation between the Christian faith and the intellectual work of higher education the center of the whole question of the definition of a specifically Christian education and Christian college. Although for the most part these emphases really fell short of taking up the fundamental challenge posed to faith by the dominant university conceptions of knowledge, they, nevertheless, kept alive a concern with the problem.

A few participants actually came close to raising the question of whether the world being created by modern technology and instrumental rationalism was one which by its nature was rapidly coming to exclude not only everything pertaining to the Divine, but to the fully human as well. "In a world which we have designed and created and made to operate on our terms," said physicist William G. Pollard,

> to what or to whom can we turn to seek for guidance and mercy? Indeed neither science nor technology have any means of coping at all with such a thought. Nothing that is taught in any standard course in psychology, sociology, economics, political science, or history would even suggest what possible connection the act of seeking guidance and mercy could have with the real world, the world as these subjects believe it to actually be. Our whole educational system has conformed itself to this quest for omnipotence which has been empowering our culture for a century. Education has cooperated with this quest by thoroughly and consistently removing every evidence of God from every area of human inquiry and so has prepared the way for man himself to seek to appropriate to himself the throne of God.[102]

But the deeper question, implied here, whether faith could have any meaningful relation to modern knowledge, and to the world created by that knowledge, without a fundamental transformation of our ways of knowing ourselves—this question was by and large skirted. It was, nevertheless, as Pollard's analysis itself implied, the primary question facing the church, in the university and in the world.

The two main conceptions of the relationship between faith and knowledge that were explored tended to see each—faith and knowledge—as having basically separate realms of truth. One such approach was to say that there is, on the one hand, reason (the knowledge realm) and, on the other hand, "more than reason" (the faith realm). As a critique of a narrow conception of reason, and as an effort not to allow the intellectual task to be defined in terms of a narrow and arid "intellectualism," this was a promising approach, but only if the "more than reason" side could be regarded as potentially a source and a deepening of knowledge, not as an avoidance of knowledge. The possibility of such a potentially deeper, more capacious way of knowing as the "more than reason" was never taken up. The other approach was to speak of the production of knowledge as given by reason and of the responsible uses of knowledge as mandated by faith. But this begged all the questions and left the modern split between faith and knowledge as wide as ever.

As long, however, as the intellectual concerns of the Christian in higher education—especially the critical questioning of the disciplines, the uncovering and probing of presuppositions, and the raising of basic life questions—remained alive and vital, the possibility of a deeper wrestling with the faith-knowledge relationship would not be wholly lost. The search for the identity of the Christian college would continue, thereby, to impinge on the primary, and not only the secondary, matters of higher education.

In 1961 Merrimon Cuninggim returned to the scene to examine again "the Protestant stake in higher education."[103] Cuninggim presented a rather devastating analysis of the reality of the Christian college—"Where are the key ideas for higher education coming from today? The answer has to be frankly made that, on the whole, they are not coming from the church-related college."[104] He concluded, nevertheless, by underscoring the hopes aroused by the theological renaissance for the church-related college and for the whole of Protestant higher education. Protestant higher education, he said, "can become the conscience for the totality of higher education" by showing that it is "devoted to the discovery and spread of knowledge, to the activity of the mind, and to the relevance of knowledge and thought for the whole life of man."[105]

On the face of it, this affirmation made very clear that the church in higher education had to deal above all with the question of knowledge. In Cuninggim's statement of the issue, however, there was nothing to suggest any of the problematic dimensions of knowledge as understood and furthered in modern higher education. It did not augur well for the birth within the church-related college, or within Protestant higher education more largely writ, of a vital grappling with the deeper problems of faith in the world of modern knowledge. By the beginning of the 1960s, therefore, the role of the church-related college, while still being given much energy and attention, seemed as elusive as ever. In this area, the church's campaign was already showing signs of stalling.

THE ACADEMIC REVOLUTION
AND THE NATURE OF KNOWLEDGE

The academic revolution was not only structural and social but also, at bottom, epistemological. It represented the culminating institutional embodiment of the centuries-long development of the exclusive conception of knowledge as bound to sense experience and abstractions from sense experience. Coming to grips with this conception of knowledge was the primary challenge facing the theological reformers in the university. In seeking to establish a beachhead for faith in the modern world and modern education, they had embarked on what, under the best of circumstances, would have been an enormous undertaking. If they were to achieve any kind of success, it would be imperative that they have an unclouded, unyielding grasp of the absolute necessity of dealing radically with the knowledge side of the faith-knowledge relationship. A few reflections on the nature of knowledge at work in the academic revolution, and at aspects of its curricular consequences, might help illuminate some further dimensions of the challenge confronting the reformers.

The conception of knowledge as power and control was thoroughly utilitarian and instrumental. The research university, of course, was committed to the higher utilitarianism of providing theoretical knowledge for the management and advance of a complex, industrial-technological culture. The less prestigious institutions farther down the tail of the academic snake pursued the lower utilitarianism of immediate community service and vocational training. In the overall competition for resources the higher utilitarianism usually prevailed, for it could argue that in the long run all else depended on the high-level, theoretical advances it made possible.

In neither of the emphases, however, was there much concern for what had been called the "basic questions" of life, and very little concern, except in an instrumentalist way, for an education devoted to the deepening and enrichment of personal and cultural existence. That other conceptions of knowledge other than "knowledge is power" might be possible and might reveal dimensions of reality as real and important as the instrumental, quantitative, and technical, was as foreign to the one as to the other.

One result of these developments, beginning in the early 1960s, was a rapid fading of interest in the humanities and in general education. During the 1960s, in fact, the social sciences became the subjects dearest to social reformers and social managers of every kind. Funding from government and foundations that did not go to the natural sciences went more and more to the social sciences. When the humanities did partake of an overflow of monies available, it was usually for research, for the "production of new knowledge," not for teaching and not for cultural deepening.[106]

The idea that the humanities could provide the required core for a general education also came under attack—from various sources and for different reasons. Research-oriented faculty were mostly indifferent toward general education, since the trend during the 1950s and 1960s was to redesign the undergraduate curriculum to encourage early disciplinary specialization and graduate work. For these faculty the tendency was to redefine general education in terms of providing the necessary interdisciplinary and methodological breadth thought necessary for specialization.[107] Or, just as often, general education came to function in fact mainly as an administrative, bureaucratic solution to the politics of departmental representation in the curriculum.[108] In both cases general education served less and less its original purpose of keeping alive the questions of meaning, ethics, and purpose in higher education.

Moreover, many students, and some of their faculty sympathizers, began to reject the idea of a required core curriculum as really a form of enforced indoctrination into an abstract mind-set and a way of life that had little to do with either the personal concerns of the students or the real problems of the society. For such reasons, the increasing popularity during the early 1960s of the demand raised by restive students for "relevance" was often directed against the ideal of the humanities as the core of the curriculum.[109] The social sciences, however, did seem relevant. It was increasingly thought that they could be carriers of moral earnestness, and actually change things in the process. Even the teaching of ethics gravitated increasingly from philosophy departments to the applied social sciences, where the real problems of life were now thought to be addressed.[110]

The "academic revolution" had a dual significance for the churches' new endeavors in higher education. On the one hand, the emphasis on research and the production of knowledge underscored the importance the original theological reformers had placed on the intellectual task of the Christian in the university. If they were to be taken seriously, the reformers would have to prove their ability to move at ease within the intellectual and academic atmosphere of the university.

On the other hand, the growing loss of interest in the humanities, and in general education, would increasingly pose a real problem for the religious reformers. The humanities had shifted from being liberal arts to becoming academic disciplines, increasingly disabled thereby from contributing much to the search for meaning. Moreover, the original claim of the humanities to being able to raise issues of meaning and truth had been fundamentally called into question by the instrumentalist and sense-bound conception of knowing dominant in the academy. The theologians had pinned much of their original case for religion and theology in the university on the importance of the humanities, and on what they had perceived as a widespread sense of the need for greater intellectual and curricular integration. By the mid-1960s it would become increasingly difficult to get much of a hearing by appealing to either of these.

The churches then would come to have three main possibilities before them: (1) They could deepen their analysis of the presuppositions of the various university disciplines, of both the humanities and the natural and social sciences. (2) They could abandon this effort and simply adopt the social sciences as defined by the university as the main vehicle for their purposes as social activists. This option would come increasingly to the fore with the growing political tensions and student unrest of the 1960s. (3) The churches could begin to respond to the deep currents of cultural change that would also soon come to be a distinguishing mark of the 1960s. The first choice, that which dealt with knowing and knowledge, could include the other two and potentially provide a sound basis for them. Separated from the intellectual and epistemological tasks, however, both social action and cultural experimentation would find themselves increasingly impotent to effect fundamental changes, in the university and in the culture alike.

It is here that we must now ask, What kind of help in dealing with the underlying problems of knowledge was being provided by the most important American theologians, the leaders of the theological renaissance? How were they dealing with the faith-knowledge issue? The church's engagement with higher education inspired by the theological renaissance depended ultimately on the understanding its best theologians provided of the relation of faith to knowledge.

NOTES

1. David Riesman, *Constraint and Variety in American Education* (Lincoln, Nebr.: University of Nebraska Press, 1956).

2. Christopher Jencks and David Riesman, *The Academic Revolution* (Garden City, N.Y.: Doubleday & Co., 1968)

3. Lawrence A. Cremin, *American Education: The Metropolitan Experience, 1876–1980* (New York: Harper & Row, 1988), 252.

4. In these paragraphs on general developments in higher education during these years, I have found, in addition to the books by David Riesman, help in G. Kerry Smith, ed., *Twenty-five Years: 1945 to 1970* (San Francisco: Jossey-Bass Inc., 1970); Verne A. Stadtman, "Happenings on the Way to the 1980s," in *Higher Education in American Society*, ed. Philip G. Altbach and Robert O. Berdahl (Buffalo, N.Y.: Prometheus Books, 1981), 101–10; Fred E. Crossland, "Foundations and Higher Education," in Joseph Froomkin, ed., *Crisis in Higher Education; Proceedings of the Academy of Political Science* 35, no. 2 (1983): 48–60.

5. See John Coleman, *The Task of the Christian in the University* (Geneva: WSCF, 1946), 10; and Charles McCoy, "Revolution in Higher Education," in *On the Work of the Ministry in University Communities*, ed. Richard N. Bender (Nashville: Board of Education, Methodist Church, 1962), 24.

6. See Fritz Machlup, *The Production and Distribution of Knowledge in the United States* (Princeton, N.J.: Princeton University Press, 1962).

7. Hal Viehman, personal interview, 11 November 1987.

8. Leonard Sweet, for instance, points out the growth in the Protestant churches during this period, while at the same time depicting it as the result of the extension of American consumerism into religion, not of the deepening of religious interests and sensibilities. Leonard Sweet, "The Modernization of Protestant Religion in America," in *Christianity in America 1935–1985*, ed. David Lotz et al. (Grand Rapids, Mich.: Wm. B. Eerdmans Publishing Co., 1989), 24–25.

9. See, for example, Roger Ortmayer, ed., *Witness to the Campus* (Nashville: Board of Education of the Methodist Church, 1956); Richard N. Bender, ed., *Campus Evangelism in Theory and Practice* (Nashville: Board of Education of the Methodist Church, 1957); Charles S. McCoy and Neely D. McCarter, *The Gospel on Campus: Rediscovering Evangelism in the Academic Community* (Richmond: John Knox Press, 1959); Richard S. Bender, ed., *On the Work of the Ministry in University Communities* (Nashville: Board of Education of the Methodist Church, 1962).

10. Ortmayer, *Witness to the Campus*, 3–4; Julian Hartt, *Theology and the Church in the University* (Philadelphia: Westminster Press, 1969).

11. McCoy and McCarter, *The Gospel on Campus*, 47.

12. Bender, *Campus Evangelism in Theory and Practice*, 3.

13. Julian Hartt, "A Theology for Evangelism," in Ortmayer, *Witness to the Campus*, 45.

14. Thomas F. Driver, "The Church amid the Forms of Social Experience," in Bender, *Campus Evangelism in Theory and Practice*, 29–42.

15. Hendrick Kraemer, *The Communication of the Christian Faith* (Philadelphia: Westminster Press, 1956); Driver, "The Church amid the Forms," 29–30; McCoy and McCarter, *The Gospel on Campus*, 74.

16. McCoy and McCarter, *The Gospel on Campus*, 72–74.

17. Viehman, interview.

18. See Parker Rossman, *Ecumenical Student Workbook* (New York: United Student Christian Council, 1949).

19. See Robert H. Eads, "A Brief History of Student Christian Movements," in *The Campus Ministry*, ed. George L. Earnshaw (Valley Forge, Pa.: Judson Press, 1964), 65–80.

20. The four uniting denominations in the UCCF were the United Church of Christ, the United Presbyterian Church, U.S.A., the Christian Church (Disciples of Christ), and the Evangelical United Brethren Church. See Verlyn Barker, "The United Campus Christian Fellowship," in Earnshaw, *The Campus Ministry*, 277–99.

21. See ibid.

22. See Herluf Jensen, "The National Student Christian Federation: As Community and as Organization," *Student World* 55, no. 1 (first quarter 1962): 484.

23. In this and the following paragraph on the social-political activities of the student movements, I am especially indebted to the fine study by Franklin Woo, "From USCC to UCM: An Historical Inquiry with Emphasis on the Last Ten Years of the Student Christian Movements in the U.S.A. and Their Struggle for Self-Understanding and Growing Involvement in Social and Political Issues" (Ed.D. diss., Teachers College, Columbia University, 1971).

24. J. Robert Nelson, ed., *The Christian Student and the World Struggle* (New York: Association Press, 1952); The other two books produced by Nelson were *The Christian Student and the Church* (New York: Association Press, 1952) and *The Christian Student and the University* (New York: Association Press, 1952). As the titles indicate, Nelson's study program embraced all three main themes of the theological renewal within the student movement at the time: the church, the university, and the world.

25. Richard Shaull, *Encounter with Revolution* (New York: Association Press, 1955); Paul Converse and M. M. Thomas, *Revolution and Redemption* (New York: Friendship Press, 1955); Keith Bridston, *Shock and Renewal* (New York: Friendship Press, 1955).

26. Woo, "From USCC to UCM," 88.

27. Charles West, *Outside the Camp* (Garden City, N.Y.: Doubleday & Co., 1959).

28. Ibid., 96.

29. Philippe Maury, *Evangelism and Politics* (Garden City, N.Y.: Doubleday & Co., 1959).

30. Woo, "From USCC to UCM," 149–52.

31. My description of the Christian Faith and Life Community is drawn from a personal letter from W. Jack Lewis, February 27, 1990; from Parker Rossman, "The Austin Community: Challenge and Controversy," *The Christian Scholar* 45, no. 1 (spring 1962): 44–51; and from a 1964 study of the community, Millard Research Associates, Ltd., *The College House of the Christian Faith and Life Community at Austin, Texas*. Typed manuscript report (Austin, Tex., and Pelham, N.Y., 1964).

32. In 1956, for instance, of the forty-two names on the honor roll, fourteen were

members of the Faith and Life Community. *Letter to Laymen* 2, no. 2 (February 1956): 1.

33. Joseph Mathews had been a doctoral student of H. Richard Niebuhr at Yale University Divinity School, and at Perkins School of Theology he had been professor of Christian ethics.

34. See Myron M. Teske, "Creative and Experimental Ways of Ministering to the College Mind," in Earnshaw, *The Campus Ministry*, 101–38; also *Letter to Laymen* 5, no. 7 (March 1959): 2.

35. Samuel Norris Gibson, *The Campus Ministry and the Church's Mission in Higher Education: A National Study of the Campus Ministry of the Methodist Church in Tax-Supported and Independent Colleges and Universities* (Nashville: Division of Higher Education, Methodist Church, 1967), 86.

36. My description of the Christian Faith and Higher Education Institute is drawn from Teske, "Creative and Experimental Ways of Ministering to the College Mind"; W. Haydn Ambrose, *The Church in the University* (Valley Forge, Pa.: Judson Press, 1968), 74–78; Jack Harrison, memo to author, 24 March 1978; Jack Harrison, "Dwelling with Man," unpublished manuscript; and Jack Harrison, "Stones and Ponds: An Illustration of the Work of the Institute," unpublished manuscript.

37. The phrase, "to think theologically what they are doing" was later always quoted by others as "to think theologically about what they are doing," but Harrison contended that the original was correct and that the amended version missed the point. Harrison, "Memo."

38. See William A. Overholt, *Religion in American Colleges and Universities*. Student Personnel Series, no. 14 (American College Personnel Association, n.d. [probably about 1971]), 20.

39. John D. Perry, Jr., *The Coffee House Ministry* (Richmond: John Knox Press, 1966), 19.

40. Some of the serious rationales given for the coffee house appear in retrospect like bad caricatures of the new theology of evangelism. One chronicler of the movement wrote, for example, "The chief heuristic value of the coffee house ministry may well be that it serve as a testing ground for the churches' dialogue with the post-Christian world. . . . The first step in the process requires the church to listen in the coffee house to what the world is saying." Ibid., 48.

41. For my description of *motive*, I have drawn largely on the fine study of the magazine by Frank Dent, "*motive magazine*: Advocating the Arts and Empowering the Imagination in the Life of the Church." (Ed.D. diss., Teachers College, Columbia University, 1989).

42. *Newsweek*, 14 February 1966, 60. Quoted in Gibson, *The Campus Ministry and the Church's Mission in Higher Education*, 327.

43. See Gibson, *The Campus Ministry and the Church's Mission in Higher Education*, 327–28. Dent reports that as early as 1942, *motive* defender Methodist Bishop G. Bromley Oxnam had to exert influence to prevent suppression of the magazine by Methodist parents angry over the magazine's dealing with issues of segregation and sex. Dent, "*motive magazine*: Advocating the Arts and Empowering the Imagination."

44. In 1969 Stile's social engagement incurred the only incidence of censorship by the magazine's denominational publisher, and Stiles himself resigned—a series of events to which we will return.

45. See some examples in J. Gordon Chamberlin, *Churches and the Campus* (Philadelphia: Westminster Press, 1963).

46. Lane C. McGaughy, "What Students Are Thinking," in *On the Work of the Ministry in University Communities*, ed. Richard N. Bender, 50.

47. See Allen J. Matusow, *The Unraveling of America: A History of Liberalism in the 1960s* (New York: Harper & Row, 1984); Helen Lefkowitz Horowitz, "The 1960s," chap. 10 in *Campus Life: Undergraduate Cultures from the End of the Eighteenth Century to the Present* (Chicago: University of Chicago Press, 1987).

48. William L. Kolb, "The Faculty Christian Movement, As Seen by a Participating Faculty Member" in *On the Work of the Ministry in University Communities*, ed. Richard N. Bender, 128.

49. Such as "The Relation of Christianity to the Disciplines," "Changing Values in College," "Politics for Christians," "The Relevance of Technology to Higher Education," and "Faith and Education in a Changing World." Taken from reports in *The Christian Scholar*. The second national conference of the FCF, held in Chicago in 1964 on the theme, "Faith and Learning in the University," with a subtheme, "The University: A Critique," drew two hundred participants, mainly faculty with some campus ministers, from about one hundred seventy campuses. John Coleman, "From Chicago," *The Christian Scholar* 47, no. 4 (winter 1964): 368–74.

50. *The Christian Scholar* 37, no. 1 (March 1954): 167.

51. This is what a perusal of regular reports in *The Christian Scholar* of conferences and campus seminars and other events would indicate.

52. *Faculty Forum*, 18 (October 1961).

53. Robert Michaelsen, "The Study of Religion: A Quiet Revolution in American Universities," in *Religious Studies in Public Universities*, ed. Milton D. McLean (Carbondale, Ill.: Central Publications, Southern Illinois University, 1967), 9–14. This book was largely a compilation of lectures given at a 1965 conference on the topic.

54. See Claude Welch, *Graduate Education in Religion: A Critical Appraisal* (Missoula, Mont.: University of Montana Press, 1971), 15, 127–28; Martha H. Biehle, *Fifty Years: 1923–1973: A Brief History of the National Council on Religion in Higher Education and the Society for Religion in Higher Education* (Society for Religion in Higher Education, mimeographed, 1974), 18–19.

55. Robert A. Spivey, "Modest Messiahs: The Study of Religion in State Universities, *Religious Education* 63, no. 1 (January–February 1966): 6; Claude Welch, *Religion in the Undergraduate Curriculum: An Analysis and Interpretation* (Washington, D.C.: Association of American Colleges, 1971), 53–54; Claude Welch, *Graduate Education in Religion: A Critical Appraisal*, 58–62.

56. Wilber G. Katz, "Religious Studies in State Universities: The New Legal Climate," in *Religious Studies in Public Universities*, ed. Milton D. McLean, 15–21.

57. For an excellent account of the social science traditions of the study of religion, see Michael G. Murphey, "On the Scientific Study of Religion in the United States, 1870–1980, in *Religion and Twentieth-Century American Intellectual Life* ed. Michael J. Lacey (Cambridge, Mass.: Woodrow Wilson International Center for Scholars and Cambridge University Press, 1989), 136–71.

58. McLean, *Religious Studies in Public Universities*, viii–ix; Michaelsen, "The Study of Religion," 4–5; Michael J. Lacey, ed., *Religion and Twentieth-Century American Intellectual Life*, 4.

59. Welch, *Graduate Education in Religion*, 204, 208.

60. Paul Ramsey and John F. Wilson, eds., *The Study of Religion in Colleges and Universities* (Princeton, N.J.: Princeton University Press, 1970), 10–11; Clyde Holbrook, *Religion, A Humanistic Field* (Englewood Cliffs, N.J.: Prentice-Hall, 1963),

chap. 8; Douglas Sloan, "The Teaching of Ethics in the American Undergraduate Curriculum 1876–1976" in *Ethics Teaching in Higher Education*, ed. Daniel Callahan and Sissela Bok (New York and London: Plenum Press, 1980).

61. See, for example, Jacob Needleman, *The New Religions* (Garden City, N.Y.: Doubleday & Co., 1970); Theodore Roszak, *Where the Wasteland Ends: Politics and Transcendence in Postindustrial Society* (Garden City, N.Y.: Doubleday & Co., 1972); Harvey Cox, *Turning East: The Promise and the Peril of the New Orientalism* (New York: Simon & Schuster, 1977).

62. Welch, *Religion in the Undergraduate Curriculum*, 53.

63. Henry F. May, "Religion and American Intellectual History, 1945–1985: Reflections on an Uneasy Relationship," in *Religion and Twentieth-Century American Intellectual Life*, ed. Michael J. Lacey, 15.

64. Spivey, "Modest Messiahs," 9.

65. See, for example, Michaelsen, "The Study of Religion," 1–3. Michaelsen writes, "During the last ten years of his life the late Paul Tillich probably spoke to more American students than any other man in academia."

66. "Studying God on Campus," *Time*, 4 February 1966, 72ff.

67. See chapter 5 below.

68. Robert Spivey's description of the development of these stages at the University of North Carolina is particularly suggestive and helpful. Spivey, "Modest Messiahs," 7–8.

69. Welch, *Religion in the Undergraduate Curriculum*, 73–77; Spivey, "Modest Messiahs," 9; Ramsey and Wilson, *The Study of Religion*, 10–11.

70. Ramsey and Wilson, *The Study of Religion*, 10–11.

71. Peter Slater, "Religion as an Academic Discipline," in Welch, *Religion in the Undergraduate Curriculum*, 26.

72. See, for example, Spivey, "Modest Messiahs"; and Ronald E. Cottle, "Religion in the University: 'Messiah' or 'Antichrist'?" *Religious Education* 66 (July–August 1971): 254–56.

73. See, for example, F. Ernest Johnson, ed., *Religious Symbolism* (New York: Institute for Religious and Social Studies, 1955).

74. Paul Tillich, *Theology of Culture* (New York: Oxford University Press, 1959), 68–75. Often, thought Tillich, explicit religious subject matter was a reflection of artistic and religious impoverishment and superficiality.

75. See James Luther Adams, *Paul Tillich's Philosophy of Culture, Science, and Religion* (New York: Schocken Books, 1965), chap. 2, "The Theology of Art and Culture," 65–115.

76. Amos Wilder, "The Church's New Concern with the Arts," *Christianity and Crisis* 17, no. 2 (18 February 1957): 13.

77. Ibid., 12.

78. Ibid.

79. In this section I am greatly indebted to the case study of the National Council of Churches' programs in religion and the arts that has been done for this project by Frank Dent. Unless otherwise indicated, I have relied for my account on this study. See Frank Lloyd Dent, "The Arts in the NCCCUSA: A Case Study," manuscript, 1991.

80. The Department on Worship and the Arts was actually a reconstituted form of the Commission on Worship, established in 1932 as part of the Federal Council of Churches. *Biennial Report*, NCCCUSA, 1952, 60; *Triennial Report*, NCCCUSA, 1957, 127.

81. *Biennial Report*, NCCCUSA, 1952, 60; *Biennial Report*, NCCCUSA, 1954, 54.

82. Amos Wilder, "The Department of Worship and the Arts: Its Task in Christian Life and Work; Statement for Consideration and Study," mimeographed manuscript. Also see the attached memorandum: Amos Wilder to Morgan P. Noyes, Vice-Chairman, Department of Worship and the Arts, To the Members of the General Committee and the Commissions of the Departments, 24 June 1955. Archives of the NCCCUSA, 1952–1972, Presbyterian Church (USA), Office of History, Philadelphia.

83. Until otherwise indicated all quotes are from the memorandum cited in the previous footnote.

84. Joseph Sittler, "Christ and the Cosmos—God's Work and Man's Search," *Report of the Special Committee on the Council's Role in the Field of Religion and the Arts* (New York: National Council of the Churches of Christ in the U.S.A., 1965), 39.

85. *Triennial Report*, NCCCUSA, 1957, 127.

86. Frank Dent has pointed out the committee's low budget from the start.

87. See, for example, *Triennial Report*, NCCCUSA, 1960, 31–33.

88. Roswell Barnes, Associate General Secretary, for example, commended the worship/arts program, while cautioning against "warm aesthetic experience" that fails to question "American technological culture." *Triennial Report*, NCCCUSA, 1957, 23–24, 26.

89. See *Triennial Report*, NCCCUSA, 1957.

90. Wilder, "The Church's New Concern with the Arts."

91. Joseph Sittler, "The Church and the Arts," *Report of the Special Committee on the Council's Role in the Field of Religion and the Arts* (New York: National Council of the Churches of Christ in the U.S.A., 1965), 31.

92. Amos Wilder, *Theopoetic: Theology and the Religious Imagination* (Philadelphia: Fortress Press, 1976), 44–45. Joseph Sittler was chair of the special committee, the members of which included Wilder, Roger Ortmayer of *motive*, Robert Seaver, dramatist and theologian of Union Seminary, Robert Baker, director of the School of Sacred Music at Union Seminary, and others.

93. Merrimon Cuninggim, *The College Seeks Religion* (New Haven, Conn.: Yale University Press, 1947), 289.

94. Howard Lowry, chap. 4 in "Liberal Education and Religion: The Church College," *The Mind's Adventure: Religion and Higher Education* (Philadelphia: Westminster Press, 1950), 99–123.

95. *The Christian Scholar* 37, no. 1 (March 1954): 3.

96. *The Christian Scholar* 37, Supplement (autumn 1954).

97. Albert Outler, "Theological Foundations for Christian Higher Education," ibid., 202.

98. *The Christian Scholar* 41, Special Issue (autumn 1958).

99. Jerald C. Brauer, "The Christian College and American Higher Education," ibid., 240.

100. "As Christians," said John Dillenberger of Harvard, in a statement repeated by others, "we ought to know our own corruptions. But the fact is that history—and our so-called enemies continually have to show them to us." John Dillenberger, "Christianity Not the Only Option," *The Christian Scholar* 37, no. 1 (March 1954): 21.

101. Robert Lowry Calhoun, "Christian Vocation on the College Campus," *The Christian Scholar* 37, Supplement (autumn 1954): 273–74.

102. William G. Pollard, "The Relation of the Christian College to the Scientific World," ibid., 250–51. Also see Kathleen Bliss, "The Christian College and

the Contemporary World," *The Christian Scholar* 41, Special Issue (autumn 1958): 265–67.

103. Merrimon Cuninggim, *The Protestant Stake in Higher Education* (n.p.: Council of Protestant Colleges and Universities, 1961).

104. Ibid., 18.

105. Ibid., 66.

106. See Fritz Machlup, *The Production and Distribution of Knowledge in the United States* (Princeton, N.J.: Princeton University Press, 1962).

107. See Daniel Bell, *The Reforming of General Education* (New York: Columbia University Press, 1966).

108. See Sloan, "The Teaching of Ethics" in *Ethics Teaching in Higher Education.*

109. Harold Taylor, a main administrator-faculty champion of the students on this score summarizes most of the arguments brought against a prescribed core curriculum. See Harold Taylor, *Students without Teachers: The Crisis in the University* (New York: McGraw-Hill Book Co., 1969), 131ff.

110. Philosophical ethics, once a required course of every college student, was now largely a highly technical, elective course for a few philosophy majors. See Douglas Sloan, "The Teaching of Ethics" in *Ethics Teaching in Higher Education.*

CHAPTER 4

The Theologians and the
Two-Realm Theory of Truth

THE AMERICAN THEOLOGIANS

What was the main understanding of the faith-knowledge relationship at work within the theological renaissance, and what were its consequences for the church's engagement with the university? Here I will focus mainly on the three most influential theologians on the American scene—Reinhold Niebuhr, his brother H. Richard Niebuhr, and Paul Tillich. While others might provide some important variations of the positions they represented, and might even require some qualifications of my generalizations, still these were the main American theologians during this period.

Focusing on them will mean, admittedly, ignoring important European theologians, whose work was crucial to the theological renaissance, though the Americans and the Europeans did not always agree. However, there are several good reasons why we can concentrate on the Americans in this context: Paul Tillich and the two Niebuhrs were by far the best known among Americans; main European influences in American theology were often mediated and filtered through them; and together they represented the main dimensions of the theological renaissance in America. Their grappling with the faith-knowledge relationship is revealing of the basic issues involved, especially as these affected the churches in American higher education.

The intellectual respectability that theology and the study of religion came increasingly to enjoy in postwar American higher education, probably against all expectations, was mainly because of the work and public prominence of these three. Each carried out his work in university divinity schools connected with the most prestigious of American academic centers: Reinhold Niebuhr at New York's Union Theological Seminary, H. Richard Niebuhr at Yale University Divinity School, and Paul Tillich, first for years with Reinhold Niebuhr at Union Seminary, then at Harvard Divinity School— brought there largely at the instigation of Harvard University President, Nathan Pusey—and finally at the University of Chicago.

Tillich's concern to demonstrate the religious dimensions of the whole of human culture brought a hearing to his ideas in nearly every academic field. Even those who disagreed with him often felt it necessary to pay attention to his work. Reinhold Niebuhr's lifelong efforts to join political analysis and action with Christian theology and ethics made him probably the best known and most publicly influential of the three. He was a voluminous writer, an indefatigable and highly sought-after speaker, preacher, and consultant, and a political activist and a critical analyst of almost every facet of America's changing political life. His influence was felt in the World Council and Federal Council of Churches, in American theological seminaries, in academia, and in foreign affairs. He was, among many other things, a member for a time of the policy planning staff of the U.S. State Department and a member of the Council on Foreign Relations, and a key founder of several such organizations as the Committee for Cultural Freedom, the American Palestine Committee, and others. *Life* magazine featured stories on him in 1946 and 1948, and in 1948 *Time* carried his picture on the cover of its 25th anniversary issue.[1] In 1959 Harvard philosopher Morton White dubbed as "atheists for Niebuhr" the many intellectuals, both in and outside academia, who, without counting themselves fellow believers, nonetheless, found great stimulation in Niebuhr's theological analyses of human nature, politics, and culture.[2]

Although H. Richard Niebuhr was not the public figure that either of the other two were, he inspired great devotion among his students, who often still speak of him as the most profound theologian of the three. Many of his students became, in the 1950s and 1960s, leading faculty members in seminaries and religious studies departments across the country.

While none of these theologians wrote extensively on higher education as such, their work was filled throughout with manifold implications for higher education. All would have agreed with Reinhold Niebuhr that the most important task facing religion in higher education was to take up and grapple with the center of university existence, the intellectual domain. "If the academic work of the college is basically hostile or indifferent to religion," Niebuhr wrote at the end of the war, "the extracurricular religious activities can serve to maintain the religious loyalty of the minority but will accomplish little to give our whole culture a more positive religious content."[3] All three dealt in so many ways with the relation between faith and knowledge that they provided the major theological underpinnings for what we have been calling the Protestant churches' new engagement with higher education.

At first glimpse it might seem that in dealing with the faith-knowledge relationship these theologians adopted a fairly uncomplicated two-realm theory of truth in which it is held that, on the one side, there are the truths given by our ways of knowing, and, on the other, there are the truths given by faith, feeling, action, morality, tradition, and so on. After all, they were among the great twentieth-century theologians of faith.

Consider, for example, the affirmation, which all three shared, about the nature and necessity of faith as trust.[4] All argued that every human being requires some unifying faith in something absolute to give coherence, meaning, and purpose to life. "We must never forget," wrote Reinhold

Niebuhr, "the religious significance of ostensible irreligion. . . . No one lives without some sense of meaning and every universe of meaning has a 'God' in it."[5] Coupled with this emphasis that no one escapes having a faith of some kind was the insistence that the Divine alone is absolute and, therefore, worthy of faith and commitment. This was "radical faith" in H. Richard Niebuhr's terms, faith as "ultimate concern" in Tillich's phrase. As Tillich was fond of putting it, only the truly ultimate is worthy of our ultimate concern. If we had to select one all-important emphasis of the neo-orthodox influence in the theological renaissance, perhaps it would be its constant demand that all absolutizing of the relative, all attempts to make divine what is only creaturely, is idolatry and the essence of sin. The pervasive modern faith in what Tillich described as "self-sufficient finitude" could only lead to destructive pride and finally to despair.

This conception of faith certainly sustained the injunction to analyze the faith presuppositions at work in every field and discipline of knowledge and to test their adequacy in comparison with Christian presuppositions. "The god of a universe of meaning," said Reinhold Niebuhr, "is that which is not explained but by which things are explained. It is the final source of meaning. The God of modern naturalism is 'nature.' "[6] These hidden, lesser gods were to be exposed, and their poverty held up for all to see. Their inadequacy alongside the ultimate assumptions of the Christian view could then be made apparent.

At the same time this conception of faith also supported the critique of the fragmentation of the modern curriculum and the call to seek a larger, integrating unity that would bring coherence to modern culture. Every academic discipline, Reinhold Niebuhr said, "is inclined either to pursue its interests without asking fundamental questions about the meaning of the whole, or it elaborates an implicit philosophy, drawn from its own characteristic modes of procedure or the 'behaviour' of reality upon the level of its investigation."[7]

Coherence was to be found in the fractured world of meaning by pressing the different disciplines to recognize that they all raised, as Tillich never tired in trying to show, basic, existential questions of life that only the ultimates of theology could answer. The integrating unity could be found in H. Richard Niebuhr's terms by entering into the different disciplines in the "radical faith" that the many diverse commitments and paths of inquiry point finally to "the One beyond the many," to the larger meaning of which all lesser meanings partake, provided that one maintained a never-ending criticism of the pretensions of the lesser. Both the tyranny of hidden, inadequate explanatory assumptions about reality and the meaninglessness of a fragmented world of discourse were seen as the result of an inadequate conception of faith.

All the theologians maintained that "radical faith," "ultimate concern," is a gift that arises out of an encounter with the absolute Other, an encounter that demands an existential decision committing us in every dimension of our lives. The existentialism of these theologians also had direct implications for higher education. The emphasis on commitment encompassed every human endeavor and demanded bringing the faith to bear on scholarship, on politics, on vocation, and so forth.[8] It also meant that there was a natural affinity between the new theology and certain strong, existentialist philosophical currents present in postwar American higher education, an affinity that helped enhance the intellectual standing of theology in the university. However, the emphasis on an ultimate decision seemed to draw a sharp line between faith and knowledge: faith being a kind of existential leap into the unknown; knowledge being identified with that which can be objectified, dissected, and manipulated.

Yet it was more complicated than this. The theologians did not want to reject modern science, historical criticism of the scriptures, and the general attainments of secular knowledge. "The presuppositions of faith by which the whole of life is conceived as a unity are not the simple achievements of rational analysis," Reinhold Niebuhr said, "but neither can they stand in contradiction to the scientific and rational analyses of experience."[9] The theologians had a deep appreciation for the achievements of modern consciousness—its capacity for critical understanding, for rational control, and for individual selfhood and freedom. Indeed, Reinhold Niebuhr himself, for instance, was most eloquent in identifying the essence of human selfhood as its capacity for freedom, for transcendence of self and nature—and its unique propensity to abuse and to corrupt this freedom. In this all the theologians agreed, and in this they were all thoroughly modern. Above all, they did not want in any way to be taken for fundamentalists or religious dogmatists of any kind. "The culturally obscurantist versions of the Protestant faith," said Reinhold Niebuhr, "are so irrelevant to religion in higher education that no policy in the academic program can hope to overcome the irrelevance."[10] They wanted to represent a faith that could speak the language of the modern world and thus address with real consequences for the larger culture, the problems of the modern world.

Nevertheless, they recognized that one major problem of the modern world is the dominance of a narrow objectifying way of knowing applied to every level of reality. They also saw that because it could claim precision, verifiability, and public use, and because of its great success in the areas of science and technology, it was the only conception of knowing recognized by the modern public. "The triumph of autonomous reason," said Paul Tillich, "particularly in the natural sciences, has pushed aside religious knowledge. Either it is repudiated altogether or it is relegated to a corner, or it is transformed by secular interpretations."[11] The results were, as he put it elsewhere, "a rapid decay of spiritual (and not only the Spiritual) life, an estrangement from nature, and most dangerous of all, a dealing with human beings as with things."[12]

The dominance of a narrow quantitative, instrumental conception of knowing meant, in H. Richard Niebuhr's words, that we live "in a depersonalized and often disenchanted world in which we are taught to doubt the primary realities that we experience—the self and its companion selves."[13] Hence, the theologians found it necessary to show how the most important realities of our life, human and divine, can be acknowledged, responded to, and talked about, despite their exclusion from modern knowledge.

In order to carry out this project they had at least to edge toward the development of a more encompassing rationality than that represented by an objectifying, sense-based reason. The desire to make affirmations of faith required at least some grounding in knowable reality, a grounding not afforded by the dominant modern conceptions of how and what we know. As a consequence, the theologians began, really by necessity, to explore other ways of knowing, even if they themselves did not quite conceive of what they were doing in these terms.

They went about it in three ways: they began to attempt to broaden the conception of reason itself; they began to develop the concept of "knowledge of persons," and thus embarked on a genuine foray into the realm of qualitative knowledge, as distinct from the dominant modern quantitative, discursive, and instrumental knowledge; and they looked toward metaphor and symbol as a way of knowing the intangible and the invisible realms spoken of by religion, again invoking the possibility of genuine qualitative ways of knowing. Whether they carried these efforts far enough to provide the basis for a genuine bridging of faith and knowledge is the central question we must explore.

In working to make a case for ways of knowing that are more encompassing and penetrating than our ordinary conception of knowing, Paul Tillich distinguished between what he called "technical reason" and "ontological reason." Technical reason, dealing only with the discovery of means for ends, with the external relations among objects given primarily in sense experience, dominates our time. Technical reason is essential in dealing with the objects of finite experience, in establishing the means to achieve given ends, and in setting up logical, coherent systems of thought. At this level the theologian is as dependent on technical reason, and must value it as highly, as anyone else. By itself, however, technical reason cannot deal with ends, purposes, and meanings; it has no way of recognizing their reality. The human being understood solely in the light of technical reason is dehumanized; a God proved by technical reason is no longer God, but only another object among objects, albeit, perhaps, the most important or powerful of objects. Technical reason lacks, in a favorite phrase of Tillich, "the depth dimension of experience."[14]

"Ontological reason," by contrast, is that deeper rationality that grasps those elements of reality that cannot be reached by technical, controlling reason. Ontological reason points to the depth dimension, to the ultimate source of our necessarily finite and relative experiences of truth, beauty, goodness, and love.[15] Ontological reason is also at work in our awareness of the relationships among wholes, Gestalt processes, meanings, values, and qualities.[16] Since the mid-nineteenth century, Tillich pointed out, technical reason has become the exclusive conception of reason recognized by the modern world. The result has been that this narrow reason has itself fallen more and more into the service of irrational and nonrational ends and forces, for in itself it has no access to the dimension of depth.[17] Technical reason is not to be rejected, but it is "adequate and meaningful only as an expression of ontological reason and as its companion."[18]

Ontological reason opens up into "ecstatic reason"—reason that is transparent to the ground of being, to the "depth dimension of reality." It is reason "grasped by an ultimate concern."[19] It is the possibility of reason as a union of the detachment, analysis, and objectification of technical reason with the depth dimension of ontological reason.[20] And it is ontological reason as ecstatic reason in which the affirmations of faith in the ultimate have their grounding, and which secures them against the attacks of a noncomprehending technical reason.[21]

The Niebuhrs also spoke of other ways of knowing beyond those of technical reason. They emphasized, however, the peculiar nature of practical reason and knowledge of persons over against theoretical, objectifying reason. Since faith is by its nature personal, the theologians had perforce to develop some concept of knowledge of persons, as distinct from knowledge of things.

The primary concern of H. Richard Niebuhr was with revelation as the encounter with Being itself that makes possible faith as trust and trustworthy action in response to Being. The response of faith and trust is the essence of being a person. Knowledge of persons, Richard Niebuhr stressed, takes place in community, for selfhood comes to birth and is nourished only in relation to other selves.[22]

The response of faith, of radical trust, is made possible within the community whose identity has been initiated and shaped by the revelatory event. Richard Niebuhr's position is well-described as a kind of "social existentialism" in which the response of faith is inextricably entwined with the identity and relationships of the whole community and with the memory and recounting of the community's history. There are, Richard Niebuhr said, two kinds of history. There is an outer history, as a detached observer might tell it, of events and objects without existential, personal meaning. And there is an inner history of selves in relationship, a history conveyed through the community's own retelling of the narrative of the meaning of its life together.[23]

The importance that H. Richard Niebuhr saw in the story, in narrative, as the source of communal identity over time actually contained two important emphases that opened the way for a deepening of knowing into the qualitative. It emphasized, as we have just noted, the importance of selves and the relationships among selves. It also assumed the importance of language as a bearer of not only instrumental and discursive meanings but also intrinsic, qualitative meanings.

This larger conception of language, as we have seen, has been adamantly denied by the positivisms prevalent in the nineteenth and twentieth centuries, for it necessarily implies a larger realm of meaning beyond the visible and tangible, a realm usually denied by, because it is inaccessible to, a knowing based exclusively on sense experience and abstractions from sense experience. To make narrative language central, redolent as it is with images and metaphors, is also to raise the question of the role in all knowing of the image-making capacities of the human mind. In short, it is to raise the question of the paramount role of imagination in all our knowing—of nature and of the spirit. There was, therefore, in H. Richard Niebuhr's interrelated conceptions of faith, person, community, and narrative, rich possibilities both for the beginning of a fundamental transformation of the dominant modern conception of knowing and for placing technical reason within a larger, more capacious qualitative and imaginal rationality.

Likewise, for Reinhold Niebuhr, "knowledge of persons" as selves in community is also central.[24] The essence of selfhood Reinhold Niebuhr saw in the human being's capacity for freedom. The two great modern threats to the self—and these were Niebuhr's constant foes—were idealism and naturalism. "Both," he argued, "obscure the dimension of selfhood."[25] Idealism, he believed, does so by absorbing the individual into the universal categories of abstract reason. Naturalism does so by reducing the human being to the mechanisms and the determinative structures of causal regularity. Both are temptations of the human being, for the human being seeks to avoid freedom either by abusing it in a denial of creaturely finitude, or by denying it and sinking into an identification with the subhuman.[26] The reality of guilt and sin, which Niebuhr was a master in delineating, was itself a witness to the potential dignity of the human self.

In Reinhold Niebuhr's view, the possibility of personal knowledge is given from beyond in the encounter with the personal God of the biblical tradition, just as is the possibility of human meaning in history. The problem of meaning is solved, maintained Niebuhr, only by "the introduction of a principle of meaning which transcends the world of meaning to be interpreted."[27] The true nature of the human being is to be known and judged only by means of "a source of light and truth beyond him."[28]

But this meaning from beyond was itself to be understood in terms of knowledge of persons. Knowledge of persons Reinhold Niebuhr saw not only as essential to understanding the nature of personal responsibility but also as analogous for talking about our relationship to the Divine.[29] Our relation to the other, our response of trust and faithfulness, and our deficiencies in both, are dependent on our knowledge of the other as person. We know something about the other from our observations of their behavior (our use of technical and empirical reason). But it is not until they begin to reveal their inner being, that is, it is not until they speak to us, that we can begin to have an understanding that compels our deepest response as persons in our own right. Likewise, the revelation of the Divine is to be understood in an analogy with the self-disclosure of a person. Again, there was in this beginning conception of knowledge of persons, and in its accompanying realization of the importance of the word, of qualitative language, the starting point for a deeper, more encompassing conception of qualitative knowing.

Tillich also spoke of the difference in kind between knowledge of persons and knowledge of things.[30] He was, however, more reticent, more chary than the Niebuhrs of speaking unguardedly about the personal nature of the Divine, since he wanted always to avoid any suggestions that the reality of the Divine is amenable to our finite conceptions, most especially our finite conceptions of personality.[31]

Nevertheless, particularly in his emphasis on existential meaning and decision, Tillich also stressed the unique nature of personal existence, and of knowledge of persons, in contrast to the existence and knowledge of things. In fact, one of Tillich's main criticisms of the disciplines of the modern university was that, in thrall to technical reason, they had narrowly pursued their own aims and had lost a sense of the underlying unity of being. In the process they also had lost a sense of the unity and wholeness of the human being. The human person had been divided among the disciplines and reduced to yet another object, or rather a conglomeration of disparate objects, "a physical object, a chemical object, a biological object, a psychological object, a sociological object."[32] "Above all what is lost," in this fragmentation and objectification, Tillich said, "is the central self that makes it possible for us to have language, to make tools, to make decisions, to deliberate, and even to come in conflict with ourselves—which no other being can."[33] Once more the conception of knowledge of persons pointed to another larger, more fundamental transformation of all our knowing.

For all three theologians the nature of personal knowledge and of the meaning of the encounter with the Divine are disclosed only through symbols, not through the propositions of discursive, analytical reason. Here again was an attempt by necessity to broaden the dominant modern conception of knowledge by arguing that the denotative signs and labels of ordinary reason can not express the nuances and connotations of the fullness of reality. Religious language and religious knowing, they maintained, are essentially symbolic. All drew on the classic Coleridgean concept of the symbol as that which participates in the reality it represents. There is, therefore, no such thing as "just a symbol."[34] Nor is the symbol ever to be rendered literally. "It is important," said Reinhold Niebuhr, "to take Biblical symbols seriously but not literally."[35] The symbol both embodies and points beyond itself to the reality it discloses.

The concept of the symbol could be developed with different emphases.

For Tillich the ultimate, the holy, to which ontological reason points, can only be grasped through metaphor and symbol, otherwise it too would be reduced to the objectifications of technical reason.[36] But in his view anything could potentially become a religious symbol of the holy, "a dimension of reality which shines through the bearers of the holy, be it stars and trees, ocean and earth, paintings and buildings, music and words, or persons and historical events."[37] The only nonsymbolic statement about God, Tillich maintained, is that God is being-itself, because this statement does not point beyond itself.[38] In his later work, Tillich was even to qualify this.[39]

The two Niebuhrs also emphasized a similar conception of the religious symbol, but stressed more its role as essential in the knowledge of persons as selves in community. Reinhold Niebuhr's repeated emphasis was on the symbols of God and of the self conveyed in the biblical tradition. The nature of the self and the personal nature of God (a stress that Tillich was more ambiguous about) could only be expressed in poetic, religious, and metaphoric images and symbols. For Reinhold Niebuhr these can be appropriated in faith and then become the presuppositions of interpretation and understanding of all human history. Reinhold Niebuhr's argument was that the dramatic categories of freedom, encounter, and dialogue presented in the images, myths, and symbols of the biblical tradition provided the most adequate and penetrating of all presuppositions for understanding and making sense of life. In his preaching, especially, Reinhold Niebuhr showed himself to be a virtuoso in bringing the symbols and images of the biblical tradition to bear in vivid, compelling fashion on the tasks of human beings in modern society.

The symbol was also central to H. Richard Niebuhr's conception of religious knowing as personal. He, however, gave much more attention than did the others—and probably more than did any other contemporary theologian—to the importance of imagination and the image in all our knowing. Like Tillich, he distinguished between two kinds of reason, but rather than Tillich's ontological and technical reason, Niebuhr spoke of practical reason, "the reason of the heart," which works with personal, relational images, and theoretical reason, the "reason of the head," which works with impersonal, objectifying images.[40] Both realms of reason require the image-making and image-using capacities of the human being. It is the image—the pattern, the form, the symbol—which gives us our world or worlds with which reason in both spheres must work.

What must not be done is to use images in those spheres of meaning where they do not apply: the application, for example, of mechanical imagery to persons and personal relationships. Another error to be always avoided is the hardening of images in a literalistic identification with that which the image is intended to illuminate. Both are "evil imaginations" that wreak havoc with our life and world.[41] The reason and images of the heart reveal the "internal history" of selves in community; the reason and images of the head reveal "the external history" of impersonal things and objects. Here H. Richard

Niebuhr's conception of imagination is seen to be part and parcel with his social existentialism and the importance of narrative in the life of the community of faith.

Despite its attempts to strengthen the knowledge claims of faith through a conception of personal knowledge and symbolic truth, the position of the theological reformers broke down at crucial points. In the end the theologians pulled back from affirming unambiguously the real possibility of knowledge of God and of the spiritual world. They again and again resisted seeking or talking about knowledge of God for fear of the danger of applying objectifying and manipulative modes of thought where they did not belong. At the same time, however, they wanted to affirm fully and without question, lest they be thought religious fundamentalists, the same objective, analytic modes of modern science and historical analysis in every other domain besides faith. The result was a split that forced the theological reformers back onto faith presuppositions whenever they spoke about religion and onto an increasing reliance on naturalistic approaches to the sensible world whenever they wanted to speak about ethics, science, or knowledge in general.

In order to avoid literalism and objectification of the spiritual, the theological reformers, for all their forays into personal and symbolic knowledge, tended to make the encounter with the holy utterly ineffable. This is true of Paul Tillich, for instance, in his conception of ontological reason, which gives him the basis for criticizing the pretensions of controlling and technical reason. At one point, he does seem to connect ontological reason with knowledge of qualities, which he says includes such things as "the quality of a color, or the meaning of an idea, or the nature of a living being."[42] However, this all-important connection made in passing is never pursued, and all mention of qualities and of knowledge of qualities is dropped.

Tillich, consequently, is unrelenting in holding that ontological reason and revelation do not provide any knowledge other than an awareness of the presence and utter mystery of the holy. "But revelation," he writes, "does not dissolve the mystery into knowledge. Nor does it add anything directly to the totality of our ordinary knowledge about the subject-object structure of reality."[43]

Tillich never entertains the possibility that an awareness of the mystery of being, and wonder and reverence before it, might become an unending source for ever-new, but real knowledge of the infinitely rich, qualitative dimensions of reality, if the requisite capacities for qualitative knowing were also to be developed. Rather, the depth dimension, the ground of being, remains a sea of unknowing. It can inspire, as it does for Tillich, a sense of the mystery of existence and an existential quest for the meaning of existence. But it leaves the structures of reality as given by our ordinary discursive and technical ways of knowing completely unaltered, even potentially. And so, despite all, the realm of religious meaning and the realm of ordinary reality remain in Tillich's system essentially two different worlds.

Similarly, for H. Richard Niebuhr; his strong concept of knowledge of persons ultimately did little to bridge the split between faith and knowledge. It is true that Richard Niebuhr, like Tillich, wanted to eliminate any conflict between faith and reason, and he spoke of faith seeking knowledge and reason acting faithfully. At the same time, however, Niebuhr continually subordinated the knowledge dimensions of faith to faith as trust and faith as relation. The importance of knowledge always tends to recede before the demand for relationship and response. This is the case even with knowledge of persons; it is all the more so with the Divine. In the encounter with Being there is given no knowledge of the spiritual, except, as John Cobb has observed, knowledge of "the sheer being of Being."[44] And its import for us can only then be explicated in existentialist fashion.

The existential demand for commitment, response, and relationship swamps even the development of the personal knowledge needed to make that response ever more intelligible, despite Niebuhr's own description of revelation as "this intelligible event which makes all other events intelligible."[45] Before the inscrutable being of Being, the tendency always is present for personal meaning and intelligible response to be swallowed up in existential arbitrariness. Niebuhr's own conception of confessional relativism seems to have been an admirable recognition of this on his part.[46]

Ultimately, Reinhold Niebuhr's faith presuppositions, and his view of persons and personal knowledge, also remained dissociated from other kinds of knowledge. Paul Tillich once criticized Reinhold Niebuhr's conception of reason as being, in Tillich's terms, exclusively that of "the calculating type of reason," "scientific, arguing, technical reason"; a narrow conception of reason "which has been peculiar to us [only] since the middle of the nineteenth century."[47] Tillich was correct: Always when Reinhold Niebuhr talked about knowledge, he assumed knowledge of this sort. This meant eventually that his view of persons and of personal knowledge, as given in the biblical revelation, often remained hanging because he could provide them with no integral connection to knowledge of the world, as this is given by our ordinary reason in the exclusively modern, restricted sense that Niebuhr accepted.

This same narrow conception of reason further encouraged Reinhold Niebuhr to invoke the mystery of God, rather than to talk about the possibility of knowledge of God, since in his view the latter would imply subjecting the Divine to the mechanistic, objectified, and manipulable structures given by technical reason.[48] This meant, however, as with the others, that the presuppositions of faith, which were held to make personal experience possible, seemed increasingly to be nothing more than just that, assertions that demanded arbitrary, existential decisions.

Thus, for all their emphasis on personal and symbolic knowledge, the role of symbols for these theologians remained curiously elusive, even vague. Despite the insistence that there is no such thing as "just a symbol," that a true symbol, as opposed to a mere sign, participates in the reality it represents, it was never clear exactly what the symbol did represent for these theologians. If it was not genuine knowledge of the Divine, which had consequences also for knowledge of the world, what was it? If it was personal knowledge, did this have any connection with other kinds of knowledge? Indeed, symbols as described by the theologians seemed to serve more for eliciting moods, feelings, energies, and existential commitments than for conveying qualitative realities having cognitive significance.

The results could be seen, for example, in their approach to the study of scripture. The biblical images, myths, and symbols were to provide the affirmations of faith in a god beyond the world of natural necessity, in a nonobjectifiable and nonreducible personal reality, and in a meaning to historical events given from beyond history. Yet the scriptures were also to be subjected to all the assumptions of modern analytic reason and historical criticism, which by their nature had no place for any of these affirmations of faith. This conflict between faith and knowledge within the approach to scripture itself, the main source of symbolic affirmations by the theological reformers, was never clarified or eased.[49] In such a situation the faith assertions, unsupported by the results of analytic historical criticism, could only eventually seem to be referring either to something unknowable and unreal or to the subjective convictions of the theologians themselves.

The theologians' portrayals of the Divine-human encounter drawn from the dramatic myths, stories, and images of the Bible had initially a fresh and bracing quality about them. Eventually, however, they seemed increasingly to be couched in a language and in concepts that had little connection with knowable reality as experienced and shaped by the modern mind. As presuppositions, the assertions of faith took on more and more a dogmatic quality, or of a worldview that is imported from without. Such a worldview can interpret the world, but it does not in any fundamental way alter the content and structure of that world, since these have been given already by our ways of knowing. Thus the theologians' faith presuppositions came to carry a double burden: They appeared increasingly dogmatic and, at the same time, more and more dispensable as only one possible way among others of interpreting a world already given without them. It would become ever more tempting for many others to begin to focus exclusively on that given world.

A similar situation pertained with respect to ethics. For the theologians, the analysis of any given situation was provided entirely by technical reason—increasingly in its pragmatic, instrumental versions. The affirmations of faith—say, for example, the importance of persons in just and caring communities—could then be brought into the situation as goals to be sought. Once introduced, however, the attainment of the faith goals and values would be carried out again exclusively by technical reason—often by out and out conniving, *the* political mode par excellence of technical, instrumental rationalism.

It was not unlike the ethical emotivism of the logical positivists, otherwise the archenemies of the theological renaissance. The logical positivists had maintained that we can have knowledge only of empirical facts and abstractions, primarily mathematical abstractions, based on those facts. In this view all statements referring to metaphysics, religion, and ethics, if not utterly meaningless, were simply expressions of emotional feelings and preferences—hence the term emotivism to describe an ethics in which all ultimate goals and values are seen as having their roots in the unknowable and irrational. In actuality, as Weber pointed out early in the century, this has long been the major conception of ethics in modern culture.[50]

The ethics of the theological reformers were perilously close to further reinforcing, rather than in any way overcoming, the fundamental emotivism of the modern world, with its split between a rationalism of means and an irrationalism of ends and values. On at least one occasion, Reinhold Niebuhr commended the logical positivists' notion of ethical values as emotive because he thought this protected values from being subsumed under the categories of a calculating, scientific rationalism. But this also meant that faith and its accompanying value assertions had no rational grounding; thus they were delivered all the more firmly to that same narrow reason for their implementation. It was a dilemma for which on Niebuhr's terms there was no solution.[51]

Moreover, as can be seen especially in some of the "realist ethics" of Reinhold Niebuhr, even the values and goals of ethical action themselves seemed to be supplied less and less by faith and instead to be taken increasingly from the available alternatives of the given political left or right—with faith being reduced to a mere source of energy and willpower for their attainment. Despite Niebuhr's attacks on the naturalism of John Dewey, for example, the two were in many ways very close: Dewey pursuing an ethics of pragmatism in the context of his "natural piety"; Niebuhr pursuing an ethics of pragmatism in the context of his "biblical piety." It would be relatively easy for critics to take the next step and to say, "Let us just be pragmatists in whatever context we find ourselves."

Finally, the inability of the leading theologians to overcome the separation between faith and knowledge was especially reflected in their view of science and in the sharp separation they made between nature and history. For these theologians, nature is the realm of objects, strict regularities, and mechanical determinism and necessity. History is the realm of persons, of freedom, of transcendent meaning. Science gives us the one; faith—and knowledge of persons—the other. Because each dealt with different and separate realms of meaning, so it was argued, there need be no conflict in principle between them. This neat division fit well the desire to be able to affirm both science and religion. But the connections between the two remained unclear, and in this lack of clarity lurked a host of serious, unaddressed problems and inconsistencies.

It is true that the nature-history, nature-person dichotomy undergirded the main and harshest criticism the theologians brought to bear on science. This criticism lay, as we have seen, in their attempt to limit science to the realm of things and to decry its extension to the world of persons. The threat of the dehumanizing "tyranny of science" over persons they took very seriously. That many thinking people seemed oblivious to it was to Reinhold Niebuhr, for example, a kind of modern scandal. "The elaborate reverence of even religious thinkers before the pretensions of science," he said, "is a measure of the decadence of our culture."[52] However, as long as science represented the way of knowing determinative for all experience, and not only for that of the laboratory, it was not self-evident that it could so easily be kept within its proper boundaries—especially given that the realities of ordinary experience were being increasingly decided within the laboratory. This problem the theological reformers did not consider.

Critical rigor at this point was further weakened by another, related approach the theologians took toward science. This was the argument that, although science has been implicated in all the great problems of the modern world, the main fault lay not with science nor with scientists, but with society's misuse of both.[53] This enabled the theologians fully to embrace science, technology, and technical reason as the good moderns they so wanted to be, and at the same time to exercise their prophetic judgment on the foibles of the modern world and its sinful inhabitants. It also avoided completely the necessity of looking more closely and critically at the adequacy of the kind of knowing that was shaping the modern world.

Nevertheless, the theologians tried to avoid a complete separation between science and religion. They sought the unifying bridge, however, solely in an extension of faith without a corresponding consideration of the knowledge side of the relationship. They were fond, for example, of pointing out that theologians and scientists both began their reasoning on the basis of faith. H. Richard Niebuhr was especially strong in describing the faith commitments and personal loyalties of scientists on which their scientific endeavors themselves rested: faith in the intelligibility of the universe, faith in the scientific community, faith in the search for truth, and so on.[54] This was well-taken, and it was an effective antidote to the positivist claim that science proceeds solely on the basis of a neutral, detached intellect. By itself, however, the analogy between scientific and religious faith had the effect of bypassing the really difficult conceptual and ethical questions. In itself, the analogy always tended toward a kind of uncritical religious sanction and legitimation of science, since, after all, the scientists too were "men of faith," just as were the theologians.

With all their emphasis on ethics, the theological reformers never were able to conceive as within the realm of possibility that perhaps the paramount ethical injunction of our time is not simply the moral use of the products of knowledge—important as that is, but, more important, the transformation of knowing—*metanoia* in its deepest and most radical sense. Such a transformation of knowing would require the concomitant transformation of feeling and willing and the development of these in their cognitive capacities. The theological reformers did stress, and the Niebuhrs often graphically, the involvement of feeling and willing in knowing and the recognition of both as essential to grasping the full truth beyond that given by a narrow, intellectualistic rationalism. But the possibility of developing feeling and willing, so as to open wider domains of reality to actual knowing of a new and deeper kind, was in the end foreclosed by the fears we have seen that knowledge threatened mystery. The uncritical acceptance of the dominant, modern conceptions of knowing ran too deep.

It was this nearly complete acceptance of the scientific description of nature that posed problems that the theological reformers were often unable even to recognize, much less to deal with. For one thing, it meant their acceptance without question of the scientific description of nature as a world of impersonal objects related exclusively by physical cause and effect. To put it in H. Richard Niebuhr's terms, while history has both an inside and an outside, nature has only an outside, an outside of mechanical, quantifiable, objects. The possibility that nature might have, as do human beings, both a mechanical, quantitative outside and a meaningful, qualitative inside, is not one these theologians entertained. Their view as a result left nature fully vulnerable to human manipulation and control.

It was not a good basis on which to develop a radical ecological ethic, nor a vigorous medical ethic. It precluded nearly from the outset any radical critique of the adequacy of the scientific view of nature. It is symptomatic in this regard that the theological reformers never tired in heaping ridicule on all religious persons who rejected Darwinism, lumping them all together as unreconstructed fundamentalists—even though Darwinism represented in fact the extension of the mechanical philosophy to everything, including persons and spirit, and was a direct challenge to any theological conception of a meaning in history that transcends history. That there have always been reputable biologists who have entertained evolutionary views and at the same time have been highly critical of Darwinian and neo-Darwinian evolutionary explanations simply escaped them, so eager were they not to be seen as antiscience.

It might seem that Paul Tillich offered an exception to this acquiescence in science's mechanistic view of nature. Almost alone among the mainstream theological reformers, Tillich responded to nature with a sense of awe and wonder. He himself spoke of his "romantic relationship toward nature." Nature inspired in him as he described it, "a predominantly aesthetic-meditative attitude . . . as distinguished from a scientific-analytic or technical-controlling reaction." This was essentially his complaint against Calvinism and Puritanism, and against the Ritschlian ethical theology (and here he may well have been taking an oblique swipe at the Niebuhrs), that in these "there is no mystical participation in nature, no understanding that nature is the finite expression of the infinite ground of all things, no vision of the divine-demonic conflict in nature."[55] This awareness of the mystery of nature could make nature an ally and source of inspiration of the existential quest for meaning. By the same token it would also presumably discourage the technological abuse and exploitation of nature. Tillich's own deep sense that there are vital life-forces at work in nature suggested that for him nature is more than the outside that meets the eye.

Yet, because Tillich refused to draw implications for our ways of knowing from his sense of the mystery and inner life of nature, he offers no more than a romantic mood of wonder and awe. The world of nature as it is determined and given by the technical reason of science remains as little changed for Tillich as for any neo-orthodox, or any naturalist for that matter. "Science," Tillich said,

> is the cognitive approach to the whole of finite objects, their interrelations and their processes. Religion is the total approach to that which gives meaning to our life. . . . All statements about facts, structures, processes and events in nature, man and history, are objects of scientific research and cannot be made in the name of religion.[56]

As long as religion was conceived as having no cognitive dimension, then, of course, Tillich was correct that it should make no statements about our knowledge of the world.[57] By the same token science had nothing to contribute to religion. In making this separation, however, he rejected entirely the possibility of an imaginative deepening that could cut across both science and religion, opening up new possibilities in each and a more radical critique of both.

The desire to reconcile is overwhelming. Science and religion could not conflict because "scientific truth and the truth of faith do not belong to the same dimension of meaning. . . ."[58] In essence Tillich's was a total embrace of the dichotomy between science as fact and religion as meaning, and in the end a simplistic one at that. Because they belong, Tillich insisted, to "different dimensions," he was able to claim that there was no conflict between science and religion. "There is no religious statement," he said, "that can contradict a scientific statement if religion is understood in its fundamental sense as ultimate concern and science is understood as the inquiry into the finite facts and their relations."[59] The reconciliation thus effected enabled Tillich to claim a place for religion in the modern world. But it was a reconciliation purchased at a very high price. At bottom the two-realm theory of truth remains for Tillich, as for the others, fully intact, and with all its problems.

To make the story complete, it must be added that in his last years H. Richard Niebuhr took up his earlier reflections on imagination, and the importance of image and metaphor, in a way that could have had implications for bridging the nature-history dichotomy. Influenced by the work of Cassirer, Gombrich, Auerbach, and Stephen Pepper, Niebuhr turned anew to the importance of the human being as an image-maker. Our perceptions, conceptions, organization, and understanding of the world, all, he wrote, "are guided and formed by the images in our minds." This is true, he pointed out, in religion, art, science, and philosophy alike: "They are all symbol systems."[60] In later notes he speaks of the role of image, metaphor, and symbol in what may be a suggestion of genuine non-sensory and qualitative knowledge in "dealing with realities that are not objects of sense perception, such as conscience, or the form of the state, or patriotism or human freedom." He even speaks, in their relationship to faith, of "the difficult knowledge of such qualities as we encounter in painting and music, the even more difficult knowledge of good and evil, above all the most difficult knowledge of the Transcendent."[61] Here were points where an integral connection between faith and knowledge, nature and history, science and religion, might have been developed. These, however, were fragments, intimations only, and, unfortunately, they were published posthumously.

In the theologians' manner of speaking about the mystery and transcendence of the Divine there always seemed to hover in the background the specter of a Kantian-like thing-in-itself that could never be known—Tillich's unfathomable ground of being and "God above god"; H. Richard Niebuhr's God as "that great Void," "the great abyss."[62] There also seemed to be at work a Kantian-like distinction between the realm of faith and freedom and the realm of knowledge and necessity, a dichotomy that they never overcame. Indeed, their work seemed to represent an extension into the twentieth century of the basic Kantian project to find a grounding for faith apart from knowledge. Recall Kant's famous, "I have found it necessary to deny *knowledge* of *God, freedom,* and *immortality* in order to find a place for *faith.*" If knowledge left no room for faith, perhaps "a place" for it could be established within the realms of feeling or of ethical action.

The two major streams of nineteenth-century, post-Kantian Protestant theology, emanating from and symbolized by Schleiermacher and Ritschl respectively, attempted to carry out the Kantian project by finding a solid foundation for faith either in the nature of religious experience (feeling) or in ethical action (will), as distinct from knowing. It may not be too grand an oversimplification to see these two major streams of modern Protestant theology reaching their twentieth-century culmination in the work—and perhaps even in the temperaments—of Paul Tillich and Reinhold Niebuhr especially: Paul Tillich with his "ecstatic reason," "ultimate concern," and sensuous feeling for the depth dimension of experience; Reinhold Niebuhr with his ethical earnestness and relentless testing of the origins and implications of faith in political-social action—with H. Richard Niebuhr in a real sense attempting to encompass both. It may be that one way of viewing the whole theological renaissance is as a major twentieth-century expression of the great Kantian and Protestant two-realm theory of truth as a solution to the problems of faith posed by the acceptance of an exclusively sense-bound reason and mechanistic science. It was a noble attempt, and its failure all the more momentous.

Addressing the leaders of the theological renaissance directly, Harvard analytic philosopher Morton White, writing in 1959, stated the problem they faced in just these terms. Challenging the theologians to come to grips with the question of knowledge (and shrewdly alluding to their own oft-expressed appeal to the needs of the whole man and turning it ironically against them), White wrote,

> I suggest . . . that the cease-fire proposed by the twentieth century for the war of the nineteenth, the attempt to arbitrate the nineteenth-century struggle by granting science a sphere of influence over knowledge and religion a sharply separated sphere of influence over feeling and will, is unworkable and necessarily unstable. For being religious in the sense of the question "Should I be religious?" involves commitment on all levels of experience, including one that is cognitive or taken to be cognitive by the religious man. Far from catering to the whole man in whose interest the cease-fire is often signed, the compromise view of religion as a purely emotive, or esthetic, or social affair encourages the most far-reaching kind of fragmentation.

Then drawing out the implications for higher education itself, White added, "and I suggest that any educational effort to nourish religious feeling or to stimulate religious action by trying to present an abstract essence of religion, conceived as the life of feeling and willing (as opposed to knowing), will fail."[63]

White had identified the heart of the problem. But, if the theologians were to respond to it on his terms, then he had, of course, also left them with a Hobson's choice: either to continue in the unsatisfactory split between knowledge and faith or to join the two in terms of the modern conception of knowing that had "no place" for faith. The theological reformers, by and large, attempted to defuse the problem, essentially by arguing that faith itself provided the bridge and could be found extended into and necessarily at work in even the most positivist of scientists—but, since in the end it did not at all change the scientists' positivism, such a bridge built from the faith side turned out to be a fragile structure that could bear little weight.

The so-called radical theologians of the 1960s took up the kind of challenge posed by Morton White and addressed the problem of knowledge. And they chose to do so on his terms. They would bravely accept—indeed they would embrace as returning prodigals—the modern world, its culture, its totally empirical, pragmatic ways of knowing—and then see what, if anything, could be salvaged from and for faith.

Ten years after heralding the theological renaissance, the editor of *The Christian Scholar* found cause to ask, "Whence the theological doldrums? Why is there so little intensive theological work being done today?"[64] Apparently the new radical theologies, which were beginning to occupy the theological spotlight did not yet count as serious, even though the *Scholar* had been among the first to introduce them.[65] With his eye on the mainstream, however, the editor was giving expression to a widespread sense that the theological enterprise was stuck.

THE SECULAR THEOLOGIANS

The emergence in the early 1960s of the self-named "secular" and "radical theologians" reflected a deep sense that the neo-orthodox-inspired theological renaissance had run its course and had proved wanting. There were varieties of radical theology, as exemplified in the thought of the major American figures of the movement: Harvey Cox, William Hamilton, and Paul van Buren.[66] In their works can be seen clearly the main dimensions of what was suddenly being widely embraced and proclaimed by a host of theological writers as Christian secularism. With their differences, the various secular theologians all agreed in taking the modern mind-set as normative and definitive for all statements about reality, theological statements especially. All shared the further conviction that the modern mind simply had no place for traditional theological affirmations, in fact had little inkling even of what they meant, above all those faith affirmations that spoke of realities transcending the world of empirical, sense experience. All had a deep appreciation for the potential that they detected within modern consciousness and culture for new possibilities of human freedom and responsibility, which they wanted to protect and nourish.

Weaving throughout the whole radical theology movement was the influence of the German theologian Dietrich Bonhoeffer.[67] In his letters from prison, while awaiting execution for his part in the plot against Hitler's life, Bonhoeffer had suggested that the human being has now "come of age" and no longer needs God as a stopgap problem-solver to take over where human weakness fails; he suggested that a "religionless Christianity" is demanded for modern human beings. Whatever Bonhoeffer himself meant, his fragmentary thoughts from prison came to have a wide influence, first among the neo-orthodox in their efforts to engage the world seriously, then more radically among the secular theologians in their wholehearted affirmation of secularity and human autonomy.

Probably the most popular of the new theologians, Harvey Cox, was also the least radical. His book, *The Secular City,* had been written originally as an NSCF study book, before it made the best-seller lists. As Langdon Gilkey has pointed out, Cox's thinking was still cut very much in the neo-orthodox pattern.[68] Almost all the main themes of neo-orthodoxy are present in his work but, at crucial points, are given a new twist and emphasis. What Cox did essentially was to join the biblical theology of the neo-orthodox with a renovated version of an older progressive faith in the divine immanence, now seen to be working through the structures, processes, and values of modern secularized society. As we have seen, this sense of progress was also present in the neo-orthodox theologians' affirmation of the secular, despite their criticisms of liberal versions of progress. Cox fastened on this theme from the neo-orthodox and highlighted it, extolling the benefits of the modern world, while downplaying its shadow side in a way the older neo-orthodox seldom would have done.

Employing the neo-orthodox strict dichotomy between nature and history, Cox affirmed the latter as the sole arena of divine activity and human meaning.[69] Secularization with its rejection of all forms of transcendence in nature, its desacralized natural world given by science, its pragmatic instrumentalism in politics, its destruction of traditional institutions and values in an urban-industrial culture, and its exaltation of human capacities and responsibility—all he interpreted as "an authentic outcome of the impact of biblical faith on western history."[70] The process of secularization, interpreted in light of the biblical imagery of the creation, Sinai, the exodus, Easter, and so on, has been, Cox said, "a glorious liberation," a progressive striving toward an ever greater potential for peace, justice, and ecumenical harmony.[71] Cox could affirm the meaningfulness of history, and more specifically of its secularization, because he could view it through the spectacles of the neo-orthodox understanding of the biblical story. Thus, he could have both God and secularization—the latter as the working out of the divine will in history.

Not so, the others. They were more consistent than Cox and saw that the biblical story, myths, and images were no more plausible to the modern mind than any other transcendent references. Modern ways of knowing and speaking simply had no place for affirmations of spiritual reality. The modern mind found them, therefore, to be meaningless; hence, the Nietzschean expression of the "death of God" to characterize the outlook of the radicals.

The "death of God" did seem to mean different things. Since Thomas Altizer was also a major spokesman for the use of the term, and was often identified as one of the secular theologians, a couple of observations about him might be helpful. Altizer was not only the most interesting but also the most orphic of the new theologians. For him, God seems to have once existed but then to have really died in the crucifixion of Christ in a kind of kenotic emptying into the world as we now experience it. Transcendence had emptied itself, died into immanence—"the newly discovered radical immanence of modern man, an immanence dissolving even the memory or the shadow of transcendence."[72] It is still possible to be a Christian, in Altizer's view, but, radically, to follow Christ in his humanness means rejecting all traditional expressions of faith in a God of transcendence, a transcendence that now threatens to stifle the new freedoms and responsibilities that God in dying has opened up to man. In this Altizer sounded much like the secular theologians, and as a consequence was often considered simply one of them.

In many ways, however, as Langdon Gilkey has pointed out, Altizer, far more than the others, has a close affinity with older Christian traditions, beginning with the Pauline. Altizer's own emphasis on immanence contains within it the possibility and hope of an inner transformation of the world into which the transcendent God died. There is the strongest of suggestions that, if "the Word became flesh," the flesh might yet become Word. "It is," Altizer writes,

> precisely by a radical movement of turning away from all previous forms of light that we can participate in a new totality of bliss, an absolutely immanent totality embodying in its immediacy all which once appeared and was real in the form of transcendence, and a totality which the Christian must name as the present and living body of Christ.[73]

Here Altizer's use of the word immanence was ambiguous. Although immanence is supposed to have wiped out all memory and shadow of transcendence, Altizer himself, perhaps alone, seems to have been exempted from having forgotten since he continued seemingly to remember and to talk a lot about it.

But Altizer's immanence is really not that of the modern world. His is too full of the reality of the potential, *potentia,* the one dimension of reality above all that modern modes of knowing refuse to recognize and are incapable of dealing with. While he does not seem to have considered the possibility of developing qualitative ways of knowing capable of grasping *potentia* cognitively, Altizer clearly did not belong to the camp of the secular theologians. His primary significance for our purposes is that at the time he helped give currency to the phrase "the death of God," which the truly secular theologians employed for their own purposes but actually very differently from Altizer.

In the work of William Hamilton and Paul van Buren the main characteristics of the rapidly spreading, radical secular theology are most clearly seen. For William Hamilton the death of God seems to have meant that God never existed, but that it is only now that the human being is fully awakening to the fact of the divine absence and unreality.[74] Hamilton began his move from neo-orthodoxy in the realization that his faith in the wholly other of revelation no longer carried the persuasive power needed to outweigh and overcome his doubts.[75]

Langdon Gilkey has helpfully discussed Hamilton's radical turn and in such a way that shows its direct relevance to the faith-knowledge issue.[76] Within neo-orthodoxy there was sometimes thought to be one point at which knowledge of God was generated; namely, at the moment of the decision of faith when one could be said to "know" the brute fact of the divine existence.[77] From this point one then could go to the scriptures, to the church tradition, and to human experience, and from these develop further deductions of the probable nature of the Divine, the latter to be further tested in faith through life. But this was all secondary to and dependent on the initial knowledge of the brute fact of God given in the faith encounter. "Outside of that relation to the 'Wholly Other,' " writes Gilkey, "experience in general was devoid of God, the world was secular, and no theological language was possible." At the point where doubt overwhelmed faith, then, it was, as Hamilton himself put it, "a short step, but a critical one, to move from the otherness of God to the absence of God."[78] And once that move is made, and if the modern conception of knowing, with its elimination of the Divine from every realm but faith, is accepted as normative and beyond the possibility of being transformed, then the conclusion must be that God is dead.

It was Paul van Buren, however, who brought into clearest relief the epistemological issues that lay at the heart of the whole new secular theology. Van Buren was a philosophical theologian working out of the perspective of linguistic analysis, which he took to be the most recent and careful articulation of what the modern world agreed on as the canons of meaningful discourse. Van Buren maintained that, whatever it may have meant to past generations, language about God is no longer meaningful to modern consciousness, which demands empirical verification of all reality claims. Van Buren fully accepted the finality of the ways of knowing that dominate and shape modern science, technology, and "the whole industrial process." These are what increasingly form the modern experience of the world.[79] The empirical base of this way of knowing makes language of a transcendent God—in fact, it makes the entire notion of a spiritual world—unintelligible to modern human beings.

The idea of God, van Buren said, "has been ruled out by the influence of modern science in our thinking." And, in words that applied as well to the entire secular theological movement, he made it clear that "in making such statements, we reveal our own commitments to modern science."[80] He regarded any appeal to special religious ways of knowing set off from the scientific methods by which he assumed we come to know the sense world as misconceived and, in any case, doomed. This meant that for the theologian, who carried the same assumptions about knowable reality as everyone else in the modern world and thereby was no less secular than anyone else, the only intellectually honest course was to abandon talk about God and transcendence entirely. "We do not know 'what' God is," he said, "and we cannot understand how the word 'God' is being used."[81] It must be given up. Neither faith assertions nor metaphysical speculations are meaningful to the modern secular mind-set, so, for all practical purposes God is dead to the modern world.

Nevertheless, all the secular theologians argued that it is still possible in the time of the death of God to be a Christian. Van Buren's way of explaining how this could be is the clearest, and it seems to express what most of the others meant. It is still possible to be a Christian, if what were once regarded as statements about God are really seen as descriptions of specific attitudes and outlooks on life. The language of faith has a meaning, he maintained, if it is taken to refer to the "Christian way of life," rather than to something having cosmological being and significance.[82] The Christian faith has meaning then as "a certain form of life," "a way of life," which shapes attitudes, influences behavior, and gives patterns to human relationships.[83]

The secular theologians, as their name suggests, had a deep appreciation for the achievements and potential for the future that they discerned in modern secular consciousness. Radical possibilities for human freedom, new opportunities and capacities for self-determination and responsibility, new forms of interhuman relationships, and enhanced scientific-technological control of nature for human betterment—all these the theologians saw as possibilities for modern human beings that had not been available to earlier generations.

Their challenge to those who would try to bridge the gap between faith and knowledge was, therefore, twofold. They made unmistakably clear the difficulty of maintaining and speaking about faith in a spiritual world while simultaneously participating in the assumptions of the modern secular world. At the same time, they challenged those who would criticize the modern mind-set, first, to show that the critics themselves were not already irremediably shaped by it and unable really to transcend it and, further, that if, nevertheless, they did claim to be able to criticize and go beyond the modern mind-set, to demonstrate that they could do so without sacrificing the new potentials for enhanced human freedom, responsibility, and rational control of nature that the modern world uniquely seemed to offer.

Running throughout the secular theology is great enthusiasm for these possibilities of modern secular consciousness, an optimism about its prospects, and a desire not to be left out. As Hamilton plainly said, the theologians wanted desperately to be part of the movement "from cloister to world," which meant, "from place of protection and security, of order and beauty, to the bustling middle class world of the new university, of politics, princes, and peasants."[84]

In their enthusiasm for modernity, however, the secular theologians seemed to have sensed, somewhat inchoately, that the potentials for progress they found so appealing in the modern world also were endangered by that world. This led them, therefore, to stress three things in addition to their otherwise unqualified celebration of modernity. First, they affirmed that, in the man Jesus, the modern Christian, who is now pursuing a totally secular "way of life," has a model of what it means to be truly human. Second, the meaning of the truly human is to be further filled out and nourished, not by drawing on theological analyses of human nature, but through the insights afforded by literature and the humanities. Altizer draws on Blake, Hegel, Melville, Freud and Nietzsche; Hamilton calls on Dostoevsky, Shakespeare, T. S. Eliot, Saul Bellow, and others for insight into the human and speaks of "a Hamlet theology" and "an Orestes theology"; van Buren moves from the theological seminary to teaching in the university and makes the humanities the prime source and context for what is now going to be called theology. Third, they all affirmed the importance, again with Jesus as the model, of working for liberating social change. In all of this, however, the secular theologians were caught in a number of inconsistencies and problems.

For one thing, their appeal to the picture of Jesus that emerges from the historical analysis of the scriptures was a problem in itself. Since they could by no means have been oblivious of the uncertainties about Jesus resulting from historical biblical criticism, it is difficult not to conclude that their "Jesus" was a conscious projection of their own making, a construct on which to hang their own ethical and political predilections. However, the favored place of Jesus also may have represented the vestige of an older piety not yet completely expunged from their thinking.

Second, in translating God statements into statements about the human being with a humanistic content and, at the same time, to profess allegiance to the modern mind-set is certainly less than consistent. After all, the humanities as much as theology had been on the defensive in modern culture since at least the middle of the nineteenth century. As the neo-orthodox had seen clearly, to speak of "the truly human" as other than a machine or a higher animal is already to move well beyond the limits of modern secular reason. "Freedom," "self-giving love," "commitment"—all the things the secular theologians loved to speak about in describing the truly human and the possibilities of secular man, are categories of the spirit, and have no more place than God in a purely quantitative, instrumentalist, and utilitarian way of knowing. If the modern mind-set results in the death of God, it leads just as inexorably, as C. S. Lewis once put it, to the "abolition of man." For scientifically committed secular theologians to turn to the humanities for their primary sources seems curiously old-fashioned and, in light of the fate of the humanities during the past two centuries, exceedingly naive.

Third, the attempt to translate theological statements into "life forms," dispositions, moral patterns—in short, in van Buren's phrase, into "a Christian way of life" also had its peculiar problems. What it represented was essentially a kind of refined emotivism or decisionism, since the ultimate basis for the preferred "way of life" was essentially arbitrary preference. To the extent that this "way of life" arose solely out of the linguistic conventions of the Christian community and tradition, it represented a kind of communal positivism—a communal, linguistic *positing* of life forms and moral givens— which in the end is about all that the modern mind-set permits as the ultimate moral reality. In effect, it made communal convention the ultimate—hardly an assuring safeguard for the flowering of human freedom, spontaneity, and creativity.

Finally, the theologians' call to work for liberating social change also was problematic. Again Cox's version of liberating social change was by far the most popular and influential, but it did not differ basically from the others.

For the secular theologians it is in transforming, often revolutionary, social change that the truly human—and for Cox, the Divine in the world—manifests itself. The task of the church, then, as Cox put it, is "to help the world to be the world." The church could do this in two ways: one, by encouraging the secularization process through science and technology so as to extirpate from the world any last traces of mystical and magical enchantment that might otherwise threaten the human sense of self-determination; two, by finding out where the movements of revolutionary change are at work and identifying with them. The primary task of the church is, therefore, in a striking reversal of the neo-orthodox approach, "the discussion of social change" and "finding out where the action is," and only then to do theology.[85] Faith exists here primarily as an attitude that energizes action; and success in action becomes the test of truth.

As a consequence, social action would become increasingly disconnected from any kind of rational reflection, theological or otherwise, that was not either, simply, tactical scheming or mere articulation of arbitrary value preferences. Meaning would have a tendency to collapse into power politics. And the hopes of the original theological renaissance that the university might be engaged at its intellectual center would become about as intelligible to the followers of the new secular emphasis as God-language.

The radical theologians saw the inconsistency in the neo-orthodox attempt to affirm a faith in transcendence and simultaneously to accept the strictures of modern sense-bound ways of knowing. They accordingly eliminated the transcendent and kept the world as the modern mind-set knew it. That they then went ahead, as scientific naturalists have always done, to smuggle in their own value preferences for what constitutes the truly human, in the theologians' case under the cover of the man Jesus, was their own inconsistency.

On their own grounds, they had no basis for affirming their particular, intangible human values any more than for affirming the transcendent. Neither had a place in a purely quantitative, instrumentalist world. The separation between a narrow sense-bound world of knowledge and the other dimensions of human experience (including what little etiolated vestiges of faith were left) remained as gaping as ever.

Nature was rendered all the more vulnerable to technological and industrial exploitation. After all, the call was to demystify the world completely, scouring from it any shade of inner life, so that there should be nothing left in nature to give second thoughts about taking it apart for human purposes. It is characteristic of both the neo-orthodox and the secular theologians that nature has no place in either. In seeking to affirm the human potential, the secular theologians had actually sanctioned all the characteristics of modernity that most threaten that potential.

The secular theologians had adopted unreservedly the conception of knowable reality that had long been conventional in the modern West. As van

Buren phrased his own position, and it applied equally to the others, they had accepted uncritically the methods of the thinking of "an industrialized, scientific age." They had, in his words, "taken them seriously and accepted them without qualification."[86] In their eagerness to be part of things, they had adopted without hesitation all the epistemological conventions and habits of "the bustling middle-class world of the new university." At bottom they were not radical theologians so much as they were conventional epistemologists.

THE RADICAL EMPIRICISTS: THEOLOGIANS ON THE MARGIN OF THE MAINSTREAM

Very much part of the theological renaissance, yet in many ways rejected or ignored by mainstream representatives of that renaissance, was a theological perspective that can be variously described as neo-naturalist, process, and radical empiricist, or all together, depending on the emphases and nuances of the individual thinkers involved. This perspective received its original impetus and articulation among theologians and students associated with the Federated Theological Faculty of the University of Chicago. Its leading representatives included such persons as Henry Nelson Wieman, Charles Hartshorne, Bernard Loomer, Bernard Meland, and younger theologians such as Daniel Day Williams and John Cobb.

All in this tradition were concerned to take with full seriousness the challenge posed by the dominant modern mentality to the Christian faith and to religious-ethical-cultural meaning of every kind. They seemed to grasp the radicalness of this challenge with a clarity not shared by most other Protestant theologians. This alone makes even a brief look at them important. They were all deeply influenced in one way or another by the process philosophy of Alfred North Whitehead, upon which they drew directly. For many of them, Charles Hartshorne's exposition and development of Whitehead's view was especially influential.

All were concerned and convinced that it is possible to overcome the dualism between the modern mind-set and the experiences and affirmations of faith. But they were also convinced that this overcoming of dualism could be achieved only through a work of radical theological-philosophical reconstruction carried out on both sides of the faith-knowledge relationship. That they took up this task in ways that suggested far-reaching implications for the possibility of enlarging our conceptions of how and what we can experience and know makes taking note of them in our story essential—especially since their work in this respect was, and continues to be, widely ignored in much of mainstream Protestant theology. We will undertake here only a brief, and I fear all-too-summary, look at mainly the epistemological implications and promise represented by this theological perspective. More than that would quickly outrun the scope of this study. The focus will be primarily on three theologians of the tradition: Henry Nelson Wieman, Bernard Meland, and John Cobb.[87]

These theologians had a contact point with the mainstream of the theological renaissance in their conception of faith as ultimate concern. Much more than most of the mainstream, however, they saw faith not only requiring a cognitive context but also containing an essential cognitive drive and function. As Bernard Meland put it, faith is "a psychic and social energy" that orients the human being toward the ultimate creative and qualitative sources of life.[88] Faith nurtures the sensibilities, "the instruments of perception, conscious awareness, imagination and feeling," that give knowledge. Faith itself is "an act of inquiry."[89] From this perspective alone, the basic Kantian dualisms between knowledge and faith, knowledge and ethics, nature and history, which otherwise ran so deep through the theological renaissance, were being fundamentally called into question.

Henry Nelson Wieman attempted to follow consistently the modern demand that religion and ethics must be grounded, not in dogma nor in rational speculation, but in concrete, empirical experience.[90] "More than any other major theologian prior to World War II," wrote John Cobb, "he [Wieman] took his stand within the modern vision of reality."[91] The position Wieman developed is accurately described as neonaturalism: It is a naturalism because in taking experience as ultimate, it rejects all forms of dualistic separation between faith and knowledge, religion and science, nature and history. It is a neonaturalism because it rejects the reductionism of modern science, holding that a real empirical stance, attentively adhered to, will reveal the fundamentally qualitative nature and richness of experience. It was in this sense, very much in the spirit of William James, a radical empiricism.

Wieman took as his starting point the late modern conviction, articulated especially by Whitehead (as well as others), that the world consists not of changeless being nor of substantial entities but is an ongoing process of events. These events, Wieman pointed out, are qualitative in their basic nature. "Quality," he wrote, "is the ultimate substance of the world out of which all else is made."[92] The events of experience are apprehended directly by feeling as qualities. The transformation of this primordial and preconscious experience of quality into what Wieman calls "qualitative meaning" is the experience of the good, of intrinsic good.

Wieman affirmed always the possibility of a "creative increase in qualitative meaning."[93] God is to be found in experience as "creative good," as the creative process or the "creative event" that makes possible and works for ever greater achievement of "qualitative meaning." "What human life is all about," wrote Wieman, "is to achieve forms of thought and action which are as rich as possible with felt quality."[94] In short, experience itself has the possibility for an ever enriching experience and knowledge of qualities and qualitative meaning. Faith presses for and orients the human being toward this deeper knowledge and experience of the qualitative and the good, of the divine.[95] Thus, the qualities of beauty, love, truth, and the grounds of faith itself in its many dimensions are not excluded from potentially knowable experience.

Some aspects of Wieman's thought came under criticism from colleagues in his own tradition. While highly appreciative of Wieman's efforts to speak meaningfully of God and of the reality of qualities, Bernard Meland and John Cobb, for example, criticized him for being at important points too much in thrall to certain aspects of modernism. Meland saw him, like John Dewey (whose thought Wieman was very close to at many points), too attached to the modernist emphasis on novelty and change to be able adequately to consider what needs to be conserved and transmuted from the past.[96] Cobb saw Wieman as too tied to a particular ontology of process that arbitrarily made it impossible to take into account the full nature of personal existence.[97]

At other places Wieman seems unable to free himself from even more naive expressions of the modern mind, in the process seriously violating his own commitment to radical empiricism. Wieman, for example, did not accept all of Whitehead uncritically, especially what he considered to be White-head's notion of an organic "cosmic consciousness." Wieman appealed, however, for his main evidence against organicism at this point to the characteristic modern picture of the universe as an inanimate, mechanistic, meaningless affair except for the singular and isolated experience of the human being.[98] Here his own radical empiricism seemed to desert him and to collapse into the narrowest, naive empiricism of the modern mind-set.

Just as serious, Wieman never seems to have been able to bring himself to follow through on the full cognitive implications of his conception of qualitative meaning. He frequently seemed ambivalent about whether the deeper intuition of qualities could properly become knowledge, perhaps sharing with the neo-orthodox the fear that the modern narrow conception of knowledge would drag down the fullness of the intuitive encounter.

On the one hand, for example, Wieman spoke of deep feeling that can provide the basis for developing genuinely cognitive feelings, as distinct from unformed feelings that are merely self-referencing.[99] In this respect he spoke of "deep intuition," in which we can know other minds, and in which we know God.[100] On the other hand, however, he sometimes tended to draw a sharp and unbreachable line between the primary experience of qualities and knowledge strictly conceived.[101] When he drew this line, he identified intuitive insight with experience and reserved the term knowledge solely for the work of discursive and controlling reason.[102] If studiously adhered to, the distinction becomes self-cancelling. It cuts the ground from under a deepening of qualitative experience and qualitative meaning themselves. It makes even talking intelligibly about the deep sources of qualitative meaning an impossibility.[103] Most of the time, however, Wieman seems not to have stuck to this distinction in so total a way. He was usually able, therefore, to describe a primary encompassing form of cognition, variously called insight, intuition, and appreciative awareness, that can be the deep source and context for reason itself.

Important as they may be, the various criticisms of Wieman do not negate his achievement. He saw clearly the dangers to faith itself of a split between faith and knowledge, and he realized that this dualism could be surmounted only through an ever deepening qualitative experience and knowledge. Wieman himself attempted to give concrete expression to his commitment to the overcoming of the dualism of faith and knowledge by bringing his apprehension of qualitative meaning to bear on a variety of human disciplines and endeavors in education, economics, government, and history.[104]

Bernard Meland turned much more to Whitehead for his philosophical framework than did Wieman.[105] The task of the theologian in our time, said Meland, is to set the affirmations of faith "in a context which will give them intelligible and communicable power as meaningful."[106] That context could be provided, he thought, by a radical empiricism that sees that experience is fundamentally a flow of creative events all internally (not mechanistically) interrelated.[107] This flow of events is meaningful, qualitative, and woven together at the deepest level through feeling.[108] While feeling at this deep level is unconscious, the qualities and meanings it apprehends can be brought more and more into the consciousness of both the individual and the wider culture.[109] The expansion of meaning and qualitative enrichment depend, therefore, on ways of coming to know and bring to realization the qualitative dimensions of the world.

Meland's favorite expression for this fundamental qualitative way of knowing was "appreciative awareness."[110] Although Meland sometimes groped for an adequate characterization of "appreciative awareness," still he was able to depict with clarity essential aspects of what he meant. First, appreciative awareness is deeply cognitive. It is not merely an experiential response to the world; creative appreciation yields knowledge. Appreciative awareness he describes as "intellect deepened, sensitized, and informed by feeling which arises from sensibility."[111] It provides the knowledge of the non-sensory, relational, and qualitative realities—truth, beauty, the good, and so forth—that faith requires for its own substance.[112] In fact, he even described appreciative awareness as faith, the attitude of trust "assuming an explicit cognitive concern."[113]

Second, appreciative awareness is both objective and subjective. Meland moved to break out of the modern notion that all statements about values, purposes, meaning, and qualities are only subjective because they are thought to be tainted with feeling. Here, as with all Whiteheadians, feeling reaches out beyond itself as a fundamental fact of experience and source of knowledge.[114] Third, appreciative awareness does not reject technical and critical reason, but provides the qualitative context necessary for these more restricted modes of knowing to have intrinsic meaning and direction, which in themselves they lack. Appreciative awareness joins perceptive and imaginative understanding with critical and technical thought.[115] Finally, appreciative awareness can be nourished and further developed. It is "a form of thinking, or a level of thinking, which can be awakened and nurtured just as surely as discipline in logical analysis or precision in scientific thought can be achieved within the education process."[116]

It was from this perspective that in 1953 Meland wrote *Higher Education and the Human Spirit*.[117] Meland began this book by pointing out that the basic issue in higher education has to do with "the nature of thinking" that pervades the college and university. Attempts to bolster morals, aesthetics, or religion will all come to naught, he argued, if "the mode of thinking which defines the intellectual experience of a school" undercuts or has no place for these concerns.[118] To focus on morality without paying attention to thinking is to overlook the fact that goodness at its deepest level often lies well beyond ordinary morality and must be grounded in the human being's best imaginative, poetic, and perceptive capacities. Where these are ignored, morality quickly hardens or is extinguished.[119] Similarly with religion: The main problem facing religion in higher education, Meland wrote, "is basically a problem in the nature of thinking."[120]

In his treatment of higher education, Meland had three primary goals. In the first place, he developed, along the lines we have noted, his conception of the transformation of thinking as appreciative awareness. His second purpose was to show that higher education has as its main responsibility the nourishment of appreciative awareness as the necessary foundation and framework for all the disciplines of knowledge. Third, he tried to explore and set forth concretely the ways the curriculum and pedagogy of higher education could best serve these goals.

Meland did much to show that the arts of every kind, including those literary subjects that deal primarily with meaning and quality, are essential in developing cognitive, imaginative capacities in all areas. Much of Meland's attention in this book and elsewhere was given to the arts, symbolism, myth, and religion as sources and modes of appreciative awareness. He did not direct the same attention to the sciences and to the questions of what the transformation of thinking in these fields might require, and what its implications might be. A certain important dualism still remained, but in showing the aesthetic nature of all knowing, he had identified an essential point of departure for surmounting that dualism.

Meland's book received little attention from other Protestants deeply involved with American higher education. The emphasis on thinking and imaginative transformation did not appear to them a compelling priority.

The most comprehensive attempt to deal with the problem of the Christian faith in the modern world was that undertaken by John Cobb. As Cobb put it, the basic issue could be simply stated. For more and more people in the culture, and not just for a few intelligentsia, the Christian vision was fading because the term God had lost its meaning. It had become "an empty word."[121] Certain presuppositions of the modern worldview—that reality is at bottom physical and mechanistic and can be apprehended only through sense experience—made meaningful discourse about God impossible. Associated primarily with the rise of modern science, and widely thought necessary to it, these assumptions, consciously and unconsciously, had come increasingly to shape people's experience and understanding of the world.

Pointing at the incompatibility of the Christian faith with the dominant modern worldview was, of course, not especially novel with Cobb. The larger theological renaissance itself had its origins in what were initially thought to be solutions to the problem. These attempted solutions had taken primarily two forms. One, they were expressed as some kind of dualism, such as that between nature and history, that attempted to preserve a separate realm for faith and ethics apart from the realm of knowledge. Two, they took the form of advocating one or another alternative categories in place of God, categories variously thought to incorporate the ultimacy and basic meaning of God, but in terms more congenial to modern consciousness and sensibilities—categories such as "authentic existence," "being and the ground of being," "creativity," "the depth dimension," "love," "presence in suffering," "the truly human," and others.[122]

The dualistic solution Cobb rejected as inadequate simply because if the Christian faith could not be shown to correspond meaningfully with our larger view of reality, it had in all honesty to be abandoned. He pointed out further, however—and the clear grasp of this seems repeatedly to have eluded almost all mainstream theologians, including, and sometimes especially, the most "secular"—that attempts to replace God with other concepts and categories would also not work. These other categories had been emptied of their meaning by the modern mind-set every bit as much as the term God. What was demanded was a critique of the underlying presuppositions of modernity and, at the same time, the development of a convincing vision of reality that made discourse about God meaningful and compelling. The continuity of this analysis with the initial aims of the theological renaissance and the determination to pursue those aims consistently were both apparent.

Drawing deeply on Whitehead and Charles Hartshorne, Cobb attempted with philosophical rigor and precision just such a critique and constructive vision of reality. Without presuming to do adequate justice to the full philosophical-theological vision set forth by Cobb, we can take note of certain central emphases within it that addressed the faith-knowledge issues directly. In these Cobb was genuinely radical—far more radical than most of those who went by that title.

One consequence of a process, event-centered, and organic view of reality, as Cobb developed it, was that it made possible a thoroughgoing critique of naive conceptions of the ultimacy of physical matter. In a world of events interrelated directly in organic feeling awareness, the invisible and non-sensory are seen to have the primacy and ultimate actuality usually ascribed by the modern mind naively to physical matter. The physical is seen to be a product of more fundamental processes that can include, as Cobb put it, "what we usually call mental and spiritual phenomena."[123] An ultimate dualism between mind and matter becomes untenable, as does also the primacy of mechanistic relationships and physical causality. A view of the world in organic, process terms makes life, order, growth, and subjective experience, and all that these imply in qualitative richness and meaning, not secondary and ephemeral but primary and of the essence of things.

The human being, therefore, rather than having to be explained in terms of something else that reduces away the essentially human, becomes the starting point for all understanding. This the tradition of radical empiricism consistently stressed.[124] This need not, however, lead to ultimate relativism. An organic, qualitative view of reality makes it possible once again to recognize the importance of human experience as a clue to the universe, rather than as an anomaly to be explained away.[125] The human experience of feeling awareness—of the other, of qualities, and of meaning—becomes the starting point and analogue for understanding and talking about both nature and the spiritual.

An aesthetic awareness of the qualitative is the primary form of experience and the basis for all knowledge. Experience and knowledge of truth, beauty, and goodness, as well as ordinary qualities of color, sound, and so forth, is not that of a subjectivity enclosed within itself, but of a feeling, participatory subjectivity that is the underlying characteristic of the world.

In the human being, above all, the primacy of the non-sensory and of the invisible in all experience becomes apparent. At the most fundamental level, Cobb pointed out, for example, we do not experience another human being through our senses (or extensions of our senses through scientific instrumentality, such as microscopes and X-rays). "We never see other persons," writes Cobb, "only their bodies."[126] The human being as such is an invisible being and to proceed otherwise ultimately results in all kinds of theoretical and practical mischief. While, indeed, most of our ordinary experience is conveyed in conjunction with sense experience, or inferred from it, this experience itself presupposes for its possibility the non-sensory and invisible. Memory, temporal experience, a sense for the reality of the world, the felt grasp of internal relations with other events—the essential foundations of human experience, all are fundamentally non-sensory.[127] The possibility is, thus, opened for genuine non-sensory knowledge of the kind essential to knowledge of life and beauty in nature, as well as knowledge of the deepest human personal, ethical, and spiritual realities.

Cobb did not hold back in pointing out the implications. The recovery of a vital Christian vision that connected with the whole of life was now possible. Meaning could be restored to central concepts and categories of faith and experience that for many mainstream theologians had become painful embarrassments, almost taboos, to be avoided if possible, at most to be merely alluded to, and then only if absolutely necessary.

It now became possible, for example, to speak meaningfully and directly, and with prospects for increasing precision, about the reality of the human soul.[128] What is required for the expression and nurturing of the soul in all its dimensions—thinking, feeling, willing, valuing—could now also be considered. Intuitive knowledge of non-sensory realities also becomes of utmost importance for both science and religion. In the natural world it would become possible to speak meaningfully of action at a distance, to consider the reality and importance of other kinds of causality besides the purely mechanical, and to develop knowledge of the potential.[129] Religious intuition, the "nonsensuous perception of meanings," "extrasensory perception," a knowledge of moral ought in "imaginative feeling"—all could be talked about meaningfully and the conditions of their further development considered.[130] Language is recognized as the distinctively human carrier of qualities and meanings that point beyond language itself.[131] Body-free experience and knowing come to be seen as centrally important and not of merely peripheral interest.[132] The possibility of life after physical death is established and can be forthrightly taken up as a subject of utmost importance, to theologians especially (a subject which most mainstream theologians assiduously sought to avoid, as though broaching it were the height of bad taste).[133]

Most of Cobb's work remained within the domain of what could be established as philosophically and theologically necessary and possible. The emphasis was on the interpretation of existing science and of ordinary experience in the light of a new worldview. What was required for the actual transformation of knowledge and for the development of new capacities of intuitive insight remained to be developed. But Cobb had shown the importance of doing so, and he had advanced a daring and comprehensive philosophical-theological foundation for making it possible.[134]

The theologians of radical empiricism and process, however, continued throughout to be a marginalized group, on the edges of the mainstream theological renaissance. They had seen more clearly than others the extreme challenge to faith posed by the modern mind-set. And they had taken some bold measures to meet that challenge. By and large, however, the radical empiricists received little serious attention from the mainstream of the theological renaissance. The mainstream, including its secular versions, seemed unable even to grasp the radical empiricists' analysis of the seriousness of the threat posed by modern conceptions of reality to vital faith and meaning in all forms. Consequently, the radical empiricists' analysis of the problem, along with their attempted solutions to it, remained on the margins of the theological renaissance. Even as the renaissance began its decline, the new possibilities proposed by the radical empiricists were not considered seriously by most other mainstream Protestant theologians.

CONCLUSION

The mainstream Protestant theologians had come to embrace totally the conventions about knowing and the knowable world dominant in the university and modern culture. Neither the neo-orthodox nor those theologians, like the Niebuhrs and Tillich, who often went far beyond a strictly neo-orthodox position, were able to bridge the two realms of truth. The consequent adoption by the secular theologians of only one realm, that of modern scientific and technological truth, effectively eliminated the theological basis for the church's engagement with higher education. The theological collapse was complete by the mid-1960s. It would take only a short time, given a shove by the forces of social upheaval, for the rest of the church's efforts in higher education to tumble in on themselves as well.

NOTES

1. Larry Rasmussen, "Reinhold Niebuhr: Public Theologian," *Cross Currents* 38, no. 2 (summer 1988): 204. Rasmussen's article has a still more complete account of Niebuhr's activities, and, in addition, of his writing.

2. Morton White, *Religion, Politics, and the Higher Learning* (Cambridge, Mass.: Harvard University Press, 1959), 88–89.

3. Reinhold Niebuhr, *The Contribution of Religion to Cultural Unity*. Hazen Pamphlets, 13 (n.p., 1945; 3rd impression 1950), 10.

4. As distinct, for example, from faith as belief in propositions, derived from dogma or scripture or elsewhere, about the nature of reality.

5. Reinhold Niebuhr, "Religion and Modern Knowledge," in *Man's Destiny in Eternity*, ed. L. Lyman Windolph. The Gavin Lectures (Boston: Beacon Press, 1949), 121.

6. Ibid.

7. Reinhold Niebuhr, *The Contribution of Religion to Cultural Unity*, 5.

8. See, for example, Paul Tillich, *The Spiritual Situation in Our Technical Society*, ed. J. Mark Thomas (Macon, Ga.: Mercer University Press, 1988), 71ff.

9. Reinhold Niebuhr, *The Contribution of Religion to Cultural Unity*, 11.

10. Ibid.

11. Ibid., 31.

12. Tillich, *Systematic Theology* (Chicago: University of Chicago Press), 1: 99.

13. H. Richard Niebuhr, *Radical Monotheism and Western Culture* (New York: Harper & Row, 1970), 140–41.

14. Tillich, *Systematic Theology*, 1: 71–81.

15. Ibid., 79–80.

16. Ibid., 72–75.

17. Ibid., 73

18. Ibid.

19. Ibid., 53–54, 79, 111–12.

20. Ibid., 99–100.

21. Ibid., 74; also Tillich, *The Spiritual Situation*, 44–45.

22. See especially H. Richard Niebuhr, *The Meaning of Revelation* (New York: Macmillan Co., 1941).

23. Ibid., 139–40.

24. See Reinhold Niebuhr, *The Nature and Destiny of Man* (New York: Charles Scribner's Sons, 1953), 2: 64ff.

25. Reinhold Niebuhr, *The Nature and Destiny of Man*, 1: vii.

26. A constant theme for Reinhold Niebuhr; see, for example, ibid., 68ff.; 74ff.

27. Reinhold Niebuhr, *The Nature and Destiny of Man*, 1: 164.

28. Ibid., 2: 67.

29. Ibid., 64.

30. Here, in all three theologians as throughout the whole of neo-orthodoxy, the influence of Martin Buber's conceptions of I-Thou and I-It relationships is patent.

31. See, for example, Paul Tillich, *Theology of Culture* (New York: Oxford University Press, 1959), 61ff.

32. Tillich, *The Spiritual Situation*, 100–1.

33. Ibid., 102.

34. Tillich, *Systematic Theology*, 1: 131, 238–41; H. Richard Niebuhr, *The Responsible Self: An Essay in Christian Moral Philosophy* (New York: Harper & Row, 1963), 157.

35. Reinhold Niebuhr, *The Nature and Destiny of Man*, 2: 50.

36. Tillich, *Systematic Theology*, 1: 79.

37. Paul Tillich, "The Relationship Today Between Science and Religion," in *The Student Seeks an Answer*, ed. John A. Clark, Ingraham Lectures in Philosophy and Religion at Colby College, 1951–1959 (Waterville, Maine: Colby College Press, 1960), 298.

38. Tillich, *Systematic Theology*, 1: 238.

39. Tillich, *Theology of Culture*, 61–62.

40. H. Richard Niebuhr, *The Meaning of Revelation*, 94–95.

41. Ibid, 97.

42. Tillich, *Systematic Theology*, 1: 72–73, 109.

43. Ibid., 1: 109.

44. John B. Cobb, Jr., *Living Options in Protestant Theology: A Survey of Methods* (Philadelphia: Westminster Press, 1962), 289.

45. H. Richard Niebuhr, *The Meaning of Revelation*, 93.

46. Ibid., 176ff.

47. Paul Tillich, "Reinhold Niebuhr's Doctrine of Knowledge," in *Reinhold Niebuhr: His Religious, Social, and Political Thought*, ed. Charles W. Kegley and Robert W. Bretall (New York: Macmillan Co., 1961), 36–43. As we have seen, for all practical purposes, despite his concept of ontological reason, Tillich does not end up far removed from Niebuhr. This will be even more apparent in the discussion of the theological reformers' attitude toward science below.

48. See, for example, Reinhold Niebuhr, *The Nature and Destiny of Man*, 2: 60–61.

49. Langdon Gilkey has made this point very strongly. See Gilkey, *Naming the Whirlwind: The Renewal of God-Language* (Indianapolis and New York: Bobbs-Merrill Co., 1969) 95–104.

50. Weber's view of ethics is often described as "decisionism," since, if ultimate ends and values are seen as having no rational grounding, they can only be decided on arbitrarily. "Decisionism" and "emotivism" both describe the arbitrariness of all ethics in the modern world in which all knowledge has been delimited by instrumental rationalism. See Stephen P. Turner and Regis A. Factor, *Max Weber and the Dispute Over Reason and Value: A Study in Philosophy, Ethics, and Politics* (London: Routledge &

Kegan Paul, 1984). Recall Alasdair McIntyre's contention that emotivism still describes the specific character of the modern age. Alasdair McIntyre, *After Virtue: A Study in Moral Theory* (Notre Dame, Ind.: University of Notre Dame Press, 1981), 21.

51. Reinhold Niebuhr, "The Tyranny of Science," *Theology Today*, 10 (January 1954): 468.

52. Ibid., 472–73.

53. See, for example, H. Richard Niebuhr, *Radical Monotheism*, 138.

54. Ibid., 78–89, 127–41.

55. Paul Tillich, *The Essential Tillich*, ed. F. Forrester Church (New York: Macmillan Publishing Co., 1987), 212, 251.

56. Paul Tillich, "The Relationship Today between Science and Religion," in *The Student Seeks an Answer*, 302.

57. Tillich, *Systematic Theology*, 1: 11.

58. Paul Tillich, *Dynamics of Faith* (New York: Harper & Row, 1957), 81.

59. Tillich, *The Spiritual Situation*, 165.

60. H. Richard Niebuhr, *The Responsible Self*, 151–52.

61. H. Richard Niebuhr, *Faith on Earth: An Inquiry into the Structure of Human Faith*, ed. Richard R. Niebuhr (New Haven, Conn.: Yale University Press, 1989), 38–40.

62. Paul Tillich, *The Courage to Be* (New Haven, Conn.: Yale University Press, 1952), 186–90; H. Richard Niebuhr, *Radical Monotheism*, 122.

63. Morton White, *Religion, Politics, and the Higher Learning* (1959), 92–93.

64. *The Christian Scholar* 47, no. 1 (spring 1964): 3.

65. For example, John Wren-Lewis, "Science, the World, and God," *The Christian Scholar* 42, no. 3 (September 1959): 169–84; Ronald Gregor Smith, "A Theological Perspective of the Secular," *The Christian Scholar* 43, no. 1 (March 1960): 11–24; William Hamilton, "Daring To Be the Enemy of God," *The Christian Scholar* 46, no. 1 (spring 1963): 40–54; William Hamilton, "The Death of God Theology," *The Christian Scholar* 48, no. 1 (spring 1965): 27–48.

66. William Hamilton, *The New Essence of Christianity* (New York: Association Press, 1961); William Hamilton and Thomas Altizer, *Radical Theology and the Death of God* (Indianapolis: Bobbs-Merrill Co., 1966); Paul van Buren, *The Secular Meaning of the Gospel* (New York: Macmillan Co., 1963); Harvey Cox, *The Secular City: Secularization and Urbanization in Theological Perspective* (New York: Macmillan Co., 1965); Thomas Altizer, *The Gospel of Christian Atheism* (Philadelphia: Westminster Press, 1966). I have also found extremely helpful Gilkey, "The Radical Theologies," chap. 3 in *Naming the Whirlwind*, 107–46; and Thomas W. Ogletree, *The Death of God Controversy* (Nashville and New York: Abingdon Press, 1966).

67. See, for example, William Hamilton, "Dietrich Bonhoeffer," in Altizer and Hamilton, *Radical Theology*, 95–112. Also see Harry E. Smith, *Secularization and the University* (Richmond: John Knox Press, 1968), 44–66.

68. Gilkey, *Naming the Whirlwind*, 25–26.

69. Cox, *The Secular City*, 25.

70. Ibid., 20–21.

71. Ibid., 49.

72. Altizer, *The Gospel of Christian Atheism*, 22, passim.

73. Ibid., 153.

74. Hamilton and Altizer, *Radical Theology*, 37.

75. Hamilton, *The New Essence*, 55; Hamilton, "Thursday's Child," in Hamilton and Altizer, *Radical Theology*, 87–93.

76. Gilkey, *Naming the Whirlwind*, 115–24.

77. It was a kind of positivism of the divine fact. Indeed, it is remarkable the extent to which neo-orthodox descriptions of the divine-human faith encounter are sometimes couched in language filled with overtones of the naive realism of nineteenth-century science and twentieth-century logical positivism. "Faith," wrote Richard Niebuhr, for example, "is at least as much an unavoidable counterpart of the presence of God as sense experience is an unavoidable counterpart of the presence of natural entities or powers . . . but faith and God belong together somewhat as sense experience and physical reality do." H. Richard Niebuhr, *Radical Monotheism*, 12–13. Elided in the quote is Niebuhr's acknowledgment that the analogy is inadequate. What is lacking in the original quote is any awareness of the crucial importance and presence of the *concept*, without which sense experience by itself is totally helpless to give us any kind of world at all. But the willingness of Niebuhr to use this flawed analogy is significant. Perhaps in part because they feared the snares of idealism, the neo-orthodox, when they considered the problem of knowledge, were constantly prone to fall into the problems of naive realism.

78. Gilkey, *Naming the Whirlwind*, 117; Hamilton, *The New Essence*, 55.

79. Van Buren, *The Secular Meaning of the Gospel*, 17.

80. Ibid., 100.

81. Ibid., 84.

82. Ibid., 100–101.

83. Ibid., also Ogletree, *The Death of God Controversy*, 63.

84. Hamilton and Altizer, *Radical Theology*, 36.

85. Cox, *The Secular City*, 126.

86. Van Buren, *The Secular Meaning of the Gospel*, 102.

87. Although in many ways certainly sui generis, Wieman is important here because he identified central issues early and clearly, and he was among the first to maintain that modern experience on its own grounds demands a much richer, more comprehensive understanding of reality than the dominant modern mind-set is itself ready to recognize. Meland attempted to bring the process perspective to bear explicitly on higher education, and just at a moment when the theological renaissance was at its height and when the prospects for the church's engagement with the American college and university seemed most promising. John Cobb is the most important of the three. His development of a Christian natural theology based on Whitehead was the most systematic and comprehensive of all; and, in developing it, Cobb made clear its stunning implications for the possibilities of our experience and knowledge of the world. Moreover, Cobb has continued to develop his perspective in many areas, actually carrying out perhaps more fully than anyone, the original concern of the theological renaissance to bring theology to bear on the various disciplines of knowledge.

88. Bernard Meland, *Faith and Culture* (New York: Oxford University Press, 1953), 63ff.

89. Ibid., 112–16; also see Wieman, *Religious Inquiry: Some Explorations* (Boston: Beacon Press, 1968), passim.

90. My account of Wieman is based mainly on Henry Nelson Wieman, *The Source of Human Good* (Chicago: University of Chicago Press, 1946); idem, *Man's Ultimate Commitment* (Carbondale, Ill.: University of Illinois Press, 1958); and idem, *Religious Inquiry*. I have also found extremely useful the chapter on Wieman in Cobb, *Living Options in Protestant Theology*.

91. John B. Cobb, Jr., *God and the World* (Philadelphia: Westminster Press, 1969), 128.

92. Wieman, *The Source of Human Good*, 302.

93. For example, see Wieman, *The Source of Human Good*, 31–39, 162, 219; idem, *Religious Inquiry*, 24–27.

94. Ibid., *Man's Ultimate Commitment*, 96–97.

95. Ibid., 20–21.

96. Meland, *Faith and Culture*, 108–10.

97. Cobb, *Living Options in Protestant Theology*, 114–19. Later Cobb also criticized Wieman's notion of God as "creative good" as carrying "overtones of meaning which are not really accessible within the modern vision," which Wieman's radical empiricism demanded that they be. See Cobb, *God and the World*, 128–29.

98. Wieman, *Religious Inquiry* 40–45.

99. Wieman, *The Source of Human Good*, 306; 142.

100. Ibid., 185–86.

101. See, for example, Wieman, *Man's Ultimate Commitment*, 136ff.

102. Dewey, even more than Wieman, restricted the conception of knowledge itself, as distinct from experience, entirely to operational and controlling modes of knowing. Fortunately, Wieman was not as consistent as Dewey on this point. For the baneful consequences of this restriction in Dewey's thought, see Douglas Sloan, "John Dewey's Project for Saving the Appearances," *Revision* 13, no. 4 (summer 1991): 23–41.

103. Wieman's concern here seems to have been twofold: to maintain that there can be no knowledge that sacrifices the tests of reason (analysis, logical coherence, verification, and so forth); and, more important, to protect the priority in all things of primal life experience—to ensure that the richness of qualitative experience not be diluted and impoverished by the dominance of an abstract and manipulative conceptuality. Both concerns are extremely important, but the total separation of insight and reason is highly problematic. The strict separation of insight and reason tends to leave insight totally in the realm of the vague and spontaneous, making the systematic nourishment of capacities for more powerful insight exceedingly difficult. It also makes any real interaction between insight and reason, and their mutual fructification and purification, one of the other, just as difficult. By denying to insight a genuinely deep and incorrigibly cognitive character, which the word itself surely suggests, the sharp separation would seem to make it impossible for reason even in the narrow sense to draw on insight.

104. See, for instance, Wieman, "Institutions under Commitment," Part 2 of *Man's Ultimate Commitment*.

105. See Meland, *Faith and Culture*, 57, 126.

106. Ibid., 57.

107. Ibid., 132–46; also, Bernard Eugene Meland, *Higher Education and the Human Spirit* (Chicago: University of Chicago Press, 1953), 24.

108. Meland, *Faith and Culture* 112, 142.

109. Meland, *Higher Education*, 24–25; idem, *Faith and Culture*, passim.

110. See especially, Meland, *Higher Education*, 16ff., 48–78. As we have seen, Wieman also used the expressions "appreciative awareness" and "appreciative consciousness."

111. Meland, *Higher Education*, 19.

112. Ibid., 19–20.

113. Meland, *Faith and Culture*, 120.

114. Ibid., 94–95, 112; also Meland, *Higher Education*, 65.

115. Meland, *Faith and Culture*, 125; Meland, *Higher Education*, 23ff.

116. Meland, *Higher Education*, 75.

117. See note 107 for full citation.

118. Meland, *Higher Education*, v.

119. Ibid., 1ff.

120. Ibid., 22.

121. See John B. Cobb, Jr., *A Christian Natural Theology: Based on the Thought of Alfred North Whitehead* (Philadelphia: Westminster Press, 1965), 13–14; also see idem, *Living Options in Protestant Theology*, 317–23; and idem, *God and the World*, 117ff.

122. Cobb, *A Christian Natural Theology*, 14–15.

123. Cobb, *God and the World*, 71.

124. For example, see Wieman, *Religious Inquiry*, 6; Cobb, *A Christian Natural Theology*, 27.

125. Cobb, *God and the World*, 73ff.

126. Cobb, *A Christian Natural Theology*, 239; also Cobb, *God and the World*, 73–74.

127. Cobb, *God and the World*, 76; idem, *A Christian Natural Theology*, 240–41.

128. See especially Cobb, *A Christian Natural Theology*, 47–91.

129. Ibid., 53, 240, 203 n. 53. Mental and final causality, impossible to admit within exclusively mechanistic models of nature, are essential for dealing with organic phenomena, such as form and growth; and they have great relevance for religious and historical experience. Likewise, knowledge of the potential is of essential importance for theology and for science, which, even in its most mechanistic forms, must presuppose the reality of the potential for working purposes, but must in its mechanism just as quickly finesse that assumption by declaring it purely formal or adapting it to hedging concepts, such as latent heat, latent energy, and emergence.

130. Cobb, *A Christian Natural Theology*, 53, 77; 115ff.; 233–34; 240; also see idem, *God and the World*, 66–86.

131. Cobb, *A Christian Natural Theology*, 59, 61–62.

132. Ibid., 66ff.

133. Ibid., 63–70; also Cobb, *God and the World*, 100–102.

134. Cobb continued to develop his theological-philosophical vision. Furthermore, he worked over the years to give concrete expression to his conviction of the need to overcome the dualism between faith and knowledge, bringing his theological vision to bear on one major field of knowledge after another—on science, ecology, ethics, religious dialogue, and, most recently, economics. As a consequence, the perspective represented preeminently by Cobb, and now more recently also by his student David Ray Griffin, has emerged as a major contender for the basis of a genuinely postmodern Protestant theology. In our concluding chapter, therefore, we will look at the process perspective as it continues to be developed by Cobb and Griffin. In addition to other books by Cobb already cited, see among his wider work especially John B. Cobb, Jr., *Christ in a Pluralistic Age* (Philadelphia: Westminster Press, 1975); idem, *The Structure of Christian Existence* (Philadelphia: Westminster Press, 1967); idem, *Beyond Dialogue: The Transformation of Christianity and Buddhism* (Philadelphia: Fortress Press, 1982); idem, *Matters of Life and Death* (Louisville, Ky.: Westminster/John Knox Press, 1991); John B. Cobb, Jr., and Charles Birch, *The Liberation of Life: From the Cell to the Community* (Cambridge and New York: Cambridge University Press, 1981); John B. Cobb, Jr., and Herman E. Daly, *For the Common Good: Redirecting the Economy toward Community, the Environment, and a Sustainable Future* (Boston: Beacon Press, 1989).

CHAPTER 5

The Campaign Collapses:
The Student Movement

STUDENT UNREST

As auspicious as the beginnings might have seemed for both the student and faculty initiatives during the 1950s, there were already straws in the wind that did not bode well. Among them were some shocks to the faith in the transformative potential of higher education that had originally helped impel the church's renewed engagement with the American college and university. A first blow came with the publication in 1957 of Philip Jacob's study, *Changing Values in College*.[1] The Jacob report, a summary of hundreds of studies made by others of the values of college students, was sponsored by the Hazen Foundation. While, thus, itself very much a product of the church's new involvement with higher education, the Jacob report was widely read and discussed throughout American higher education.

Unfortunately, concluded the Jacob report, the four years of college experience had little or no effect in altering basic student perceptions, values, and commitments. Jacob described the average college student as "gloriously contented" and "unabashedly self-centered," aspiring to material gratification with no other major aims in life. He found that although students respected traditional moral virtues, they were little disturbed by the moral laxity they thought prevalent among those around them, and they had little sense of social and political responsibility. They seemed to need religion, but did not see that it had anything to offer as a guide to life. The students valued college highly, not for the development of intellect and character, but mainly for what it had to offer in vocational training and social adjustment. And, Jacob said, the four year college experience seemed to have little influence in transforming these student values.[2]

The Jacob study was controversial; some similar studies seemed to confirm it, others to call it into question.[3] But it was the Jacob report that received the most attention, and that initially had the strongest impact on persons concerned about higher education, both inside and outside the churches. In 1962, Charles McCoy, one of the church's well-known writers on higher education, observed that the Jacob study is "the most widely known study of recent years." And in 1966, almost ten years after its publication, the authors of a major study of church-related colleges commented that the Jacob study had "probably been more widely discussed by college administrators than any other on higher education written since World War II."[4]

Reflecting the dominant response, *The Christian Scholar* expressed dismay about the challenge of the Jacob study to the faith in the transforming potential of higher education, with which, for instance, it and the Faculty Christian Fellowship had been launched. The journal noted that not only did the report not support "the widely held assumption that a college education has an important, almost certainly 'liberalizing effect.' . . . But equally or more distressing is the conclusion that the addition of knowledge and the supposed development of critical capacities does not necessarily lift the value patterns or influence value systems."[5] Even though it had been quickly challenged, the Jacob report had seriously called into question the hopes of all who had looked to higher education as the place to lay the foundations for fundamental personal and social transformation.

Further doubts along these lines were raised as studies critical of the faculty and the institution of higher education themselves began to appear. A study that received much attention, *The Academic Marketplace,* by Caplow and McGee, depicted the faculty as consumed mainly with career advancement and little interested in the integration of the curriculum, the ethical uses of knowledge, or the social role of higher education, to say nothing of "the basic questions." Another study that received even more attention, David Riesman, *Constraint and Variety in Higher Education,* analyzed higher education as a function of impersonal institutional forces over which there could be but little control.[6]

Reviewing these works, the editors of *The Christian Scholar* remarked that "most debilitating of all is the implication that at no point are academic peoples' lives determined by the basic values of the academic life," and that "the life of the mind in institutions of higher education may be eclipsed by the over-riding demands of expediency and technical adequacy."[7] A few years later, however, they affirmed again that "there must be a new and fundamental concern for the intellectual life" and for "the theological education of laymen," if there was to be "renewal in the churches" and "penetrating vitality in our academic communities."[8] However, the original faith and enthusiasm behind the church's new efforts in higher education had been sorely lamed.

No sooner had the Jacob report appeared than American campuses began to teem with new life and myriad activities that seemed to belie the picture of a complacent and socially unconcerned student body. If Jacob had sown seeds of doubt, the growing involvement of students in various social causes and protest movements may have at first rekindled some hopes, but almost just as quickly added confusion to doubt. By the end of the decade this student unrest, and the wider cultural turmoil it merged into, would become the occasion—partly causal but largely contextual—for the undoing of the church's twentieth-century engagement with American higher education.

The student unrest on American campuses during the 1960s was enormously complex. It was the peculiarly American expression of a wider movement of student protest that gripped most major universities of Western Europe as well. The civil-rights movement and the Vietnam War helped give peculiar shape and intensity to the American expression of student unrest but do not entirely explain it. Various attempts have been made to explain the student unrest of the 1960s. Most have added something to the picture; none, however, has sufficed either singly or in combination to provide entirely satisfactory causal explanations.[9]

There was, however, a certain characteristic of the student unrest of the 1960s, which, while not offering an exhaustive, causal explanation, does help to describe its peculiar nature and quality. This was that it had many of the marks of a religious movement. Both participants and observers noted this at the time and have done so since. Cultural critic Paul Goodman compared student unrest to the Protestant Reformation. Philosopher John Searle, a not altogether friendly analyst of student unrest, spoke of it as a "search for the sacred." Columbia University historian Walter Metzger said that "whatever else it may be besides, the student movement is at bottom religious." Brown University historian William McLoughlin described the upheavals of the 1960s as the beginning of the fourth American Great Awakening.[10]

The religious dimensions of the movement were manifest in two ways especially: in a search for meaning that was not bound by the confines of a narrow and thoroughly professionalized cognition; and in a moral earnestness and idealism that exhibited romantic, visionary, and prophetic attributes. That moral earnestness and the search for meaning could quickly veer off into some of their worst possible aberrations does not conflict with the religious nature of their origins.[11] These religious qualities were present in both of the main expressions that student unrest took in the 1960s: in political-social activism and in the search for new cultural values.

These two currents of student unrest—political and cultural—were often mixed and overlapped; and even later in the 1960s, when they could be clearly distinguished, they could not always be entirely separated. Often student unrest seemed to consist of a farrago of civil-rights demonstrations, antiwar protests, beards, sit-ins at the university president's office, the visions of LSD, pot-smoking, rap and rock sessions, the Beatles, Che Guevara, urban and rural communal experiments of hundreds of different varieties, Eastern philosophies, gurus, American Indian shamanism, dropping acid, passing out flowers, sitting zazen, sexual liberation, weaving, potting, gardening, rolfing, and multifarious humanistic psychologies. Nevertheless, political and cultural radicalism can be distinguished as two major expressions of student unrest in the 1960s, each of which presented its own particular challenges, to society and specifically to both the university and the church in the university.

Political Radicalism

The political activism of the student movement of the 1960s had important, specific religious roots and connections. The black civil-rights movement was probably more important for the beginnings of most American student political activism of the 1960s than the socialist traditions of some organized student political groups, such as the Students for a Democratic Society (SDS). The civil-rights movement had important direct religious roots in the traditions of the black church, and these were exemplified in the work of the Student Nonviolent Coordinating Committee (SNCC) and the preaching and example of Martin Luther King, Jr. It was the example of the black students in the civil-rights movement that began to awaken white students and to draw them first into working in the civil-rights movement and, increasingly, into activities aimed at establishing human justice and equality on a broader front. The nonviolence and moral example of SNCC was a direct inspiration to leaders of the SDS. In its beginnings the student political movement was not religious simply in a general sense, but had direct, overt connections with the prophetic tradition of biblical American religion. There was a certain biblical and prophetic quality about the earnest political faith and commitment of some, even, of the staunchest political activists of the older and newer left traditions, which stood as a model of moral seriousness to the politically concerned in the churches.

The explicit religious feeling and imagery of even the New Left, the more secular, socialist-oriented student organizations, remained unmistakable, though were usually translated into secular terms. The SDS Port Huron Statement of 1962, that remarkable document of American student dissent, set forth the SDS program with a declaration of faith in the human being worthy of the most venerable American transcendentalist and liberal religious traditions. "We regard *men*," the manifesto read, "as infinitely precious and possessed of unfulfilled capacities for reason, freedom, and love."[12] Staughton Lynd, old Leftist, used even more explicit religious imagery. "What I think I mean by being a radical," he said, "is functionally equivalent in many ways to what people have meant for two thousand years by being a Christian. . . . the radical is or should be someone who has a coherent vision of a better way that men can live, a paradise, as it were, which he continually endeavors to create on earth." Paul Potter, president of SDS, came to feel that the movement had missed its fullest possibility by not sufficiently heeding its deepest religious being. "Increasingly," Potter said,

> I am attracted to religious *images* like love and communion and soul and spiritual and church. . . . Not of any church I have directly known or experienced, but of the church I have heard some churchmen talk about, the early revolutionary church, whose followers lived in caves and shared their bread, their persecution and their destiny.[13]

Here were points at which the mainline Protestant churches could connect, and they frequently did. The social gospel emphases of neo-orthodoxy had long found cooperation on this front possible, even when it necessitated stern critiques alike of Marxist and liberal utopianism. The new secular theology with its call to identify with the world encouraged the church to make common cause with political groups of every kind. But there were also serious problems for the church in this relationship. The nature of the problems can be seen in the words of a student radical cited by Kenneth Keniston:

> But my vision had always been that all of a sudden a million people would march on Washington, singing "A Mighty Fortress is Our God," and the government would come tumbling down. I would feel much more identified with that than if a million people marched on Washington singing "The Internationale." . . . My basic rhetoric is a very theological one. . . . My problem is that the basic rhetoric is one that's irrelevant. . . . [It] just doesn't work.[14]

The Protestant reformers and activists wanted to connect with this moral earnestness, and they wanted somehow to recover the relevance of the religious roots, and even the rhetoric, from which it had sprung. To do so, they would have to speak to the larger desire for meaning in which the moral drive for social justice was really set. And they would have to do so in a language that was, indeed, relevant. If, however, they went too quickly for relevance, they would have to give up the larger meaning, as the secular theologians had done without a second thought. But if they did not address the intellectual grounds of meaning more satisfactorily and persuasively than the neo-orthodox had, they would sacrifice relevance. If they could not bring together ethical earnestness, and the deeper faith it evinced, into an integral connection with the acknowledged realities and possibilities of the knowable world, their ethics, like their faith, would have no more standing than anyone else's arbitrary ethical and religious preferences.

If the church reformers failed to keep the concern with social justice and action integrally tied to a concern with the intellectual tasks and responsibilities of the university, they would lose whatever claim they originally might have had to a respectful hearing from the university. At the same time they would be made totally dependent on those who had made social action and political tactics their major preoccupations, unburdened by extraneous intellectual and faith commitments.

The various stages of the developing course of student unrest in the 1960s can almost be charted exactly in terms of students' changing attitudes toward the university. The public's love affair with higher education, with all the ambiguities that entailed, continued throughout the 1950s. It was given a renewed boost by Sputnik, which ensured that increased public funds would continue to pour into the university, and that its research would be seen as ever more essential to the technological, economic, and military strength of the nation. The momentum established in the growth of the university during these years continued on through the rest of the decade, in spite of the troubles the university and the rest of the society were soon to be plunged into.

Probably the high point of relatively unambivalent celebration of the university's role as service station to the nation was, as we have already noted, Clark Kerr's 1963 *The Uses of the University*. "Intellect," wrote Kerr, "has . . . become an instrument of national purpose, a component part of the 'military-industrial complex.' "[15] A year later on Kerr's own Berkeley campus the Free Speech Movement erupted, triggered by a spontaneous demonstration at an "unauthorized" recruiting table at Sproul Plaza. The early stages of the emerging student critique of the university reflected in many ways aspects of the earlier Protestant theological critique: fragmented courses, unethical uses of knowledge, lack of concern for the needs of students. Although it was now given a sharper and more intense political orientation, the new critique still took the form of "helping the university to be the university," that is, of calling it to return to its own best nature. The undercurrent of anger that was present among students in these early years reflected in part their feeling of disappointment that the university had turned from a primary concern with the needs of the student to catering to the needs of the power forces in society without a critical thought and, in the process, was happily reaping the benefits of doing so—grants, prestige, growth—regardless of what this entailed for the unprivileged outside the university or for the neglect of the privileged within.

Even in this, and even if negatively, as historian Walter Metzger's diagnosis of student dissent later indicated, a further religious dimension of the movement can be seen. A major cause of student unrest, according to Metzger, was the failure of the faculty to fulfill its traditional "pastoral" responsibilities to students. The "close historical and functional connection between the academic's profession and the priest's vocation," Metzger argued, had been ignored by the modern university faculty. As a result, he said, "In the modern university, where many students recoil from academically-favored paths of life and doubt the virtue of increasing knowledge, the academic faculties have also lost their capacity to steer their flocks, their power to preach a persuasive gospel." And, in the modern university, he further argued, we see no movement among the faculty "to rehabilitate those special talents . . . to set forth a more insistent ethic, to recruit more dedicated acolytes, or to reconstruct seminarial (that is, graduate school) instruction," in short, to recover and "to increase its pastoral skills."[16]

This was an eloquent vindication from an unexpected source of the considerable attention given by the Protestant theological-educational reformers since Moberly to the neglect by modern university faculties of their responsibilities and relationships to students. Although there is no indication that any of the students' developing critique of the university was drawn from the already extant church critique, still they had much in common and several important, potential points of contact and cooperation.

It was not unnatural, therefore, that leaders of the student Christian movement and alert campus ministers felt a natural affinity in the beginning with the new expressions of student unrest, its criticism of the university and its call for a self-conscious attention to the ethical uses of knowledge. What, however, had been for the educational reformers of the Protestant theological renaissance mainly an attempt from the side of concerned faculty to call themselves and their colleagues to account, was now arising as an accusation from the side of the students. The students' sense of being a neglected and aggrieved partner in a relationship in which traditionally they could have expected to have received special nurturing—intellectual, parental, and pastoral—now took on political dimensions as they looked about to identify with others whom they could regard as having also been wronged by the powers that be—black citizens, the urban and rural poor of America, the peasants of Southeast Asia, and so on. It is ironic that at the moment that the young secular theologians were hastening to affirm the university as the hope for liberating social change, the students were already moving into a more radical stage in their relationship to the university, condemning it for its uncritical ties with the privileged and powerful sectors of society and its lack of larger social responsibility.

The next stages in student revolt soon followed: the attempt to shut the university down, until its administrators, faculties, and boards of trustees should come to their senses and mend their ways; then, this hope failing, to try in disappointed rage actually to damage the university, "to trash" it, with no hope that in doing so something better might follow, either from their actions or from the university. Yet, even these later stages of destructive anger and violent *ressentiment* still concealed a sense among the students of a trust betrayed, a sense that they had looked to the university as something special—like their parents—and had been let down. The most radical moment of all came, then, when the students finally began to give up on the university as something special, regarding it instead (often using quasi-Marxist modes of analysis to articulate their feelings and perceptions) as merely a function of the larger social order, no more important than any other social institution. In the end the university was not even regarded by the more radical students as an especially opportune place from which to launch the larger revolution. For the less radical students, the majority, higher education by the 1970s was becoming more and more simply an irremovable given, the unavoidable doorkeeper to social standing and advance, with which they would have to settle.[17]

Throughout, the political activists, moderate and radical alike, almost never challenged the university's claim to be the prime source and guardian of genuine and normative knowledge. When questions of knowledge were raised, it was almost always in connection with the ethical uses of knowledge and the control of knowledge. The university discipline of the sociology of knowledge, and associated Marxist conceptions of ideology, provided the main categories for challenging the university's claim that it simply was pursuing value-free inquiry and that it was, therefore, not basically responsible for the uses to which society put the knowledge thus gained. Against this claim, the sociology of knowledge and Marxist modes of analysis were often used to good effect to show that nonrational, nonobjective interests were as much at work in the university's production and certification of knowledge as elsewhere.[18] But beyond this, by now, entirely conventional criticism, the political activists did not go. Most of them did not even raise the question, which the theological-educational reformers had long seen as essential, of the hidden presuppositions about the world at work in the university disciplines.

The modern assumptions about knowing and about the known world were as firmly lodged in the collective mind-set of the politically active students, at least as far as their political activism itself was concerned, as they were in the university and culture at large. As secular theology baptized these modern assumptions as God's own, the possibility was pretty well lost for good that perhaps the student Christian movement at least might be able to keep alive the deeper connection between knowledge and political-ethical action, a connection which, we have seen, was already becoming ever more tenuous even among the older neo-orthodox.

The student Christian movement, like the wider student movement, was, thus, losing any essential reason for maintaining a critical engagement with the central intellectual understanding and work of the university. The students in their political theory simply accepted without question that an adequate understanding of the world was given by the dominant university modes of inquiry and discourse and their ethical emotivism. Within this modernist conception of knowledge, ethical ends and purposes could not be rationally considered and established, they could only be emotively asserted, arbitrarily, and in extremis fought over. It also became more and more difficult, therefore, for the students to argue persuasively that their political views and activism as such had any special claims on the university, and to which the university owed a hearing.

Separated from knowledge, except in the shallow and by now thoroughly conventional sociology of knowledge sense, political activism on all sides began, as a consequence, to devolve increasingly into unmitigated power politics. Thus, political action on all sides began to fall into and to reinforce ever more strongly the emotivist, irrational nature of most ethics and value assertions in modern culture. It also represented an embodiment and carrying out into the public realm of the exclusive and prevailing definition in modern education of "knowledge as power." And the more the political activists relied, usually for want of any other source of help, on Marxist modes of analysis, the more totally they were disabled from bringing a really radical epistemological-ethical critique to bear on the university and society, since these modes of analysis, despite their other refinements, rested on the most naive acceptance of the nineteenth-century mechanical philosophy, its worldview, and its ethics of power.

Cultural Radicalism

The other main manifestation of student unrest, the countercultural, presented a different and more difficult challenge to the religious student movements, campus ministers, and theological reformers. Political activism of the most radical sort was not far removed from Protestant social gospel traditions; it could be interpreted as an expression of faithful, ethical response to the biblical concern for justice; and through the black church and civil-rights movement it had a concrete connection with some of the deepest Protestant religious traditions in America. The countercultural movement, however, with its sexual exuberance, its hallucinogenic cults, its interest in Eastern religions, native North American shamanism, new and older esoteric and occult religions, and its communal experimentation, was to most Protestants, from theologians to campus ministers to lay people, a strange, new world, or perhaps an all-too-familiar world of suppressed primal drives and pagan temptations. Even the ecstatic existentialism of Paul Tillich seemed, next to much of the counterculture, decidedly tame and staid.

Moreover, the overtly Eastern and mystical religious interests of the counterculture appeared often as a direct challenge to both neo-orthodox and secular theological renderings of the biblical tradition—smacking for the neo-orthodox of all the pride of the finite creature rebelling against the divine creator, for the secular theologian of an escapist relapse into the magical womb of a world not yet demystified. It was difficult in the extreme for the churches to come to terms with this new religiosity appearing in the university, and often among their own children—and appearing ironically just at the moment when the Protestant theological critique of the university had reached its most complete articulation, just at the moment, furthermore, when secular theology was proclaiming the death of God and the end of religion.

The one place where the new religious interests of the students were finding a positive response within the university, and a place at which the church had concentrated many of its educational reform efforts, was in the newly developing departments of religious studies—but even here the reception of the new was frequently at the expense of the established Western religious traditions.

By the end of the 1960s some important efforts were being made, mostly from outside the churches, but a few from within, to recognize the best within the counterculture, especially in its new interests in religion and communal experimentation.[19] Two of the most important of these attempts were represented in Theodore Roszak's *The Making of a Counter Culture* (1969) and in Jacob Needleman's beginning reappropriation of the primordial religious tradition, which he first began to articulate in his 1970 survey of leading countercultural religious movements, *The New Religions*.[20]

Both Roszak and Needleman were intent on safeguarding the counterculture against irrational tendencies to which it was prone. Both were opposed to the drug culture as a destructive dead-end, and both were insistent that the counterculture not reject clear reason in its search for deeper sources of meaning. The healthy appetite of the students, Roszak said, "requires mature minds to feed it."[21] Most important, Roszak and Needleman were concerned to develop from the counterculture a radical critique of the foundations of modern Western, technological-industrial society and to enunciate a new alternative cultural vision.

In their work it was necessary for them also to wrestle in their own way with the modern split between faith and knowledge that had confronted the Protestant theological renaissance. In their work can also be seen a deeply critical appraisal (made explicit by Needleman) of the failures of mid-twentieth-century mainstream Jewish and Christian religious bodies. Whether Roszak and Needleman dealt any more satisfactorily, or ultimately any differently, with the problem of faith and knowledge than did the Protestant theologians can be a useful question in our context.

In many ways Roszak was attempting to show that political action and dissent by themselves could not effect any fundamental social change because the political in itself shares in and reinforces all the basic assumptions of the society against which it rebels. Political revolution, he argued, often becomes the mere handmaiden of the technocracy in the latter's "great project of integrating ever more of the world into a well-oiled, totally rationalized managerialism."[22] Roszak saw the counterculture attempting to bring meaning to the movement: "Before we act in the world," he said, "we must conceive of a world; it must be *there* before us, a sensible pattern to which we adapt our conduct."[23] It was this larger meaning, which alone could make political action truly radical, that he wanted to rescue from the counterculture's irrational aberrations.

The counterculture Roszak saw as basically a rejection of what he called the reigning technocracy, the governance of society by scientific-technical experts and managers, whose authority rests in their uncontested appeal to scientific forms of knowledge grounded in what Roszak described as "the myth of objective consciousness."[24] The elaboration of scientific modes of knowing into the dominant influence of our age, Roszak maintained, had produced three major characteristics of modern culture: (1) its "alienative dichotomy"—the split between a world of inner subjects and outer objects, with all the exploitation and manipulation that makes possible; (2) its "invidious hierarchy," in which the experts govern in the name of scientific knowledge, and the rest submit to their management; and (3) its "mechanistic imperative," which insists on reducing everything to explanations of physical cause and effect, thus leaving no place for ideals, mind, and other nonmaterial realities.[25] The modern worldview tends to appropriate for itself the whole meaning of reason, reality, progress, and knowledge. Those who suggest that this view does not give expression to the fullest dimensions of human experience are then accused of trafficking in the irrational.[26]

Nothing less is required, Roszak argued, than "the subversion of the scientific world view." And this could only occur through the emergence of a new culture in which the "non-intellective capacities of the personality" become the arbiters of reality.[27] The significance of the students' new interest in non-Western and esoteric religious traditions was for him precisely that it represented an exploration of the nonintellective consciousness as "a critique of the scientific world view upon which the technocracy builds its citadel and in the shadow of which too many of the splendors of our experience lie hidden."[28]

Although the terminology and feeling tone differ between the critique of modern culture and education set forth by Roszak and that developed within the Protestant theological renaissance, it is remarkable how much they had in common. Roszak spoke of the deeper commitments and meanings beyond technical reason; the theologians spoke of "ultimate concern," "radical faith," and "the depth dimension of experience." Roszak stressed the exploration of "the nonintellective capacities of the personality"; the theologians attempted to develop "knowledge of persons" as a realm beyond that given by a sense-bound reason. Roszak dissected "the myth of objective consciousness"; the theologians criticized "the cult of objectivity." Roszak wanted to bring to light the underlying mechanistic and objectivistic worldview of the technocracy; the theologians called for examining the hidden, usually naturalistic, presuppositions of modern knowledge. Such similarities and potential points of contact, nonetheless, seem to have escaped the Protestant cultural critics and reformers, for they offered no response.[29]

What is of most interest, however, is that Roszak's solution to breaking the cultural hold of a narrow scientistic mode of reason was at heart essentially the same as that of the theological renaissance—and with all the same problems. Roszak had the same fear we have seen among the theologians of bringing what he called the deeper, nonintellective dimensions of experience into an integral connection with knowing and knowledge: the fear that to do so would result in forcing the richness of experience once more into the narrow and arid confines of technical reason. Like the theologians he did not entertain the possibility of a deeper rationality that could encompass both.

Roszak, therefore, wanted to speak of the chief problems of the technocracy, which he had identified as its "alienative dichotomy," its "invidious hierarchy," and its "mechanistic imperative," as belonging not primarily to the epistemology but to the psychology of science, to its "psychic style."[30]

His solution to the inadequacies and aggrandizing tendencies of this psychic style was to place it within and confine and check it by another: the psychic style of poetic-religious vision.[31]

His solution in the end, then, came down to an argument for the poetic and religious visionary imagination to provide the meaning and goals for technical reason, and to set limits to it. He wanted to place science in the context of a "rhapsodic intellect" that "would subordinate much research to those contemplated encounters with nature that deepen, but do not increase knowledge." This was at heart the same solution to the faith-knowledge problem as that offered by the theologians. The facts of the world are still given by discursive, empirical reason; their meaning and uses are to be supplied by myth, image, symbol, and vision. But that the latter should have genuinely cognitive possibilities for either the world of nature or of the spirit, rather than merely a different psychology, a different psychic style, Roszak denied.

There still remained the two unbridged realms of truth, the scientific-technical and the poetic-religious, just as with the theologians. The theologians would take their overarching framework of meaning from the myths and images garnered from their reading of the biblical tradition; Roszak would take his from a wider compass of poets, mystics, and ancient forms of participatory religious wisdom. Tillich had his "ecstatic reason," which did not yield knowledge; Roszak his "rhapsodic intellect," which did not increase knowledge. The theologians would speak of the "eyes of reason" and the "eyes of faith"; Roszak would speak of the "eyes of flesh" and the "eyes of fire." In neither case was there achieved an integral connection between the two realms of truth.

The weakness of this kind of solution was dramatically illustrated at the very time Roszak was presenting his version of it. The same year, in 1969, Norman Mailer, himself no stranger, nor unsympathetic, to countercultural enthusiasms, brought out *Of a Fire on the Moon*, his account of the Apollo moon landing.[32] In this work Mailer confessed his helplessness as an artist to compete with the accomplishments of the scientific way of knowing.[33] As an artist, Mailer found he had nothing to add that might deepen understanding of the technological marvel, and certainly nothing to compete with it as drama. And, on top of that, science had usurped for its own purposes—in this case, Apollo and the moon—the artist's most powerful resource, the myths and images of imagination, in short, the sources for Roszak's "magic vision."

What Mailer had vividly illustrated was the constant vulnerability of faith, value, and vision, where these are not grounded in knowledge, or themselves do not serve as potential sources of knowledge. In a two-realm theory of truth, in which only one side has to do with knowledge, there is always a twofold problem. There is the tendency for the nonknowledge side to assert itself in a paroxysm of irrationality and violence—if the counterculture had its share of drug-blasted minds and helter-skelter Manson murders, political extremism also had produced its full complement of violence and assassination—and this Roszak had wanted to safeguard against. The other problem, however, which Mailer illustrated, is that in a two-realm theory of truth, in which only one side has to do with knowledge, there will always be a constant pressure to fit the sources of experience and inspiration to the framework of reality provided by the recognized ways of knowing. The pressure is always in one direction, from the side of knowledge, to eliminate or appropriate for its own purposes, and often in truncated and debased versions, the realm of experience, value, and vision. This is what the secular theologians, through their concession to scientific naturalism, had signified for the neo-orthodox; it was what Norman Mailer, via NASA, signified for Roszak and like-minded countercultural poets and visionaries.[34]

Jacob Needleman seemed to offer a different possibility in his sympathetic presentation of the new religions of the counterculture. Needleman introduced his book by describing his own turn from a thoroughgoing, existentialist neo-orthodox theology (he had spent a year as visiting scholar at Union Theological Seminary in New York City), which he saw as dominant in mainline seminaries, churches, and synagogues, to a new appreciation of ancient Eastern and esoteric Western religious traditions.

The religious situation of the West was characterized overwhelmingly, Needleman thought, by the loss of a meaningful cosmos. In the West "the scientific revolution destroyed the idea of a sacramental universe," and religion became at most a matter having to do with ethical and legal relations among human beings.[35] Mainstream Western churches and synagogues were losing increasing numbers of their students during the 1960s to Eastern and new religions, Needleman thought, because mainstream Western religion had itself accepted the desacramentalized universe of modern science.

Specifically, students were leaving their churches and synagogues because they found them lacking in three crucial ways: (1) the churches had acquiesced completely in the modern exclusion of mind and intelligent purpose from the cosmos, and so they had nothing of genuine religious significance to speak about; (2) they had abandoned any concept (which they once had) of paths of spiritual methods and disciplines for the development of body, mind, and emotions, necessary for real religious insight and life; and (3) they had underestimated the full human possibilities of spiritual freedom, immortality, and higher stages of consciousness, having totally accepted for daily life the reductionism of the human being by modern psychology and sociology. Students were leaving the old and taking up, what were for them, the new (often ancient, traditional) religions because the familiar old ones had surrendered their religious substance.

Needleman offered a beginning opening for a whole new look at the possibilities of a genuine knowledge of realms being excluded by the modern mind-set as either unknowable or unreal. There were many problems not addressed by Needleman: What, for example, of the relation between religious knowledge and scientific knowledge? What might be the relation of the ancient wisdom to the modern possibilities of individual responsibility and new forms of communal relations? Was the ancient wisdom as accessible to modern consciousness as Needleman seemed to think, even with the requisite paths of inner discipline? There were other questions, but Needleman's was a beginning effort, and one that also pointed Western religions to some of their own forgotten roots and possibilities. It was a potential opening, however, which found little response from the churches.

THE STUDENT CHRISTIAN MOVEMENTS

For the Christian student movement, as well as for the mainline campus ministry, it was "the movement," the call for liberating political action and social change, that commanded their interests and commitments. Political action was crowding out not only any real interest in countercultural religious currents but the earlier concern of the SCM and of the whole theological renaissance in the intellectual dimension of higher education. As early as the late 1950s, in fact, a major shift in emphasis within the American national student Christian movement was well under way. The shift was from a primary focus on "the university question" to a concern with the pressing political and social problems of the larger society. As we have seen, both emphases, the intellectual and the political, had been present in the student movements from the 1930s on. However, as we have also seen, no integral connection was ever drawn between them. Consequently, as the balance tipped toward social action, the earlier concern with the intellectual and conceptual background of the problems of modern culture tended simply to disappear. Both the analysis of the problems and the prescriptions for change were taken increasingly from the self-understanding, the dominant conceptuality, and the given political forces and ideologies of modern society itself.

Several influences were at work in this shift toward social action. It was never clear, for instance, just how committed American students ever were to the university question. Despite the talk among leaders (mostly among theologians, campus ministers, and student movement professional staff) about the need for students to become lay theologians, and despite the founding of many intentional communities with this as their aim, the readiness of most American students to make the intellectual life their dominant collegiate commitment was never blindingly apparent.

By the late 1950s, also, the thoughts of Dietrich Bonhoeffer were beginning to have wide currency in the WSCF, and from there were percolating into the American student Christian movement.[36] Bonhoeffer's words on the need for Christians to identify with the world further encouraged a concentration on political and social issues seen as the manifestation of concrete opportunities for discovering the Divine at work in the world. The older,

Social Gospel traditions, as well as the central stress of the theological renaissance on social ethics, further strengthened the new emphasis on "being in the world." As the notion of "identifying with the world," of "letting the world set the agenda," was developed into a full-blown "secular theology" in the mid-1960s, about the only thing left by then was political-social action.

Thus, with the eruption of social problems and social unrest at the end of the 1950s and the early 1960s, the American student Christian movements were poised, ready to be propelled headlong into an exclusive concentration on social action. The civil-rights movement, the Angola crisis, the Cuban crisis, the South Africa crisis, the invasion of the Dominican Republic, and finally the Vietnam War provided a host of burning issues that moved to the center of the student Christian movement concerns.[37] But these issues were also the concerns of others—others, like the black students of the civil-rights movement, who were among the actual pioneers of radical social action.

The birth of the free speech movement on the Berkeley Campus in 1964 suddenly put the whole of American higher education at the heart of the social unrest engulfing the nation. Now, ironically, the university question was being posed anew and on all sides. In the shift toward redefining the university question increasingly in terms of social action and of the university's responsibility for and complicity in the nation's social problems, the national student Christian movements now found themselves outpaced by others. By 1964–1965 the student Christians were facing the dual question: What was their proper task in the university, and what were to be their relations to other student groups and movements who now seemed to be leading the way in the same political-social action they had identified themselves with?

In order better to answer these questions the National Student Christian Federation in 1966 reorganized as the University Christian Movement (UCM).[38] The reorganization was intended to decentralize the movement and thus to facilitate initiatives and leadership at the level of the local campus. The national organization was now to serve mainly as a resource center and facilitator of a plurality of student groups engaged in political action for social change.

A wide net was cast by the reorganization. The new movement was to bring together not only the various mainline Protestant student groups but also Orthodox and Roman Catholic university communities. Further, the UCM saw as part of its main mission to reach out in cooperative work to a variety of nonreligious student organizations, now incorporated into the UCM organizational structure as "related movements." These included the Students for a Democratic Society (SDS), the National Student Association (NSA), the Student NonViolent Coordinating Committee (SNCC), the Southern Student Organizing Committee (SSOC), the Northern Student Movement (NSM), and the United States Youth Council (USYC).[39] As the

UCM groped to find its new identity, it made strenuous efforts to strike a working relationship with radical student movements, especially the Students for a Democratic Society. Various action-oriented caucuses—the radical caucus, the black caucus, the women's caucus, and the international caucus—quickly formed within the UCM.

Over Christmas and New Year's week of 1967–1968 the UCM organized, with substantial funding from the Danforth Foundation, a major conference with over a thousand students attending. Called "Process '67," and held in a large Cleveland hotel, chosen as symbolic of the secular urban environment, this conference was to be the last positive undertaking of the UCM.

As described in a detailed study conducted for Danforth by two sociologists shortly afterward, the conference was held in an ambience of peace symbols, draft-card burning to punctuate worship services, rock dancing, and an experimental device called Depth Education Groups (DEGS). Consisting of groups of fifteen to thirty students, the DEGS were based on the "free university" ideas of radical economist Robert Theobald and cultural critic Paul Goodman and were intended to provide a model of inquiry as an experimental alternative to that of the university.[40] The conference focused on issues of social inequity at home, American militarism abroad, and the need for both to be opposed by student "revolutionary" action. As the authors of the follow-up study noted, there was in all the talk about revolution, changing the world, and participating in God's redeeming work in the world, a pronounced "messianism," a "playing at power," power that the students simply did not possess.[41]

Increasingly fragmented, the UCM in 1968 appointed a task force on ideology and charged it with developing clarity for the UCM's future identity and goals. In early spring of 1969, the general committee of the UCM met in Washington, D.C., to hear the report of the special task force. The report called on the UCM to commit itself to radical social revolution, and its members to subordinate their individuality to the requirements of collective action.

In the midst of intense, often vituperative debate, the black caucus suddenly took the floor, charged that the UCM had no grasp of the real needs of blacks, and demanded that, to show its good faith, the UCM should give its main budget of fifty thousand dollars to the black caucus for it to use for its own purposes. Unable to resolve the impasse that had now arisen, faced with its actual inability to be an organization of revolutionaries, and void of any other source of self-understanding, the UCM adjourned for the evening, and the next morning voted itself out of existence.[42]

The collapse of the UCM was complete, and it left the mainline Protestant student movements bereft of a national, ecumenical organization. Robert Rankin of the Danforth Foundation later commented, in an oft-quoted statement, that the UCM "sank out of sight, vanished from the scene without a trace . . . ; that at my urging, the Danforth Foundation had furnished the

UCM with sufficient funds to purchase a fifty-thousand-dollar gun with which they committed suicide."[43] A New England fragment of the UCM continued,[44] and the older UCCF kept alive a remnant of working ecumenical cooperation among its four constituent churches. But all semblance of a concerted national, to say nothing of an international, interdenominational Protestant student movement had come to an end.

Even *motive* magazine, the only remaining national voice for the different Protestant student groups, in 1969, that year of collapse, ran into serious resistance, and finally in 1972 ceased publication. Soon after becoming the official journal for the UCM in 1966, which it had been de facto for the whole student movement for over a decade, *motive* began to have identity problems of its own. It too began to move toward a more activist orientation, but at the same time tried to maintain its experimental commitment to joining the arts and the Christian faith.

By 1969 *motive*'s focus had begun to splinter as it attempted to identify with a variety of different constituencies. Unfortunately, it had long incurred the suspicion and displeasure of some officials of the Methodist Church for its unconventional ways. That year, Editor B. J. Stiles, under pressure from Methodist church officials, handed in his resignation. The magazine limped on for another three years, and was finally discontinued. With the death of *motive* there remained nothing resembling a national, student Christian movement journal, and certainly none of any kind that approached the editorial excellence and daring of *motive*.[45]

It is interesting to note that the British student Christian movement followed a course very similar to that of the United States. The coupling of the intellectual task of the university with the concern for social justice and action, which had really begun in the WSCF and the British SCM, came undone there as in the United States. More and more in thrall to the worldview and instrumental rationalism of the university, and extolling the virtues of a secular world, the British student Christian movement increasingly found the only justification for its existence in working for the success of the "revolution." The entire intellectual dimension of its original critique of the university simply evaporated. During the 1950s and 1960s the WSCF quarterly journal, *Student World*, had continued to explore for its readers the meaning of an authentic Christian presence in the academic world, intellectually, theologically, and ethically. As late as 1966, for instance, *Student World* carried a book-length, WSCF executive committee study on the topic "A New University for a New World," which still preserved the original breadth of interest in the aims of the university, in the curriculum, in the structures and teaching of the university, and in the Christian engagement with the scientific worldview and technological orientation of the university. Even in this study, however, can also be seen a clear tendency to accept uncritically a technical reason's account of the world, and then to try to bring the faith to bear on that world by means of what had become the standard neo-orthodox "in spite of."[46]

An exclusive emphasis on political action continued to move into the faith-vacuum left by secular theology. In 1969 *Student World* ceased publication, and its place was taken by *WSCF Books,* which were entirely concerned with political action and with furthering the revolution.[47] By the early 1970s the British SCM was barely alive in the university and was devoted entirely to funding communes and social projects, which a *Christian Century* editorial described as carrying "the unmistakable marks of the revolutionary left" and as having "inevitably driven the movement into the position of an even smaller minority."[48] With nothing of either religious or educational significance to offer, the British movement, like its United States counterpart, was left with social action as this was defined by the secular world and with secularists better equipped for carrying it out than the church folk.

A final comment may be in order with respect to the phrase, "To help the university be the university"—a cry of the student Christian movement for nearly three decades. By 1969 the phrase had undergone several metamorphoses of meaning. In the early years, in the hands of Moberly, for example, the phrase pointed to the need to identify an older ideal of the university that the actual, modern university was thought to be in danger of betraying. There may have been a good deal of nostalgia mixed in with the conception of this ideal, but it did supply the phrase with a content that could be discussed objectively and critically. As the emphasis on the intellectual issues began to wane, the phrase remained, but more and more as a formula for inspiration—increasingly talismanic, presumptuous, and cant.

Secular theology gave the phrase new content, but changed its meaning. With secular theology's virtual apotheosis of the university's instrumental, narrowly empirical, and utilitarian modes of knowing, the phrase in effect now meant, "Let the university be the university—as it is" (a nice secular turnaround of the neo-orthodox "Let the church be the church"). A study book for Baptist students, in discussing the church's responsibility to the university, said, for example, "The church needs to begin by learning to accept the university *as it is.* . . . The university is called by God to be the university . . . ; the church is called to help it to be true to its heritage as a community of persons united in the rational pursuit of truth."[49] Another study of students on campus urged that "churches can make an important contribution to higher education only if they accept the college *as it is.* . . ."[50]

In other words, to help the university be the university now meant, in a complete reversal of the original meaning, to free it of any ideal obligations—metaphysical, religious, or ethical. It meant, in effect, abandoning the original call to bring to light and critically examine the underlying presuppositions at work in the university and its disciplines. If there were to be any guiding ideals for the uses of knowledge, these were to be sought and applied somewhere else. The old positivist notion of value neutrality and objectivity never had a better representative. Nevertheless, not a little presumptuousness was still involved in the use of the phrase. Within a couple of years, however, by the late 1960s, the phrase had all but disappeared, having yielded to feelings of disillusion, betrayal, and anger, as the involvement of the university in many of the social, political, and military problems of the country became undeniably apparent.

THE CAMPUS MINISTRY

The campus ministry, though not dependent directly on the UCM, also fell into disarray. During the years after the war, the campus ministry grew apace with the expanding university, and by the mid-1960s few campuses were without its presence.[51] Its members were the intellectual and theological elite of the Protestant ministry itself: more highly educated, more interested in world events, more involved in ecumenical endeavors, more liberal and socially active than their counterparts in the traditional parish.[52] Many of them trained in university seminaries, they were enthused by the theological emphases of the mid-century and were at least acquainted with major social and intellectual issues of the times. Among them were many creative, often charismatic, figures determined to bring their theological and ethical concerns both to faculty and students in higher education.

Yet the role of the campus minister was highly ambiguous.[53] On the one side, the campus minister often rejected the model of the traditional parish minister and the conception of the ministry held by denominational leaders. In turn the latter frequently failed to understand the unique problems and tasks of the campus minister, even at times regarding the campus ministry as a less serious form of the ministry than that of the parish. At the same time, however, the major financial support for the campus ministers came from the traditional churches and denominational structures.

On the other side, the campus ministers were desirous of being accepted as full-fledged members into the university community, and often they took the scholar and the teacher as their main models. Yet in most cases the ministers lacked the requisite teaching appointment and credentials (namely, the Ph.D.) necessary for full university status. Worse, they were often regarded by university administrators and faculty—or almost as bad, feared they were regarded—in the images of the disdained traditional clergy, which they had often gone into the campus ministry to escape. It is not surprising that a sense of marginality suffuses the literature of the campus ministry during these years, nor that the turnover rate of campus ministers was extremely high in relation to other callings.[54]

Of the two major waves of upheaval we have looked at that swept the 1960s, political activism and cultural experimentation, the campus ministry, like the student Christian movement generally, found its raison d'être increasingly in the former. There was an occasional tipping of the hat to the quest for new values and sources of meaning apparent among the cultural radicals. Most campus ministers were eager to be sufficiently "with it" as not to be seen as condemnatory of the looser life-style and, sometimes, even the drug ethic of the students. The real sympathies and energies of the campus minister, however, went to the political radicals.

There was some concern, it is true, especially at the end of the 1960s, that the campus ministry, by virtually ignoring the cultural radicals, had turned its back on one of the most important expressions it would ever encounter of a deep student interest in religion. One leading campus minister, referring to Roszak's book and alarmed at his colleague ministers' lack of awareness, wrote,

> One way of interpreting the situation is to suggest that nothing freaks out a campus minister faster than a student who wants to talk about religion, particularly so if he pushes questions about the value of meditation, prayer, and the like. What does he think we were trying to avoid when we came to the campus in the first place? . . . True enough, the kids' religious trip is grass-colored and Zen-flavored; they are not asking for Vacation Bible School. But they *are* into mystical experience, spiritual awareness, you name it. Are campus clergy so alienated from the resources of the Jewish and Christian traditions (to name only two!) as to be unable or unwilling to relate them to this basic hunger of the counter culture? . . . Like it or not, any attempt on our part to survive *solely* as radicals-in-residence not only denies the clear implications of our credentials, but also—at this stage of the game at least—amounts to a copping out on the greening process itself.[55]

A few others also began gradually in the 1970s to try to make contact with the spiritual core of the counterculture, but their numbers were small, and by then it was too late.[56]

The political orientation of the campus ministry was fully in keeping with the long-standing WSCF and neo-orthodox concerns for social ethics. Given their identification with the world of the university, the campus ministers really had little other choice. To have sided with the cultural radicals, especially in light of their often florid expressions of irrationalism, would have alienated the campus ministers completely from their university models. As it was, they could take up the banner of applied social science as a medium for their ethical concerns and, in so doing, at once ally themselves with the most *au courant* university discipline of the 1960s.

Increasingly the tendency was to define the campus ministry solely in terms of the pioneering of ethical social policy and action. The advent of secular theology, which found ready acceptance among many campus clergy, mainly in the conservative Cox variety, forced them farther in this direction, since it left them little alternative other than social action, if as good secularists they were to have anything to do with at all.

This notion of the ministry found its fullest expression in the concept of the campus minister as "prophetic inquirer" advanced in the 1969 publication of the Danforth Study of Campus Ministries.[57] Often referred to as the

Underwood Report, the study was directed by Kenneth Underwood, professor of social ethics at Wesleyan University, sometime professor of theology and ethics at Yale Divinity School, and an esteemed and influential figure among leading campus ministers. The study was in two volumes: the first by Underwood himself set forth the conception of the campus ministry as "prophetic inquiry"; the second consisted of various case studies and analyses by others describing the campus ministry as it existed and exploring prospects and proposals for its future. Intended as a major reorientation and proposal for the future development of the campus ministry, this large, lumbering work expressed, and in many ways embodied unwittingly, the major problems in which the campus ministry was enmeshed.[58]

The Underwood Report was based on the assumption that the university is the most influential of modern institutions and that the campus minister, therefore, is in a position of pivotal importance in relation to the church, the university, and the wider culture. Underwood drew on biblical and church traditions to speak of the normative roles of the minister as pastor, priest, king, and prophet. While he affirmed all of these as important, he urged that the campus ministry adopt primarily the prophetic role. Coining the phrase "prophetic inquirer" for the campus minister, the Underwood Report called for combining the university social science disciplines with a biblically based ethic of justice. The social sciences would provide social analysis and understanding; the biblical ethic would provide goals for social action. The union, however, was a forced one, since no essential connection was shown to exist between the social sciences and any particular ethical position, biblical or otherwise. The concept of prophetic inquiry was basically a rhetorical not an integral joining of the two.

Indeed, this conception of the ministry raised the question, Why the campus minister as "prophetic inquirer" rather than the university social scientist? It was, after all, the latter who in fact had the prized training, expertise, and degree. Again, there was no small element of presumption in the suggestion that the social scientist needed to be guided, either in the intricacies of the applied discipline or in ethical sensitivity and insight, by the campus minister. A certain awareness of this problem seems to have been reflected in a growing interest during the 1960s in proposals for the professionalization of the campus minister, in which the minister would be trained and credentialed, not in the seminary, but in the university.[59]

This desire for professionalization reflected a further embrace of the university ethos. It did attempt to make provision for what was now seen as the main task of clerical preparation; namely, to "open up for the clergy the major alternative types of social action in the modern world."[60] However, it left unraised the questions, Why the campus ministry at all? Why not simply the committed Christian social scientist—the "lay theologian" that had been talked about for so long? The issues of what theological deepening might have been required by either the social policy–oriented campus minister or the lay theologian social scientist—and how and where this was to be acquired—were skirted altogether.

This pointed to an even deeper problem that haunted the Underwood Report throughout, but that was never really faced. This had to do with the reality and nature of the religious-theological dimension on which the whole possibility of distinctively religious-based social policy and action presumably depended. Only on occasion does the problem emerge in full view, as it did, for example, in a poignant report from campus minister Donald Shriver, who worried that "the professional ministry, as well as the most profoundly devout laity, have reached in many congregations an almost incapacitating cynicism of doubt as to whether the images and principles which pervade the language of the pulpit and theologian have empirical reference outside the mind of the speaker."[61] In other words, people were finding it harder and harder in the modern world to believe in the religious realities that could make a biblically based social ethic any more compelling than some other ethic. What would seem to have been the study's most urgent concern, the modern erosion of a convincing sense of religious reality, is never confronted.[62]

This is not to say that many campus ministers did not perform valuable services, and perhaps most of all in just the role of prophetic inquirer envisaged for them by Underwood. As confrontations on many campuses became increasingly antagonistic, frequently it was the campus minister who alone was in position and able to mediate between the contending parties. One account reported that in California alone, at Los Angeles State College, Valley State College, the Claremont Colleges, Los Angeles City College, and the University of California at Santa Barbara, campus ministers had played key roles in resolving or alleviating tensions.[63] At a number of universities, at the University of California in Los Angeles, at Indiana University, and at about a dozen others, the campus minister was named as the official university ombudsman.[64] At Los Angeles State, at the University of North Carolina, and at the University of Michigan, veteran campus ministers were appointed to high student personnel and administrative positions. Elsewhere campus ministers provided similar valuable service to the university.

Ironically, however, the mediating position of the campus ministry and the move toward an ever more exclusive concern with social policy and action further exacerbated the problems of identity and marginality.

The reports of a major consultation of campus ministers and theologians meeting to reflect on the Underwood Report indicate some of the problems and the different groupings and positions that had developed around them.[65] All groups tended to accept the emphasis on social policy and action, but with different views on what was required. One group consisted of those who wanted to do justice to both sides of Underwood's image of prophetic inquirer. The minister, they felt, still carried a religious symbolism that could be mobilized in the interests of social action. The primary task of the university chaplain was, therefore, "the exploitation of that symbolic potency" by what seemed to be any means possible, "sensitivity training, psychodrama, art, drama, poetry, and dance," and "the liturgy." In keeping with this thoroughly utilitarian understanding of the prophetic, this group also urged the professionalization of the campus minister in order "that his credentials . . . be recognized in both Jerusalem and Athens."[66]

Another group consisted of those who basically accepted the Underwood conception, but who did not want to ignore the important issues raised by the cultural radicals among the students with their new interest in the occult, in the feeling life, in their "insatiable search for the real." How they were to respond to these interests was not made clear. A third group included those campus ministers who, having been disillusioned with the university, identi- fied with the most radical student political activists. Their call was for building a network of campus ministers and all others "who see the revolutionary demands of the Epoch as we do." The Underwood study drew from them the reproach that it was proposing essentially "that the campus ministry should be conducted by academic types congenial in university establishment circles," and that "nothing of an embarrassing nature will ever again emanate from it."[67]

To these groups should also be added those who simply confessed their loss of any firm sense of identity and their uncertainty about the future. There were also those who affirmed marginality as an opportunity for experimentation and risk-taking free from the worries of tenure and ordinary parish pressures. A few others saw the campus ministry as wholly rudderless and the participants of the consultation as engaged in a massive effort at rationalizing the validity of whatever position they found themselves in.[68]

Also indicative of the unraveling of a national and ecumenically oriented campus ministry was the decision of the Danforth Foundation in the early 1970s to redirect its resources away from support of the campus ministry toward its home city, St. Louis. The president, Merrimon Cuninggim, resigned in protest, and his staff scattered. The Danforth Foundation not only had funded the Underwood study but, for years, with its Danforth Fellows and other projects, had been one of the most creative sources of support and development of the Protestant campus ministry. Nearly three decades of major ecumenical planning and support were at an end. It would probably not be too great an overstatement to say that, far from heralding new directions, the Underwood Report signaled, and was in many ways itself symptomatic of, the shattering of the twentieth-century Protestant campus ministry.

THE PARADIGMATIC STUDENT EXPERIENCE

During the 1960s the various student movements, not just those of the churches, found themselves in a dilemma of which they were seldom actually cognizant. Deeply disturbed by the university's involvement in national policies of economic and military oppression, they sought ways to direct its uses of knowledge in morally responsible directions, as they conceived them. Two primary ways opened for them as we have seen. Although these were sometimes mixed, they remained nevertheless distinguishable: political radicalism—activist challenging of the existing institutional structures and powers; and cultural radicalism—experimentation with alternative personal and communal values in an attempt to find fundamentally new sources of cultural reconstruction. In both cases, however, the students tended to accept without question, as definitive and simply given, the dominant university conception of knowing and knowledge.

The political radicals found themselves being told that, even if their activism was the way to change society, the university, which dealt primarily with knowledge, was an ill-chosen and inappropriate arena for their political activities. Likewise, the cultural radicals were told that even if their alternative values might conceivably be more attractive than those of the larger society, the university, which dealt primarily with knowledge, was not the place to launch a cultural renaissance. If they wished to cultivate their alternative life-styles, they were advised to do so not in the university but in their urban and rural communes. In both cases the students were told that they endangered academic freedom and the orderly pursuit of knowledge.

In the end the students had no effective answer. With their political and cultural radicalism they had failed to develop a corresponding epistemological radicalism that would have enabled them to address the heart of the university and its life.[69] Without a deeper grounding in the world of knowable reality, political and cultural radicalism were always in danger of sliding off into very conventional forms of anger, romanticism, hedonism, resentment, messianism—all the irrational abuses of the movements that their critics were more than glad to pounce on. By the mid-1970s the university administrators had begun successfully to reassert the university ideal of detached research, teaching, and the production of "useful knowledge." Already refugees from the 1960s were conspicuous misfits.

From this perspective the student experience was paradigmatic, and the breakdown of the theological version of the two-realm theory of truth can be seen in similar light. The truths of knowledge were ceded to the university and its dominant conception of instrumental rationalism. Thus, the truths of faith and ethics were left without grounding in knowable reality. The attempt to realize them through action (will) became either unknowing, willful assertion of interest or a playing out of the given political positions of the times, albeit in traditional faith language. The attempt to realize the truths of faith through ecstasy (feeling) became, without the development of cognitive implications, arbitrary and sentimental. For many unable to conceive of alternatives to the dominant modern modes of cognition, the temptation would be, however reluctantly, to give up faith altogether and to settle for some available utilitarian ethic.

It remains to be seen to what extent the faculty supporters of the theological renaissance in the university found themselves in the same dilemma as the students.

NOTES

1. Philip E. Jacob, *Changing Values in College: An Exploratory Study of the Impact of College Teaching* (New York: Harper & Row, 1957); see the Hazen pamphlet discussion of Jacob: John E. Smith, *Value Convictions and Higher Education* (New Haven, Conn.: Edward W. Hazen Foundation, 1958).

2. See especially Jacob, "A Profile of the Values of American College Students," in *Changing Values in College,* 3–4.

3. Jacob's findings seemed corroborated by Edward Eddy's study of a year later: Edward D. Eddy, Jr., *The College Influence on Student Character* (Washington, D.C.: American Council on Education, 1959). The so-called Cornell study confirmed some of Jacob's conclusions, but presented a more complex picture of student attitudes and values: *What College Students Think* (Princeton, N.J.: D. Van Nostrand Co., 1960). Others, however, challenged Jacob. Max Wise, *They Come for the Best of Reasons* (American Council on Education, 1958), presented a much more sympathetic view of student values and aspirations. And Robert Pace in 1960, analyzing specific studies rather than combining data from different colleges as Jacob had done, concluded that "significant changes in students' values took place, and in a number of instances appeared to last after graduation." C. Robert Pace, "The College Environment as an Exemplar of Values," in *Higher Education in California: Its Responsibilities for Values in American Life* (Commission on Higher Education of the California Teachers Association, 1962), 10–20. Later studies presented conclusions more similar to Pace's than to Jacob's, but it was Jacob's study that had the most immediate impact and received the most attention

4. Charles S. McCoy, "The Nature of the University," in *On the Work of the Ministry in University Communities,* ed. Richard N. Bender (Nashville: Division of Higher Education, Methodist Church, 1962), 41; Manning M. Pattillo, Jr., and Donald M. MacKenzie, *Church-Sponsored Higher Education in the United States* (Washington, D.C.: American Council on Education, 1966), 73.

5. *The Christian Century* 41, no. 4 (December 1958): 599.

6. Theodore Caplow and Reece J. McGee, *The Academic Marketplace* (New York: Basic Books, 1959); David Riesman, *Constraint and Variety in American Education* (n.p.: University of Nebraska Press, 1956).

7. *The Christian Scholar* 42, no. 2 (June 1959): 83–84. Also see Roland Mushat Frye, "The State of Learning Examined," A Review of Caplow-McGee and of Riesman, *The Christian Scholar* 44, no. 1 (spring 1961): 88–92.

8. *The Christian Scholar* 45, no. 1 (spring 1962): 3–5.

9. Explanations have been offered in terms of generational conflict, child-rearing practices, an outgrowth of the civil-rights movement, a general crisis in authority, the Vietnam War and the draft, the sheer numbers of students on the modern campus (over seven million American students by the fall of 1969), the complicity of the American university in racial discrimination and military planning and research, the unresponsiveness of modern institutions to humane purposes and the need for

large-scale social change, and so on. One of the most sensible discussions of the multiple causes of American student unrest during the 1960s is John R. Searle, *The Campus War: A Sympathetic Look at the University in Agony* (New York: World Publishing Co., 1971), 152–82.

10. Searle, *The Campus War*, 5–8; Paul Goodman, *New Reformation: Notes of a Neolithic Conservative* (New York: Random House, 1970), 162; Walter Metzger, "The Crisis of Academic Authority," *Daedalus*, summer 1970, 587; William G. McLoughlin, *Revivals, Awakenings, and Reform: An Essay on Religion and Social Change in America, 1607–1977* (Chicago: University of Chicago Press, 1978), 179ff.

11. In fact, the ideological fervor of many students, and even the turn toward violence of some more radical political groups, resembled nothing so much as similar traits of religious fanatics.

12. Quoted in Todd Gitlin, *The 1960s: Years of Hope, Days of Rage* (Toronto and New York: Bantam Books, 1987), 108.

13. These examples are from Edward E. Ericson, Jr., *Radicals in the University* (Stanford: Hoover Institution Press, Stanford University, 1975), 198–208. Ericson provides many more examples as well.

14. Kenneth Keniston, *Young Radicals: Notes on Committed Youth* (New York: Harcourt, Brace & World, 1968), 31.

15. Clark Kerr, *The Uses of the University* (New York: Harper & Row, 1963), 124.

16. Metzger, "The Crisis of Academic Authority," 602–3.

17. See, for example, Arthur Levine, *When Dreams and Heroes Died: A Portrait of Today's College Student* (San Francisco: Jossey-Bass, 1980).

18. For one influential example, see Theodore Roszak, ed., *The Dissenting Academy* (New York: Pantheon Books, 1968).

19. An example from within is Harvey Cox, *Turning East* (New York: Simon & Schuster, 1977), but this appeared almost ten years too late.

20. Theodore Roszak, *The Making of a Counter Culture: Reflections on the Technocratic Society and Its Youthful Opposition* (Garden City, N.Y.: Doubleday & Co., 1969); Jacob Needleman, *The New Religions* (Garden City, N.Y.: Doubleday & Co., 1970). Each of these were beginnings for both writers. Roszak went on to explore the further possibilities of a counterculture. Needleman became, with Huston Smith, a main American representative of the primordial tradition.

21. Roszak, *The Making of a Counter Culture*, 46.

22. Ibid., 266.

23. Ibid., 80.

24. Ibid., 7–8, 21, 205ff.

25. Ibid., 217ff.

26. Ibid., xiii.

27. Ibid., 50–51.

28. Ibid., 83.

29. My search in the theological journals for a response to Roszak, or to any wide discussion of the religious potential of the counterculture, has yielded only occasional reviews. Of course, I may have missed something of importance.

30. Ibid., 217.

31. Ibid., 253–54.

32. Norman Mailer, *Of a Fire on the Moon* (Boston: Little, Brown & Co., 1970).

33. See Alvin Kernan, *The Death of Literature* (New Haven, Conn.: Yale University Press, 1990), 204, 207.

34. Of course, the now famous, high resolution lens photo image of the earth taken

from Apollo 8 has and continues to evoke a poignant feeling for the earth as a living being. But if we really begin to treat her as a living being, and not merely as an inanimate machine to be used, and at best managed, it will depend on a transformation of our knowing, not only of our feeling, such that we will be able to derive from our scientific knowing deeper insight than the current, dominant mechanistic imagery can provide.

35. Needleman, *The New Religions,* 4–5.

36. Woo traces nicely the movement of "worldly theology" from the WSCF into the American movements. See Franklin Woo, "From USCC to UCM: An Historical Inquiry with Emphasis on the Last Ten Years of the Student Christian Movements in the U.S.A. and Their Struggle for Self-Understanding and Growing Involvement in Social and Political Issues" (Ed.D. diss., Teachers College, Columbia University, 1971), especially 95ff.

37. The 18th Ecumenical Conference on Christian World Mission in 1959 had as its main study book Philippe Maury's *Politics and Evangelism* (Garden City, N.Y.: Doubleday & Co., 1959). The 19th Conference in 1963 had as its theme "For the Life of the World" and included, along with major lectures on the church in the world, lectures on Brazil, Angola, South Africa, Czechoslovakia, and "Christian Participation in Nation Building." See *Wind and Chaff* 2, no. 2 (January 1965): 11. *Wind and Chaff,* the quarterly newsletter of the NSCF, provides a good running picture of the many various social issues that occupied the attention and energies of the students during the early 1960s.

38. John Coleman had long before called for abolishing the Student Christian Movement and establishing instead a "University Christian Movement" of students and professors. Here again, in the 1966 reorganization, key phrases that had long been common currency in the movement were mobilized, but metamorphosed fundamentally in the process. John Coleman, *The Task of the Christian in the University* (Geneva: World Student Christian Federation, 1946), 19.

39. Woo, "From USCC to UCM," 38–59.

40. David S. Wiley and Jackson W. Carroll, "Process '67 and the University Christian Movement: A Report and Interpretation of a Survey of Conference Participants," manuscript, 1971, 1.

41. Ibid., 26.

42. Woo, "From USCC to UCM," 203ff; the events of these last days are also recounted nicely by Dorothy Bass, "Revolutions, Quiet and Otherwise: Protestants and Higher Education during the 1960s," in *Caring for the Commonweal: Education for Religion and Public Life,* ed. Parker J. Palmer et al. (Macon, Ga.: Mercer University Press, 1990).

43. Robert Rankin, ed., *The Recovery of Spirit in Higher Education: Christian and Jewish Ministries in Campus Life* (New York: Seabury Press, 1980), 12.

44. Bass, "Revolutions, Quiet and Otherwise" in *Caring for the Commonweal.*

45. Frank Dent, " '*motive magazine*': Advocating the Arts and Empowering the Imagination in the Life of the Church" (Ed.D. diss., Teachers College, Columbia University, 1989).

46. Jean Joussellin, "A New University for a New World," *Student World* 59, no. 1 (first quarter, 1966): 3–89.

47. *WSCF Books* (Geneva: World Student Christian Federation, 1971–1974). Eight *WSCF Books* were published altogether, most of them under the editorship of Bruce Douglass, a leading figure in the social action programs of the American NSCF. In 1974, as far as I have been able to learn, even this series ceased being published. The

titles were, Bruce Douglass, ed., *Trying Times: American Politics in Transition from the Sixties to the Seventies* (1971); *The Fourth Man and the Gospel* (1971); *Hope against Hope* (1971); *China: The Peasant Revolution* (1972); *A New Look at Christianity in Africa* (1972); *The Evolution of the Modern Idea of Revolution* (1972); Thomas Derr, ed., *Ecology and Human Liberation* (1973); *Women in the Struggle for Liberation* (1974).

48. *The Christian Century*, May 17, 1972, 570. Also see the account of the British Student Christian Movement demise in Steve Bruce, *A House Divided: Protestantism, Schism, and Secularization* (London and New York: Routledge, 1990), 132–34.

49. W. Haydn Ambrose, *The Church in the University* (Valley Forge, Pa.: Judson Press, 1968), 18 [emphasis added].

50. J. Gordon Chamberlin, *Churches and the Campus* (Philadelphia: Westminster Press, 1963), 143 [emphasis added].

51. Philip E. Hammond, *The Campus Clergy* (New York: Basic Books, 1966), 8–14; Jeffrey K. Hadden, *The Gathering Storm in the Churches* (Garden City, N.Y.: Doubleday & Co., 1969); Kenneth Underwood, *The Church, the University, and Social Policy*, The Danforth Study of Campus Ministries, 2 vols. (Middletown, Conn.: Wesleyan University Press, 1969), vol. 1, 47–78.

52. Hammond, *The Campus Clergy*, 42.

53. Ibid., 10–11; Dorothy Bass, "Revolutions, Quiet and Otherwise" in *Caring for the Commonweal*.

54. Hammond, *The Campus Clergy*, 16; Underwood, *The Church, the University, and Social Policy*, 1: 212ff.

55. Donald Shockley, "If the Campus Ministry Dies, Call It Suicide," *NACUC News*, National Association of College and University Chaplains and Directors of Religious Life (winter 1970–1971), 1–2.

56. See, for example, Myron Bloy, ed., *Search for the Sacred* (n.p.: Church Society for College Work, 1972).

57. Underwood, *The Church, the University, and Social Policy*.

58. The second volume of analytical articles ironically provides in many areas almost an autopsy of the campus ministry at the end of the 1960s.

59. This was a major proposal of the Underwood study itself. Also see [Church Society for College Work], *The Professional Identity of the Campus Minister: Report on the First Consultation on the Future of the Campus Ministry* (Cambridge, Mass.: Church Society for College Work, 1970); Hammond, *The Campus Clergy*, chap. 2.

60. Kenneth Underwood, "Foreword," in *The Church, the University, and Social Policy;* Hammond, *The Campus Clergy*, viii–ix.

61. Underwood, *The Church, the University, and Social Policy*, vol. 1, 240.

62. The point is not to criticize the commitment to radical social action, far from it, but simply to point to the problems that ensued from the dissociation of that action from the deeper intellectual critique and grounding that was necessary for its realization as "prophetic."

63. F. Thomas Trotter, "The Campus Ministry as Normative," Guest Editorial, *The Christian Century*, June 4, 1969, 766.

64. Hal Viehman, interview by author, 11 November 1987.

65. [Church Society for College Work], *The Professional Identity of the Campus Minister*. The lack of agreement at the consultation was such that three separate reports of its meetings, each representing a different position, had to be made.

66. Ibid., 30.

67. Ibid., 45.

68. Ibid., 20.

69. One university faculty member who recognized the inadequacy of the conceptions of knowledge dominant in the university was Henry David Aiken of Brandeis. Aiken wrote, "My complaint against contemporary versions of rationalism is that the only form of intelligent work that they are prepared to acknowledge are those which culminate in the achievements of the formal and natural sciences and their simulations of the 'sciences of man.' What is wanted, of course, if the university as the central institution of higher learning is to survive, is a more subtly and complexly inflected philosophy of human nature and culture that will do better justice to all the ranges of human intelligence, achievement, and perplexity." Henry David Aiken, *Predicament of the University* (Bloomington, Ind.: Indiana University Press, 1971), 10, also see 349–82.

CHAPTER 6

Collapse and Rout:
The Faculty

The highest hopes for the church's new engagement with American higher education depended on those college and university faculty members who had come under the influence of the theological renaissance. In several areas, in fact, faculty involvement had for a time begun to give substance to the hope that the Protestant church, and religion more generally, might be able to reclaim an important presence within American higher education. The efforts of the faculty theological-educational reformers had begun to bear fruit in the pages of *The Christian Scholar,* in the organization of the Faculty Christian Fellowship, in continuing discussion about the role of church-related colleges, in the innovative experiments in religion and the arts, and in attempts by theologically adept scientists to reexamine the relation between science and religion. By the end of the 1960s, however, nearly all these undertakings were in deep trouble, and the hopes that had attended them were fading, if not already dead. To be sure, the expansion of university departments of religion continued in full swing, but even here the original hopes of the theological reformers, as we shall see, were being thwarted.

THE DEMISE OF THE
FACULTY CHRISTIAN FELLOWSHIP

The success of the theological-educational reform probably depended to a large extent on the existence of a fairly stable institutional and social situation in which the reform movement's still fragile forces could be developed, strengthened, and deployed to greatest advantage. It was just such stability that disappeared in the social and educational turmoil of the 1960s.

The theological-educational reform would have been difficult in the best of circumstances. As it was, the unexpected upheavals of the 1960s by themselves may have been enough to derail it. It is conceivable, nonetheless, that a foothold might have been secured that later could have served as a foundation for renewed efforts. Essential to such a foothold would have been the development of a vigorous and penetrating examination of the university disciplines. Undertaking this critical examination had initially been the most important purpose in the founding and early self-understanding of the Faculty Christian Fellowship.

Some important first steps were made in this direction. *The Christian Scholar* repeatedly attempted to carry out an ongoing examination of the disciplines. The *Scholar* continued well into the 1960s to devote articles and whole issues to the relation between faith and various academic subjects and disciplines, exploring what the editor identified as "the frontier between faith and scholarship." In 1964 the Faculty Christian Fellowship did finally commission a series of small pamphlets, after the manner of the English Dons' Group, on the relation between the Christian faith and some of the disciplines.[1] Of course, Reinhold Niebuhr and Paul Tillich especially had made important breakthroughs in bringing the Christian faith to bear in a probing examination of the assumptions of the modern mind and of many academic disciplines. It was Niebuhr's ability to cast new light particularly on the social sciences, history, and political theory that won him followers among many persons outside the churches, as well as within. Tillich likewise had distinguished himself in dealing with the foundations and meaning of a range of subjects, especially those pertaining to philosophy, the arts, and psychology.

Although Tillich and Niebuhr never overcame the basic modern dualism between faith and knowledge, they had made important and impressive beginnings. It is certainly conceivable that others could have built on their achievements and carried them forward in response to the original call of the theological-educational reformers for an intense and sustained probing by theologians and committed Christian faculty of the presuppositions of the modern fields of knowledge. But this did not happen. In the end, the full-scale examination of the presuppositions of the modern university disciplines never took place.

Sensing that the critical encounter with the disciplines was not occurring, a 1961 editorial in the *Faculty Forum*, the FCF newsletter, lamented that "there is much conversation *about* conversation, but too little conversing."[2] The failure on this matter, however, meant that the linchpin of the entire theological-educational reform was coming undone.

In addition to the difficulties posed by the general turmoil of the 1960s, two other developments further hampered a radical examination of the disciplines. One of these was the changing nature of the professoriat itself during these years. The other was in part related to this and had to do with the disappearance of any strong theological support for a critical dialogue with the university disciplines.

The postwar expansion of American higher education continued unabated during most of the 1960s. Not only did the numbers of students relentlessly increase, but there was also a concomitant growth in the numbers of people teaching. In the twenty years from 1940 to 1960 the size of faculty doubled from 147,000 to 244,000; in only ten years after that, faculty ranks nearly doubled again by more than 200,000 to an estimated 509,000 in 1970.[3] There were more *new* positions filled in the 1960s than the total number of faculty slots existing in 1950.[4] This immense quantitative increase reflected fundamental qualitative changes also taking place in higher education. Institutionally, the larger numbers represented the development of huge state systems of higher education with enormous and newly diverse student bodies. At the center of these systems, the research university reigned supreme, setting research and prestige standards for the whole.

The ascendancy of the research university represented the continuing importance of the university as the prime source of the scientific-technological knowledge required by modern society. The government especially looked to the research university to supply its needs for new knowledge. In 1968, 88 percent of all faculty research funds was provided by the federal government, much of it by this time for military-related projects.[5]

One result was the realignment of university faculty and disciplines along the lines of those who could command research grants and those who could not. Another result was to extend the dominance of the research emphasis into all subjects even more completely than before, accentuating the century-long tension within modern higher education between teaching and research.[6] As David Riesman and Christopher Jencks remarked in *The Academic Revolution*, there now existed "no guild within which successful teaching leads to greater prestige and influence than mediocre teaching."[7] The reward system that governed promotion and tenure was determined in all subject areas almost entirely by success in research and publication. The emphasis on research added fuel to the flames of student unrest, on the one hand, strengthening complaints by students of neglect and poor teaching by the faculty, and, on the other hand, provoking from them charges of faculty and university research complicity in an unjust war.[8]

The increase in numbers of faculty also brought a new kind of faculty member: younger—about one third of all faculty in the 1960s was now under thirty-five years of age; from a more socially diverse background—for the first time the working-class student had made it into university faculties in significant numbers; and more sympathetic to their students' concerns—most of them themselves barely out of graduate school.[9] This newer breed of faculty also came to the university with high expectations for themselves with regard to salary, support, and prestige. What they often encountered, however, were the unceasing pressures of a reward system based on success in research and publication and simultaneously a student body demanding more attention and accusing them of "selling out to the powers."

Many of these new faculty often sympathized with the student critics of the university. In a large Carnegie Commission survey of thousands of faculty members, over half agreed that "big contract research has become more a source of money and prestige for researchers than an effective way of advancing knowledge"; and a large percentage felt that most American colleges "reward conformity and crush creativity," and that the concentration of research grants in the major universities had been "corruptive" of the institutions getting them.[10] At the same time, the faculty remained loath to endanger a newly launched academic career and to reject funding, with all the perquisites it brought for the older faculty and the enhanced opportunities it offered younger faculty on the tenure track of the inescapable reward system.

In this kind of situation, one that had been relatively rapid in developing, the call to carry out a critical examination of the basic university disciplines must have seemed to most faculty exceedingly utopian, if not downright strange. For most scholars, especially the younger ones, to have raised truly critical questions about the basic presuppositions of their own disciplines, which they were being expected on the contrary to develop and promulgate, would have been just about as much as their own academic lives were worth.

It is significant in this respect that the university reward system itself never received critical scrutiny from Christian scholars. Although Arnold Nash had early on advocated a sociology of knowledge approach to raise critical questions about the relation between the university reward structures and the intellectual views and assumptions dominant among its members, no one ever followed up on his call.[11] (When this kind of questioning did begin to come, it was not from Christians so much as from university sociologists and young, critical theorists who, in publishing their critical analyses of the reward system, managed at the same time, of course, to satisfy its demands and to reap its benefits.) The overwhelming pressures of the university reward system thus worked against one of the central tasks for a vital Christian presence in the university as envisaged by the theological-educational reformers.

Yet the discontent with the university emphases, which we have seen was shared by large percentages of faculty, and not just by younger faculty, suggests that the possibility of carrying out this critical wrestling with the disciplines was not entirely closed. It suggests that there may well have been situations in which older, and perhaps even younger, faculty touched by the theological renaissance would have found it not uncongenial to continue a radical probing of basic presuppositions. Even if this were to have occurred only here and there, essential resources would have been laid for resuming the task on a larger scale in more settled and favorable times. For this to have taken place, however, required a clear vision of its importance. And it was just this clarity of vision, on which everything depended, that was removed by the theologians themselves.

The original call to examine the presuppositions of the modern mind-set had potentially radical epistemological implications. The pervasive assumption of the modern mind, for instance, that the animate derives from the inanimate, the living from dead matter, has a close affinity with mechanistic images and modes of explanation, and it lends encouragement to an exclusive reliance on quantitative ways of knowing. The contrary assumption (one, by the way, much closer to our ordinary experience, since we never, ever encounter life emerging from what is dead) would not exclude quantitative ways of knowing, but would demand and encourage the development of qualitative ways of knowing every bit as rigorous as the purely quantitative. The failure of the theological reformers, however, to make an integral connection between faith and knowledge seriously blunted such radical epistemological possibilities. They tended to regard the presuppositions of thought only in the secondary sense of providing explanatory worldviews that give order and meaning to knowledge already derived apart from them. Worldviews in this sense provide meaning, but they have no direct epistemo-logical or methodological significance. Even in this weaker form, however, the critical examination of the presuppositions of thought was of crucial importance and, had it been pursued, could have kept alive the possibility of the emergence of a still more radical, epistemological probing.

The turn to secular theology took even this away. The underlying concern of the secular theologians was to affirm the human being's "coming of age" as a newly autonomous, freely responsible, and self-determining agent. The way they went about it, however, simply pulled the backbone from any deep examination of the modern mind-set and its assumptions about knowable reality. The problem can be clearly seen, for example, in Harry Smith's 1968 book, *Secularization and the University*, in which he attempted to apply secular theology directly to the university question.[12]

Smith identified the essence of secularization as the rejection of all unified worldviews and metaphysical systems that claim to provide overarching explanations and ultimate meaning to human experience. All such total worldviews—scientistic, positivistic, metaphysical, and biblical alike—were to be rejected as either mythic escapes from the world, remnants of a still enchanted, undemystified and undemythologized world, or ideological con-structs designed to provide a security within the world, but a false security that entailed the loss of human agency and freedom.[13] To avoid the suffocating imposition of such total worldviews, modern human beings should remain content with purely functional, problem-solving instrumental reason, which had no metaphysical or meaning-giving pretensions. There seemed to be only two choices: coercive, all-encompassing worldviews or a totally functional, means-oriented instrumental rationalism. Given these alternatives, Smith and the other secularists opted for the latter.

This meant for Smith that theological educational reformers should cease their complaining about the intellectual fragmentation of the university, for that could only be a misconceived pining for lost metaphysical absolutes. Rather, they should affirm without reservation the autonomous use of instrumental reason in the academic community and celebrate "the dynamic differentiation in higher education"—its "diversified and specialized truth-seeking, the integrity of its several disciplines, and the legitimate pluralism which this produces."[14] In other words, as the major cultural-institutional expression of man's coming-of-age, the university and its instrumental ways of knowing were to be accepted as fundamentally unproblematic. What was once condemned as destructive fragmentation was now to be welcomed as commendable diversification.

Smith, however, gave indication occasionally that he himself was a bit uneasy about some implications of this enthusiastic embrace of the modern mind-set. At times, the otherwise unrestrained affirmation of secularization was tempered by a recognition of "the various forms of ideological reductionism" prevalent in the university and of "the domination of means over ends and techniques over values" that stemmed from " 'the technical reason' which permeates the current campus scene."[15] At these points Smith reverted to a neo-orthodox, two-realm theory of truth as though it presented no problems whatsoever. When he was in this mode, he urged that faith in God as the sole source of meaning and wholeness could counterbalance the exclusive emphasis in the modern world on means and techniques and that a sense of awe before the mysteries of creation (shades of the enchanted world!) could offset the modern emphasis on empiricist, instrumental reductionism. Here he even recommended the humanities as a source of human values and goals to balance the raw instrumentalism of technical reason.[16] The central modern dualisms kept reasserting themselves with a vengeance.[17]

In his introduction to Smith's book, Harvey Cox had identified and raised the difficulty that confronted Smith (as well as Cox himself and the other secularists). "The question left unanswered by this book, as it has been left unanswered by most theologians today," Cox rightly observed, "is how the church can proclaim the positive side of the gospel without lapsing again into closed world-views and static systems. If, as Bonhoeffer insisted and Smith reminds us, secularization is 'a clearing of the decks for the God of the Bible' what happens after the decks are cleared?"[18] Having rejected all possibility of transcendence and having proclaimed the unproblematic nature of technical reason along with the fundamental integrity of the university and its "diversified disciplines," the secular theologians left the original theological-educational reform with neither positive vision nor critical mission. There was no longer any reason for pursuing a radical critique of the university disciplines and their underlying presuppositions.

If the student Christian movement had exited the university with a flourish, the Faculty Christian Fellowship seems to have just faded away. In the summer of 1967 the editor of *The Christian Scholar* announced that the journal would cease publication with the forthcoming winter issue. The editorial of that last issue, entitled, "An Ending, Not an End," was more wistful than accurate, for an end it surely was.[19] Although the *Faculty Forum*, the newsletter for the FCF, continued to be published (and circulated free-of-charge) into the 1970s, the Faculty Christian Fellowship, long moribund, was now indeed dead.

The demise of *The Christian Scholar* and of the Faculty Christian Fellowship signaled that the mainstream Protestant churches' critical, scholarly engagement with American higher education was all but over.

THE TEACHING OF RELIGION

The study of religion in the university also turned out far different from what had been envisaged and hoped for within the theological renaissance. We have seen important changes already beginning to take place in the early 1960s. The first thing that had to be given up was the long-standing hope (from William Adams Brown through Moberly, Nash, Miller, and others) that theology broadly conceived might provide the unifying and integrating principle for what was perceived as an overspecialized and fragmented curriculum. Versions of this conception did continue to appear to the end of the 1960s.[20] But nothing happened as a result of them, and the ideal became increasingly suspect as anachronistic, as a disguised attempt to hold on to an outmoded ideal of cultural unity and metaphysical certainty.[21]

More enduring had been the other hope that through departments of religious studies the basic human issues, including the theological, could find a firm lodging in the university. We have seen how, during the 1950s and 1960s, departments of religious studies continued to spread in private nondenominational as well as in public colleges and universities. Part of this growth represented both a readiness to apply the academic disciplines to the study of religion, as well as a nascent sense of the religious dimensions of those disciplines. We have also seen that a further contributing factor to the growth of the new departments was the availability of highly trained graduates from interdenominational seminaries to staff them. In fact, during the 1950s and well into the 1960s, the original hope that theology would find a firm place within the university was for a time realized through the presence in these departments of young faculty imbued with the intellectual and theological excitement of the theological renaissance.

It was also in the departments of religious studies that there was to be found the major, significant university response to student interest in Eastern, archaic, and esoteric religious traditions. This in itself was a turn away from the neo-orthodox conception of the proper encounter between Western theology and world religions. Protestant theology in general and the neo-orthodox orientation in particular, with its suspicion of all religions that suggested God might be more than the simply Wholly Other, were ill-prepared for this growing pluralism, and unreceptive to it. At the same time, many of the young faculty in the new religion departments, including many recent seminary graduates, often seemed more interested in the Eastern and new religions than in the Western traditions. Religious studies began to move increasingly to the margins of Protestant concerns, and, in turn, the influence of Protestant seminaries in departments of religion diminished rapidly during the 1960s.[22]

By the end of the decade the teaching and study of religion had become fully part of the university intellectual and institutional structure. The place of the study of religion in the university, however, was decidedly ambiguous. The members of these relatively new departments, eager to establish their bona fide university credentials and scholarly rigor, accommodated themselves, perhaps even more readily and uncritically than others, to the full panoply and apparatus of the university reward system. They were fond of pointing out that the study of religion was at last a full-fledged academic discipline in its own right, with its own departmental organization alongside all the other disciplines.

One effect was that the professional standards of the guild (read: research, publication, and a noncommittal relationship to the subject) competed with, and had a strong edge over, concern with the "basic questions" of life. In this respect it would be unlikely to find religion departments any more diligent than others in challenging the university to be concerned with the larger truth, meaning, and ethical dimensions of its work. In 1970, sociologist and ethicist James Gustafson, urging greater professionalization in the teaching of religion, also noted with approval that "religious studies is becoming less important as a part of a general liberalizing education and more important as a potential field of research leading to a professional academic career."[23] The study of religion was truly taking its place as one more academic discipline among the others.

Moreover, there were strong tendencies to view the study of religion as the application of the other disciplines to the explanation of religious phenomena. Religion from this perspective tended to become merely another object for sociological, historical, and psychological analysis, something to be reduced to the categories of the disciplines being applied. This was certainly proper as one important approach to the study of religion. It is interesting to note, however, that, on this thoroughfare, there has seldom been much two-way traffic. Rarely has the study of religion worked the other way; that is, back on the other disciplines, calling their presuppositions into question, reducing them to something else, or demanding that their ways of knowing be transformed if they were to have access to the truth about reality.

Of course, the truth claims of religion were usually regarded as outlandishly at odds with those of the university disciplines. It was much easier, therefore, either to reinterpret them as something else or to dismiss questions of knowledge and truth altogether, and to settle instead for description, function, and meaning. The consequence was, as one leading figure in religious studies acknowledged in 1970, that there reigned within the field itself "a fundamental skepticism about the status of religious truths."[24]

Yet, these trends did not reveal the whole story. The place and role of religious studies in the university was more many-sided and ambiguous than they indicated. The department of religious studies was, for instance, the one point where a more thoroughgoing pluralism than elsewhere in the university was tolerated and even sought. This included not only a pluralism of content—other cultures, other religions—but also a pluralism of theoretical and methodological approaches to the study of human culture. Robert Bellah argued in the early 1970s that three forms of religious consciousness and method had arisen in the study of religion in American higher education: the older approach of church and seminary, which, in its cruder forms, often saw the study of religion as a means of proselytizing in the university; the Enlightenment orthodoxy of the university, with its narrow conception of reason that had shaped and continued to dominate the university disciplines; and an increasingly influential approach, which Bellah called "symbolic realism," that stressed understanding and interpretation and a recognition of the integrity of religion in its own right.[25]

What Bellah seemed to have in mind with this last was the tradition of the cultural, human sciences (*Geisteswissenschaften*). This tradition had its roots in the nineteenth century, and it is associated with such figures as Wilhelm Dilthey and Heinrich Rickert who argued for a separation in purpose and method between the natural and cultural sciences. This tradition, developed further in various ways and from diverse sources, in the twentieth century had produced a number of theoretical and methodological approaches to the study of human beings and culture—among them those approaches associated primarily with phenomenology, hermeneutics, existentialism, the history of religion, aspects of critical theory, and variations on these. This tradition continued to resist the reduction of human beings and culture to narrowly rationalistic and objectivistic, causal explanations. It was just this tradition of the human sciences that Bellah argued had been largely excluded from the Enlightenment orthodoxy of the American university and its disciplines.

In the study of religion, however, this tradition had its own leading scholars in such persons as Ernst Cassirer, Mircea Eliade, Norman Brown, Herbert Fingarette, and Paul Ricoeur—and in the rise of the departments of religious studies, this tradition had managed to gain an important toehold in the university. The real significance of the new religious studies departments, Bellah argued, was that they offered an arena within the university in which ways of understanding entire dimensions of reality inaccessible to a narrow empirical and discursive rationalism were being harbored and developed. "There are few places in the university," Bellah said, "and the department of religion is perhaps chief among them, where it is possible to say that cognitive rationality is only one human good among others, and that unless it exists in the context of the cultivation of moral, religious, and aesthetic sensitivity the consequences may be monstrously destructive."[26]

The phenomenological-hermeneutical tradition, Bellah's "symbolic tradition," represented basically an attempt to develop what we might call a strong version of an institutionalized two-realm theory of truth in the university. The older, weak version we recognize, of course, in its earliest institutionalization in the university in the strict division that developed between science and the humanities. Any balance between these had repeatedly broken down as the humanities' claims to provide genuine knowledge on an equality with science had been progressively eroded and called into question by the positivistic assumptions of the modern mind-set.[27] The tradition pointed to by Bellah can be seen as a strong version effort to shore up the humanities and reinstate them as genuine sources of knowledge on an equal standing with science.

That this tradition had found its main lodging in the departments of religious studies may, in effect, have undercut its relatively strong epistemological claims. It was as though the new, strong claims of the humanities, once granted entrance, were then to be isolated from the rest of the university—quarantined as it were within the religion department lest the infection spread to other fields. There the new tradition would remain relatively innocuous, restricted as it was to religion, which elsewhere could continue to be regarded according to the canons of the modern mind as, at best, a matter of arbitrary preference or linguistic, communal custom. It promised to be an effective quarantine for it preserved the older dichotomy in which science produces knowledge and the humanities, even in this resuscitated form, traffic primarily in meaning.

In many ways it was a quarantine congenial to the professional interests of the religion faculties themselves, for it afforded them full standing in the university, but, also in modern university fashion, relieved them of any uncomfortable obligation to raise critical and challenging questions about the assumptions at work in the wider university outside their own department. The religionists were freed to tend their own professional garden, to revel in a lush growth of meanings and interpretations, and to not have to worry themselves about truth and wider implications beyond. It was not a bad arrangement, but it was a far cry from the original intentions and hopes of the theological renaissance.

More recently, of course, the infection has spread, and the hermeneutical-phenomenological-symbolic tradition has found a much wider response in other fields, particularly in literature departments, where it has taken extremely relativistic, at times, nihilistic forms. This is a larger part of the story that we will touch on in the concluding chapter. At this point, suffice it to observe that religious studies, regardless of its ambiguities and difficulties, still presents a place within the university of opportunity and possibility. In many colleges and universities the departments of religious studies often served during the 1980s as the "pluralistic wing" of traditional philosophy departments, frequently being one of the few places in the university where the full range of metaphysical, ethical, and religious subjects once at the center of philosophy could be pursued. In a similar way religious studies departments also have functioned sometimes as the "pluralistic wing" of university-based theological seminaries, providing the main access for interested seminary students to the study of non-Western, archaic, and Western esoteric-occult traditions.

Although the emphasis may continue to be mainly on description and comparison, there is often the possibility within religious studies for persons such as Huston Smith and Wilfred Cantwell Smith to raise harder questions of truth.[28] These openings and possibilities are, to be sure, weakened considerably by the two-realm theory of truth that pervades religious studies, even, or perhaps especially, at those places where the hermeneutic-phenomenological tradition is most strong, with its tendency to divide nature and history, much as the neo-orthodox theologians did, though the current dichotomy is more likely to be between nature and culture. But these are recent developments.

By the end of the 1960s the original ideas of the Protestant theological renaissance for the teaching of theology and religion in the university were dead, or had been transformed out of recognition. The alternative possibility of establishing a new approach in this area was not one in which the theologians and churches now seemed much interested.

In 1975 the Society for Religion in Higher Education changed its name, after some heated discussion, to the Society for Values in Higher Education. This name-change was perhaps as symbolic as anything of the full extent of the collapse of the church's engagement with twentieth-century American higher education. The Society for Religion in Higher Education, recall, had been formed in the early 1960s by a merger of the Fellows of the National Council on Religion in Higher Education (the Kent Fellows) with the Fellows of the Danforth Foundation. These two organizations had been among the most active and effective influences in promoting the teaching of religion in higher education and in providing support for the actual training of teachers of religion. By the 1970s the many changes that had taken place in the teaching of religion and in the church's longer relationship to higher education would seem to have made the Society's name-change eminently reasonable.

The growth of national professional groups of scholars, such as the American Academy of Religion and the reorganized Society for Biblical Literature, had gradually taken over much of the role played earlier by the Society, especially through the Kent Fellowships, in supporting graduate study in religion. A name-change would perhaps encourage a yet wider redirection of interests. The shift in emphasis we have just looked at in the understanding of religion—from a primary concern for moral and spiritual dimensions in higher education to an interest in religion as a professional academic discipline—this shift favored a name change in which the older meaning was not so definitely suggested. Professional concerns probably also stood behind the desire for a name-change on the part of the large numbers of persons in the Society with Danforth Fellowships who had doctorates in areas other than religion (although presumably they had, in good faith, accepted their Danforth Fellowships out of a deep interest in the basic issues of religion). And because the Society hoped to receive federal matching grants in its fund-raising drive, a change of name was considered advisable to avoid church-state legal problems. The choice of such a bland but modish term as values seemed a way of satisfying all these interests. That in itself indicated some considerable fading of original intentions.

But the name-change and choice of the term values were symbolic of an even deeper issue. In the modern world the term values carries overwhelmingly subjective connotations. Values are for the modern mind subjective preferences, personal and social, over against the objective realities provided by scientific knowledge. Because of the narrowness of modern reason, the appeal of the term values, as Langdon Winner has observed, is that it makes people feel that in using it "they are moving away from purely rationalistic, technocratic modes of thinking toward something more warm, caring, and humane," that they are getting down to the most important dimensions of human experience.[29] But this is an illusion since in reality it means a capitulation to the modern dualism between subject and object, value and fact, in which the most important domains of human experience can only be dealt with in arbitrary, irrational, and ultimately dogmatic ways, as in "value commitments."

In the modern world, value talk almost always represents a loss of qualities as part of knowable reality. Langdon Winner in a devastating account of the change in name of the Society, of which he was a member at the time, wrote,

> The organization chose a convenient policy, changing its name to The Society for Values in Higher Education. After all, who could possibly object to "values" in higher education? What a masterstroke! And what a great tradition it upholds! The "Ten Values" Moses received from God on Mt. Sinai, Jesus of Nazareth's "Values on the Mount," St. Augustine's treatise *The City of Values*, Tom Paine's stirring pamphlet *The Values of Man*. And who will ever forget Karl Marx's magnum opus, *Capital and Social Values*.[30]

Owen Barfield has stated the problem well. "One of the things I have particularly noticed in the course of my life," he writes, "is the ever-increasing vogue of that word *value*, and especially its plural, *values*, as well as of relatively modern concepts like *value judgments* and *value free*, in philosophy, psychology, sociology, journalism and elsewhere."[31] The Society's name-change was indicative of the loss of knowable realities once claimed by faith. "People used to talk," Barfield continues,

> about the beautiful and the ugly, noble and beastly, right and wrong; but that could only go on as long as there was confidence that qualities are objectively real. The current preference for "values" has come about because the term is one that neatly avoids any such ontological commitment.[32]

The Society's falling back on the vacuous term values was an effort to salvage something that would not give offense to modern sensibilities. Value talk made it possible for the Society to seem to be dealing with the centrally important human concerns without challenging the basic instrumentalist and materialist presuppositions of modern culture.

The failure, however, which this involved, of dealing with knowledge, was ultimately most destructive of faith. Without knowledge of the qualities of existence as objective as well as subjective, faith is left with no inner grounding and substance, with no actual reference. It can then only harden into dogmatic assertiveness, or melt away. The symbolism of the Society's name-change—the dissolution of faith, the attempt to cover this up with value talk, and the ensuing reinforcement of the modern mind-set with all its assumptions and dualisms such as the fact-value split still firmly in place—pointed to the dismal ending for yet another of the original hopes of the theological renaissance in American higher education.

SCIENCE AND FAITH

Throughout we have seen that at the core of the church's attempt to engage modern higher education lay the faith-knowledge issue. This meant that ultimately the church and its thinkers would have to come to grips with the relationship between faith and science. Science provides the conceptions of knowledge and of knowable reality that have most shaped the modern university and that have increasingly determined our modern experience of the world. At the heart of the faith-knowledge relationship, therefore, lay the question of the adequacy of science in providing the main and dominant conception of how and what we can know. Interestingly, it was not the theologians but, rather, some scientists who had been deeply touched by the theological renaissance who undertook the most thoroughgoing examination of their own field. It was among them, rather than among the humanists, that the deepest probes were made into the presuppositions of modern thought. This was one area, therefore, in which some basis was laid for work that still holds perhaps the most promising possibilities for a much-needed renewal of efforts to engage the faith-knowledge issue.

There are two reasons why this is not entirely surprising. In the first place, those scientists who had responded to the theological renaissance were also most painfully aware of the chasm that separated scientific ways of knowing—and the modern scientism that often sprang from them—from the affirmations of faith and the new theological understandings they had found so meaningful. Second, they found themselves already part of a lively discussion that had long been under way among some leading scientists and philosophers of science concerning the foundations of scientific knowledge. The crisis in physics of the 1920s, with its challenge to classical mechanistic and objectivistic conceptions of knowing, had been the most important influence in provoking the discussion, one which by its nature swept up anyone seriously concerned with larger questions of the nature of ultimate reality and of how we might know it. For these reasons it is important to take a brief look at the efforts of a few theologically interested scientists to reconcile faith and knowledge.

There was no uniform outlook or program among these scientists, but they did share certain central concerns and convictions. All of them were deeply influenced by the theological renaissance, but they all attempted to move beyond the separation between religion and science, history and nature, faith and knowledge, that had come to characterize main currents of the new theology. These scientists were convinced that for the sake of both religion and science the separation had to be overcome.

It is significant that three of the major intellectual movements of the time—the biblical theology of neo-orthodoxy, modern existentialism, with which neo-orthodoxy was inseparably interwoven, and twentieth-century positivism and its variants, with which neo-orthodoxy usually felt itself at odds—had in common that they all made a sharp cleavage between religion and science. For the neo-orthodox, science deals with a world of secondary relationships—finite, causal relationships—in space and time; theology deals with personal-social meanings and with God as the Wholly Other, the transcendent prime cause and source of the entire world process. But beyond this, for the neo-orthodox, science and theology are essentially distinct, and they have little to say to one another.

This separation was further reinforced by existentialism with its sharp contrast between the commitment, concreteness, and passion of personal life and the detached, abstract, and cold nature of rational cognition. Lending its support to this dichotomy, linguistic analysis, drawing on Wittgenstein's notion of different "language games," spoke of science as a language for description, correlation of empirical data, and for technical problem-solving, and of religion and ethics as very different language games having to do with the subjective expression of desire, attitudes, and life forms.[33]

Some theologians were not comfortable with this isolation of science and religion from each other. We have noted the problems Tillich encountered in his particular attempt to reconcile the two. Another theologian, also very much part of the theological renaissance, who resisted what he called "neo-orthodoxy's almost proud repudiation of earth," was the Lutheran Joseph Sittler. Sittler wrote, "There is a meaning in the non-human world of nature"; and he thought, "The largest, most insistent, and most delicate task awaiting Christian theology is to articulate such a theology for nature as shall do justice to the vitalities of the earth. . . ." Sittler sought the basis for such a theology in a renewal of the arts, the sacraments, and the theological doctrine of the Incarnation.[34] The radical empiricists and process theologians also had dramatically portrayed nature as qualitative and alive through and through.

But it was the theologically informed and committed scientists—their numbers were not large—who went furthest in trying to bring theology and science together.[35]

These scientists were all agreed that the most important problem facing the modern world is the knowledge issue. "Our thought patterns today are dominated largely by those appropriate to the kind of knowledge that comes to us through the natural sciences," wrote physicist Harold K. Schilling. "The fundamental issue, then," he continued, "is this: Does the universe include any reality other than that recognized by the sciences?"[36] There were two further, interrelated questions involved. One was whether there are ways of genuine knowing other than those of the sciences. The other was whether the dominant assumptions and images currently at work in scientific knowing were adequate for the tasks of science itself.

Both questions were addressed by the biologist L. Charles Birch. The pervasive way in which modern science views nature, Birch pointed out, is in terms of the mechanical philosophy. To those who would object that twentieth-century developments in modern science have made mechanism obsolete, his answer was that, true, this seems to be the implication of much in modern science, but that, in spite of this, mechanistic images and modes of explanation continue to predominate. "Mechanism is the orthodoxy of modern science," he wrote.[37] The theory of mechanism, he observed, is constantly being refurbished and outfitted anew, as, for example, "in the current craze of cybernetics."[38] In fact, regarding his own field, Birch noted that biologists on the whole are still more thoroughly mechanistic than ever.[39]

The trouble with the theory and method of mechanism, Birch pointed out, is that it omits—by definition it can do no other—the entire realm of qualities. In the mechanistic view of nature there are neither the qualities occasioned by sense experience—color, sound, and so forth—nor those qualities having to do with aesthetic and moral experience, with mind, meaning, and purpose. Yet these qualities constitute the most important experiences we have as human beings.[40] Without them nature is impoverished and religion and ethics are impossible. Mechanism is a useful abstraction for certain purposes, but there has been no justification for making it an all-embracing view of the universe.[41]

William Pollard, Episcopal priest, physicist, and executive director of the Oak Ridge, Tennessee, Institute for Nuclear Studies, analyzed the problem in much the same way. Then he gave it an emphasis that would have had the most radical consequences for the transformation of modern consciousness and knowledge had he followed through on it. Referring to Alfred North Whitehead's comment that "every philosophy is tinged with the colouring of some secret imaginative background," Pollard asked what are the chief characteristics, "the secret imaginative background," of our contemporary style of thought.[42] The answer, he said, is that it is pervaded by the quantitative and sense-bound assumptions of modern science such that whole segments of external reality are excluded from our apprehension and understanding.

Because of this "secret imaginative background" of the modern mind—here Pollard was very much engaged in the task of bringing to light the unexamined presuppositions of modern thought and consciousness—because of these assumptions, the transcendent and the supernatural have no place in our contemporary understanding of the world, and are, consequently, disappearing from our understanding of ourselves as well. The arts, music, poetry, painting have lost their external reference and have become mere expressions of the artist's inner, subjective emotional experiences and imaginary fancies. Religion and theology have become even more vapid, "possessing no external reference in objective reality."[43]

It was in this connection that Pollard was more radical than anyone we have looked at in his assessment of modern consciousness. "My thesis," he said, "is that modern man has lost a capacity to respond to and to know a whole range of reality external to himself which Western man in earlier centuries quite naturally possessed." In other words, Western consciousness once had the capacity to know supersensible realities but has lost that capacity and is now faced with the question of whether and how it might be regained. "Throughout the whole wide range and diversity of human experience," said Pollard,

> with the sole exception of the West in the nineteenth and twentieth centuries, the world of nature has been alive with, and immersed within, a supernatural world which everywhere made contact with it, although was transcendent to it. It is this whole dimension of reality which the scientific age has lost the capacity to experience or know. An age such as ours which has lost a genuine capacity for knowing and responding to some great segment of reality is actually, without knowing it, in a dark age. . . . We really have lost a genuine capacity which the rest of mankind has possessed and actively exercised, and we have become a people trapped and in bondage within the prison of space, time, and matter.[44]

He added that, consequently and unfortunately, "It is primarily the business of the university . . . to maintain the imprisonment of our time." "It saddens me," he said, "to see a new generation being victimized by this all pervasive spirit of this epoch."[45]

It is difficult to see how anything less than Pollard's strong formulation of the problem—that is, in terms of the need to develop new capacities for knowing qualitative, supersensible realities in nature and spirit—could ultimately bridge the faith-knowledge dichotomy for modern consciousness. Therefore, it will be all the more disappointing to see that Pollard's own solution fell far short of any such thing; in fact, it took the form of a fairly standard neo-orthodoxy, with some tantalizing openings in it.

Nevertheless, the most interesting aspect of these scientists' wrestling with the faith-knowledge, religion-science issue was that they did go beyond merely criticizing the hidden presuppositions of thought to attempting their own positive approaches. We will look briefly at three main forms of their positive attempts to reunite science and religion. One was simply to point out, which all of them took pains to do, that the ambiguities of science that had emerged in the twentieth century, especially in quantum physics, called into question a thoroughgoing mechanistic and reductionist interpretation of nature.[46] Most were careful to emphasize that the new physics did not support positive affirmations about human freedom or purpose and meaning in the universe, but that it could not be used to deny these either.

Pollard did attempt to find in the indeterminacy in nature posited by physics at the quantum level an opening for God's action in the world as understood in the light of the biblical narratives.[47] Ian Barbour criticized Pollard's position here as providing no common terms for connecting language about physical entities like electrons with biblical or any other language about God.[48] The being of God as presented in the Bible becomes for Pollard at this point a faith affirmation that he attempts to make credible by appealing to atomic indeterminacy to show how divine agency in the world might be conceivable; but this remains very much a kind of faith-knowledge separation that avoids most of the basic issues Pollard himself at other places takes pains to bring out.

The scientists' second type of positive approach to the issue was to show the many parallels between modern science and religion and from these parallels to argue that both revealed important domains of experience and that they were not unconnected. Barbour was especially active in surveying all the ways in which these parallels and likenesses could be drawn.[49] This was again a kind of "strong version" of the two-realm theory of truth. What made it a strong version was that most of these scientists insisted on finding ways of talking about religion (and art) alongside science as also having to do with knowledge. Harold K. Schilling, for example, spoke of "the three facets of experience," science, art, and religion, and he attempted to show not only that all three arise out of experience, but more important that all have to do with knowledge, with what we "know as a result of that experience," which is more than a product of our inner states and desires.[50] But this was more of an assertion than it was a statement about the nature and possibility of aesthetic and religious knowledge. Pollard also tried to tighten the connection between the two realms by speaking of "conceptual knowledge," which is the domain of science, and of "nonconceptual knowledge," which is the province of religion and poetry.[51] This distinction was his attempt to indicate that true knowledge included much more than what is provided by discursive, empirical reason, with which the conceptual is usually identified. But his acceding to this narrow definition of conceptual was unfortunate, for it forced Pollard, in order to speak of a deeper knowledge, to adopt the phrase "nonconceptual knowledge," an exceedingly vague and almost oxymoronic expression.

A third way taken by some scientists was potentially the most far-reaching of all. Although this approach never really got beyond the speculative, it pointed the direction that would have to be followed if a truly radical joining of faith and knowledge was ever to be achieved in a way that maintained the integrity of both. This was the recognition of the qualities of existence as both subjective and objective in nature. The biologist L. Charles Birch was the clearest and most forceful in setting forth this recognition.

Birch was deeply influenced by the process metaphysics of Alfred North Whitehead with its view that an adequate understanding of the world must make a central place for the objective realities of life, feeling, and qualities. Birch argued that to understand the universe we should begin with that experience most complete and nearest to us; namely, the experience of ourselves. Rather than reducing the human being to something else, we should see the entire universe in the light of human experience. "The most directly accessible clue we have to the nature of the universe," said Birch, "is neither the electron, nor amoeba, but man."[52] If we begin with the human being, then we begin to see that nature is itself permeated at every level with life, feeling, mind, and purpose—that these are the essence of what makes human experience human. Rather than being epiphenomenal or secondary after-thoughts, they actually provide the primary basis for understanding everything else. All these qualities the mechanistic theory of nature leaves out. Eventually, Birch would say that the universe most adequately under-stood is a "humiverse."[53]

Birch, however, did not carry through the full implications of his recognition of the importance of qualities for our ways of knowing. Like his fellow Whiteheadians, Birch remained largely within a speculative metaphysics, an interpretation of the world that, on principle, is open to realities excluded by positivism and mechanism, but one which has usually stopped short of exploring what this philosophical perspective might entail for the develop-ment of new capacities of knowing and for actual scientific research methods and strategies.

Birch did not raise the possibility of developing qualitative ways of knowing. He tended to remain instead with only a vague feeling-awareness of the qualities of the world. For Birch, we can at most have "the accurate knowledge of science" set against "a dim background of *invincibly indefinite* feeling for the 'life of things.' "[54] Science, in other words, remains pretty much what it is, but needs to be supplemented by feelings. Birch did not ask whether it is possible to go further and, through heightened awareness and attentiveness, to develop the feelings as disciplined cognitive capacities that could yield not merely dim awareness, but increasingly precise and rigorous knowledge of qualities as both subjective *and* objective. As it was, Birch's approach remained a version of the two-realm theory, but it was perhaps the most open and promising of all the versions of it.

For all their efforts to bring a critical perspective to bear on their disciplines, these scientists had yet to make real inroads into overcoming the deep modern breach between religion and a purely quantitative science. One step they might have taken in this direction would have been to explore the participatory nature of all knowing, since modern physics was itself suggesting this as a possibility. The twentieth-century crisis in physics had seriously challenged the traditional objectivist, onlooker view of the knower as detached and uninvolved in the known.[55] Philosophers of science, such as Thomas Kuhn, Michael Polanyi, and Norwood Hanson, already had begun to explore the participatory nature of all knowing, not least scientific knowing.[56] All these writers (including Kuhn, though he is better known for his emphasis on the communal nature of science) had pointed to the primacy of imagination and of the participatory involvement of the knower with the known as the source of all knowledge. Here might have been a point at which, for example, Birch's insistence on the primacy of mind in nature and in the human being alike could have been given a concreteness and methodological penetration it otherwise lacked.

Was it not possible, and what would be required, to raise systematically the imaginative powers of the mind beyond mere fancy (to use Coleridge's distinction) to the level of what the physicist David Bohm has called insight? Insight, Bohm has argued, is a deep, concentrated attentiveness that is the source of all newness in knowledge and the essential foundation for the meaning of logic, calculation, and technical reason.[57] What is required for the development of capacities of insight and imagination capable of penetrating with power and discrimination not only the quantitative but the qualitative dimensions of reality? This was not a question the theologically interested scientists took up, although their concerns touched on it at point after point.[58] It was a question that, had it been pursued, would have been crucially important not only for science, but for religion and art as well.

Such questions are especially intriguing in the light, for example, of Michael Polanyi's efforts to show the real unity between knowledge and faith, since Polanyi was frequently referred to by the American, theologically interested scientists.[59]

Polanyi pointed out that the problem of the relationship between faith and knowledge was an ancient one, but that it is only in the modern world, as a result of the influence of science, that it has taken on totally new and global dimensions.[60] If the relationship between faith and knowledge is to be adequately dealt with, it will require, Polanyi said, that we pay heed to essential features of the process of knowing that are "disregarded by the modern conception of positive, scientific knowledge."[61]

Polanyi distinguished between two kinds of processes that are involved in every comprehensive act of knowing. There is, first, the awareness of particular entities and the explicit forms of logical reasoning, deductive and inductive, that connect the particulars. But these are impotent in themselves, for they depend on deeper, more hidden, and more encompassing processes of knowing. There is in all knowing, Polanyi maintained, another deep, subsidiary awareness (later he called it a "tacit awareness") of the whole that includes the particulars, and actually is the basis of our knowledge of them.[62] Yet this deep, tacit knowledge of a more comprehensive, coherent whole makes possible and gives significance to the conscious perception and analysis of the parts. This essential tacit knowledge is ignored by the dominant modern views of knowing.

The implications for faith of this deeper understanding of the process of knowing were clear. In the first place, it established the reality and efficacy in all knowing, not only of the empirical but of the invisible and intangible as well.[63] In the second place, Polanyi's account of knowing spoke to the anxiety often expressed by the neo-orthodox that too much attention to knowing might destroy the mysteries of faith. In Polanyi's view, it is incorrect to contrast faith as mystery with knowledge as certainty, since both faith and knowledge have their mysteries and uncertainties, and they are related. In knowing, as in faith, all progress involves entrusting ourselves to the intimations of the unseen. And, in our doing so, mystery never disappears since we can never tell "in what new way reality may yet manifest itself."[64] In the third place, very much in line with Birch's grasp of the importance of the human being, Polanyi makes knowledge of persons central to all knowing. I-It knowledge remains of great importance but is seen as dependent on a wider, more fundamental context of I-Thou knowledge.

Nearly all the theological reformers, including the neo-orthodox among them, had emphasized knowledge of persons, but then had left the concept suspended with no integral connection between it and other domains of knowing. With Polanyi this emphasis of the neo-orthodox now had the possibility of becoming the all-important point for deepening our knowledge of the full reality within which faith operates. In Birch's terms, knowledge of the qualities of persons implies the possibility, and necessity, of further knowledge of the qualitative in all other realms. Understood in this way, personal knowing, Polanyi said, is "the true transition from the sciences to the humanities and also from our knowing the laws of nature to our knowing the person of God."[65] In this conception of knowing, he argued, we see that we have the possibility of uncovering ever deeper levels of, hitherto, hidden meanings, and of opening the way to knowing the Divine. "Thus," he said, "natural knowing expands continuously into knowledge of the supernatural."[66] And knowledge, then, like faith, would pertain to both realms, the natural and the supernatural.

Polanyi himself, however, did not really deal with the further question of how we might develop such knowledge. His primary concern was to show that we cannot begin to understand our ordinary ways of knowing apart from deeper intuitive processes, which modern consciousness is ignorant of or tends to deny, even though it depends on them in all that it does. He does not consider the larger question, whether it is possible, and perhaps is now necessary, consciously to develop further those tacit, intuitive capacities—in short, to strengthen their qualitative sensitivity and grasp. His entire approach, however, was pregnant with such questions, and provided a basis for taking them up. But they were not pursued by him or by the other theologically concerned scientists.

It may be worth noting in this connection that Birch, Schilling, and Pollard especially, did have a lively sense of the importance of the arts and the entire realm of aesthetic experience. Qualities and the qualitative are the substance of art, and imagination is its life's blood. The scientists recognized this, and seemed to sense that in the experience of art the imaginative, intuitive capacities and sensitivities for apprehending and working with qualities are brought to birth and nourished. At the very least the arts serve to heighten and keep alive that dim awareness, of which Birch spoke, of the qualitative context omitted by a purely quantitative, instrumentalist science. That the nourishing of artistic capacities might also be essential to the development of qualitative ways of knowing in science itself, however, was not explored.

Curiously, these scientists seemed to have had little, if any, awareness of the lifelong and ground-breaking scientific work of Goethe—in botany, morphology, meteorology, and color theory—in laying a real foundation for just such a science of qualities. Pollard did once refer briefly and positively to Goethe, having been alerted by Heisenberg's challenge to the scientific community to reevaluate Goethe's scientific work and to cease automatically rejecting it because it did not fit Newtonian theory and the Newtonian-Kantian worldview. But Pollard seemed to have no awareness of Goethe's real potential for his own concerns.[67] Barbour, much in keeping with a venerable Protestant suspicion of the Romantics and the Romantic imagination, dismissed Goethe, wrongly, as a vitalist and nature romantic.[68] Birch, oddly, since he was a biologist and had a high regard for the Goethean-influenced biologist Agnes Arber, seems to have been unaware of the potential importance of Goethe for developing a science of an objective knowledge of qualities and of living nature, Birch's two major concerns.[69]

Although they did not pick up the Goethean possibility, these scientists all had a deep appreciation of the potential of art as the pivot for once more joining science and religion—art as the qualitative bridge between a broadening of science to include the qualitative dimensions of nature and a grounding of faith in genuine qualitative knowledge of soul and spirit. It will, therefore, be all the more important for us to ask, as we will in the next section, about the fortunes of the efforts arising out of the theological renaissance to bring together religion and the arts.

These theologically interested scientists had probably gone the farthest of all the faculty touched by the theological renaissance in taking a critical look at their own disciplines. Science was by far the most important of all fields to be looked at in this way. They had, furthermore, emphasized the necessity of transforming and deepening the kinds of knowing that shape modern consciousness and its experience of the world. They had done this in ways that, regardless of shortcomings, did open possibilities for future dialogue. By and large, however, they had not begun to effect a real joining of religion and science.[70]

Probably most theologians, and theologically concerned scientists and other faculty, still held much the same position regarding religion and science as that expressed in a special issue of *The Christian Scholar* on science and theology. The human being, said the editors of the *Scholar*, lives in a world that is given— nature—and in a world that humans make through "action, thought, and imagination"—history; and that the joining link between them is ethics.[71] That nature and history are both given and made; that action, thought, and imagination play no less a role in shaping the one as the other; that ethics and epistemology are intricately and inseparably intertwined and can only artificially be separated—nothing of this was considered. The great split between nature and history, and finally, therefore, between knowledge and faith continued, and, as ever, to the detriment of the faith side of the relationship.

RELIGION AND THE ARTS

The effort to move the churches into a new understanding of the culturally formative role of the arts, and to take renewed responsibility for their own aesthetic life and that of the wider culture, gave many signs by the early 1960s to be taking hold. A place for the arts within the National Council of the Churches of Christ in the United States of America (NCCCUSA) had been established, and a base for a yet wider involvement seemed to have been secured with the founding of the Society for the Arts, Religion and Contemporary Culture (ARC). Both of these undertakings, as we have seen, involved leading theologians, some outstanding literary scholars and other faculty—a few of them, like Nathan Scott of the University of Chicago, also active in the Faculty Christian Fellowship—and an increasing number of artists. These efforts were finding reflection and support in the growing interest among many regional and local church groups in modern drama, literature, and painting. In *motive* magazine, furthermore, the concern with religion, culture, and the arts had a major voice on the college campus.

The attention to the arts held great promise for the church's involvement with the university. Here was a point at which the imaginative sources of knowing could be dealt with directly. For decades religious leaders (neo-orthodox and secular theologians alike) had championed the crucial importance of the humanities, including religion, as the prime carriers of meaning, value, and qualitative awareness within the university curriculum. Since the rise of the modern university, however, the arts and humanities as a whole, though not quite as much as religion specifically, had been kept on the defensive, having constantly to justify their place in the curriculum as equals with science and technology. The attempt to ground the importance of religion in modern higher education by an appeal to the humanities was, therefore, hamstrung from the start.

In turning renewed attention to the arts, the churches and their faculty members in the university were potentially taking up the question of the fundamental role of imagination, and of what is required for the development of imagination, in all knowing—in the humanities and ultimately in science as well. The implications for the church's engagement with higher education could be profound, indeed, but only if they were consciously recognized and pursued.

Unfortunately, persistent problems continued to sap the strength of the religion and art movement.

The decade of the 1960s itself began ironically on something of a symbolic sour note for those sensitive to the aesthetic quality of the church's contributions and witness to the wider culture. In 1960 a twenty-page report of Dr. Roy Ross, general secretary of the National Council of Churches, heralded the completion of the Interchurch Center, the new headquarters for the national, interdenominational Protestant organization. As head of the Department of Worship and the Arts, Marvin Halverson had already exercised his critical, religious-artistic-architectural judgment on behalf of the National Council. The original plans for the Interchurch Center strongly echoed the neo-Gothic spirit of nearby Riverside Church. Convinced that Gothic was neither aesthetically nor theologically the order of the day, Halverson, with the help of Paul Tillich and Alfred Barr of the Museum of Modern Art, had orchestrated sharp criticism of the initial Gothic design. The critics' efforts, which involved not only internal meetings within the council but also leaks and letters to the New York City press, were successful, and the Gothic blueprints were scrapped.

It was a Pyrrhic victory, however, since further planning for the headquarters was pursued without consultation with Halverson and the Department on Worship and the Arts. The result was an utterly utilitarian office building, a concrete cubic structure, occupying a city block and resembling nothing so much as a huge filing cabinet. It was immediately dubbed "The God Box," and has been widely known as such ever since. Located at 475 Riverside Drive on Manhattan's Upper West Side, near Columbia University and overlooking the Hudson River, the Interchurch Center stood across the street from the even more gigantic, neo-Gothic Rockefeller-funded, once Baptist but by now pan-Protestant, Riverside Church. The two buildings together, the neo-Gothic and the unrelievedly bureaucratic, presented to some ungenerous critics a fitting tribute to the twentieth-century Protestant imagination. At the least, the juxtaposition of the two seemed to capture in stone a basic dilemma facing the theological renaissance: How to be true at the same time to the traditions of faith and to the demands of the modern world without succumbing to the worst in both?

The difficulties of obtaining funding and, more important, understanding from the denominations and from most of the National Council of Churches' officials themselves, continued to impede the work of Halverson's committee.[72] In 1962, as was noted earlier, Halverson resigned. Still, one extremely important source of hope for the work of the committee was the president of the National Council of Churches himself, J. Irwin Miller. An industrialist and Disciples of Christ layman from Indiana, Miller remained throughout his tenure the strongest advocate within the council of the need to seek a new relationship between religion and the arts. His grasp of the dimensions of this task seems to have been of the same depth as those of Wilder, Halverson, Joseph Sittler, and others.[73] At the resignation of Halverson, it was Miller who appointed the special committee, headed by Sittler, that proposed a reorganized and full Department of the Arts within the National Council. This reorganization culminated in 1966 with the forming of a full-fledged Department of Church and Culture.

Roger Ortmayer (earlier editor of *motive*) became director of the new department. Funding problems, however, remained as persistent as ever. The staff of the new department consisted basically only of Ortmayer himself and a couple of sometime assistants. The arts were of low priority within the Council of Churches as such. Ortmayer's own increasing emphasis on sponsoring pop art and "happenings" made the work of his department seem all the more alien to the concerns of the Councils' constituent members, and support continued to dwindle.[74] Retrenchment and centralization of the Council, beginning in 1969, redirected the funds from J. Irwin Miller through general administrative channels, and further reduced the status and curtailed the programs of the department. Although Ortmayer remained until 1974, the work of the National Council of Churches in the field of religion and the arts had already essentially ended.[75]

A similar fate befell ARC, the Society for the Arts, Religion and Contemporary Culture. Throughout most of the 1960s, ARC maintained a vigorous and exciting program of exchange between artists, theologians, and academics.[76] It had its own newsletter, *Seedbed*, and a series of occasional publications. Funding, however, was here also difficult. Almost no support seems to have come from the churches, and during most of the 1970s there was little available from other sources, with the result that ARC became increasingly moribund.[77]

As with the arts in modern education, so too with the arts in the churches: in both situations they are among the first things to go in times of financial exigency. As the Protestant churches felt increasingly pinched for money in the late 1960s and into the 1970s, it is no surprise that programs in religion and the arts suffered first. In both cases the deeper reasons for this lack of financial support were also similar. In modern education, the arts, except in the rarest of instances, are not regarded as having any intrinsic connection with knowledge, least of all "knowledge as power," which is about the only definition of knowledge accorded recognition in modern education. Hence, the arts occupy at best a precarious position in the curriculum, especially in the modern research university. Likewise in the churches. The arts are not seen as having anything essential to do with religious truth, and at best are usually regarded as but peripheral aids to worship and the expression of faith.

Even among the most active proponents of the importance of the arts for religion there was a strong tendency to see the arts as at bottom essentially subjective and expressionistic, and not as potential manifestations of a qualitative world that is both subjective and objective. Ultimately, there was no money available because the arts were not regarded as important.

Amos Wilder later recounted an incident that illustrates the lack of understanding among church leaders that the champions of a new relationship between religion and the arts continually faced. When, in October 1963, the report on the Council's Role in the Field of Religion and the Arts, which Wilder himself was mainly responsible for, was submitted to the General Board of the NCCCUSA, a body of about a hundred members, it passed without dissent. In the discussion, however, one board member asked whether the funds that were to be assigned to the new Department of the Arts would not be better used by the Council's Department of Evangelism. Sittler, Wilder, and others on the committee argued that evangelism itself in the twentieth century was best conceived in terms of "the symbolic media and images of the age." It was, however, not this theological argument that carried the day with the board, but the observation that "in any case the main funding of the new program in the arts was to be provided out of private sources [J. Irwin Miller's it seems] and thus would not burden the Council's general budget." It had become clear, Wilder remarked, that "some of the delegates of the churches questioned any such concern with the arts, even if they paid their own way. What has Zion to do with Bohemia?"[78]

By 1969 the commitment of the churches to developing a vigorous dialogue and relationship between the arts and religion was all but dead. And almost twenty years later, Robert Seaver, another member of the Sittler committee, reflected that the ultimate reason all the NCCCUSA programs in the arts collapsed was that none of the Protestant churches at the national level had "an interest in art as a way of knowing."[79]

THE CHURCH-RELATED COLLEGE

The search for a clear meaning and identity for the church-related college also ran aground during these years. From one perspective the church-related college had continued to present the most tantalizing and frustrating problem for the educational reformers, for it was in this domain that the church seemed, from the standpoint of numbers, still to have its major and most palpable presence within American higher education. In the mid-1960s about one third of all colleges and universities in the country were private, and more than half of these (817 by one count) were affiliated with religious bodies, 57 percent of these Protestant.[80] At the same time, if these colleges were unable to achieve some sense of clear identity distinct from the other institutions of American higher education, they stood to become for the church in actuality more an albatross than a promise for the future.

A major concern of the theological-educational reformers had been to ensure that church-related colleges were intellectually and academically of the highest quality. This had long been a goal of leading Protestant champions of church-related higher education, and one in which they had actually achieved considerable success. In the phrase then already much in vogue, "academic excellence" was seen by the reformers without exception as the sine qua non of a truly Christian college and university—anything less would simply be shoddy discipleship. By the mid-twentieth century, however, "academic excellence" had become defined almost entirely in terms of the intellectual canons of the research university and its discursive, instrumentalist, and quantitative conception of knowledge. The basic assumptions of these canons meant, therefore, that now allegiance to academic excellence would, by definition, make increasingly marginal whatever distinctively religious orientation and commitments the college might have.

The most common tactic on the part of the advocates of church colleges was still to appeal to the role of the church-related college as a potential carrier of Christian values—values that determined conduct, character, and interpersonal relationships, especially teacher-student relationships, and values that guided the ethical uses of knowledge. This did ensure that the church-related college could present itself, as it had traditionally tried to do, as uniquely concerned with the humanities and liberal arts as the principal carriers of religious-moral values in the curriculum. In every case, however, this hoary tactic left values (whatever they might be) arbitrary in their sources, ancillary and subordinate to the dominant conception of academic excellence, and, in the end, artificially applied to intellectual inquiry and discovery. Moreover, since the humanities, in church-related colleges as elsewhere, were treated simply as separate academic disciplines, they were not likely, except in unusual cases, to serve as prime sources of compelling religious and ethical reflection.

The other main response of the church-related colleges, and it did not necessarily contradict the first, was to stress the academic excellence of the institution as the college's contribution to the wider society. The advantage of this was that it permitted the college to do two things simultaneously: to recruit faculty who would enhance the college's strictly academic reputation without having to worry about their religious orientation, and to present the college in doing so as fulfilling a special commitment to Christian service.

As the search for the identity of the church-related college continued to prove ever more difficult, increasing numbers of the church colleges were concentrating instead on academic excellence—even if this meant giving up their church connections, as many were doing. In mid-decade a major study of church-related colleges, again funded by the Danforth Foundation, observed, "The intellectual presuppositions which actually guide the activities of most church colleges are heavily weighted in the secular direction. . . ." The study went on to say:

> Many academic people do not think of religion as concerned primarily with the truth about ultimate reality. Rather, it is regarded as a moral code, as a set of ideals, or as a quaint and antiquated body of ideas which educated people are supposed to have outgrown . . . [and] there is good reason to believe that the church colleges are, by and large, stronger academically (in the secular sense) than they are religiously.[81]

At about the same time, another study of Presbyterian colleges showed that most Presbyterian college presidents and the Presbyterian Board of Christian Education itself tended to be increasingly concerned about their colleges' academic excellence (defined in ways acceptable to the nonchurch educational mainstream) and less and less concerned about their colleges' religious identity.[82] This was especially significant in light of the Presbyterians' long and deep commitment to higher education.

This is not to say that there was not a considerable amount of continuing experimentation and innovation aimed at making the church-related institutions unique. Much of this experimentation, however, focused on administration, on improvement of teaching (faculty development was already becoming a catchword), on student life, and, in general, on "character and values." Where there was a direct concern with knowledge and the intellectual life, it took the form chiefly of an emphasis on reinvigorating the humanities, especially through interdisciplinary studies.[83] The continual call for more attention to the humanities did reveal a pervasive sense that the humanities were being neglected in modern higher education, but rarely was there any attempt made to get at the root causes of that neglect.

When yet another major study of church-related colleges appeared in 1978, it did little more than underscore the near complete frustration of the effort to find a distinctive identity for the church-related college.[84] Arguments for the church-related college in this latest study often rose no higher than a rather lame appeal to America's need for a pluralistic system of higher education and a call for greater sensitivity to moral and religious values.[85] Among those schools that were attempting to maintain their religious identity and, just as important, their religious commitment, the engagement with the knowledge-faith relationship had been almost entirely neglected. Instead, the stress on a dualism between knowledge and values ("intellectual," "creedal," "humane," and "moral" values), or between the academic life and the campus moral-worship-communal atmosphere, was more pronounced than ever.[86]

The rhetoric of the colleges reported on in the study was familiar, unexceptionable, and tired: "the seriousness of the commitment as an educational institution," "scholastic integrity," "freedom in the pursuit of truth," "the college's concern is the liberally educated mind," "the pervasive role of values," "the dignity of each student," and so on. Again and again the call was for a church-related college "that knows itself to be, first, a seat of higher learning, and, second, a home of spiritual values."[87] As always it sounded right, but the old difficulty of bringing the two together in an integral and mutually supportive way was totally passed over, for by 1978 this task had long been abandoned. And, consequently, what it might mean to be a church-related college truly within but not of modern higher education, nobody could say.

By the end of 1969, along its entire front, the major twentieth-century engagement of the Protestant church with American higher education had collapsed, and its forces were in rout.

NOTES

1. Edited by William B. Rogers, and published by the Faculty Christian Fellowship, these included: Charles S. McCoy, *The Meaning of Theological Reflection;* W. Taylor, *Christian Faith and Historical Studies;* Joseph P. Havens, *A Religion-Psychology Dialogue;* Thomas F. Green, *Education and Epistemology;* Dante Germino, *Political Science and Christian Faith;* Philip N. Joranson, *Conservation—Theological Foundations;* John W. Dixon, Jr., *Aesthetics and Art Criticism;* Earl A. Holmer, *Presuppositions of Business Administration;* Cameron P. Hall, *Theology, Values and Economics;* Arnold S. Nash, *Sociology, Science and Theology.* To these should perhaps be added the earlier Hazen pamphlets on the Christian faith and the vocations.

2. *Faculty Forum* 18 (October 1961).

3. These figures are from Seymour M. Lipset and Everett C. Ladd, Jr., "The Divided Professoriate," *Change* 3, no. 3 (May–June 1971): 54–60

4. Ibid., 56.

5. Ibid., 57.

6. Hugh Hawkins, "University Identity: The Teaching and Research Functions," in Alexandra Oleson and John Voss, *The Organization of Knowledge in Modern America, 1860–1920* (Baltimore and London: Johns Hopkins University Press, 1979).

7. Christopher Jencks and David Riesman, *The Academic Revolution* (Garden City, N.Y.: Doubleday & Co., 1968), 531.

8. Ladd and Lipset discovered that, ironically, faculty who were research oriented were more politically liberal than those who were primarily interested in teaching, and even that those who had received federal research grants and who had consulted for federal agencies were more politically liberal and Left-oriented than the others. Ladd and Lipset, "The Divided Professoriate," 58.

9. Lipset and Ladd, "The Divided Professoriate," 57.

10. Ibid., 57–58.

11. Arnold Nash, *The University and the Modern World* (New York: Macmillan Co., 1943), 226ff.

12. Harry Smith, *Secularization and the University* (Richmond: John Knox Press, 1968).

13. In this respect, Smith, with the other secularists, clearly saw the tendency at work in neo-orthodoxy for the concept of worldview, biblical or otherwise, to become merely an arbitrarily chosen framework of interpretation.

14. Ibid., 147–48.

15. Ibid., 138–39.

16. Ibid.

17. Also see, for example, ibid., 144ff.

18. Ibid., 10.

19. *The Christian Scholar* 50, no. 4 (winter 1967): 341–42. As the "ending" was presented, *The Christian Scholar* was simply giving way to a new journal, which would be its successor, *Soundings*, published by the Society for Religion in Higher Education. However, they were, in fact, two very different journals. *The Christian Scholar* had tried something new and remained, accordingly, somewhat outside the mainstream. *Soundings*, more polished, more academically sophisticated, has often carried outstanding articles, but it is little different from any other academic, professional journal.

20. See, for example, Nels F. S. Ferré, "Contemporary Theology and Christian Higher Education," in *Searchlights on Contemporary Theology* (New York: Harper & Row, 1961), 199–219; H. Richard Niebuhr, "Theology in the University," in *Radical Monotheism and Western Culture* (New York: Harper & Row, 1960), 93–99; Julian Hartt, *Theology and the Church in the University* (Philadelphia: Westminster Press, 1969).

21. See Smith, *Secularization and the University;* Kenneth Underwood, *The Church, The University, and Social Policy.* The Danforth Study of Campus Ministries, 2 vols. (Middletown, Conn.: Wesleyan University Press, 1969), 1: 214–25. Not even Richard Niebuhr's concept of "theology as servant" sufficed to renew enthusiasm for theology as a unifier. Niebuhr, "Theology in the University" in *Radical Monotheism.*

22. Wilson notes the waning influence of the Protestant seminaries in departments of religion by the end of the 1960s. Paul Ramsey and John F. Wilson, eds., *The Study of Religion in Colleges and Universities* (Princeton, N.J.: Princeton University Press, 1970), 8–10.

23. James F. Gustafson, "The Study of Religion in Colleges and Universities: A Practical Commentary," in *The Study of Religion in Colleges and Universities*, ed. Ramsey and Wilson, 344.

24. Ibid., 20.

25. Robert N. Bellah, "Religion in the University: Changing Consciousness, Changing Structures," in *Religion in the Undergraduate Curriculum: An Analysis and Interpretation*, ed. Claude Welch (Washington, D.C.: Association of American Colleges, 1972), 13–18.

26. Ibid., 18.

27. An interesting recent example of the recurrent denial of epistemological standing to the humanities comes from one of the foremost historians of American higher education and of the humanities in the curriculum, Laurence Veysey. "Those who reject the dominant scientific conception of knowledge," Veysey writes, "can only wander off in a score of mutually unrelated directions." Laurence Veysey, "The Plural Organized Worlds of the Humanities," in *The Organization of Knowledge*, ed. Oleson and Voss, 57.

28. See, for example, Wilfred Cantwell Smith, "Transcendence," *Harvard Divinity Bulletin* 18, no. 3 (fall 1988): 10–15; Huston Smith, "Another World to Live In, or

How I Teach the Introductory Course," *Religious Studies and Theology* 7, no. 1 (January 1987), 63.

29. Langdon Winner, *The Whale and the Reactor* (Chicago: University of Chicago Press, 1986), 161.

30. Ibid.

31. Owen Barfield, "Language, Evolution of Consciousness, and the Recovery of Human Meaning," *Teachers College Record* 82, no. 3 (spring 1981): 428.

32. Ibid., 430.

33. For expressions of these different positions, see the articles in Ian Barbour, ed., *Science and Religion: New Perspectives on the Dialogue* (New York: Harper & Row, 1968). Barbour's introduction is a helpful discussion of the similarities and differences among the different approaches to science and religion.

34. Joseph Sittler, "A Theology for Earth," *The Christian Scholar* 37, no. 3 (September 1954): 367–74.

35. In the following discussion, I draw mainly, though not entirely, on the work of four of these scientists: Ian Barbour, chair of the Religion Department and professor of physics at Carleton College; Harold K. Schilling, chair of the Physics Department at Pennsylvania State University; William Pollard, executive director of the Oak Ridge Institute of Nuclear Studies and an Anglican priest; and L. Charles Birch, head of the School of Biological Sciences at the University of Sydney, and a noted evolutionary ecologist. Although Birch was an Australian, he was a major participant in the American dialogue and a frequent contributor to *The Christian Scholar* and other American religious and theological journals.

36. Harold K. Schilling, "On Relating Science and Religion," *The Christian Scholar* 41, no. 3 (September 1958): 375.

37. L. Charles Birch, "Interpreting the Lower in Terms of the Higher," *The Christian Scholar* 37, no. 3 (September 1954): 402.

38. Ibid.

39. Ibid.; also L. Charles Birch, *Nature and God* (London: SCM Press, 1965), 60.

40. Birch, "Interpreting the Lower in Terms of the Higher," 403; idem, *Nature and God*, 61.

41. Birch, "Interpreting the Lower in Terms of the Higher," 403.

42. William G. Pollard, "The Recovery of Theological Perspective in a Scientific Age," in *Religion and the University*, ed. Jaroslav Jan Pelikan, et al. (Toronto: University of Toronto Press, 1964), 25.

43. Ibid., 27–28.

44. Ibid.

45. Ibid., 39.

46. See Ian G. Barbour, *Issues in Science and Religion* (New York: Harper & Row, 1971; originally published by Prentice-Hall, 1966), 276–374; William G. Pollard, *Physicist and Christian: A Dialogue between the Communities* (Greenwich, Conn.: Seabury Press, 1961), 107–9; Birch, *Nature and God*, 59ff.; Harold K. Schilling, *Science and Religion: An Interpretation of Two Communities* (New York: Scribners, 1962); also see idem, *The New Consciousness in Science and Religion* (Philadelphia: United Church Press, 1973).

47. Pollard, *Physicist and Christian*, 106–8.

48. Barbour, *Issues in Science and Religion*, 429ff.

49. Ibid.

50. Schilling, "On Relating Science and Religion," 378–79.

51. Pollard, *Physicist and Christian*, 110.

52. Birch, *Nature and God*, 60.

53. L. Charles Birch, "Nature, God, and Humanity in Ecological Perspective," *Christianity and Crisis* (October 29, 1979), 264.

54. Birch, *Nature and God*, 64. Emphasis added.

55. The physicist John Wheeler has summed up this challenge: "The quantum principle has demolished the once-held view that the universe sits safely 'out there,' that we can observe what goes on in it from behind a foot-thick slab of plate glass without ourselves being involved in what goes on. . . . We have to cross out that old word 'observer' and replace it by the new word 'participator.' In some strange sense the quantum principle tells us that we are dealing with a participatory universe." John Archibald Wheeler, "The Universe as Home for Man," *American Scientist* 62 (November–December 1974): 689.

56. Thomas Kuhn, *The Structure of Scientific Revolutions*, 2d ed. (Chicago: University of Chicago Press, 1970); Michael Polanyi, *Personal Knowledge: Towards a Post-Critical Philosophy* (Chicago: University of Chicago Press, 1958); Norwood Hanson, *Patterns of Discovery* (Cambridge: Cambridge University Press, 1958).

57. See David Bohm, "Insight, Knowledge, Science, and Human Values," *Teachers College Record* 82, no. 3 (spring 1981): 380–402; David Bohm, "On Insight and Its Significance, for Science, Education, and Values," in *Education and Values*, ed. Douglas Sloan (New York: Teachers College Press, 1980), 7–22.

58. Barbour came as close as any to pursuing the question of participation, but treated it more psychologically than epistemologically and so did not follow through any of its more radical possibilities. See Barbour, *Issues in Science and Religion*, 175–94.

59. Michael Polanyi, "Faith and Reason," *The Journal of Religion* 41, no. 4 (October 1961): 237–47; idem, *Personal Knowledge: Towards a Post-Critical Philosophy* (Chicago: University of Chicago Press, 1958); idem, *The Tacit Dimension* (Garden City, N.Y.: Doubleday & Co., 1966).

60. Polanyi, "Faith and Reason," 237.

61. Ibid., 239.

62. See especially Polanyi, *The Tacit Dimension*.

63. Polanyi, "Faith and Reason," 243.

64. Ibid., 244.

65. Ibid., 245.

66. Ibid., 246.

67. Pollard, *Physicist and Christian*, 94–95.

68. Barbour, *Issues in Science and Religion*, 324ff.

69. There has recently been a growing awareness of Goethe's importance for science. The crucial importance of Goethe's scientific method for our time was established by Rudolf Steiner, the editor of the definitive Weimar edition of Goethe's scientific works. Steiner himself took Goethe as the point of departure for an even deeper and more systematic development of qualitative ways of knowing. See, for example, Rudolf Steiner, *Goethe the Scientist* (New York: Anthroposophic Press, 1950) and Rudolf Steiner, *A Theory of Knowledge Implicit in Goethe's World Conception* (Spring Valley, N.Y.: Anthroposophic Press, 1968). For examples of the continuing and growing interest in Goethe's scientific method, see Frederick Amrine et al., eds., *Goethe and the Sciences: A Reappraisal*. Boston Studies in the Philosophy of Science, 97 (Boston: D. Reidel Publishing Co., 1987); Henri Bortoft, *Goethe's Scientific Consciousness* (Tunbridge Wells, England: Institute for Cultural Research, 1986); J. Bockemuehl et al., eds., *Toward a Phenomenology of the Etheric World* (Spring Valley, N.Y.: Anthroposophic Press, 1985). Also see especially Arthur Zajonc, *Catching the Light: The Entwined History of Light and Mind* (New York: Bantam Books, 1993). A splendid, recent English

edition of excerpts from Goethe's major scientific writings is Douglas Miller, ed., *Goethe: Scientific Studies* (New York: Suhrkamp Publishers, 1988).

70. Nor does the position of so-called critical realism, currently the favorite attempt of a number of Protestant theologians and scientists to reconcile science and religion, provide an advance over the positions we have looked at. Critical realism is characterized by Arthur Peacocke, probably its major representative, as a "cautious, skeptical and qualified realism concerning scientific models and metaphors," which also wants to take account of the social context in which scientific practice, interpretation, and understanding occur. (See citation below.) The critical realists are aware that when scientists speak of such theoretical entities as electrons and so forth, these can not be taken at face value in a naive sort of way. Nevertheless, say the critical realists, because the scientists achieve considerable instrumental success, their theoretical constructs must be granted some kind of qualified real existence. The critical realists are aware of the criticisms of naive realism but still want to maintain some kind of realism over against pure instrumentalism, on the one hand, and idealistic subjectivism, on the other. They want to have some solid grounding for knowledge and for ethical action.

As the physicist Arthur Zajonc has demonstrated, however, critical realism is a compromise position, an ad hoc solution that constantly hedges. It is full of qualifications that would attempt to ward off central problems rather than confronting and disposing of them. As Zajonc shows, critical realism turns out not to be critical at all, but rather, a form of transcendental realism justified by appeals to science's instrumental success. As a result, science in the end is left naively uncriticized, and no new epistemological ground is opened up. The "mutual modification" between science and religion, of which the critical realists are fond of speaking, is not mutual by any means. The only modification that takes place is on the side of religion as it is expected to adapt to the continued advances of an unaltered science.

See Arthur Peacocke, *Intimations of Reality: Critical Realism in Science and Religion* (Notre Dame, Ind.: University of Notre Dame, 1984); Harold Nebelsick, *Theology and Science in Mutual Modification* (New York: Oxford University Press, 1981); Arthur Zajonc, "Religion and Science: The Contemporary Dialogue" (Amherst College, manuscript, 1991). Zajonc does explore in this manuscript the kind of new "epistemological level" that is required for science itself, as well as for a new relationship between science and religion.

71. *The Christian Scholar* 46, no. 1 (spring 1963): 3–7.

72. Dr. Roy G. Ross, general secretary of the National Council, for example, in his 1960 report celebrating the opening of the Interchurch Center also portrayed the task of Worship and the Arts as mainly one of "challenging leaders in the arts to their responsibilities in the field of religion," a drastic narrowing and distortion of the Department's own understanding of its purpose. *Triennial Report*, NCCCUSA, 1960, 24. NCCUSA Archives, Philadelphia.

73. The "imagination," said Miller, must be brought into the church's "worship, liturgy, music, art, writings, and preaching . . . to reshape them in exciting and relevant terms." J. Irwin Miller, "The President's Message," in NCCCUSA *Triennial Report* 1960, 32. It was essential, he stressed again, for the church to enable human beings "to learn about God the Creator through the eyes and perceptions of the artist, and all creative humans who find knowledge of Him through their capacities for feeling and understanding beyond the power of words." Idem, "Our Mission—Servants of Our Servant Lord," *Triennial Report*, NCCCUSA, 1963, 9. NCCUSA Archives, Philadelphia.

74. Within his department Ortmayer attempted to develop three types of programs: programs in religion and architecture; collaborative programming with Pamela Ilott, director of religion for CBS, in creating television features; and the funding of special artistic works, most of them, as noted, in the nature of the current 1960s vogue of "happenings." Only the last of these received actual funding from the Council, the first two having to rely on private contributions and funds from the collaborating agencies. The evanescent nature of the happenings, which almost by definition left nothing in the way of documentation except the erstwhile memories of those who were present, makes it exceedingly difficult to obtain a concrete picture of this aspect of the department's work.

75. Frank Lloyd Dent, "The Arts in the NCCCUSA: A Case Study," manuscript. I am indebted to Frank Dent's study for many of the organizational details about the development of the National Council's efforts in the arts. Also see Nathan H. Vanderwerf, *The Times Were Very Full: A Perspective on the First 25 Years of the National Council of the Churches of Christ in the United States of America, 1950–1975* (n.p., n.d.), 85–88.

76. See John Dillenberger, *The Visual Arts and Christianity in America: From the Colonial Period to the Present,* new expanded ed. (New York: Crossroad, 1989), 178–82.

77. ARC has recently been reorganized. However, it continues to be hampered by a lack of significant funding, currently lacks administrative staff and sponsors only occasional informal publications. I am indebted to Frank Dent for this information.

78. Amos Wilder, *Theopoetic: Theology and the Religious Imagination* (Philadelphia: Fortress Press, 1976), 44–45.

79. Robert Seaver, interview by author 6 June 1988.

80. Manning M. Patillo, Jr., and Donald M. Mackenzie, *Church-Sponsored Higher Education in the United States* (Washington, D.C.: American Council on Education, 1966), v, 198.

81. The authors of the study commented, "We realize that this conclusion is directly contrary to an assumption widely held by the general public and by academic people." Ibid., 153.

82. Richard Robert Johnson, "The Developing Relationship between the Board of Christian Education and the Presbyterian-Related Colleges," (Ph.D. diss., Teachers College, Columbia University, 1968), 67–68, 89–92.

83. See ibid., 177–97.

84. Robert Rue Parsonage, ed., *Church Related Higher Education* (Valley Forge, Pa.: Judson Press, 1978).

85. Ibid., 86.

86. Ibid., 79.

87. Ibid., 89.

CHAPTER 7

Protestantism and Its Postmodern Prospects: Some Reflections on the Present and Future

The twentieth-century Protestant theological renaissance failed to penetrate the cognitive center of the modern university. The theological renewal movement had arisen in the conviction that it is possible to be at once a committed person of faith and thoroughly modern. This conviction had brought the theological reformers immediately into engagement with American higher education, and almost from the start it made them theological-*educational* reformers. They recognized that the university had become the chief keeper and cultivator of the ways of knowing and knowledge that give us the world of our modern experience. They also had a dim sense that the narrow, sense-bound conception of knowledge dominant in modern culture and higher education has by definition no way of dealing with the dimensions of experience within which faith must live. As long as this sense was alive, they could not escape having to deal with the relationship between faith and knowledge.

The reformers began to develop two main approaches to the faith-knowledge issue. One was primarily critical: identifying the limitations of modern modes of knowing and attempting to confine these to their proper domains. The emphasis of the theological reformers on bringing to light and scrutinizing the hidden assumptions of the disciplines was essential to this critical endeavor.

The second approach was constructive: to begin to demonstrate the need and possibility, if not yet the actual realization, of ways of knowing that are deeper and more encompassing of the fullness of reality than purely discursive, quantitative, and instrumental ways of knowing can be. In other words, the constructive challenge was to develop genuine knowledge of the qualities of existence on a par with and as a context for quantitative knowledge. Few ever caught more than a glimpse of the need for this positive task; fewer still the possibility of fulfilling it. Nevertheless, we have seen that the leading theologians of the movement found themselves having to move in this constructive direction in order even to talk meaningfully about faith. Their emphasis on the symbolic nature of all knowing, and their beginning efforts to develop a concept of "knowledge of persons," represented incipient efforts toward such an epistemological deepening.

Yet neither the critical nor the constructive approaches to the faith-knowledge relation were carried through, and eventually both were abandoned. Examining the presuppositions of knowledge, even when this task was attempted, tended to become an exercise in comparing abstract and arbitrary worldviews and value systems. The constructive undertaking was itself completely stillborn. "Knowledge of persons," hanging in isolation, never became the paradigm it might have been for the development of qualitative knowledge in all fields.

In the end, the churches fell back on and accepted uncritically, often enthusiastically, the dominant university conceptions of knowledge. They even gave up the critical task of showing the problems presented by an exclusively quantitative and instrumental rationalism in providing an adequate understanding of the world of nature itself, much less of the worlds of the spirit. Having once wholeheartedly adopted the dominant modern conception of knowledge, the church found that by the canons of this knowledge it had no grounding for its faith in the accepted world of knowable reality.

The possibilities then available to the church and the believer were exceedingly problematic: to give up the affirmations of faith as unknowable and perhaps unreal; to become arbitrary and doctrinaire in the assertion of faith; to attempt to secure the realities of faith in ethical striving; or to fluctuate among various combinations of these. The Social Gospel traditions of neo-orthodoxy led many in its fold to attach their hopes to political-social action as the prime witness to the power of faith commitment. But this ethical striving with no ontological underpinnings, this ethics without metaphysics (or, in the end, this ethics joined to a materialistic metaphysics), served less as a witness to the realities of faith than as a characteristic expression and reinforcement of the defining ethical emotivism of modern culture, and of the faith-knowledge dualism on which it rests. Eventually the mainline Protestant churches acquiesced entirely to the modern dichotomy between faith and knowledge, and, therefore, had no further reason to maintain the engagement with the modern university.

The collapse of the theological renaissance left in its wake a diversity of fractured theologies. A less generous observer has dubbed them "special interest theologies."[1] Many of these attempt bravely to carry on some limited aspect of the earlier reform project. Some have become platforms to ensure that the often neglected—the poor, the nonwhite, the feminine, and others—have a voice in what is left of the theological conversation, and in the politics involved. As we shall presently examine in more detail, almost all have taken note of the postmodern criticism of positivism and have garnered encouragement from it—though often what seems sometimes postmodern for one is premodern for others.

In good postmodern fashion, postmodern for the various fractured theologies often seems to be what each of them wants to make of it. Whether any of the current theologies, however, will actually go much beyond the earlier theological approach to the faith-knowledge relationship is not yet clear. There are signs that some may; it is apparent also that many, even while they are busily waving their postmodern credentials, have yet to recognize the problem.

What then of the present situation? Ironically, in its giving up of the faith-knowledge issue, the church largely bypassed other, important possibilities for actually dealing with it anew—possibilities that were already beginning to emerge in the 1960s. The ructions of consciousness and culture of the 1960s, for all their confusions and accompanying pathologies, shook loose and brought to the surface many thitherto hidden dimensions and suppressed conflicts of modern society. The place of feelings in a rationalized existence; the yearning for spiritual sustenance in a disenchanted world; the seeking for personal identity and self-development in a bureaucratized society; the demands for civil and human rights; the doubting of the total claims of the nation state, indeed, the questioning of authority of every kind; a new consciousness of nature and of the fragility of the earth; a questing for new human relationships and forms of community—all these dimensions of experience and exploration cried out for attention and, more important, though not always with the same insistence, for knowledge and understanding.

Where the knowledge and understanding were lacking, much of the nascent new awareness and sensitivity could only manifest in irrational and destructive ways, or be suppressed and work their influence through more subterranean channels. The press of events and experience, nevertheless, supplied new materials and new vantage for pursuing questions long simmering in many minds about the dominant interpretations of our world, and for developing new ways of understanding that world.

By the 1980s a remarkable upsurge of attention to the problem of knowledge began to emerge in a diversity of areas, not only in many academic disciplines, but also in the women's movement, in the peace movement, in the ecological movement.[2] The issue of epistemology was suddenly *au courant*. Questions once thought to be the province of technical philosophers—how and what we can know, who says so, and who controls the results—were being raised on every hand. The old positivism and the mechanical philosophy were reported to be collapsing.

PUTATIVE POSTMODERNISM AND THE
FAITH-KNOWLEDGE RELATIONSHIP

Today we are being told increasingly that we are about to enter a radically new period in human understanding and, consequently, of human possibilities. The claim on all sides is that positivism has at last been overcome, that the limiting assumptions of modernity are being left behind, and that we are on the threshold of an epoch so unprecedented that it can only be described as *postmodern*![3]

Perhaps. Skeptical questions aside for the moment, however, something genuinely new does, indeed, appear to be afoot. What seems to be happening is that the objectivistic conception of knowing, which is a mainstay of the mechanical philosophy and the modern mind-set, is being fundamentally challenged. Under broad attack is what Ernst Lehrs once called "the onlooker consciousness," the characteristic mode of modern consciousness.[4] This is the Cartesian view that the knower is simply a detached onlooker, describing a world of self-existent objects as though neither the knower nor the known were mutually and essentially affected in the process. This conception of knowing as involving a detached spectator observing and interpreting a world of mind-independent objects seems to be undergoing massive collapse. With the abandonment of this major tenet of the modern mind-set, talk has turned increasingly from objectivism to participation, from reductionism to holism, from positivism to postpositivism, from modernism to postmodernism.

The attack on the onlooker consciousness has been coming from all directions as in almost every field the discovery is made that the observer is willy-nilly involved in the observed. Some might be inclined to argue that this is simply the old, rock-bottom Kantian insight at last coming fully into its own. Nonetheless, it does seem to have taken a new turn.

The criticism of the onlooker consciousness perhaps has received its most important impulse from within science itself, where it has taken several forms. The involvement of the scientist and scientific instrumentation in the most internal events of scientific observation has posed the central conundrum of modern physics since the 1920s. That all facts of observation are in their nature "theory laden" is a main claim of many philosophers of science.[5] The involvement of the scientist's personal and social interests, even character, in the purest of research has been demonstrated by both philosophers and sociologists of science.[6]

The feminist critique of the detached and controlling (masculine?) modes of knowing characteristic of the onlooker consciousness has brought further awareness to the possibility of other more participatory, involved, and relational modes of knowing.[7] A growing ecological sensitivity has further underscored the exploitative, destructive power of an objectivistic, nonparticipatory consciousness. Not least, the phenomenological-hermeneutic tradition has demonstrated in the *Geisteswissenschaften* that knowledge and understanding emerge only out of a most complex circle of mutual interaction, interrelationships, and participation among knower, other knowers, and the would-be known.[8] This tradition now seems in the eyes of many to have administered the final coup de grâce to positivism in the human sciences.

The awareness of the participatory nature of knowing has also brought to the fore the ways in which the community of knowers is mutually interdependent and participant. The awareness of participation has thus been accompanied by a profound sense of the communal nature of human knowledge and the view that all knowing has its communal dimensions. The emphasis on the social nature of knowing in science has had various important sources: the role of the community of scientists in determining theory and what counts as empirical fact; the dependence of scientific observation on informal language as crucial to symbolic formulation, mediation, and interpretation; the interplay of personal and social interests and privilege in scientific research. All this has led many to conclude, as Michael Mulkay has put it, that "there is no alternative but to regard the products of science as social constructions like all other cultural products."[9]

In the social sciences there has also been an increasingly pervasive emphasis on the social construction of reality.[10] In religion a traditional emphasis on the community has lent itself easily to the widespread current interpretation of religion as itself basically a cultural-linguistic symbol system for constructing and securing communal meaning and identity.[11] All this has been part of the breakdown of the objectivistic assumption of modernity.

This rejection of the onlooker consciousness and the emphasis on participation, holism, and the social construction of reality have, interestingly, taken on increasingly nihilistic forms. Extreme expressions of subjectivism, radical relativism, and the deconstruction of everything have often replaced objectivism and hence have been characterized as postpositivist and postmodern. In fact, postmodernism and deconstructionism are in some quarters almost synonymous and interchangeable. But are radical relativism, extreme subjectivism, and nihilism really postmodern? Do they not resemble characteristics we have already recognized as central to the modern mind-set, only now carried out to their furthest extreme?

One major assumption of the modern mind-set—the objectivistic, onlooker conception of knowing—is, indeed, disintegrating. At the same time, however, other basic assumptions of modernity continue to work their influence, unquestioned and unabated. This holds for both the fundamental metaphysical assumption of modernity that the world is made up of inanimate, insentient matter related solely by deterministic, mechanical cause and effect, as well as the accompanying epistemological view that we can have knowledge only of sense experience and of abstractions from sense experience.

Question them as we might in moments of philosophical rigor and clarity, these assumptions continue to permeate our consciousness and culture and to find all manner of actual, working expression, almost as habits of the unconscious.[12] They are to be found in the commonplace modernist assumptions, for example, that all life and consciousness have arisen from chance collocations of matter in motion; that the organic derives from the inorganic and inanimate (in effect, that life arises from what is dead!); that consciousness arises from what is insentient and unconscious; that mind is to be exclusively identified with physical brain functions; that all statements about qualities—meaning, values, ideals, selves, spirit—can be reduced to some more fundamental quantitative substrata or are merely subjective expressions of arbitrary preferences, personal or collective.

The one modern assumption that has been widely challenged is that of the objectivistic onlooker as knower. The other assumptions of modernity, however, remain unaltered and in place. What is more, they are now pouring unchecked into the vacuum left by the breakdown of the onlooker consciousness. The result is a short-circuiting of what might have been a radical new possibility in human knowing; namely, the development of a genuine participatory knowledge of qualities as subjective and objective.

As long, however, as the modern assumptions that there is no reality beyond the material and no knowledge beyond the limitations of sense experience continue to accompany the breakdown of the onlooker consciousness, a genuine participatory knowing cannot develop. Instead, participation can only be conceived as self-enclosed communal interaction and social projection. The result is a radical relativism and subjectivism. What was once an individual subjectivism with respect to secondary qualities becomes now an all-consuming social subjectivism with respect to everything. Hence the doctrine that there is no truth is being presented as the very essence of postmodernism.[13]

Because it has discovered participation, but in modern fashion can only conceive of participation as locked in on itself, putative postmodernism must take the form of an absolute social subjectivism. It finds its epistemological expression in the notion of "the social construction of reality" and its metaphysical doctrine in the ultimacy of the community and the community's linguistic traditions. Within this kind of postmodernism there is a constant tendency for the group to become all-encompassing.

Furthermore, in seeing the community as primarily the linguistic community, the postmodern paradigm preserves the modern assumption that language is to be regarded as nothing apart from the social life-forms of the community. Beyond these there is no prelinguistic reality to which language can refer. There is nothing beyond the community and its linguistic forms to which appeal can be made in matters of truth and goodness. In other words, as the postmodernists reiterate, there is no truth. In its place there is only instrumentalism (that is, technical control) and conventionalism (that is, truth is what the group says it is). Since nothing new can possibly enter from without, the group is shut in on itself.

And so, philosophers and theologians of postmodernism can maintain that different linguistic communities are incommensurable—there can be no movement and connection between them. The modernist irrationality of ultimate values has been expanded into the postmodernist irrationality of incommensurate, ultimate communities. When such communities disagree, they can only contend blindly with one another, or withdraw into sectarian isolation. It is not surprising that radical ethnocentrism finally becomes the ultimate basis for choosing and championing certain values rather than others.[14] This is the logic of truth as convention, and it ends in a kind of communal positivism or emotivism.

The postmodern doctrine that there is no truth seems to have arisen in part out of the realization that the *modern mind-set* cannot attain to truth. Having come to that realization, the philosophers have made the further extrapolation that because the *modern* mind-set has no access to truth, there is no truth. This they then label postmodernism. The conclusion does not follow necessarily on the premise.

To be sure, it does seem that the call for the radical deconstruction of everything has also sprung in part from the prophetic desire to demonstrate that no one person or group has an exclusive purchase on the truth. Insofar as it helps keep this prophetic task alive, we need the "hermeneutics of suspicion" with us always. But a prerequisite for the fulfillment of the prophetic task is the larger truth that stands as fulcrum and judgment over against the immediately given. To reduce truth to convention closes off that possibility; to substitute instrumentalism for truth without a larger context is a deliberate rejection of that possibility, and is doubly dangerous for our earth because it is a worst-case combination of power and willful ignorance. In traditional language, truth as convention smacks of idolatry; truth as instrumentalism smacks of wantonness and blasphemy.

We will, of course, only approach truth asymptotically, and also have only a glimpse of it perspectivally from an infinity of vistas. But this realization does not diminish—rather, it enhances—the importance of a well-honed sense for truth. It should also begin to make us mindful of ourselves as participants and of the quality of our participation in what we would know.

Putative postmodernism consists really in taking the basic metaphysical and epistemological assumptions of modernism—minus the objective, onlooker consciousness—to their ultimate extremes. As a consequence, there is very little that is genuinely new in putative postmodernism. In fact, the problem of how genuine newness of any kind is ever to find entrance into the world created by the assumptions of modernism, and the kind of postmodernism it has produced, becomes a paramount problem of our time. Let us for a moment consider this problem of newness in a putatively postmodern world.

Basic to the modern world is the view that genuine knowledge of non-sensory, full-fledged qualitative, realities is impossible. In such a world there can be, in principle, no inbreak of radically new realities and possibilities. At best there can only be a secondary kind of novelty that results from rearrangements in what is already given within the closed system. Ideals, values, norms, aesthetic and ethical judgments, as we have seen, have in such a view no grounding other than convention. There is no prelinguistic and extralinguistic reality and meaning that language expresses and to which it points. Language is identified solely with the social life-forms of a given time and community. Words as symbols trailing meanings from beyond disappear into words as labels bearing only the meanings assigned to them, arbitrarily by usage or fiat (often fiat by the powers that be).

Cut off from a larger matrix of reality and meaning, language loses its capacity to serve either as bearer of new meaning or as source of creative criticism. It can now only mirror the already given and function merely as a lever of manipulation and control. Religious scriptures, for example, become texts—more accurately, pretexts—into which one and all can read their own interests and claims to identity.[15]

Often overlooked, moreover, is that a radical epistemology is a sine qua non for genuinely radical political-social action. In a world where there is no inbreak of essential newness, genuine liberation of the earth and its peoples becomes impossible. Where there is no genuine knowledge of the qualitative dimensions of nature and society, there can be no essentially new possibilities for deepening and transforming the overwhelmingly quantitative, mechanistic, and instrumentalist conceptions that now dominate the science, agriculture, medicine, politics, economics, and education that create the world of our modern experience. Where a radical, qualitative epistemology is lacking, truly radical political, economic, and cultural transformation is foreclosed at the outset. All that remains for those so inclined is to work for a shifting of the powers, for a change in roles of oppressor and oppressed, for a redistribution of the already given.

Where there is no knowledge of the non-sensory, qualitative dimensions of life, the capacity for experiencing and understanding the noumenal, immaterial realities that are the wellsprings of all life and meaning, and that constitute the heart and essence of all the great religious traditions, dries up. In such a world, imagination becomes, as Coleridge long ago made clear, mere fancy, a kind of associative activity that can produce hypotheses useful for the more efficient manipulation of the world, but that never penetrates into the nature of reality. In a world in which imagination is conceived in this shallow and truncated way, inspiration and revelation are meaningless expressions. Not to address the knowledge issue and the development of our capacities for newness and insight is fatal, not only to religion but, ultimately, to art and science as well.

Of course, newness does break into the modern world. In spite of its sense-bound doctrines, leakage from beyond does occur. In what is left of living language, sometimes in the artistic experience, above all in the deep unconscious sources of thinking, new, qualitative realities still slip through— else we could not recognize the threat of meaninglessness itself. Without this leakage and the occasional breakthroughs of genuine insight, new discoveries, even in the realm of the quantitative and mechanical, would be impossible.

Yet, because these sources of newness contradict the other doctrines of the

modern world, they cannot be fully acknowledged, and provision for nourishing them is not made. Imagination is permitted necessary but brief entrance
only in its most limited form—as, for example, in the need for the production
of new explanatory hypotheses—and then it is hustled quickly out-of-sight,
while calculation and observation are promoted as the primary sources of new
knowledge. Thus, writes the physicist David Bohm, our dominant view of
how genuine new knowledge is born has the process "turned upside down."
"And so," adds Bohm,

> It is not seen that the deep origins of our general lines of thinking are in creative
> acts of insight, the context of which is then further unfolded and developed . . .
> ultimately to serve as hints or clues which help to indicate or point to new acts of
> insight, and thus to complete the cycle of the process of knowledge.[16]

Unable to recognize the ultimate, nonempirical sources of all knowledge,
including the scientific, the modern world continues, as in much of the best
of modern education, to stifle and undercut its own deepest sources of creativity.

Consequently, the most important elements of genuine newness that
emerged with modern consciousness are themselves now in danger of being
lost entirely. Ironically, in the end, the modern (and putatively postmodern)
enclosure of the human being within the world of sense experience results in
the forfeiture by modernity of its own most positive and highest potentials.

With the emergence of the characteristic modern consciousness something
genuinely new and full of promise for the human being did come into the
world. This newness was intertwined mysteriously with the beginnings of
what have now become the straitjacket assumptions of modern consciousness. The positive potentials of modernity can be variously described as it
made its appearance with the Renaissance and the scientific revolution: a new
sense of wonder and respect for the material world; a clear and precise
thinking that made possible new powers of control and, accordingly, new
demands on human responsibility; and, above all, a new sense of separation
from nature—symbolized in the notorious Cartesian split—that went hand in
hand with a newly heightened experience of individual selfhood and identity. It was these positive potentials of modern consciousness that rightly
captured the attention of the secular theologians.

With the experience of individual identity and enhanced responsibility,
there came the potential for genuine freedom and love, impossible apart from
a deeply grounded individuality. With the potential for genuine freedom and
love, there also appeared the possibility of new forms of community life
and human relationships quite different from those of premodern tribalism
and communalism, in which individual identity had yet to emerge from the
relationships of blood, race, and group tradition. Initially, some, like many
leading figures of the Enlightenment, saw in this new sense of individual
worth and human possibility, which ushered in the modern age, a freeing

from the oppression of all religion and ancient tradition. Some saw it as the beginning of modern unbelief and skepticism. Later, a few would see it more complexly as the continued working of the Christ impulse ever deeper into human consciousness and experience, bringing about the possibility of an integral connection with the spirit in the very interior of the human self, grounded in the archetypal self of the Christ.[17]

Once the new concern for the material world and the experience of separation from nature hardened into sense-bound, metaphysical and episte-mological doctrines, however, the genuine new positive potentials of moder-nity also began to be undercut. Controlling reason, cut off from a larger matrix of meaning and purpose, begins to run amok, out of control. Individuality, severed from a larger and more encompassing matrix of meaning and qualitative reality, becomes in its ensuing struggle for survival, rugged and rapacious individualism—or leads to the lonely and alienated modern self, ever more vulnerable to behavioristic manipulation and social regimentation. Apart from a larger reality of meaning and responsibility, freedom disappears into deterministic mechanism or meaningless caprice. And persons and community disappear into the collective. The final tragedy of the modern mind-set, as seen most clearly in the putative postmodernism it has spawned, is that it cannot protect and nourish its own best potentials.

What then of contemporary Protestantism? What have been some of its main responses to the postmodern situation?

PROTESTANTISM AND ITS POSTMODERN PROSPECTS

Postmodern Protestantism

Much of the "postmodern" perspective has become common currency in a variety of contemporary Protestant theologies, though few seem to have recognized the implications or to have followed them through in any de-termined way. Of those who have, some have tended to emphasize mainly the deconstructive side of postmodernism, others more its communal and linguistic side. Of course, there is much overlap in each. Both illustrate the presence of the hidden modern assumptions in the postmodern paradigm and their consequences for faith when they are not recognized and dealt with.

Process theologian David Ray Griffin has made an extremely useful distinction, which I have alluded to and drawn on in discussing what I have called "putative postmodernism." Griffin distinguishes between *decon-structive* or *eliminative postmodernism* (my putative postmodernism) and *constructive* or *revisionary postmodernism*. Deconstructive postmodernism at-tempts to overcome the problems of modernism not by rejecting the basic assumptions of modernism (except that of the knower as detached, objective onlooker), but by carrying those assumptions out to their logical extremes.

This can be called "eliminative postmodernism" in that it seeks to eliminate all vestiges of premodern intimations of larger meanings, values, and realities beyond sense experience, and, at the same time, to subvert modernism's own claims to certainty from within.[18] The aim of eliminative or deconstructive postmodernism, as Griffin describes it, is to overcome the modern worldview by eliminating the possibility of any worldviews at all. The result, however, is that the modern mind-set's constant inclination toward relativism and nihilism becomes all-encompassing. Hence Griffin also calls deconstructive postmodernism, *ultramodernism* or *mostmodernism*.[19]

Here we will look briefly at three Protestant expressions of postmodern theology: first, at an example of deconstructive postmodernism; second, at a reaction in part to the implications of deconstructive postmodernism, but one that shares almost all of deconstructionism's basic premises; and, finally, at David Griffin's attempt, building on the work of John Cobb, to develop a constructive postmodern theology.

Perhaps the most thoroughgoing representative of deconstructive postmodernism applied to theology has been Mark C. Taylor in his book *Erring: A Postmodern A/theology*.[20] As already observed, much in deconstructive postmodernism has been motivated by the loftiest of ideals, and it is these that also impel theologians like Taylor to take up deconstructive postmodernism for their theological and ethical purposes.[21] Radical deconstruction is adopted out of a liberationist commitment to cut the support out from under false certainties, fixed modes of thought, and hierarchical social structures that are and have been historically used to rationalize and reinforce human injustice and oppression. God, self, truth, and purpose are all to be radically dismantled and eliminated as representing falsely reified centers of experience that have served as the justification for all manner of human inequality and exploitation.[22] Whether deconstructive postmodernist theology is capable on its own terms of sustaining its liberationist orientation is the pivotal question. Why, within this perspective of absolute flux and relativism, liberationist ideals and motives should be more compelling and less irrational than any others receives little attention.

One of Griffin's main criticisms of the eliminative postmodernism exemplified in Taylor's work is that its radical relativism, while it can be affirmed verbally, must be denied in practice and is, therefore, inconsistent and self-cancelling.[23] There is a curious logic, after all, in maintaining that "it is true, there is no truth"; in holding that the self and the possibility of intentional agency are fictions, all the while exerting self-agency in writing a book to convince other selves of their nonexistence; in denying purpose for the purpose of liberation; and in speaking of the "creativity and productivity of consciousness," at the same time arguing that consciousness and the language expressive of it are closed in on themselves.

Just as important, this kind of postmodernism seems oblivious to the unexamined modernist assumptions it unconsciously does incorporate and, therefore, fails to deconstruct. Thus, while truth is denied, all kinds of *truisms* are uncritically set forth. Many of these truisms turn out to be the naively accepted assertions of the scientific-technological worldview and its received Darwinism, as well as myriad uncontested conventions of academic social science.[24] So this postmodern theology also turns out to be not radical at all, or even genuinely postmodern. Rather, like the secular theology that preceded it, far from being radical, it is based on the conventional modern mind-set, now raised to the nth degree. For this reason, David Griffin has said that deconstructive postmodernism, and its theological expression, "for all its apparent radicality, would probably leave the dynamics of Western behavior virtually unchanged."[25]

Another postmodern approach in theology is represented by those who would try to find an anchor within the swirling flux of modern and postmodern uncertainty by fastening on the community, on the group. In this approach the community is viewed as primarily a linguistic community, shaped and governed by its language traditions and its social life-forms and practices.[26]

This approach has several potential strengths and possibilities. The emphasis on the community does underscore the social nature of human life, and, in itself, it in no way precludes the possibility of understanding the social construction of reality as a creative project of insight involving individuals in communion with one another. The emphasis also on life practices can express a basic appreciation of the importance of a deep, tacit participatory knowing that must be nourished by tradition, communal experience, and social responsibility. Above all, the central importance given in this perspective to narrative and story as providing identity and meaning to the community and its members could be truly radical. Language and narrative are potentially among our primary ways of apprehending and nurturing the qualities of existence and the immaterial relationships that are the source of its meaning.[27]

All depends, however, on whether the community participates, at least potentially, in a larger reality than its own life-forms and on whether the language it speaks is capable of referring to realities beyond the language itself. Unfortunately, in the postmodernism of the kind we have been looking at, it is precisely this wider reference and reality that are denied. There is no prelinguistic reality other than the social life-forms and practices of the group. Truth, accordingly, is determined by convention, each group the creator of its own truth.

This understanding of the linguistic community shut up within itself leaves little basis for intercommunal communication, cooperation, and rational resolution of differences. It favors, moreover, those who rise to control, for there can be no source of criticism from without that they need recognize. Nor can there be any support for the lone dissident within who would appeal to insight into a larger reality beyond the group. Truth as convention,

opportunistic instrumentalism, and sectarian ethnocentrism are the characteristics of the putatively postmodern conception of community, and they
threaten also to be those of the so-called postmodern community of faith.

In much of the current theological emphasis on the linguistic community
and its narrative traditions, the modernist and postmodernist assumption that
there is no prelinguistic reality seems often to be at work. But this is not
always clear. Two areas are especially in need of greater clarification. The first
can be discussed in traditional theological terms as having to do with the
nature of revelation.

George Lindbeck, probably the most important exponent of a cultural-
linguistic approach to religion and the faith community, often speaks as
though there is no reality other than that given and apprehended within the
language of communal convention. Yet throughout his treatment there seems
also to be lurking the unarticulated assumption that revelation does, indeed,
somehow take place in and through the linguistic traditions of the community. Else why take on the task of preserving the community and, if necessary,
working to protect and nurture its unique identity in a hostile world, if it does
not offer something of a wider truth and value worth preserving? What can
revelation possibly mean, however, where there is nothing beyond communal
life-forms and linguistic conventions? From whence would it come, and how
would it be apprehended and appropriated? What, for that matter, could
prophetic witness and criticism mean where truth is wholly communal
convention? We need to hear more from the theologians of narrative and
culture about the matter of revelation and the ways of knowing it implies.

The second area in which more clarity is needed has to do with just how
incommensurable the theologians of narrative and culture see the linguistic
community to be. The question concerns in part the possibility of communication among different religious communities. The question also has to do
with the relationships between the community of faith and the community of
science. Are these fundamentally incommensurable as some theologians
suggest?[28] If so, then postmodern theology would seem to reinforce the
central dualism of modernity. Chances are, however, that we can be reason-
ably certain that the inhabitants of the community of faith will live most of
their lives in a world and a consciousness formed and determined by the
community of science and technology. The concept of incommensurability
then will serve mainly to relieve the faith community of its responsibility for
the primary forms of consciousness that shape the rest of the world, and
probably, in fact, most of its own world. However much they may appear the
same on the surface, there is a great difference between incommensurable,
sectarian enclaves and oases of healing, hope, resistance, and unconventional
insight. The world truly needs the latter; it has more than enough of the
former. In the theologies of the linguistic community is such revelatory
insight into the realms of the prelinguistic envisioned as a possibility?

In distinction to both deconstructive postmodern theology and related postmodern communal-linguistic theologies is the attempt of certain "process theologians," theologians deeply influenced by the process thought of Alfred North Whitehead, to develop a constructive postmodern theology. This is the continuation into the present of the tradition of process and radical empiricism we examined briefly in chapter four. Particularly important in this regard are the theologians John Cobb and David Ray Griffin.[29] Their project still represents the major point within mainline Protestantism at which the necessary grappling with the knowledge side of the faith-knowledge relationship has been taken up most directly and radically, and with the greatest promise. Having already glanced at this tradition as it came to expression in Cobb's natural theology, we will focus here on its continued development into the present in the work of David Griffin.[30] Interestingly, Griffin's work also has yet to receive widespread attention from most other mainline Protestant theologians.

It is not possible here to provide an extensive and detailed analysis of Griffin's theology. For our purposes, however, it is important to underscore the two decisive points at which Griffin addresses directly the centrality of the faith-knowledge issue.

In the first place, Griffin and his fellow process theologians reject the modern, mechanistic worldview in favor of an organic worldview. In this organic worldview, mechanical cause-and-effect relationships have their place, but exist and are to be understood within the larger context of more fundamental and inclusive qualitative realities and inner relationships. From the perspective of an organic, qualitative worldview, life, feeling awareness, and internal qualitative relationships among all individuals constituting the universe are primary. Such an organic worldview lays the groundwork in principle for overcoming the great central, modern dualisms of subject and object, nature and history, nature and spirit, feeling and cognition, theory and practice, and so on. The long-standing theological separation, reinforced by the modern mind-set, between God and world is also denied in principle by such an organic metaphor, for in it "God is in the world and the world is in God."

In the second place, what distinguishes this approach, and carries it well beyond other similar metaphysical worldviews that usually remain in the realm of alternative, interpretational speculation is that Griffin stresses the epistemological implications of the organic, qualitative worldview. Our ways of knowing and the compass and quality of our knowledge must be fundamentally transformed from what they are within the mechanistic metaphor. Qualitative ways of knowing must become primary. On this point, unlike almost all mainline Protestant theologians at whom we have looked, Griffin, like Cobb, continues to address the modern limitation of knowledge to sense experience and the consequent modern denial of the possibility of nonsensory knowledge of immaterial, qualitative realities. Griffin emphasizes that we have "a nonsensory level of perception" that makes accessible to us real knowledge of moral, aesthetic, and spiritual realities.[31] In this view the necessity and possibility of a real transformation of knowing is recognized as paramount.

The affirmation of the reality and possible further development of non-sensory awareness has momentous consequences. For one thing, non-sensory awareness allows for perception and knowledge of realities that reach beyond cultural and linguistic conditioning and that, therefore, can potentially be known by all in common, and rationally discussed.[32] This possibility of rational cognition of the grounds for ethical and aesthetic judgments "reverses," as Griffin says, the pervasive modern conviction that values and ends are fundamentally irrational and not amenable to rational debate and discussion.[33] Furthermore, non-sensory awareness makes possible genuine knowledge and rational discussion of spiritual realities—the Divine, the human soul and spirit, immortality, freedom and responsibility, and the communion of souls.[34] A genuine postmodern synthesis of the best potentials of the modern discovery of individuality, clear thinking, and freedom with the reappropriation of premodern wisdom and experience becomes possible.[35]

There remain, of course, many questions, metaphysical and epistemological, which it is not possible to take up here.[36] What needs to be underscored, however, is Griffin's continued development of an epistemological radicalism rare among Protestant theologians. Griffin recognizes that worldviews and ways of knowing must both be addressed, that the knowledge side of the faith-knowledge relation in the modern world must not be ignored. More important, as Griffin shows, the requisite transformation of knowledge must involve breaking out of the modern prison-house of sense experience. The implications for religion, science, and social relations are wide-reaching and profound.

The Evangelical Surge

The passing of neo-orthodoxy was part of a larger phenomenon that involved the decline in cultural influence of the whole of mainline Protestantism itself. The abandonment of the engagement with the university was accompanied by a stunning loss of members by mainline Protestant churches. At the same time, even more dramatic, was the upsurge of conservative, evangelical Protestantism. The election of born-again Jimmy Carter as President of the United States was occasion for the media to declare 1976 "The Year of the Evangelical." The simultaneous decline of the mainline churches and the rise of evangelical Protestantism continues.[37]

Evangelicalism defies easy definition, claiming within its fold strict fundamentalists, pentecostalists, dispensationalists, scholars who find their faith and intellectual roots in Reformation Calvinist traditions of biblical authority (interpreted in diverse ways), and hosts of less well-delineated believers who combine various mixtures of allegiance to the religious authority of the Bible and a welter of borrowings from popular piety. It is these last who seem also to make up large numbers, if not the majority, of churchgoers in the erstwhile mainline Protestant denominations, churchgoers whom the theological renaissance never touched, and who now should probably also be included as part of the "new" evangelical movement.

The growth of evangelicalism and of other conservative religious movements in this country, as well as the global burgeoning of "fundamentalist" and dogmatic religions in the late twentieth century, have given rise to a controversy that bears on our inquiry. The continued and renewed vigor of dogmatic religion worldwide seems to some scholars to contradict the notion that modern secularism (its materialistic worldview, technology, bureaucracy, and rationalistic consciousness) is inherently destructive of religion. In light of the continued growth of religious movements of all kinds, predictions that the modern mind-set would lead to an irreversible disenchantment of the world and to the end of religion seem grossly exaggerated. Some now even speak of a "crisis of secularity" replacing a "crisis of religion."[38] Does this then suggest that the concern with the faith-knowledge issue is really not of primary importance after all? Is it not possible that religion will continue to reassert itself, come what may?

This way of putting the question, however, misses what is at issue. Two observations are in order.

First, the resurgence of fundamentalism is essentially a modern phenomenon and comes itself to be a prime expression of modernism. On the one hand, among fundamentalists are those who have seen most clearly that the acids of modernity have been destructive of important human values and experience. The disintegration of family; the dissolution and scattering of community, and the disregard this has involved for the virtues of loyalty, commitment, and trust; and, above all, perhaps, the unwillingness and difficulty of the modern mind to speak at all of the spiritual and qualitative dimensions of life that make human experience human—all these fundamentalism has set itself to combat. It is probably no accident that fundamentalist revivals seem most virulent in those areas of the world having recently undergone modernization (as in the Shah's Iran).[39]

On the other hand, however, to the extent that it has not taken up the epistemological task that would enable it to ground its faith assertions in knowable reality, fundamentalism becomes not only dogmatic but also vulnerable to its own inner hollowing out by the corrosions of modernity. Several commentators, for example, have begun to call attention to the pervasiveness of modern instrumental rationalism at the core of a good deal of current American evangelicalism: its uncritical embrace of technology and, especially, its well-known genius for the electronic media; its unhesitating adoption of behavioristic pedagogies in its elementary schools; its methodological rationalization of organizational structures and church management techniques; and its methodological rationalization of personal psychology, human relationships, and devotional practices.[40] The reaction against modernity, thus, frequently becomes a major carrier of it.[41]

Second, often overlooked is that the modern mind-set itself is by its nature quintessentially fundamentalistic. Weber made this clear early in the century (although he himself seems to have expected the inevitable disappearance of religion in a disenchanted world). Since modern ways of knowing cannot deal with ultimate values, meaning, purpose, and quality, these can only be asserted in the modern world arbitrarily and dogmatically. Since the need for values, meaning, purpose, and qualities does not go away, the modern world is riven with all kinds of dogmatic fundamentalism. Wherever ultimate ends and purposes are involved, we find in modernity not only religious fundamentalisms but a constant proliferation of scientific, political, and educational fundamentalisms as well. The literalism of scientific materialism and the literalism of scriptural dogmatism (as in, say, neo-Darwinism and scriptural creationism) are of a piece, and share in the common modern idolatry of the reified and hardened image.[42] On the most important of human issues, fundamentalism—the arbitrary assertion of ultimate ends and values—is the characteristic mode of modern consciousness.

In this light, it is all the more significant that a number of evangelical leaders and scholars are concerned not to be part of nor to perpetuate this kind of modern fundamentalism. In this, many critical "neoevangelical" scholars have become keenly aware of the need to wrestle with the central epistemological issues in the faith-knowledge relationship. Whether they will have more success than did the neo-orthodox members of the earlier theological renaissance, whom the neoevangelicals are coming more and more to resemble, waits to be seen.

Interestingly, the concern of neoevangelical scholars with such issues arose in connection with a new relationship of the evangelical movement with American higher education that came to the fore in the late 1960s and early 1970s, just as the mainline Protestant engagement with the university was falling apart. Throughout most of the century, evangelical education had much the quality of an underground movement. Bible institutes and colleges, and evangelical theological seminaries, separated from mainstream American higher education, carried most of the educational work of the evangelical movement, and with considerable, though, on the part of mainline Protestantism, unsuspected success.[43]

In the late 1960s the extent of this evangelical educational network began to surface. Concomitantly, a new generation of evangelical scholars began to seek to make evangelicalism a contender in American scholarly and academic life. In 1971 a number of evangelical colleges joined forces to form a Christian College Consortium, and in 1976 this was followed by the organization of the Christian College Coalition, with a membership of about seventy diverse evangelical institutions.[44] At just about the same time that the mainline

Protestant journal, *The Christian Scholar,* ceased to exist, the new evangelical academics founded their own, *The Christian Scholar's Review.* In many ways it seemed that the neoevangelical scholars had caught the falling banner of the mainline Protestant engagement with American higher education, and they were renewing the battle in their own turn.

Indeed, the correspondences and similarities between the neoevangelical and the earlier stages of the neo-orthodox engagement with American higher education are striking. First, there is the emphasis by the young evangelical scholars on the importance of the intellectual life.[45] The call by neoevangelical academics to the evangelical churches to renounce long-standing anti-intellectual suspicions of serious scholarship and to nurture the attitude that "intellectual activity can be a fundamental part of service to the Lord" is, if anything, reminiscent of the similar cry from Visser 't Hooft, Sir Walter Moberly, and the other early SCM leaders.[46]

Second, like the neo-orthodox before them, the neoevangelical scholars are shaping their critique of the secularization of the modern university.[47] Many of the same, perennial problems of modern education that drew the fire of the neo-orthodox are also prime targets of the neoevangelicals, such as the fragmentation and balkanization of the university disciplines.[48] Also in keeping with the neo-orthodox critique, the evangelicals fault the university for its failure to deal with the large questions, the "basic issues," of life (marriage, death, evil, and meaning). Like the neo-orthodox they look to the rejuvenation of the liberal arts and the humanities for raising the big issues and bringing the Christian faith to bear on them.[49] Furthermore, central to the evangelical critique is their attack on the university's adherence to "the myth of objective consciousness."[50]

In this, the evangelicals have one step on the neo-orthodox. They can now appeal to the postmodern breakdown of objectivity, whereas the neo-orthodox had to mount their attack on "the cult of objectivity" while its devotees were in full sway.[51] But the neoevangelical criticism is basically no different from that of the neo-orthodox.

Third, the neoevangelicals conceive of their task as one of bringing a biblically based conception of the Christian faith to bear on modern culture and intellectual life by demonstrating that, of all possible alternatives, such a view of the Christian faith makes the best sense of the human condition.[52] Like the neo-orthodox, the neoevangelicals want to employ "the best canons of twentieth-century cultural-historical inquiry to explore the flow of human cultural relationships in looking at their own tradition," and they want to bring the biblical message to this cultural context as it is revealed by modern scholarship.[53] How different this is from, say, Reinhold Niebuhr's understanding of the church's task of interpreting the modern predicament in the light of biblical images and stories is not clear.

Finally, the main emphasis of the neoevangelicals in their engagement with higher education, just as it was for the neo-orthodox, is the need to uncover and criticize the hidden presuppositions of modern consciousness and its intellectual endeavors. Again the evangelicals appeal to postmodernism, as the neo-orthodox could not, to bolster the contention that all knowing is based on certain unspoken, unconscious pretheoretical assumptions, and that the Christian ones are entitled to a fair hearing along with all the others.[54] But this was essentially the neo-orthodox contention as well, and in their manner of framing it, the neoevangelicals sound almost indistinguishable from the neo-orthodox.

Here we can see from yet another perspective the central issue in the problem of the relationship between faith and knowledge. Like the neo-orthodox, the neoevangelicals have identified the importance of the hidden assumptions at work in modern consciousness, and they have emphasized the need to bring these to light and to demonstrate that other assumptions about the world, with far different implications, are also available and worthy of being considered. Simply proposing alternate worldviews for interpreting the world, however, is not enough.

Unless actual new ways of knowing, new epistemological possibilities, are drawn out of these alternative worldviews, nothing essential is changed. It is our ways of knowing that give us our world, not interpretive and speculative worldviews by themselves. We may entertain any number of other metaphors than that of the machine for our understanding of the world, and theologically and philosophically they may all be more satisfying. If, however, they do not lead to new ways of knowing, then the established mechanistic and quantitative ways of knowing will continue to create an ever-more dead and mechanistic world, with little machine selves to go with it, all the while we may be comforting ourselves with meaning-filled worldviews. The neo-orthodox distinction between biblical assumptions and naturalistic assumptions did not entail merely a clash between two worldviews, but between a worldview with an established and working epistemology and one without, and the one without eventually had to give way.

Perhaps another way of making the issue clear is to realize that the metaphysical assumptions of the mechanical philosophy were fixed in the modern mind by the actual achievements of the quantitative and mechanistic epistemology of the scientific revolution. The fact that human beings began to gain control as never before over the quantitative and mechanical dimensions of the world cleared the way for the metaphysical assumptions of the material worldview to batten themselves firmly on modern consciousness. Huston Smith has observed that "worldviews arise from epistemologies."[55] Perhaps his statement requires a slight modification in that epistemologies, worldviews, and the cultural-institutional structures that arise out of them are all mutually reinforcing. But Smith is surely right in the suggestion that the ultimate hold of any worldview rests in its having its own accompanying epistemology.

Qualitative worldviews can lead to the creation of a society and a world rich in qualities only if these worldviews serve as inducements to the development of qualitative ways of knowing. This crucial step the mainline Protestant theological reformers ultimately failed to take in their call for the uncovering of hidden presuppositions and worldviews at work in our thought. On this crucial point, there is no evidence that the neoevangelicals have moved at all beyond the neo-orthodox stage of the theological renaissance.

The neoevangelicals have necessarily rejected the narrow scriptural literalism, along with what George Marsden accurately identifies as the "early modern" epistemology—a nineteenth-century Baconian common sense realism—with which the evangelical tradition has been yoked for much of its existence.[56] Marsden himself, however, has raised the interesting question whether those evangelicals who now follow through their commitment to contemporary scholarship and its thought forms have set themselves on a path leading unavoidably to their own dissolution.[57] Marsden thinks not, as long as evangelicals remain true to the biblical doctrine of the incarnation.

That response, however, seems to beg the main question; namely, whether modern thought forms by their nature make it impossible to speak meaningfully not only of incarnation but of the entire noumenal immaterial realms that are the chief occupation of the biblical, as of every other great, religious tradition. Barring their reversion to an earlier, more hardened fundamentalism, the survival of the neoevangelicals would seem to depend directly on the extent to which they succeed in moving beyond the neo-orthodox option in trying to join faith and knowledge. This would require a radical epistemological transformation. In light of the traditional evangelical suspicion of the creativeness of the human mind—a suspicion of imagination that they share in an even heightened degree with most of the rest of Protestantism—such a radical epistemological turn on their part seems unlikely.[58]

Mainline Protestantism

Mainline Protestantism continues to conceive of its task in the modern world largely within the framework of a two-realm theory of truth. Nothing is more emblematic (and symptomatic) of this than the never-ending saga of the search for the identity of the church-related college. Those colleges that declare their intention to maintain a distinctive Christian presence within higher education again and again proclaim their firm commitment both to "academic excellence," a favorite phrase of college mission statements, and to "Christian faith and values," another favorite. In this context commitment to Christian faith and values means variously: encouraging official opportunities for worship; having faculty who can "represent Christian values" in their teaching and advising; providing religion courses in the core liberal arts curriculum; raising questions of the ethical uses of knowledge; experimenting with the humanities to ensure that students are exposed to the "basic questions"; emphasizing "the importance of persons" and an active student personnel program; and so forth.[59] With their basic fact-value, knowledge-faith separation, most of these conceptions of the church-related college's task show little substantive change from what might have been written fifty years ago.

In this approach, Christian faith and values have at most a tangential relationship to knowledge and, hence, to "academic excellence." Whatever is variously conceived under Christian faith and values is, therefore, subjected to constant pressure to give way before the institutional, ideological, and individual career demands of "academic excellence," which, compared to "Christian faith and values," has a well-defined and agreed-upon meaning.

The opportunities for self-delusion and hypocrisy on the part of church-related colleges in this kind of situation are abundant. Those aware leaders who have some sense of the unequal balance between the concrete realities of academic excellence and the vague desires for faith and values expressed in their colleges' mission statements could hardly avoid a constant sense of ineffectuality. Moreover, as the various attempts are made to find some place for faith and values, the perpetual search for institutional identity continues— unless, of course, the college simply decides to settle for commitment to academic excellence alone, which can then be justified as the institution's Christian service to society. That "academic excellence" in its present, dominant form has little intrinsic place for faith and human values of any kind is a problem still seldom brought to consciousness by either college or church, much less seriously addressed.[60]

To be sure, the Protestant churches are far from being alone in their attachment to a two-realm theory of truth as their main solution to the faith-knowledge problem. That has long been a major type of response by those concerned to clear some space, some breathing room, for faith, ethics, and qualities that make human life human. And the two-realm theory of truth is better than nothing. It is better than not to preserve the memory of a realm of human selves, meanings, and aspirations in an otherwise meaningless universe. It is better than not to work repeatedly at the revitalization of the humanities in order to keep alive the important questions. It is better than not to have courses in ethics, and institutes for the study of ethics, in medicine, business, law, education, and so on. But since our experience of the world is finally shaped by our knowledge, these efforts will always be on the defensive, constantly undergoing erosion, and ever a little after the fact, a bit too late.

Our ways of knowing, and the images of the human being and of the world they work out of, already create, in the laboratory, realities that then call for practices that often stand at complete variance with meaningful human life. Ethics, therefore, is not something that comes into play only after our ways of knowing have done their work. The results of research are determined by and proceed out of the images, assumptions, and questions with which it originates. When the results are applied, the practical consequences help to create society's and individuals' views of what is real and what is right and wrong. The foundations of morality are already built into our ways of knowing. We are responsible, for example, for the kinds of images we allow to guide our attempts to integrate, understand, and interpret the world and the human being.

We can continue, as now, after the fact, trying through our ethics to alleviate the problems and ease the wrenching dilemmas created by a knowing based on inadequate images of the human being and of nature. And it is crucial that we do so as long as we have nothing else to offer. Could we not also, however, begin to work more from the center, and to ask, "What is required of our ways of knowing themselves?" From this perspective, the central task of all ethics is the transformation of our ways of knowing, what Rudolf Steiner once called, "the redemption of thinking."[61] Can anything less be an adequate understanding of the full meaning of *metanoia* for our time?

It is this possibility that at first glance might seem to make the new interest in imagination, which appears to be growing rapidly among many religious and theological thinkers, of particular importance. In many respects, of course, it is, for this interest in imagination moves the focus to the fundamentally creative and central role that our consciousness, thinking, and knowing have in all our experience. A closer look at many of the current books on imagination suggests, however, that imagination is still conceived in an exceedingly narrow way.[62]

Almost all authors on the imagination today have read their Coleridge, and they take pains to distinguish between imagination and fancy. When many of them actually treat the imagination, however, what they describe and talk about turns out, after all, to be essentially what Coleridge meant by fancy, and is far removed from his conception of the fullness of imagination with its deepest roots in the divine, creative source of the world.[63] Imagination as fancy consists in recombining and re-presenting what is already given. In science, imagination in this sense is allowed an important but restricted role in the production of useful hypotheses. Frequently this results in a kind of novelty that yields some new leverage for purposes of manipulation and control, or breathes some new life into the given framework. The framework itself, however, is seldom called into question, radically opened up, or seen to rest on grounds that transcend it. All too often, moreover, the religious imagination, usually along with the artistic imagination, is conceived of as *all* fancy, the imaginary. The result is usually an updated version of the older dualistic view that science gives knowledge while religion, poetry, and speculative metaphysics give meaning and feeling tone.

Even when the importance of a deeper conception of imagination is recognized, frequently the radical implications are not followed through. In his book on theological education, for example, Edward Farley rightly takes the nature of knowledge as his focus.[64] He looks at the dominant modern mode of knowing, which he calls the Enlightenment paradigm of knowledge, based on a narrow, but powerful, abstract, empirical reason, and at the three main corrections that it has called forth. These corrections Farley sees coming from the Romantics with their emphasis on intuitive imagination, from tradition with its concern for wisdom and a historical communal context of meaning, and from the proponents of praxis with its critical reflection on experience. The Enlightenment paradigm, taken together with its corrections, provides, Farley argues, our major present conception of how and what we can know.

Of all the components of knowing, however, Farley identifies intuitive imagination as by far the most important, but the most neglected. Intuitive imagination is the foundation of all knowing. Having made the obligatory criticisms of the various aberrations of Romanticism, Farley, nevertheless, writes, that without intuitive imagination, "the other hermeneutical perspectives fail to emerge. For it is the intuitive imagination—that central theme of romanticism—which grasps reality in its concreteness, its relationalities, its complexities." And he adds, "Without the intuitive imagination's grasp of the immediacy and complexity of reality, other hermeneutic perspectives remain undeveloped."[65] All understanding, in other words, depends on intuitive imagination. During the rest of the book, however, we hear nothing more on intuitive imagination, the development and nourishment of which one might have thought to be the central task and challenge of theological education.

And so the gap between knowledge and faith remains as wide as ever in mainline Protestantism, even at those points where we might most have expected some important progress to have been made in bridging it.

FAITH AND KNOWLEDGE: TOWARD A GENUINE POSTMODERNISM

What is required for a fundamental coming to grips with the faith-knowledge issue? What is required if faith is to seek and lead to knowledge and understanding, and if knowledge is truly to undergird and make room for faith? Another way of putting the question, in keeping with the discussion in this chapter, is to ask, What would be the criteria for a genuine postmodernism—for an approach that would move beyond the extreme modernism of deconstructive, putative postmodernism to what David Griffin has called a genuinely constructive postmodernism?

At least four essential criteria would have to be met.

The first criterion for a truly radical approach to the faith-knowledge issue, and the basis for all else, is a fundamental transformation in our ways of knowing. One way of talking about this transformation of knowing is to say that we must develop qualitative ways of knowing on par with our quantitative. Another way is to say that we must begin to develop ways of knowing the non-sensory, supersensible realities in which the sensible world has its origin, being, and becoming.

Persons as diverse as William James, Bertrand Russell, and more recently, Georg Kuhlewind and David Griffin, have shown that we must presuppose a minimum intuition of non-sensory realities as the irreducible possibility of even our ordinary, sense-bound knowing itself.[66] The task now becomes one of developing these incipient, nascent intuitive capacities into full-fledged faculties of perception and cognition.

The physicist Arthur Zajonc has described what he sees to be the critical turning point that has now been reached by science itself. If science is ever to achieve true understanding of the realms into which it is now plunging, writes Zajonc, the scientist must develop nothing less than "new cognitive faculties" for the perception and understanding of the qualitative realities that otherwise remain hidden from us.[67] And we have already seen the physicist David Bohm's description of insight as the source and possibility of new knowledge in every field. In insight, as an intensely concentrated, attentive awareness that pierces through the givens of sense experience, is to be found, Bohm argues, the source of all newness, as well as the deeper unity of the scientific, artistic, and moral imagination.[68] In the work of Rudolf Steiner (who built directly on the epistemology developed by Goethe in his scientific work) are to be found exceedingly rich indications for the development of imagination (Steiner's term for what Bohm touches on in the concept of insight), as well as deeper cognitive capacities, which Steiner describes as inspiration and intuition. Steiner's own work has had radical, wide-ranging implications for every field of human endeavor.[69] All these examples (and the reader may have others) point to the necessity and possibility of developing new capacities of perception and understanding that can make accessible the non-sensory, qualitative dimensions of reality.

The second criterion for coming to grips with the faith-knowledge issue, and for a true postmodernism, is that the positive potentials of modern consciousness must be preserved: the capacity for clear thinking consciousness, individual identity and selfhood, and the potential for freedom that individuality and clear-consciousness alone make possible. This criterion means that the necessary transformation in knowing cannot be a return to atavistic, premodern states of consciousness in which self is submerged in the Divine, in nature, or in the tribe and community. Such a going back might well be a return to greater meaning than the modern world permits but, with the loss of self it would entail, it would be meaning without freedom, responsibility, and the potential for love and new forms of community.

From this perspective the needed transformation of knowing might best be thought of as the development of imagination in the fullest sense, in Steiner's and Barfield's terms: Imagination as the involvement of the whole human being in the work of knowing, in "thought, feeling, will, and character."[70] Imagination in this deep sense gives us our world. Imagination in this sense also preserves and presupposes the reality of selfhood and its capacities for freedom and love. Furthermore, in the development of imagination in this fullest sense, the self becomes the window for the participation and actualization of universal realities and human values.

The potential for freedom and love, and the possibilities these create for new kinds of community and participative experience, are the crowning achievement and glory of modern consciousness. This consciousness, ironically, must today be liberated from its own self-imprisonment in the confines of the illusion that there can be no knowledge of the supersensory and qualitative (of which self, freedom, and love are chief). The transformation of knowing, the redemption of thinking, is essential to that liberation.

The third criterion is that a radical transformation of knowing will involve a transformation of ourselves. Knowledge of qualities in the world will depend on our being able to bring them to birth and recognize them within ourselves. All knowing is participatory. The quality of the world we come to know and live in turns on the quality of the participants and the quality of their participation. The possibility of a deepening of knowledge, thus, presupposes a constant working on oneself, on the full development of thinking, feeling, willing, and character as essential to the fullness of cognition.[71] The basic religious attitudes, for example, of wonder and reverence as readiness for what the other has to reveal, can, thereby, become more than mere inner feeling states. They can become primary cognitive organs without which nothing of genuine newness can be known.

The current "postmodern" attack on the onlooker consciousness is wrong only in assuming at the same time that what is inner cannot become a capacity for participating and knowing what is outer. Qualities are subjective *and* objective: this is the fundamental starting point for the qualitative transformation of knowing and for the qualitative transformation of ourselves that it requires.

The fourth criterion is, perhaps, less criterion than touchstone for determining that the first three criteria are being met. This criterion or touchstone is that the transformation of knowing will have consequences both for our knowledge of spirit and for our knowledge of nature. So far, almost all claims that positivism is at last being overcome fail to meet this test. The bridge that is to span faith and knowledge must be a real one. Knowledge of the qualitative realm, which both nature and spirit manifest, and from which both spring, will have consequences for both. While science, art, and religion, for example, will each have its own particular focus, objects, and tasks, they will not be in absolutely watertight compartments. The traffic between them will run in all directions, knowledge in one opening up possibilities for new insight and understanding in the others.

From the dominant Protestant perspective of a two-realm theory of truth, it has been relatively easy to see the influence of science on religion and art. The opposite movement has been almost impossible to envisage because art and religion have not been conceived as having anything to do with knowledge. But if knowledge of nature comes to have its qualitative grounding, knowledge of qualities in every other realm will have a bearing on our understanding of nature, and the opposite will also hold.

The future of the earth hangs on whether we can develop ways of knowing that can deal directly, respectfully, and precisely with the life and beauty of nature, rather than talking about these vaguely and then in practice, if not always in theory, reducing them to the inanimate, the quantitative, and the mechanistic. Similarly the renewal of religion depends on whether we can speak in knowledge, and again with precision, of the immaterial, non-sensory realm that is the source of nature and the heart and substance of religion alike. The touchstone will be whether knowledge of the one will have consequences for the other.

Owen Barfield has said, "There will be a renewal of Christianity when it becomes impossible to write a popular manual of science without referring to the incarnation of the Word."[72] What Barfield means is the exact opposite of imposing dogma—whether drawn from scripture or tradition or elsewhere—on the doing of science. Rather, he is speaking of the need for a way of knowing that opens in a new way the realm of the qualitative in both nature and spirit. Nothing less than genuine knowledge will do.

It may be argued that the development of non-sensory, qualitative knowledge is an impossibility. If such, indeed, be the case, it is difficult to see that there can be any real future, certainly for religion. And, without the development of qualitative ways of knowing, there can be little hope ultimately (and perhaps proximately) for the future of a living earth, and for the human being overall. To begin, however, to develop new capacities for knowing the qualitative can begin to open new sources for the concrete and radical renewal of science, medicine, agriculture, economics, community, art, education, and religion we so desperately need. That would be the full meaning of *metanoia* for our time.

The faith-knowledge issue turned out to be the most important issue of the modern age and of our postmodern possibilities. For a brief moment early in its twentieth-century engagement with higher education, mainline American Protestantism seems to have had a dim awareness that this might be the case.

NOTES

1. George H. Tavard, *Images of the Christ: An Inquiry into Christology* (Washington, D.C.: University Press of America, 1982), 93 n. 25.
2. For example, see Mary Belenky, et al., eds., *Women's Ways of Knowing: The*

Development of Mind, Voice and Self (New York: Basic Books, 1986); Sandra Harding and Merrill Hintikka, eds., *Discovering Reality: Feminist Perspectives on Epistemology, Metaphysics, Methodology and Philosophy of Science* (Dordrecht: D. Reidel, 1983); Ann Garry and Marilyn Pearsall, eds., *Women, Knowledge, and Reality: Explorations in Feminist Philosophy* (Boston: Unwin Hyman, 1989); Jane Duran, *Toward a Feminist Epistemology* (Savage, Md.: Rowman & Littlefield, 1990); William Irwin Thompson, ed., *GAIA: A Way of Knowing* (Great Barrington, Mass.: Lindisfarne Press, 1987); Douglas Sloan, "Education for a Living World," in *Nuclear Reactions,* ed. Evelyn McConeghey and James McConnell (Albuquerque, N.Mex.: Image Seminars, 1984), 17–32.

3. For some egregious examples, see the contributions to Frederick B. Burnham, ed., *Postmodern Theology: Christian Faith in a Pluralistic World* (San Francisco: Harper & Row, 1989).

4. Ernst Lehrs, *Man or Matter* (New York: Harper & Brothers, n.d. [1952?]), 31, passim.

5. Thomas Kuhn, *The Structure of Scientific Revolutions* (Chicago: University of Chicago Press, 1962); N. R. Hanson, *Patterns of Discovery: An Inquiry into the Conceptual Foundations of Science* (Cambridge: Cambridge University Press, 1958).

6. Michael Polanyi, *Personal Knowledge: Towards a Post-Critical Philosophy* (Chicago: University of Chicago Press, 1958); David Bloor, *Knowledge and Social Imagery* (London and Boston: Routledge & Kegan Paul, 1976); Michael Mulkay, *Science and the Sociology of Knowledge* (London: George Allen & Unwin, 1979).

7. In addition to titles cited in note 2, also see Carolyn Merchant, *The Death of Nature: Women, Ecology, and the Scientific Revolution* (San Francisco: Harper & Row, 1980).

8. A helpful presentation of the various facets of this movement is Richard Kearney, *Modern Movements in European Philosophy* (Manchester: Manchester University Press, 1986).

9. Mulkay, *Science and the Sociology of Knowledge,* 60–61.

10. See, for example, Richard Bernstein, *Beyond Objectivism and Relativism: Science, Hermeneutics, and Praxis* (Philadelphia: University of Pennsylvania Press, 1983).

11. See Clifford Geertz, *The Interpretation of Cultures* (New York: Basic Books, 1973), 87–125.

12. On the habits of the modern collective unconscious, see Owen Barfield, *History, Guilt, and Habit* (Middletown, Conn.: Wesleyan University Press, 1979).

13. See, for instance, Richard Rorty, "Education, Socialization, and Individuation," *Liberal Education* 75, no. 4 (September–October 1989): 2–9. Rorty describes truth as "whatever belief results from a free and open encounter of opinions, without asking whether this result agrees with something beyond that encounter."

14. Richard Rorty, "Postmodernist Bourgeois Liberalism," in *Hermeneutics and Praxis,* ed. Robert Hollinger (Notre Dame, Ind.: University of Notre Dame Press, 1985), 214–21.

15. The tearing apart of the intricate wholeness of scripture (often in the modernist search for the literary equivalent of the ultimate particle) and the reaction of scriptural literalism this often calls forth—both alike render inaccessible the numinous depths to which scripture witnesses and utterly destroy its essential mantric power. On the destruction of the wholeness of scripture, see the suggestive footnote comment by Owen Barfield, *Saving the Appearances: A Study in Idolatry,* (1957; New York: Harcourt Brace & World, n.d.), 175.

16. David Bohm, "Imagination, Fancy, Insight, and Reason in the Process of Thought," in *Evolution of Consciousness, Studies in Polarity,* ed. Shirley Sugerman

(Middletown, Conn.: Wesleyan University Press, 1976), 51–68. For a succinct, but extremely penetrating discussion of the nonempirical sources of all knowledge in thinking (as distinct from simply having thoughts), see Owen Barfield's introduction to *The Case for Anthroposophy,* his translation of and selections from Rudolf Steiner's *Von Seelenrätseln* (London: Rudolf Steiner Press, 1970), 7–24.

17. See, above all, Barfield, *Saving the Appearances;* also see Owen Barfield, "Philology and the Incarnation," in idem, *The Rediscovery of Meaning and Other Essays* (Middletown, Conn.: Wesleyan University Press, 1977). Jacques Ellul has described what he sees as the three great contributions of Western consciousness to the future of human development, three contributions that are now in danger of being lost: clear rationality, individuality, and freedom. Jacques Ellul, *The Betrayal of the West* (New York: Seabury Press, 1978). Also see Rudolf Steiner, *The Christ Impulse and the Development of Ego Consciousness* (Spring Valley, N.Y.: Anthroposophic Press, 1976).

18. David Ray Griffin, ed., *Spirituality and Society: Postmodern Visions* (Albany, N.Y.: State University of New York Press, 1988), x; also idem, "Postmodern Theology and A/theology: A Response to Mark C. Taylor," in *Varieties of Postmodern Theology,* ed. David Ray Griffin, William A. Beardslee, and Joe Holland (Albany, N.Y.: State University of New York Press, 1989), 29–61.

19. Griffin, *Spirituality and Society,* x; idem, *God and Religion in the Postmodern World* (Albany, N.Y.: State University of New York Press, 1989), 8.

20. Mark C. Taylor, *Erring: A Postmodern A/theology* (Chicago: University of Chicago Press, 1984).

21. In this discussion I have drawn on David Griffin's comprehensive criticism of Taylor's work.

22. Taylor, *Erring,* 140, 170, 172, 175, 180, passim.

23. Griffin, *Varieties of Postmodern Theology,* 35ff.

24. For an example of an expression of such deconstructive postmodernism rich in such truisms, see Richard Rorty, "Education, Socialization, and Individuation," *Liberal Education* 75, no. 4 (September–October 1989): 2–9.

25. Ibid., 25.

26. See George A. Lindbeck, *The Nature of Doctrine: Religion and Theology in a Postliberal Age* (Philadelphia: Westminster Press, 1984). The traditions and language of the community also figure centrally in Alisdair McIntyre, *Whose Justice, Which Rationality* (Notre Dame, Ind.: University of Notre Dame Press, 1988), and Stanley Hauerwas, *Christian Existence Today: Essays on Church, World and Living In Between* (Durham, N.C.: Labyrinth Press, 1988). Also see Stanley Hauerwas and L. Gregory Jones, eds., *Why Narrative? Readings in Narrative Theology* (Grand Rapids: Wm. B. Eerdmans Publishing Co., 1989).

27. Owen Barfield writes: "When I speak, there can be no doubt about the personal nature of the event; but equally there can be no doubt of its involving a transpersonal element, inasmuch as the words I speak have meanings that I did not originate. Moreover, if qualities are indeed the bridge between subject and object, it is by the medium of words that they become so. Viewed historically, all words, however abstract, however subjective, are seen to have a sensuous and phenomenal ingredient. It was in the process of naming nature that man became aware of her, and therefore no longer merely a part of her. And every growing child repeats that process. Words and their meanings are to qualities what numbers are to quantities. . . . It is in the very nature of words that they use the material to name the immaterial, or if you prefer it, the phenomenal to name the noumenal—and indeed the numinous." Owen Barfield, "Language, Evolution of Consciousness, and the Recovery of Human Meaning," in

Toward the Recovery of Wholeness: Knowledge, Education, and Human Values, ed. Douglas Sloan (New York: Teachers College Press, 1984), 59, 61. Also see Owen Barfield, *Speaker's Meaning* (Letchworth, England: Rudolf Steiner Press, 1967); and idem, "Language and Discovery," in Barfield, *The Rediscovery of Meaning,* 130–42.

28. See Burnham, *Postmodern Theology,* x.

29. In addition to works by Cobb cited in chapter 4, also see John Cobb and David Ray Griffin, *Process Theology: An Introductory Exposition* (Philadelphia: Westminster Press, 1976).

30. See Griffin, *Spirituality and Society;* idem, *God and Religion in the Postmodern World;* idem, *Varieties of Postmodern Theology;* and idem, ed., *The Reenchantment of Science: Postmodern Proposals* (Albany, N.Y.: State University of New York Press, 1988).

31. Griffin, *Spirituality and Society,* 5, 17; idem, *God and Religion in the Postmodern World,* 4, 6. On this, Griffin does not hedge, emphasizing that the awareness of non-sensory levels of perception demands openness to evidence scorned by the modern mind-set for parapsychology, psychokinesis, extrasensory perception, and so on. See David Ray Griffin, *God and Religion in the Postmodern World,* 6, 92–93; and idem, "Parapsychology and Philosophy: A Whiteheadian Postmodern Perspectivite," *Journal of the American Society for Psychical Research* 87, no. 3 (July 1993), 217–88. Most modern Protestant theologians seem to have an abhorrence of all notions of clairvoyance.

32. Ibid., 4.

33. Ibid., 4–7; Griffin, *Spirituality and Society,* 5.

34. See Griffin, *God and Religion in the Postmodern World,* passim.

35. Ibid., 7; Griffin, *Spirituality and Society,* x.

36. Epistemologically, for example, Griffin has yet to indicate whether and, if so, how he thinks non-sensory, qualitative ways of knowing can be further developed and strengthened, and in such a way that does not lapse into premodern, atavistic modes of participatory consciousness—as in many, and probably most, commonly recognized manifestations today of paranormal phenomena—which are ill-suited for the preservation and enhancement of individual agency, freedom, and conscious wakefulness (which agency and freedom require).

37. For comparative figures on the decline of mainline and the growth of evangelical churches, see Leonard Sweet, "The Modernization of Protestant Religion in America," in *Altered Landscapes: Christianity in America 1935–1985,* ed. David Lotz (Grand Rapids: Wm. B. Eerdmans Publishing Co., 1989), 19–41.

38. See, for example, Peter Berger, "From the Crisis of Religion to the Crisis of Secularity," in *Religion and America: Spirituality in a Secular Age,* ed. Mary Douglas and Steven M. Tipton (Boston: Beacon Press, 1983), 14–15; see also Van A. Harvey, "On the Intellectual Marginality of American Theology," in *Religion and Twentieth-Century American Intellectual Life,* ed. Michael J. Lacy (Cambridge: Woodrow Wilson International Center for Scholars and Cambridge University Press, 1989), 172–92.

39. I am aware that many American evangelicals resist the use of fundamentalism in this wider sense. Nevertheless, I find James Hunter's treatment and use of the term for these wider purposes the more convincing. See James Davidson Hunter, "Fundamentalism in Its Global Contours," in *The Fundamentalist Phenomenon,* ed. Norman J. Cohen (Grand Rapids: Wm. B. Eerdmans Publishing Co., 1990), 56–72. Whether all American neoevangelicalism can be included in this usage of the term, is, however, another question, and one to which I turn in the discussion.

40. See Alan Peshkin, *God's Choice: The Total World of a Fundamentalist Christian School* (Chicago: University of Chicago Press, 1986); John Davidson Hunter, *American Evangelicalism: Conservative Religion and the Quandary of Modernity* (New Brunswick,

N.J.: Rutgers University Press, 1983); idem, *Evangelicalism: The Coming Generation* (Chicago: University of Chicago Press, 1987).

41. Tendencies toward the inner modernization of evangelicalism seem much like the process among late nineteenth-century antimodern dissenters as described by Jackson Lears, in which many protests against the modern mind-set again and again gradually became assimilated to the rationalizing influences of that mind-set, and ended, ironically, in helping to legitimate and ease the emergence of the very modern, managerial, therapeutic, corporate society that the antimodernists were attempting to resist. Jackson Lears, *No Place of Grace: Antimodernism and the Transformation of American Culture, 1880–1920* (New York: Pantheon Books, 1981).

42. See Barfield, *Saving the Appearances*.

43. See Virginia Lieson Brereton, *Training God's Army: The American Bible School, 1880–1940* (Bloomington and Indianapolis: Indiana University Press, 1990); Timothy L. Smith, "The Evangelical Kaleidoscope and the Call to Christian Unity," *Christian Scholar's Review* 15, no. 2: 125–40; also Joel Carpenter, "From Fundamentalism to the New Evangelical Coalition," in *Evangelicalism and Modern America*, ed. George Marsden (Grand Rapids: Wm. B. Eerdmans Publishing Co., 1984), 3–16.

44. Timothy Smith, "Christian Colleges and American Culture," in Joel A. Carpenter and Kenneth W. Shipps, *Making Higher Education Christian: The History and Mission of Evangelical Colleges in America* (Grand Rapids: Christian University Press and Wm. B. Eerdmans Publishing Co., 1987), 2.

45. See Mark A. Noll, "Evangelicals and the Study of the Bible," in Marsden, *Evangelicalism and Modern America*, 106–7; see all the articles, especially those by Mark Noll, Nathan Hatch, and Mary Stewart Van Leeuwen, in Carpenter and Shipps, *Making Higher Education Christian*.

46. In Carpenter and Shipps, *Making Higher Education Christian*, see Nathan Hatch, "Evangelicalism as a Democratic Movement," 159, 170; Smith, "Christian Colleges and American Culture," 6; and George Marsden, "Why No Major Evangelical University? The Loss and Recovery of Evangelical Advanced Scholarship," 294–304. Also see David F. Wells, "An American Evangelical Theology: The Painful Transition from *Theoria* to *Praxis*," in Marsden, *Evangelicalism and Modern America*, 83–93.

47. See George Marsden, *The Soul of the American University: From Protestant Establishment to Established Nonbelief* (New York: Oxford University Press, 1994).

48. For example, see William A. Dyrness, "The Contribution of Theological Studies to the Christian Liberal Arts," in Carpenter and Shipps, *Making Higher Education Christian*, 155–71.

49. See, for example, ibid., 175.

50. Carpenter and Shipps, *Making Higher Education Christian*, xiii.

51. Ibid.

52. See Wells, "An American Evangelical Theology," in *Evangelicalism and Modern America*.

53. George Marsden, "Evangelicals, History, and Modernity," in Marsden, *Evangelicalism and Modern America*, 99; Wells, "An American Evangelical Theology," 93.

54. See, for example, Carpenter and Shipps, preface to *Making Higher Education Christian*, xiii.

55. Huston Smith, *Beyond the Post-Modern Mind*, Updated and revised ed. (Wheaton, Ill.: Quest Books, 1989 [1982]), 150.

56. Marsden, "Evangelicals, History, and Modernity," in *Evangelicalism and Modern America*, 98.

57. Ibid., 99.

58. Ironically, however, there is one point in evangelicalism's early modern tradition that might conceivably serve this transformation. Thomas Reid, the first important Scottish realist, emphasized not only the common sense presuppositions without which meaningful thought and discourse are impossible but also the creative, "active powers" of the mind. Is this, perhaps, a possible transformative *Anknüpfungspunkt* between the evangelical and the best of the romantic, imaginative tradition. On the radicality of Thomas Reid in comparison with Dugald Stewart and other commonsense realists, who were much more important to nineteenth-century Protestants than was Reid, see Sydney Ahlstrom, "The Scottish Philosophy and American Theology," *Church History* 24, no. 3 (September 1955): 257–72.

59. See the descriptions of various church-related colleges' conceptions of their tasks in Robert Rue Parsonage, ed., *Church Related Higher Education* (Valley Forge, Pa.: Judson Press, 1978). I have also drawn on a more recent study by Robert Zuber, "Ideals and Tensions in Four Church-Related Colleges," manuscript, 1991.

60. An exception to this may be the attempt at Northland College in Ashland, Wisconsin, to make an experience of the environment the epistemological basis for the entire college curriculum. Here there seems to be an awareness of the need for a thoroughgoing reform of the liberal arts curriculum in a way that has consequences for both science and the humanities. It is still doubtful, however, that the concept of the environment in this case will be much more than a poetic vessel of values within which the traditional disciplines, and the traditional academic reward system, will continue basically to operate as before. See the excellent study of Northland by Wesley Hotchkiss, which does bring out the epistemological issues in a variety of ways. Wesley Hotchkiss, "A Trip to Northland," manuscript, 1991.

61. Rudolf Steiner, *The Redemption of Thinking: A Study in the Philosophy of Thomas Aquinas* (Spring Valley, N.Y.: Anthroposophic Press, 1983; a translation of three lectures given in 1920).

62. Examples of the many books that deal with imagination in religion and theology include Gordon Kaufman, *The Theological Imagination: Constructing the Concept of God* (Philadelphia: Westminster Press, 1981); Maria Harris, *Teaching and Religious Imagination: An Essay in the Theology of Teaching* (New York: Harper & Row, 1987); John MacIntyre, ed., *Faith, Theology, and Imagination* (Edinburgh: Hansel Press, 1987); Garrett Green, *Imagining God: Theology and the Religious Imagination* (San Francisco: Harper & Row, 1989); James P. McKay, ed., *Religious Imagination* (Edinburgh: University of Edinburgh Press, 1986).

63. The best treatment of Coleridge's full concept of imagination, and of its deep implications for modern understanding, is Owen Barfield, *What Coleridge Thought* (Middletown, Conn.: Wesleyan University Press, 1971).

64. Edward Farley, *The Fragility of Knowledge: Theological Education in the Church and the University* (Philadelphia: Fortress Press, 1988).

65. Ibid., 41.

66. *William James:* ". . . the relations between things, conjunctive as well as disjunctive, are just as much matters of direct particular experience, neither more so nor less so, than the things themselves." William James, *The Meaning of Truth* (Cambridge, Mass.: Harvard University Press, 1975), 7.

Bertrand Russell:

If an individual is to know anything beyond his own experiences up to the present moment, his stock of uninferred knowledge must consist not only of

> matters of fact, but also of general laws, or at least a law, allowing him to make inferences from matters of fact. . . . The only alternative to this hypothesis is complete skepticism as to all the inferences of science and common sense, including those which I have called animal inference.

Bertrand Russell, *Human Knowledge: Its Scope and Limits.* Quoted in Owen Barfield, introduction to *The Case for Anthroposophy* (London: Rudolf Steiner Press, 1970), 13.
Georg Kuhlewind:

> The following do not designate perceptions gained through the sense-organs, but are "relationship words," as for example: *is*—to be—*as, because, then, also, otherwise, again, enough, strong,* etc. "There is nothing in the intellect that has not been first in the senses." Not a single word, not a concept in this sentence corresponds to its content since none of them originates in a sensory perception.

Georg Kuhlewind, *Becoming Aware of the Logos: The Way of St. John the Evangelist* (West Stockbridge, Mass.: Lindisfarne Press, 1985), 16–17;
David Griffin: "Sensory perception is a very high-level, specialized type of perception which may or may not occur and which presupposes the existence of nonsensory perception." David Griffin, *God and Religion in the Postmodern World* (Albany, N.Y.: State University of New York Press, 1989), 90.

67. Arthur Zajonc, "Light and Cognition," manuscript, 1989.

68. Bohm, "Imagination, Fancy, Insight, and Reason in the Process of Thought." Also see David Bohm, "Insight, Knowledge, Science, and Human Values," *Teachers College Record* 82, no. 3 (spring 1981): 380–402; David Bohm, "On Insight and Its Significance, for Science, Education, and Values," in *Education and Values*, ed. Douglas Sloan (New York: Teachers College Press, 1980), 7–22.

69. Rudolf Steiner's published books and lectures are voluminous. Among his basic epistemological works are Rudolf Steiner, *Truth and Knowledge* (1892); idem, *A Theory of Knowledge Implicit in Goethe's World Conception* (1886); idem, *The Philosophy of Freedom* (1894); idem, *The Redemption of Thinking* (1920). Most of these are available from the Anthroposophic Press, Hudson, New York. For helpful introductions to the nature and extent of Steiner's work, see A. P. Shepherd, *A Scientist of the Invisible* (London: Hodder and Stoughton, 1954); John Davy, ed., *Work Arising from the Life of Rudolf Steiner* (London: Rudolf Steiner Press, 1975); Owen Barfield, *Romanticism Comes of Age* (n.p.: Rudolf Steiner Press, 1966); also see Robert A. McDermott, *The Essential Steiner* (San Francisco: Harper & Row, 1984).

70. Barfield, *Saving the Appearances*, 141.

71. See Georg Kuhlewind, *From Normal to Healthy: Paths to the Liberation of Consciousness* (Great Barrington, Mass.: Lindisfarne Press, 1988); also idem, *Stages of Consciousness* (Great Barrington, Mass.: Lindisfarne Press, 1984).

72. Barfield, *Saving the Appearances*, 164.

Index

Printed in the United States
63125LVS00003B/1-30